DrMaster
Publications Inc.
www.DrMasterbooks.com

Author / Kotaro Mori
Translator / Misato Sakamoto
Production Artist / Primary Graphix
Cover Artist / Bryce Gunkel
English Adaptation / Benjamin Stone
Editor / Ken Li
Supervising Editor / Matthew Scrivner
Marketing / Shawn Sanders
V.P. of Operations / Yuki Chung
President / Jennifer Chen

© **Kotaro Mori 2005**

First published in 2005 by Media Works Inc., Tokyo, Japan.
English translation rights arranged with Media Works Inc.

Stray Little Devil volume 1
English translation © 2006 DrMaster Publications Inc.
All rights reserved.

Publisher
DrMaster Publications Inc.
4044 Clipper Ct.
Fremont, CA 94538
www.DrMasterpublications.com

Second Edition: January 2007

ISBN 13: 978-1-59796-043-B
ISBN 10: 1-59796-043-B

STRAY LITTLE DEVIL

Kotaro Mori

STRAY LITTLE DEVIL

1
CONTENTS

PAM.

A LONG TIME AGO...

I FELL IN LOVE WITH A DEVIL.

WEREN'T YOU SCARED?

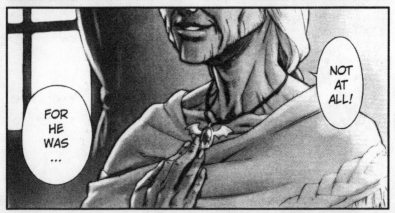

NOT AT ALL!

FOR HE WAS ...

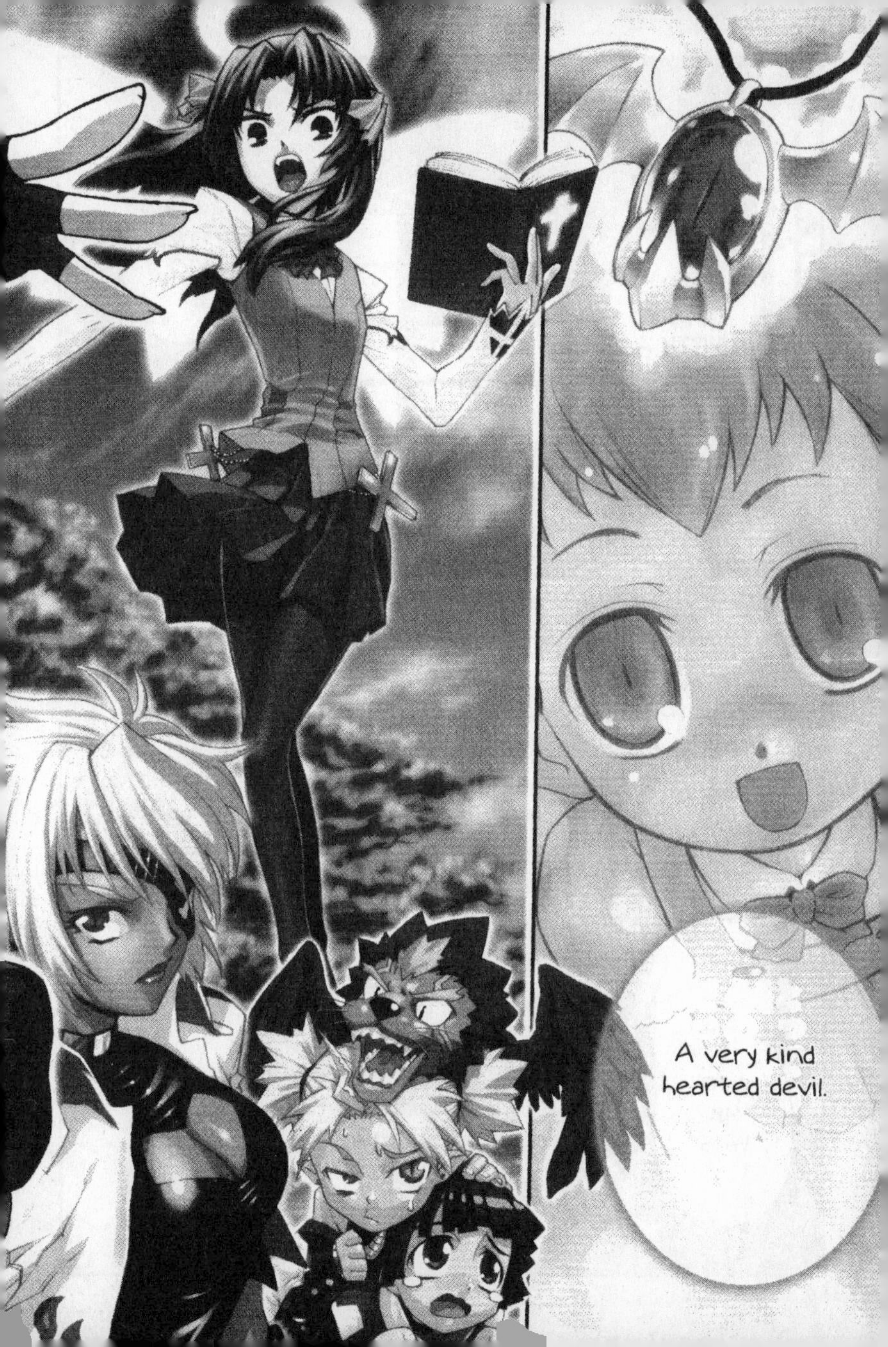
A very kind hearted devil.

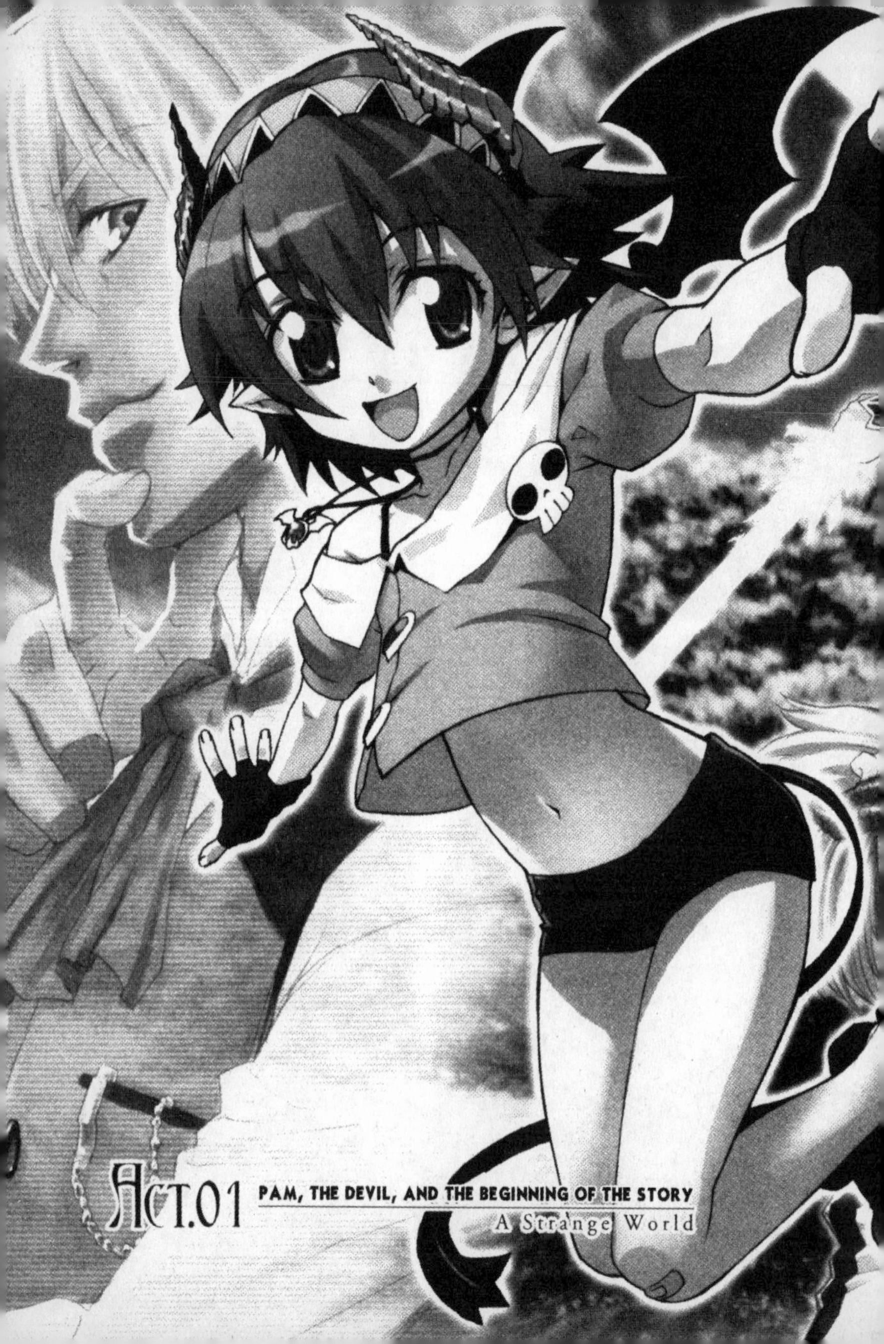
ACT.01
PAM, THE DEVIL, AND THE BEGINNING OF THE STORY
A Strange World

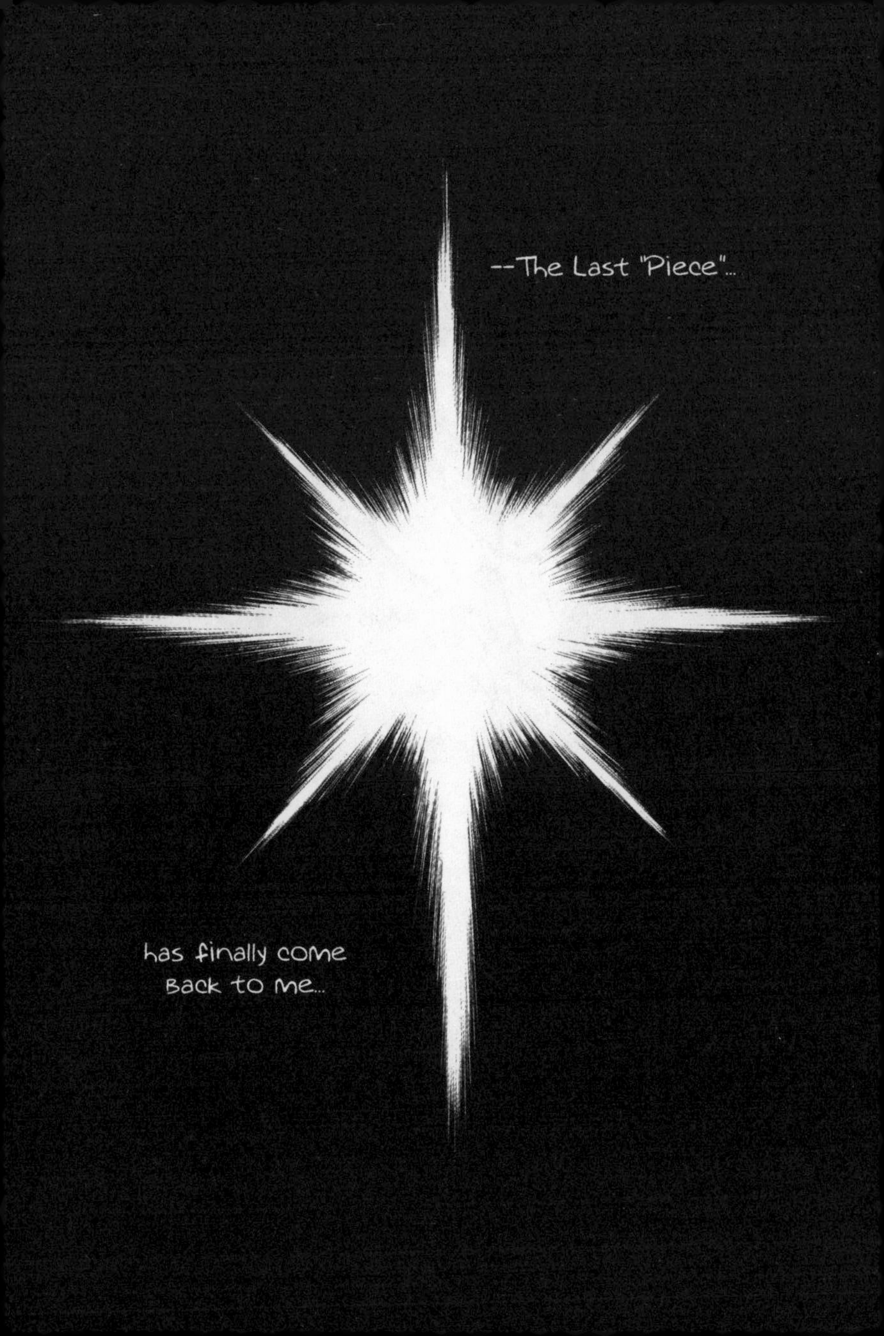
--The Last "Piece"...
has finally come back to me...

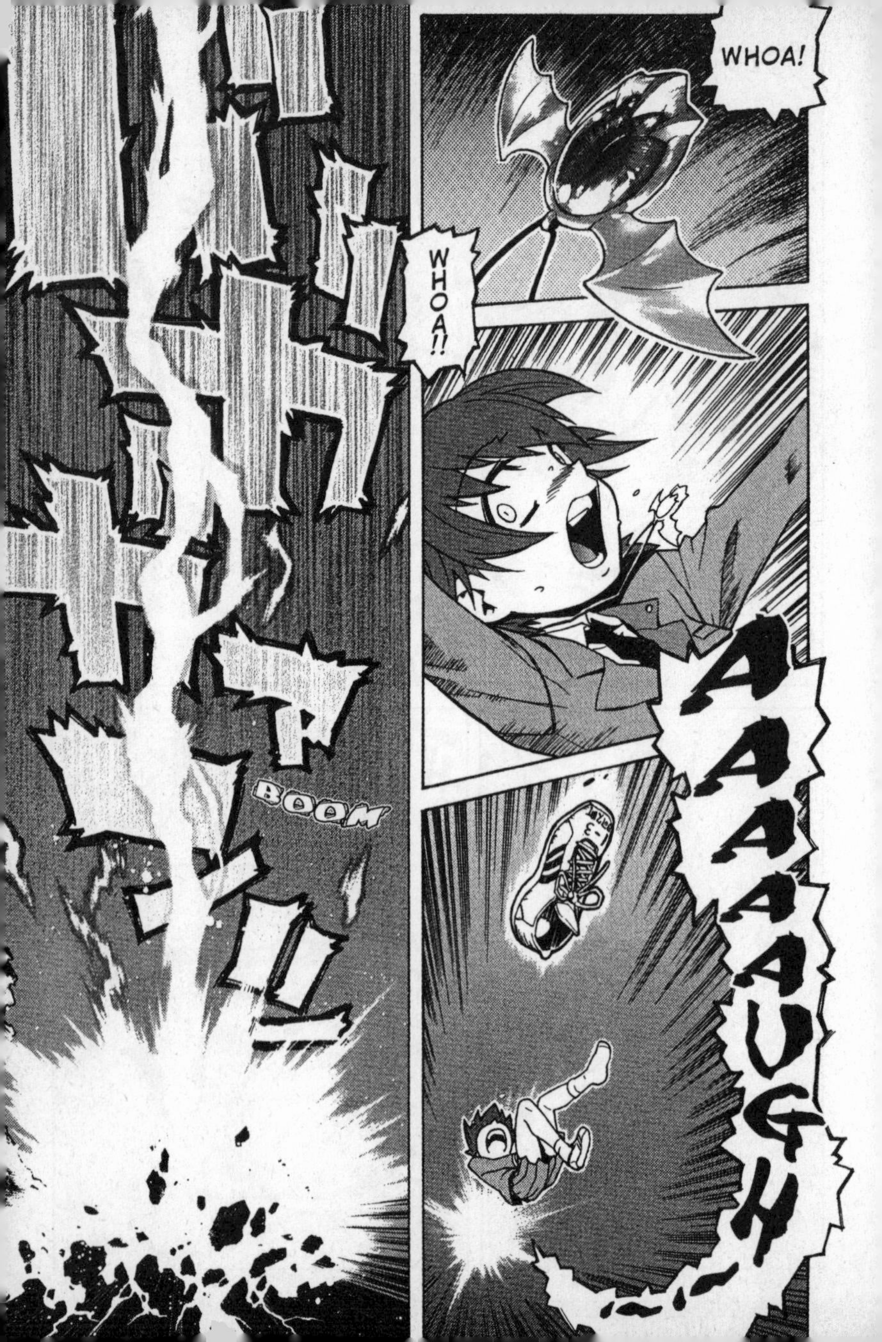
WHOA!
WHOA!!
AAAAAUGH!
BOOM

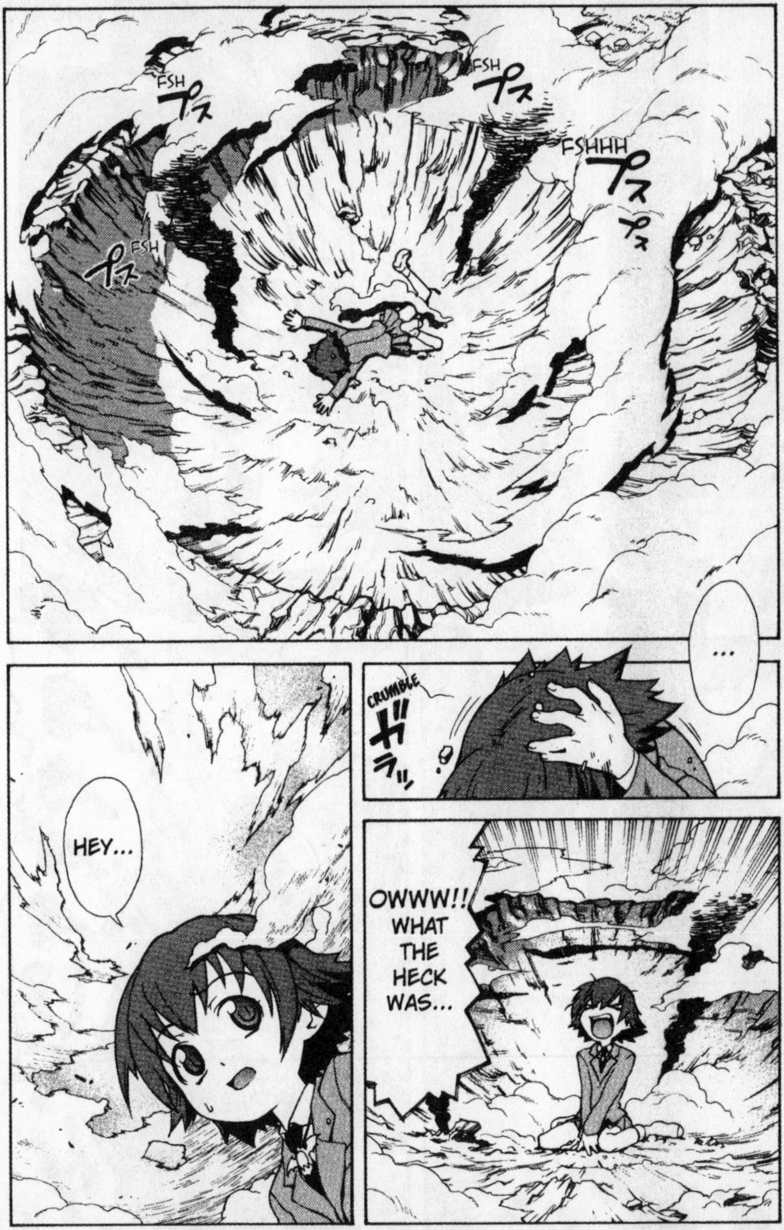
FSHHH
プス
プス
FSH
プス
FSH
プス
FSH
プス
...
CRUMBLE
ガラッ
OWWW!! WHAT THE HECK WAS...
HEY...

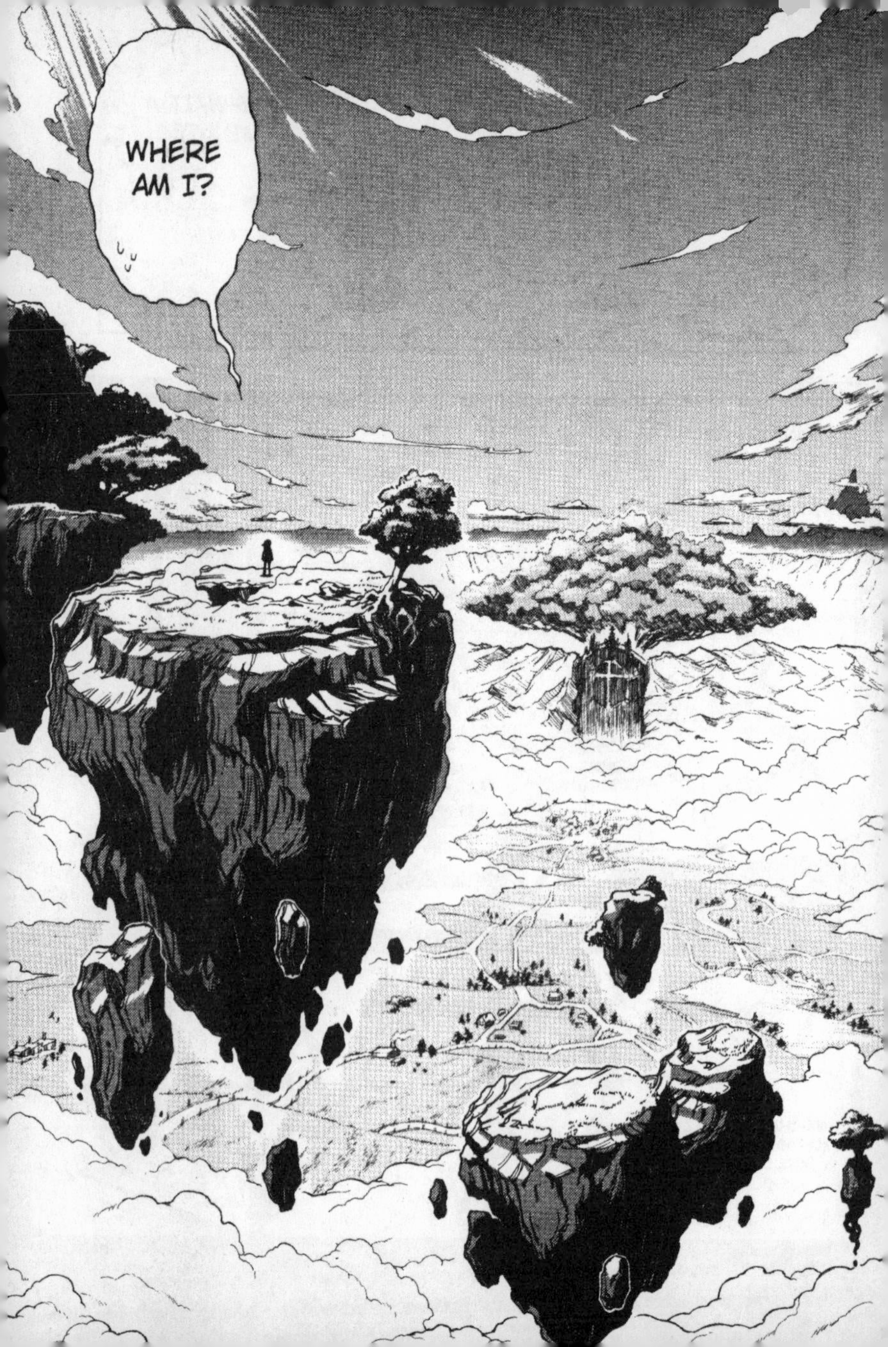
WHERE AM I?

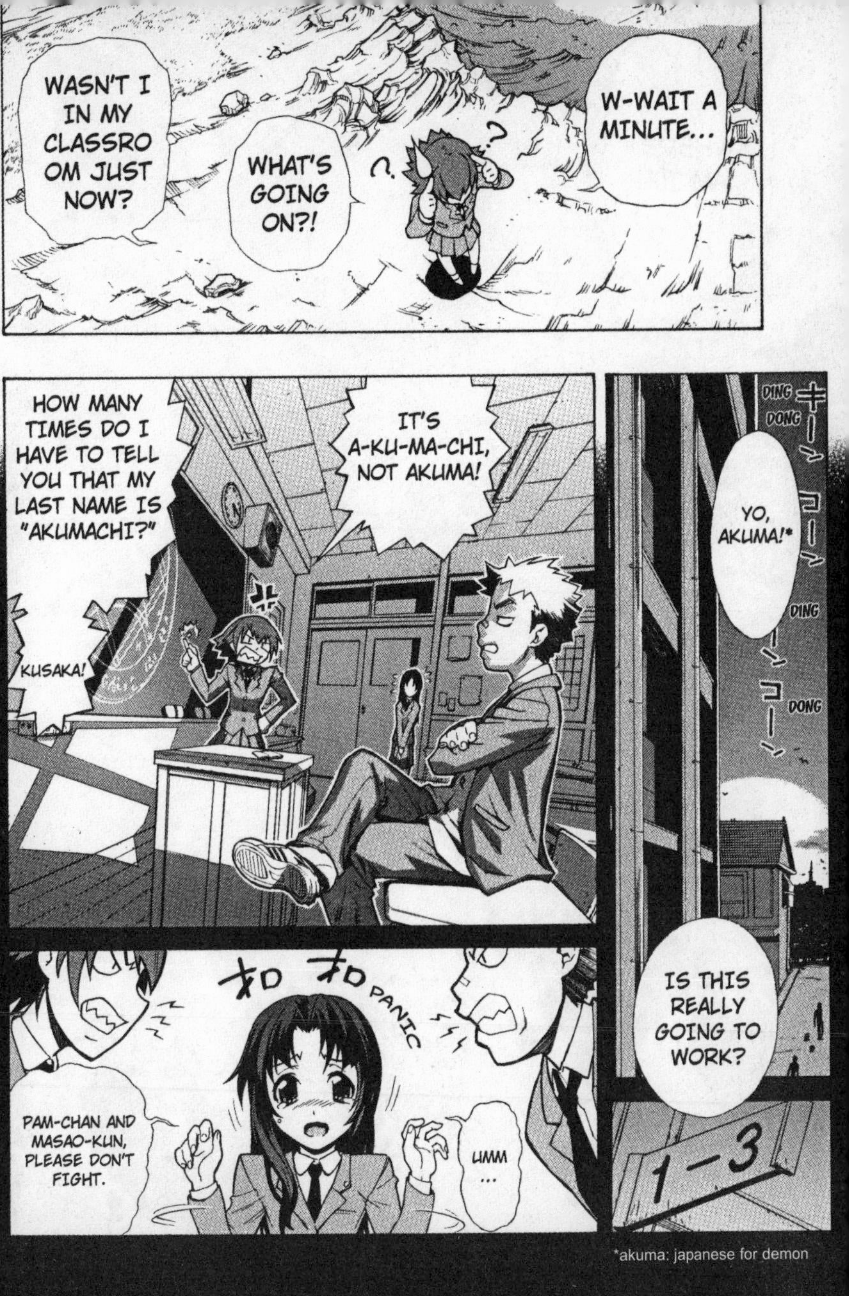
W-WAIT A MINUTE...
WHAT'S GOING ON?!
WASN'T I IN MY CLASSRO OM JUST NOW?
DING DONG
YO, AKUMA!*
DING
DONG
IS THIS REALLY GOING TO WORK?
1-3
IT'S A-KU-MA-CHI, NOT AKUMA!
HOW MANY TIMES DO I HAVE TO TELL YOU THAT MY LAST NAME IS "AKUMACHI?"
KUSAKA!
PANIC
UMM ...
PAM-CHAN AND MASAO-KUN, PLEASE DON'T FIGHT.

*akuma: japanese for demon

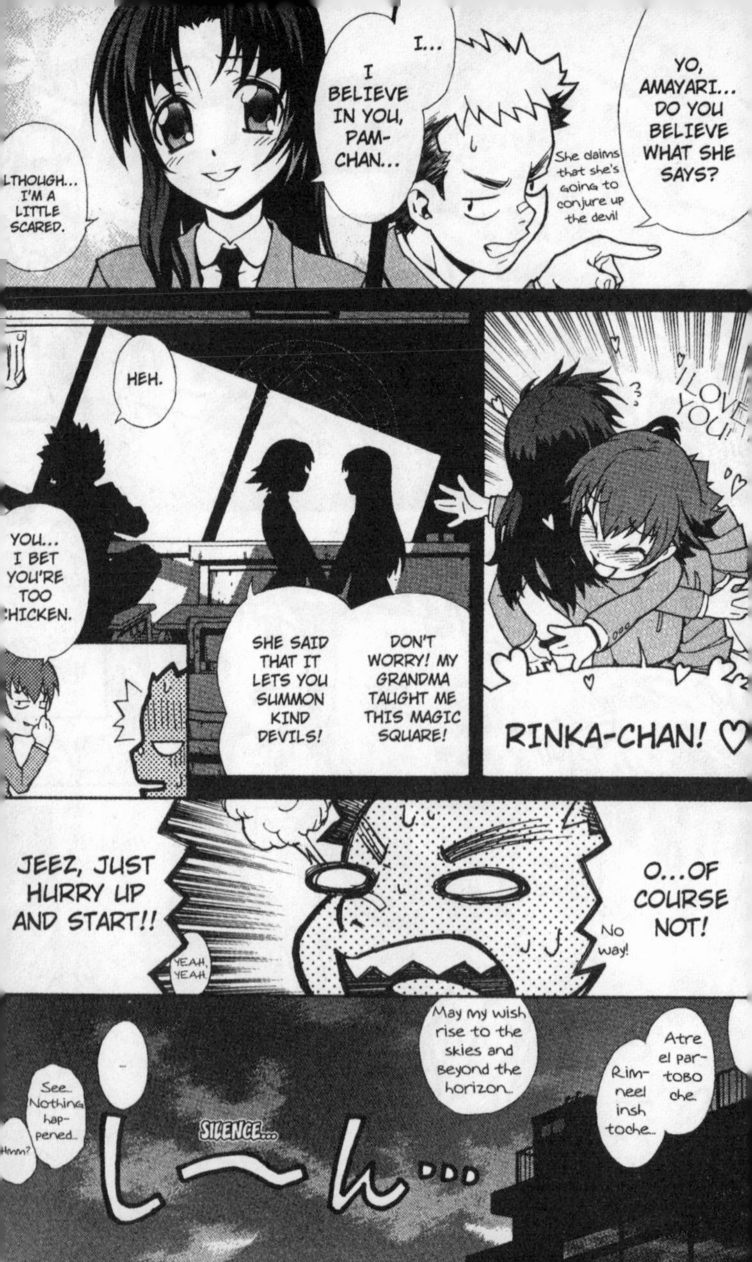
YO, AMAYARI... DO YOU BELIEVE WHAT SHE SAYS?
She claims that she's going to conjure up the devil
I...
I BELIEVE IN YOU, PAM-CHAN...
LTHOUGH... I'M A LITTLE SCARED.
I LOVE YOU!
?
RINKA-CHAN! ♡
HEH.
DON'T WORRY! MY GRANDMA TAUGHT ME THIS MAGIC SQUARE!
SHE SAID THAT IT LETS YOU SUMMON KIND DEVILS!
YOU... I BET YOU'RE TOO HICKEN.
O...OF COURSE NOT!
No way!
JEEZ, JUST HURRY UP AND START!!
YEAH, YEAH.
Atre el partobo che.
Rim-neel insh toche..
May my wish rise to the skies and beyond the horizon..
...
SILENCE...
し〜ん...
See.. Nothing happened..
mm?

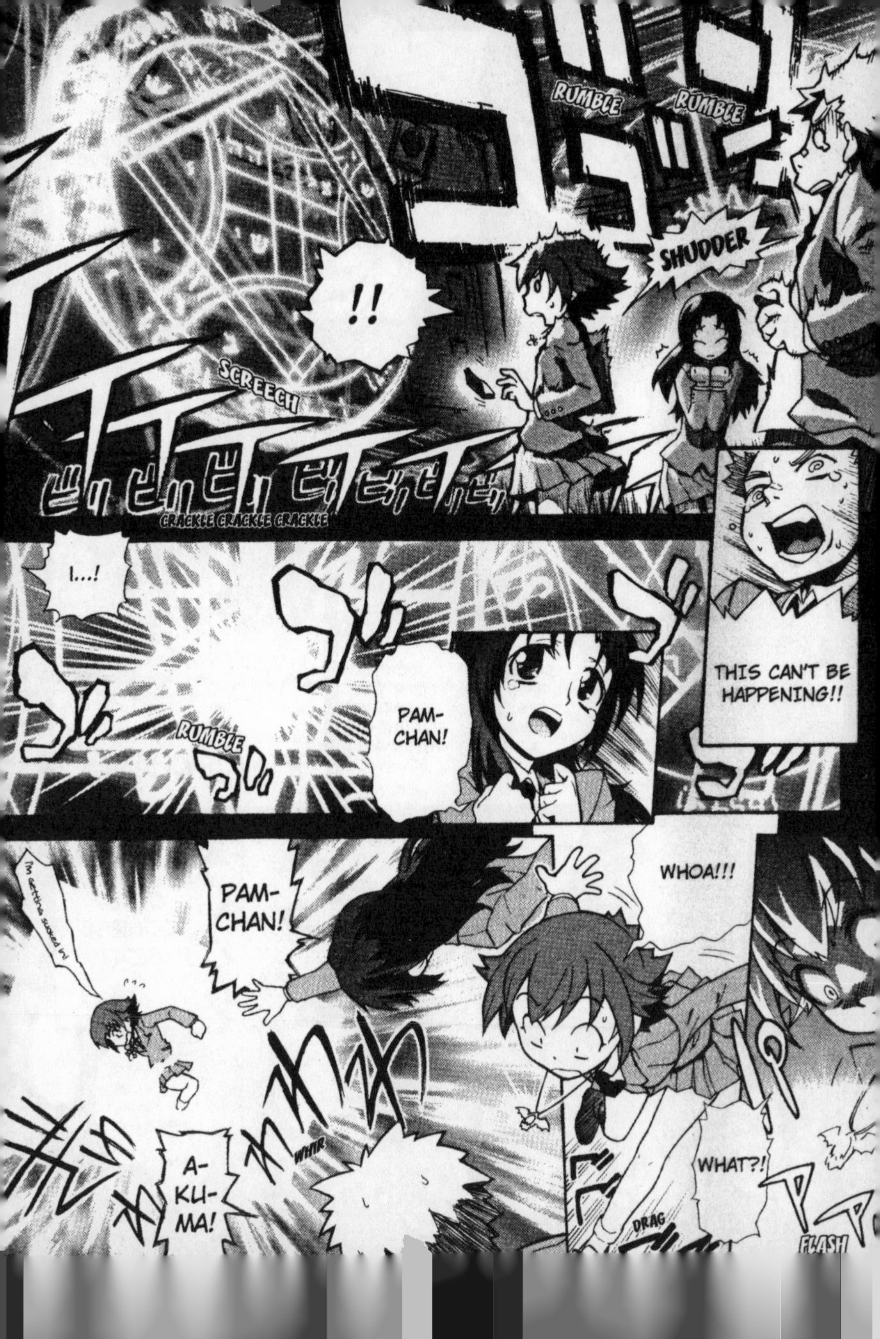
RUMBLE
RUMBLE
SHUDDER
!!
SCREECH
CRACKLE CRACKLE CRACKLE
THIS CAN'T BE HAPPENING!!
PAM-CHAN!
RUMBLE
I...!
WHOA!!!
PAM-CHAN!
I'm getting sucked in!
WHAT?!
FLASH
DRAG
A-KU-MA!
WHIR

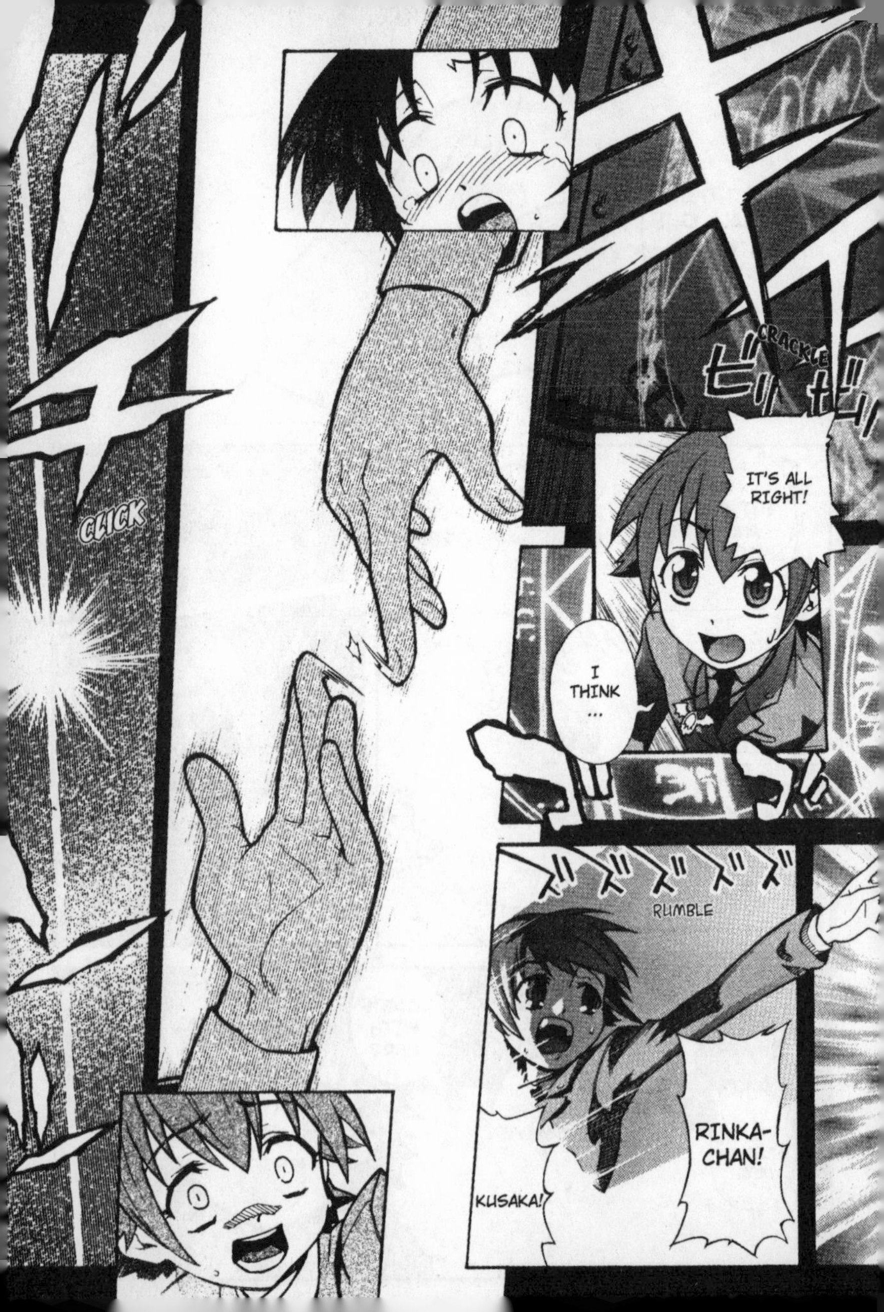
CRACKLE
IT'S ALL RIGHT!
I THINK ...
RUMBLE
RINKA-CHAN!
KUSAKA!
CLICK

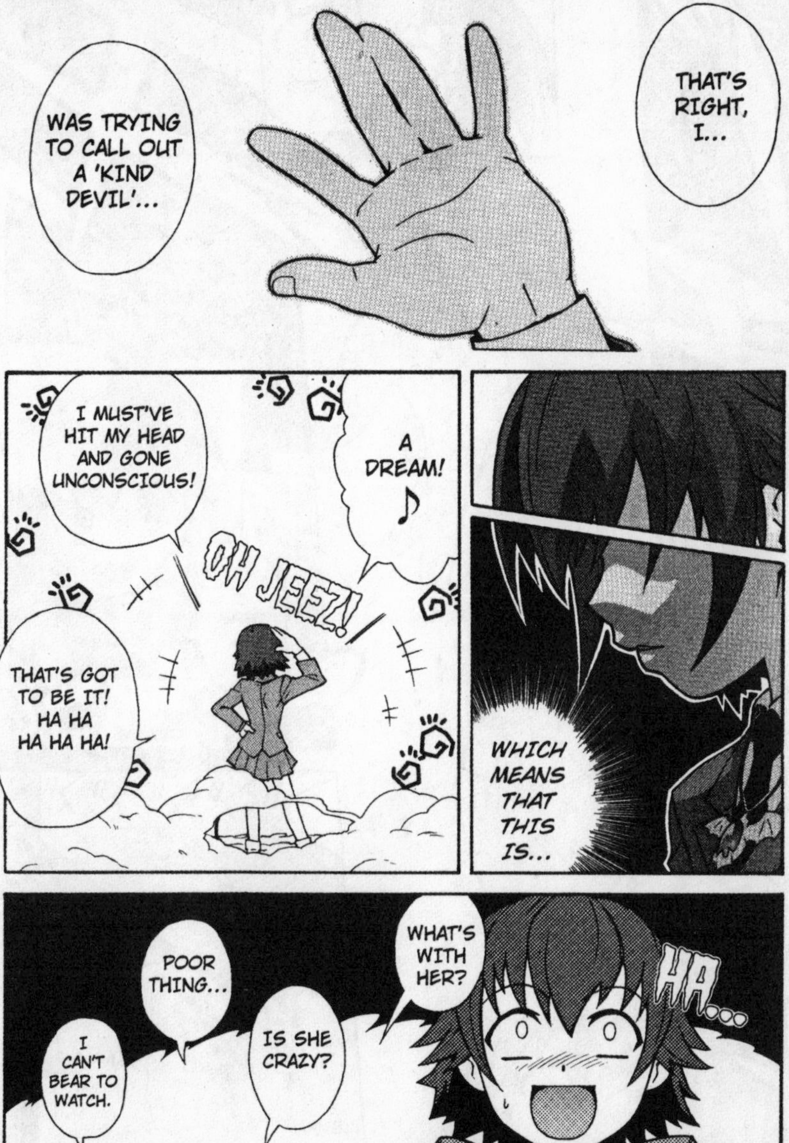
THAT'S RIGHT, I...
WAS TRYING TO CALL OUT A 'KIND DEVIL'...
WHICH MEANS THAT THIS IS...
A DREAM! ♪
OH JEEZ!
I MUST'VE HIT MY HEAD AND GONE UNCONSCIOUS!
THAT'S GOT TO BE IT! HA HA HA HA HA!
HA...
WHAT'S WITH HER?
POOR THING...
IS SHE CRAZY?
I CAN'T BEAR TO WATCH.

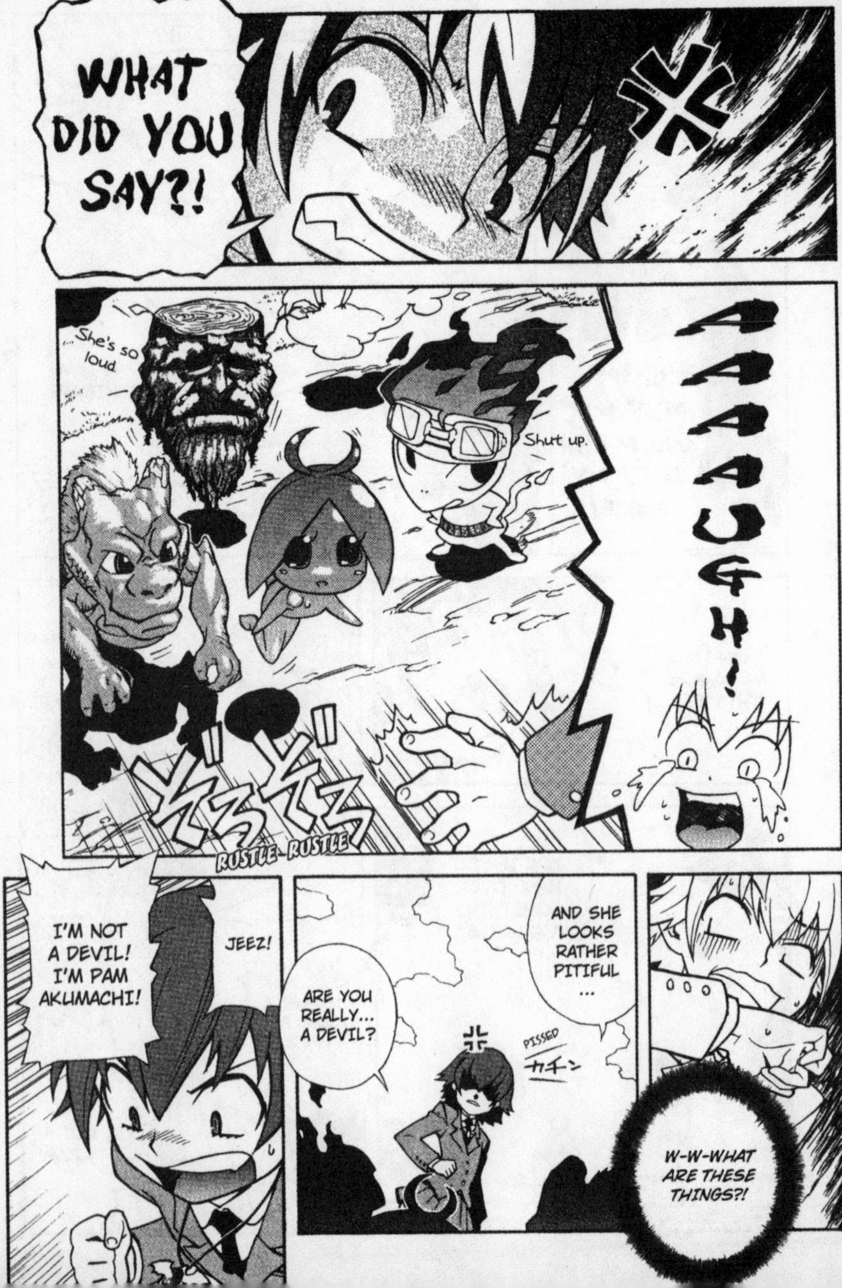
WHAT DID YOU SAY?!
AAAAUGH!
Shut up.
...She's so loud.
ぞろぞろ
RUSTLE RUSTLE
W-W-WHAT ARE THESE THINGS?!
AND SHE LOOKS RATHER PITIFUL ...
ARE YOU REALLY... A DEVIL?
PISSED
カチン
I'M NOT A DEVIL! I'M PAM AKUMACHI!
JEEZ!

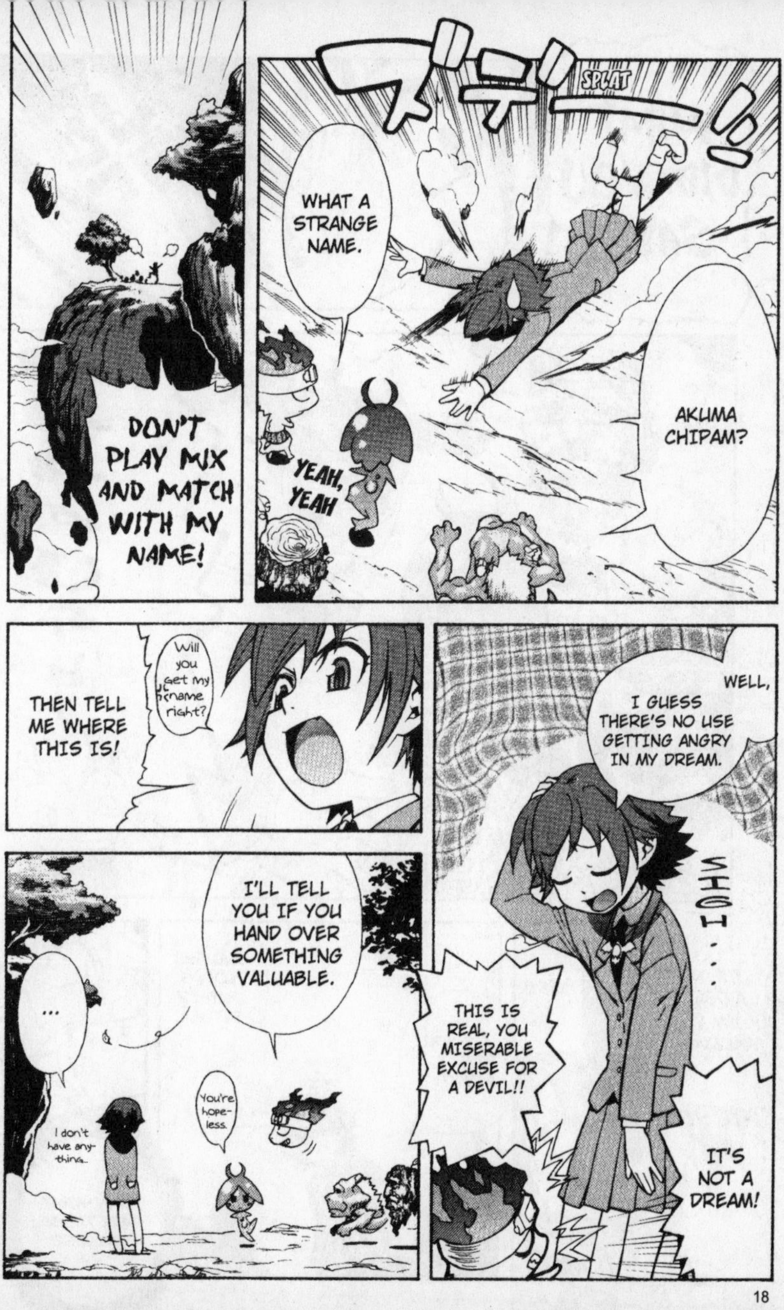
SPLAT
AKUMA CHIPAM?
WHAT A STRANGE NAME.
YEAH, YEAH
DON'T PLAY MIX AND MATCH WITH MY NAME!
WELL, I GUESS THERE'S NO USE GETTING ANGRY IN MY DREAM.
SIGH...
THIS IS REAL, YOU MISERABLE EXCUSE FOR A DEVIL!!
IT'S NOT A DREAM!
Will you get my name right?
THEN TELL ME WHERE THIS IS!
I'LL TELL YOU IF YOU HAND OVER SOMETHING VALUABLE.
You're hopeless.
...
I don't have anything...

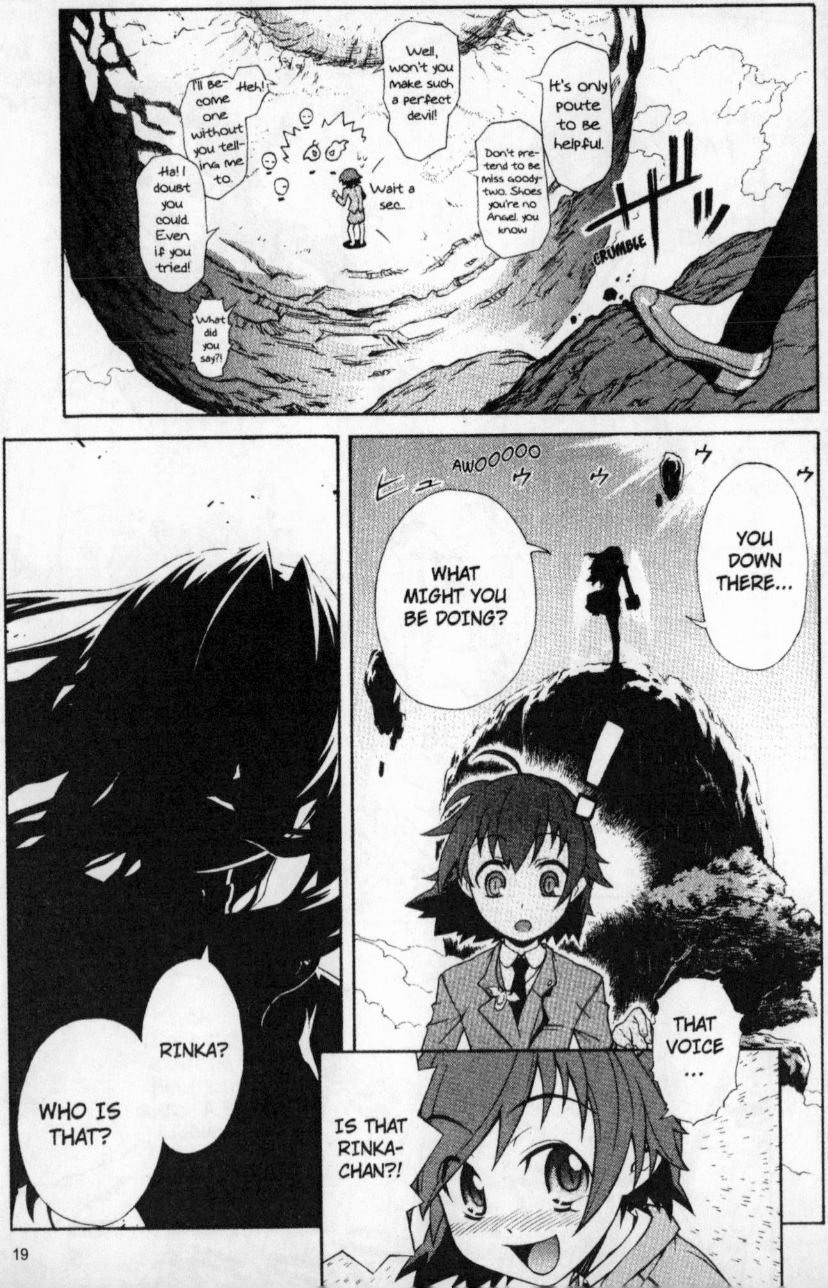
CRUMBLE
It's only poute to be helpful.
Don't pretend to be miss goody-two. Shoes you're no Angel. you know
Well, won't you make such a perfect devil!
Heh!
I'll become one without you telling me to.
Ha! I doubt you could. Even if you tried!
Wait a sec...
What did you say?!
AWOOOOO
YOU DOWN THERE...
WHAT MIGHT YOU BE DOING?
THAT VOICE ...
IS THAT RINKA-CHAN?!
RINKA?
WHO IS THAT?

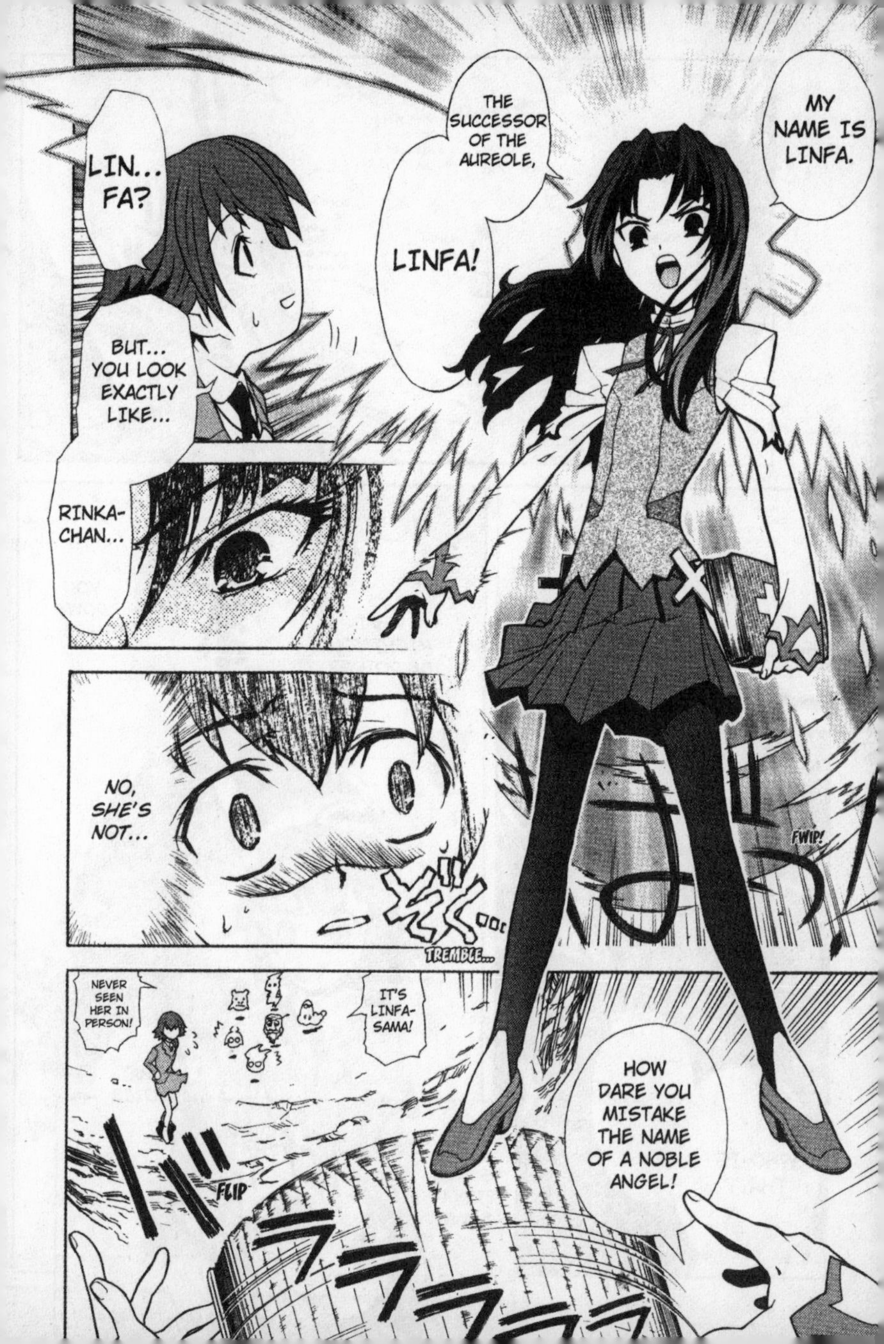
MY NAME IS LINFA.
THE SUCCESSOR OF THE AUREOLE,
LINFA!
FWIP!
LIN... FA?
BUT... YOU LOOK EXACTLY LIKE...
RINKA-CHAN...
NO, SHE'S NOT...
TREMBLE...
HOW DARE YOU MISTAKE THE NAME OF A NOBLE ANGEL!
IT'S LINFA-SAMA!
NEVER SEEN HER IN PERSON!
FLIP

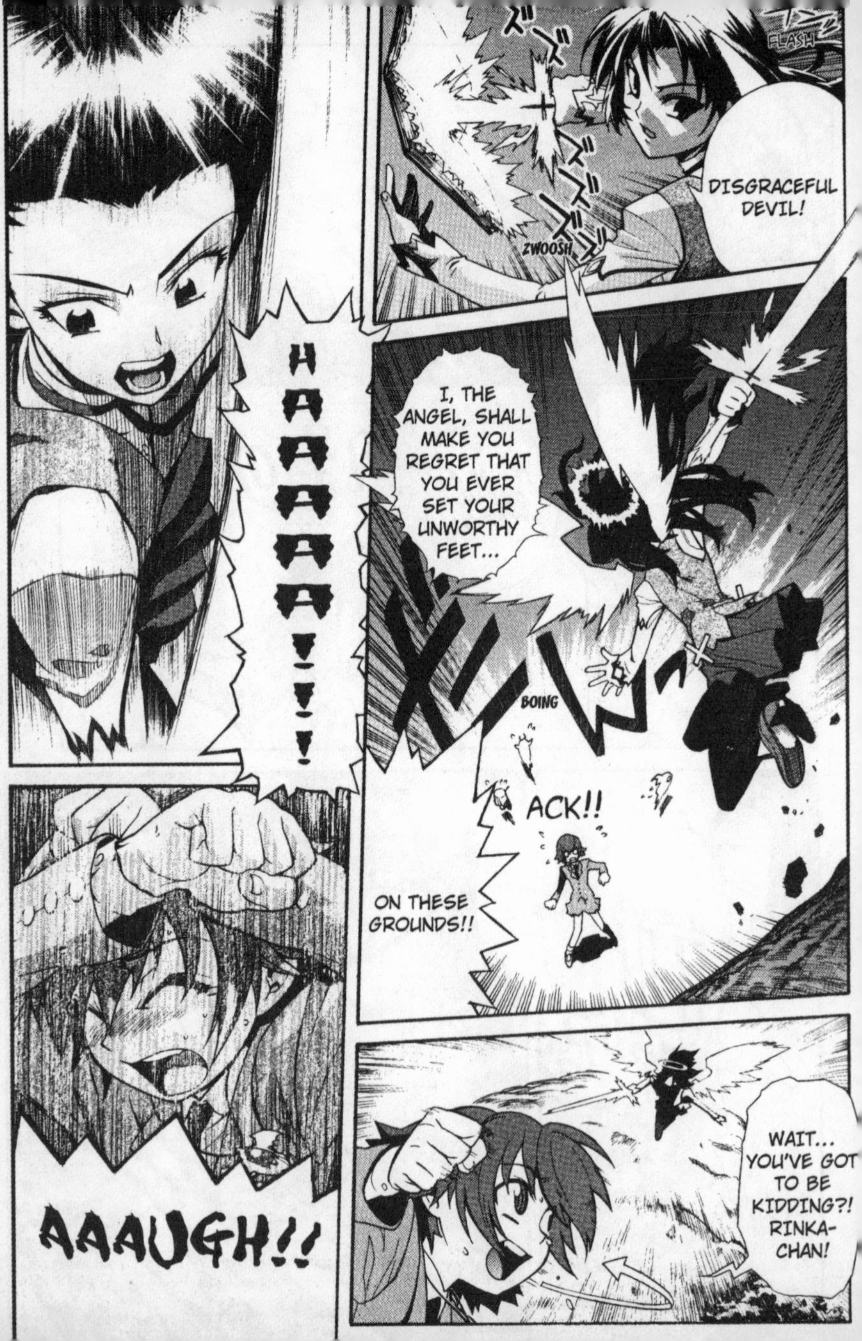
FLASH
DISGRACEFUL DEVIL!
ZWOOSH
I, THE ANGEL, SHALL MAKE YOU REGRET THAT YOU EVER SET YOUR UNWORTHY FEET...
BOING
ACK!!
ON THESE GROUNDS!!
HAAAAA!!!
WAIT... YOU'VE GOT TO BE KIDDING?! RINKA-CHAN!
AAAUGH!!

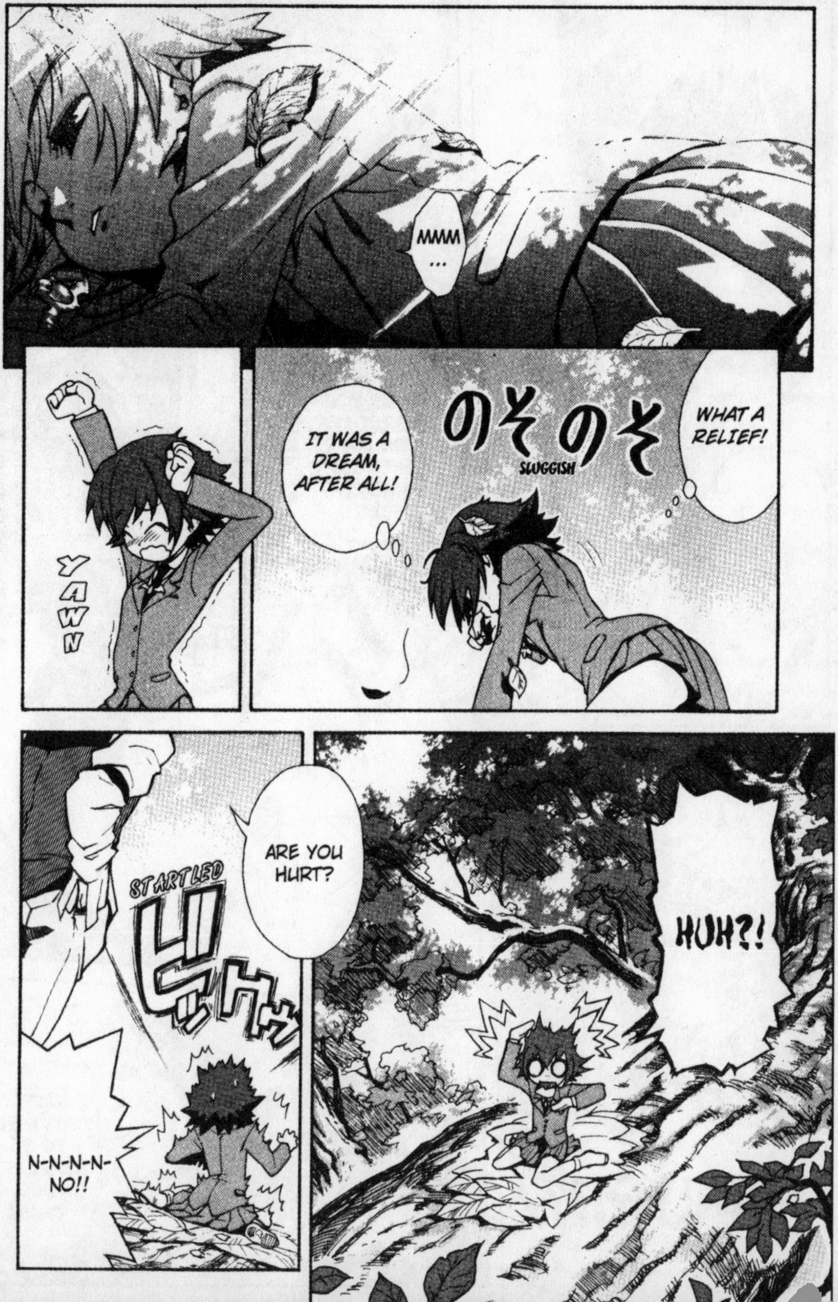
MMM ...
WHAT A RELIEF!
のそのそ
SLUGGISH
IT WAS A DREAM, AFTER ALL!
YAWN
HUH?!
ARE YOU HURT?
STARTLED
N-N-N-N-NO!!

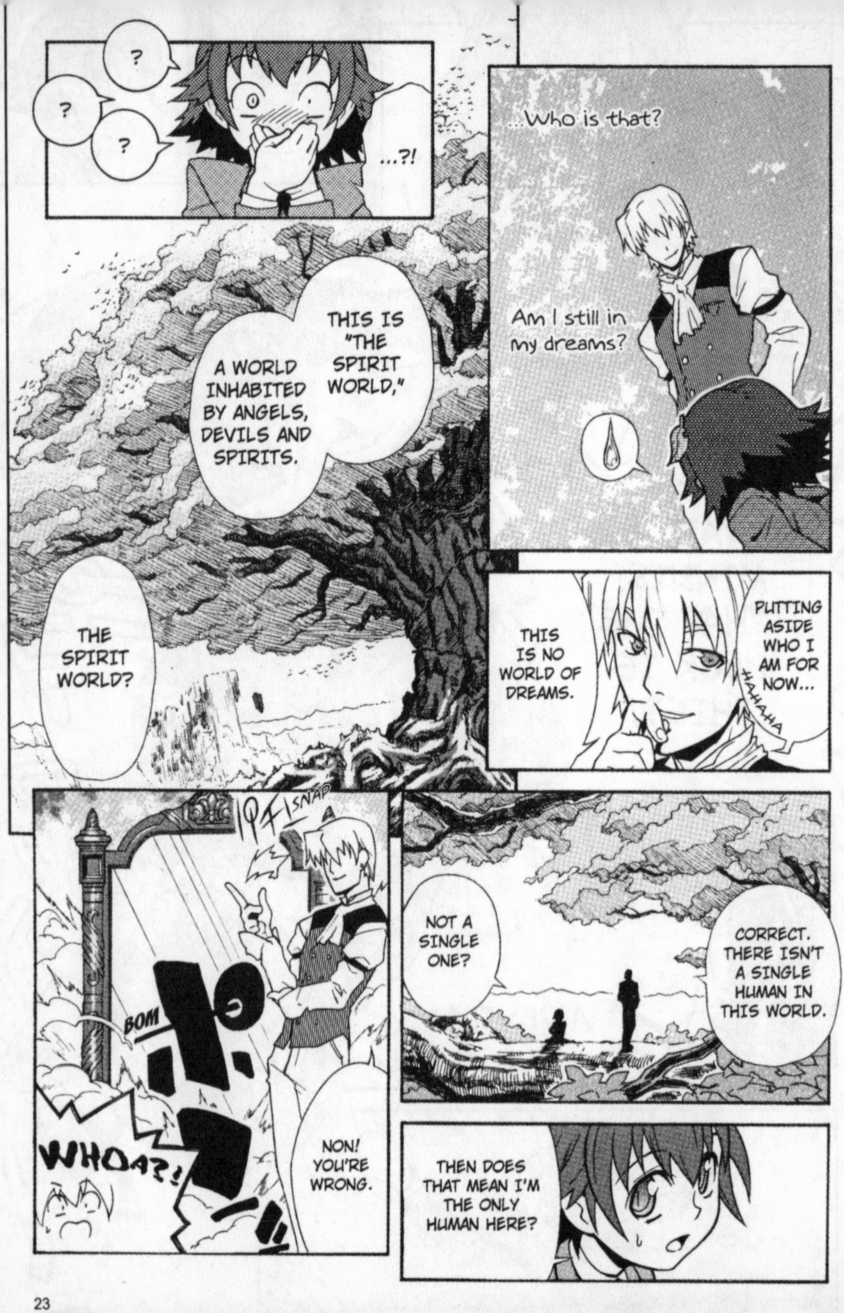
...Who is that?
Am I still in my dreams?
?
?
?
...?!
THIS IS "THE SPIRIT WORLD,"
A WORLD INHABITED BY ANGELS, DEVILS AND SPIRITS.
THE SPIRIT WORLD?
PUTTING ASIDE WHO I AM FOR NOW...
HAHAHA
THIS IS NO WORLD OF DREAMS.
CORRECT. THERE ISN'T A SINGLE HUMAN IN THIS WORLD.
NOT A SINGLE ONE?
THEN DOES THAT MEAN I'M THE ONLY HUMAN HERE?
SNAP
NON! YOU'RE WRONG.
BOM
WHOA?!

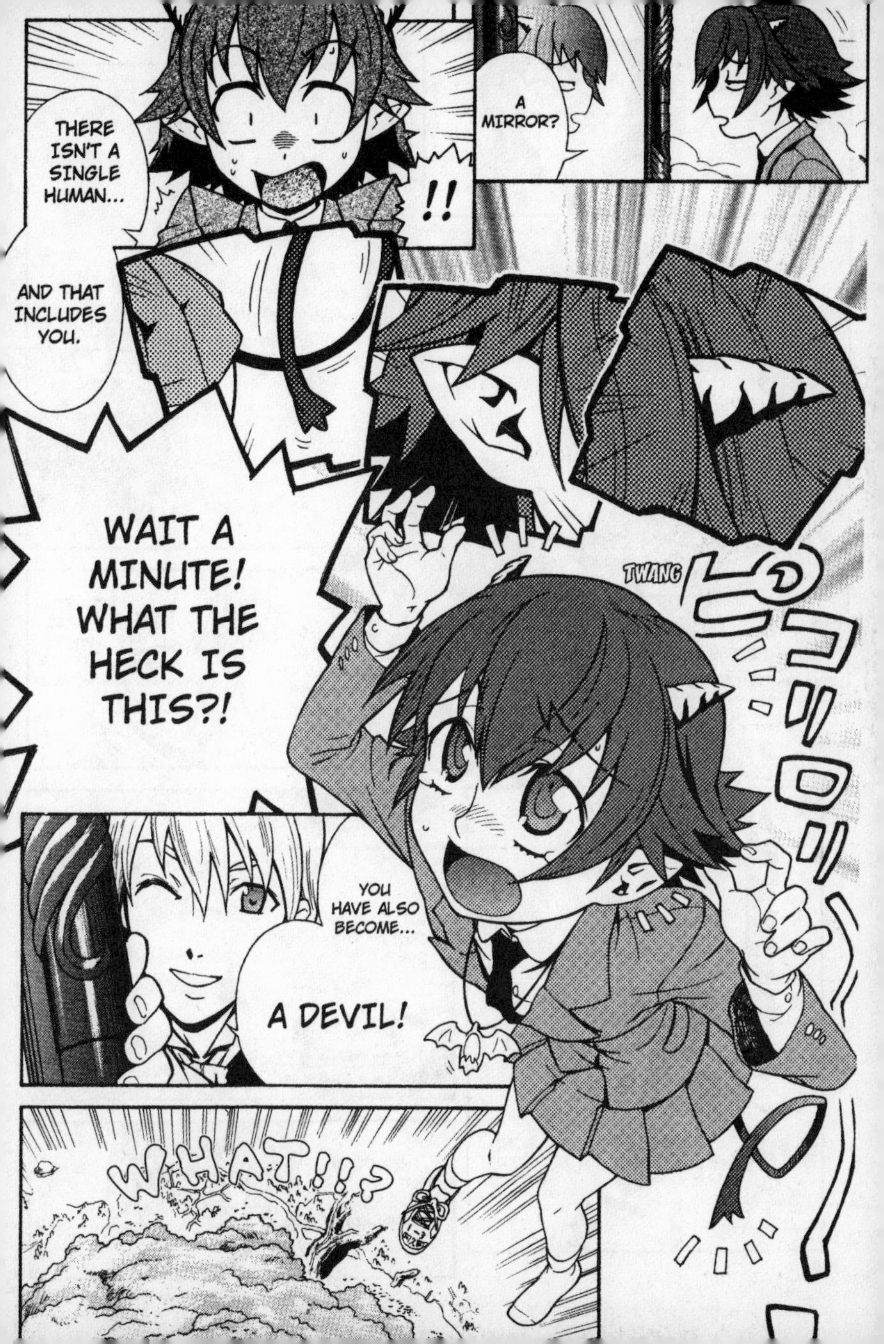
A MIRROR?
THERE ISN'T A SINGLE HUMAN...
!!
AND THAT INCLUDES YOU.
WAIT A MINUTE! WHAT THE HECK IS THIS?!
TWANG
YOU HAVE ALSO BECOME...
A DEVIL!
WHAT!!?

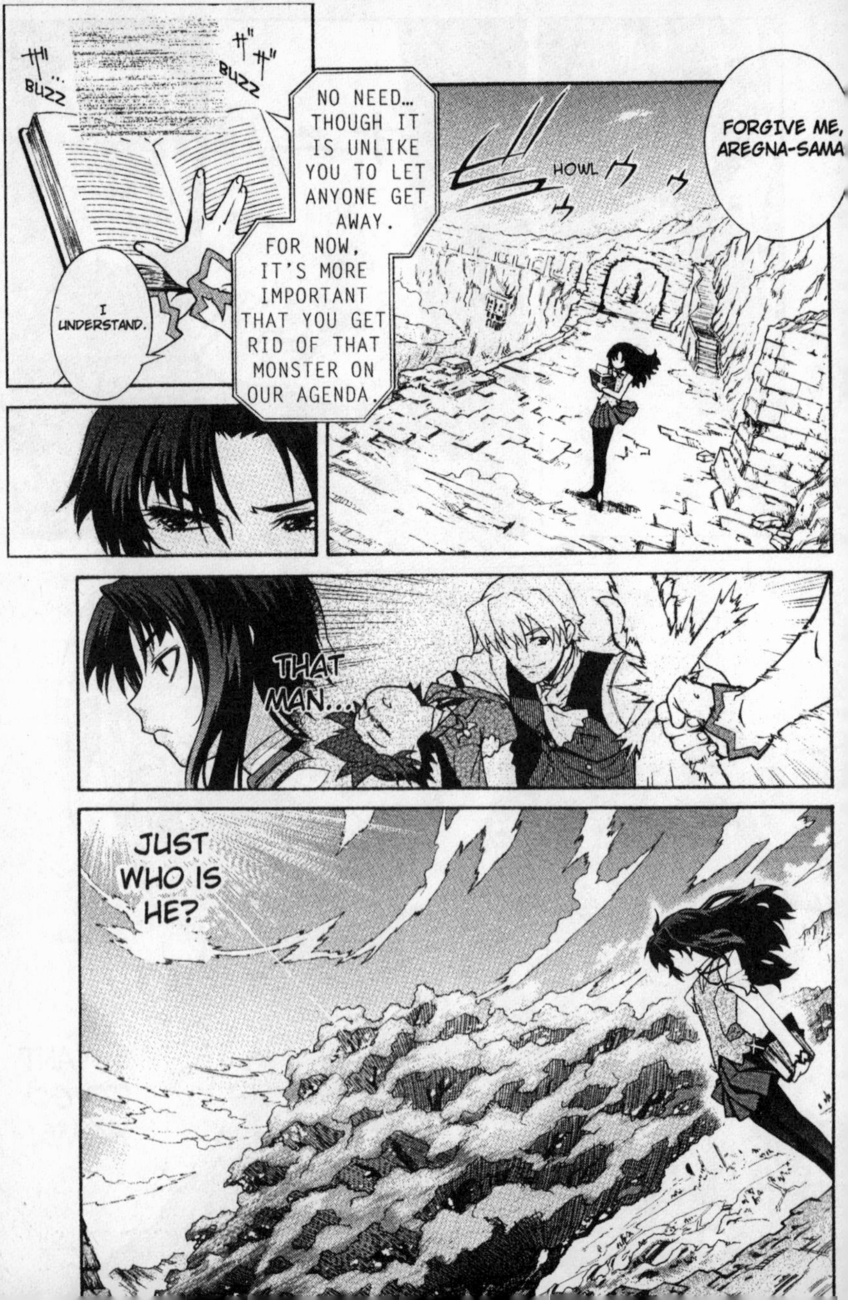
FORGIVE ME, AREGNA-SAMA
HOWL
NO NEED... THOUGH IT IS UNLIKE YOU TO LET ANYONE GET AWAY.
FOR NOW, IT'S MORE IMPORTANT THAT YOU GET RID OF THAT MONSTER ON OUR AGENDA.
BUZZ
BUZZ
I UNDERSTAND.
THAT MAN...
JUST WHO IS HE?

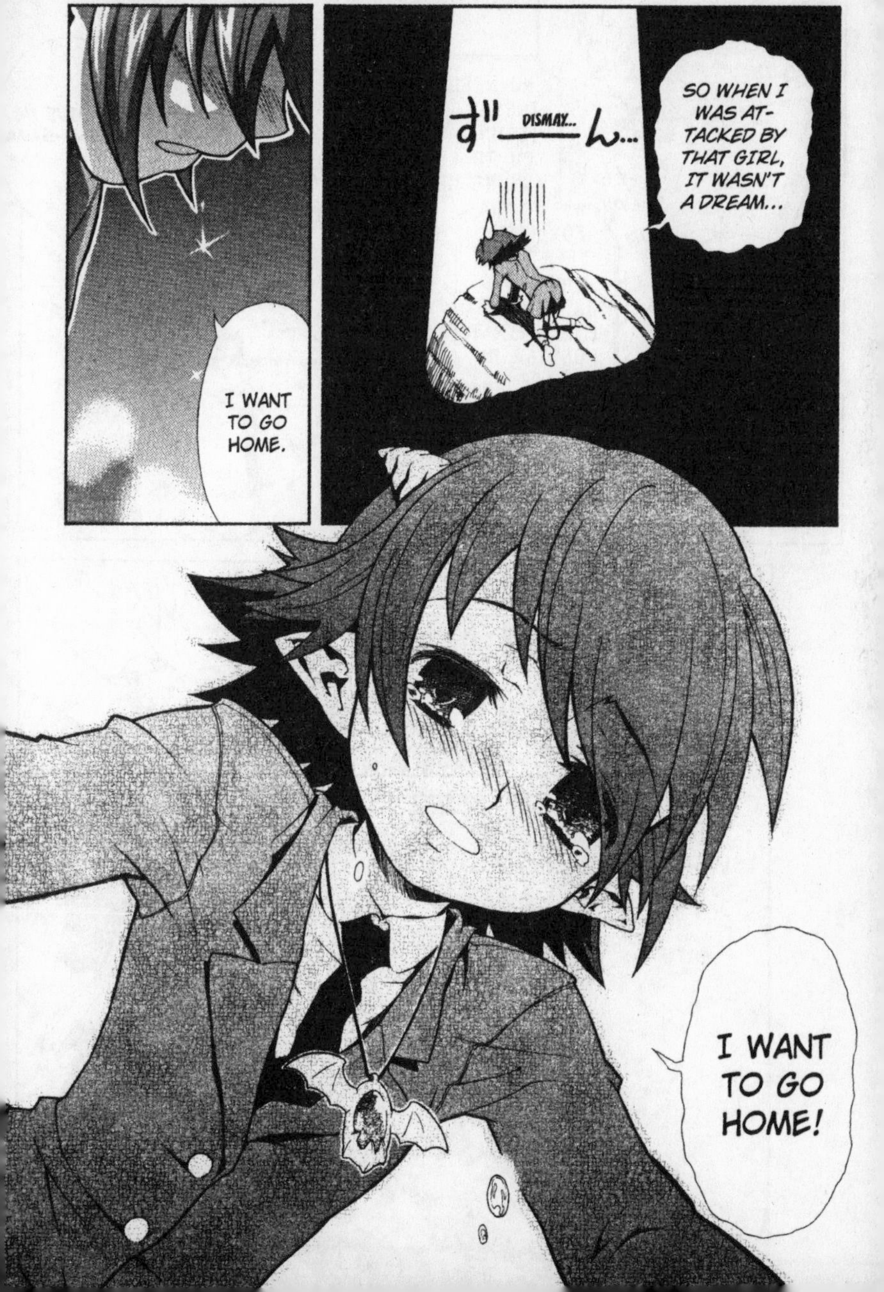
SO WHEN I WAS AT-TACKED BY THAT GIRL, IT WASN'T A DREAM...
ずーん...
DISMAY...
I WANT TO GO HOME.
I WANT TO GO HOME!

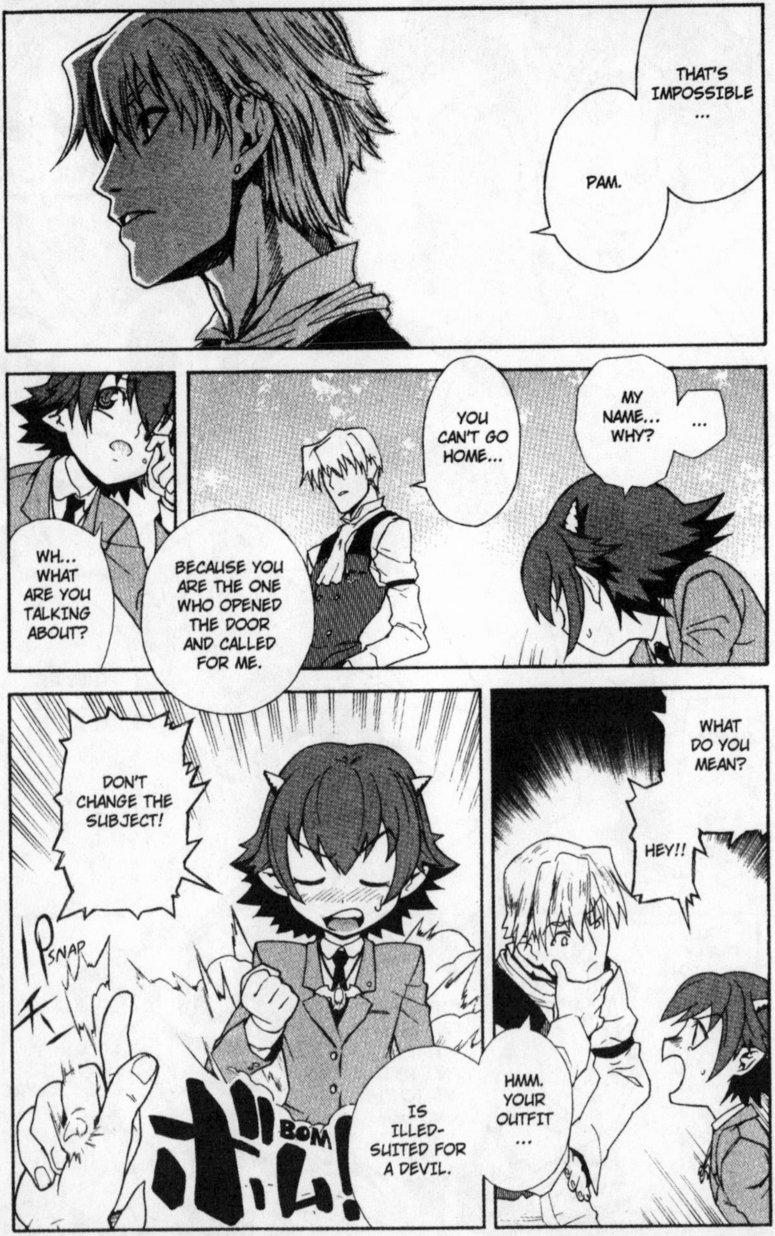
THAT'S IMPOSSIBLE ...
PAM.
MY NAME... WHY?
...
YOU CAN'T GO HOME...
BECAUSE YOU ARE THE ONE WHO OPENED THE DOOR AND CALLED FOR ME.
WH... WHAT ARE YOU TALKING ABOUT?
WHAT DO YOU MEAN?
HEY!!
HMM. YOUR OUTFIT ...
IS ILLED-SUITED FOR A DEVIL.
DON'T CHANGE THE SUBJECT!
SNAP
BOM

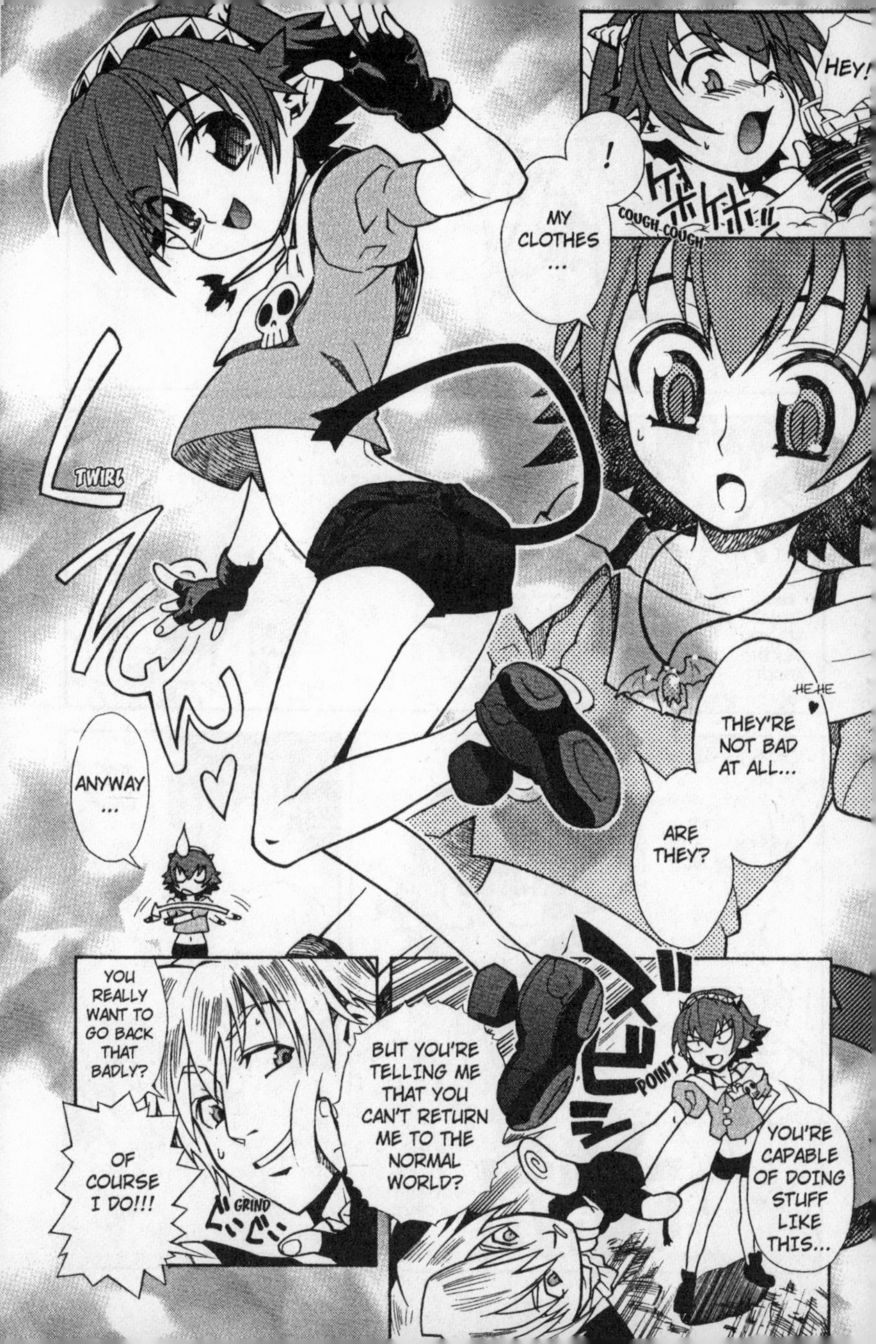
HEY!
COUGH COUGH
!
MY CLOTHES ...
HE HE
THEY'RE NOT BAD AT ALL...
ARE THEY?
TWIRL
ANYWAY ...
POINT
YOU'RE CAPABLE OF DOING STUFF LIKE THIS...
BUT YOU'RE TELLING ME THAT YOU CAN'T RETURN ME TO THE NORMAL WORLD?
YOU REALLY WANT TO GO BACK THAT BADLY?
OF COURSE I DO!!!
GRIND

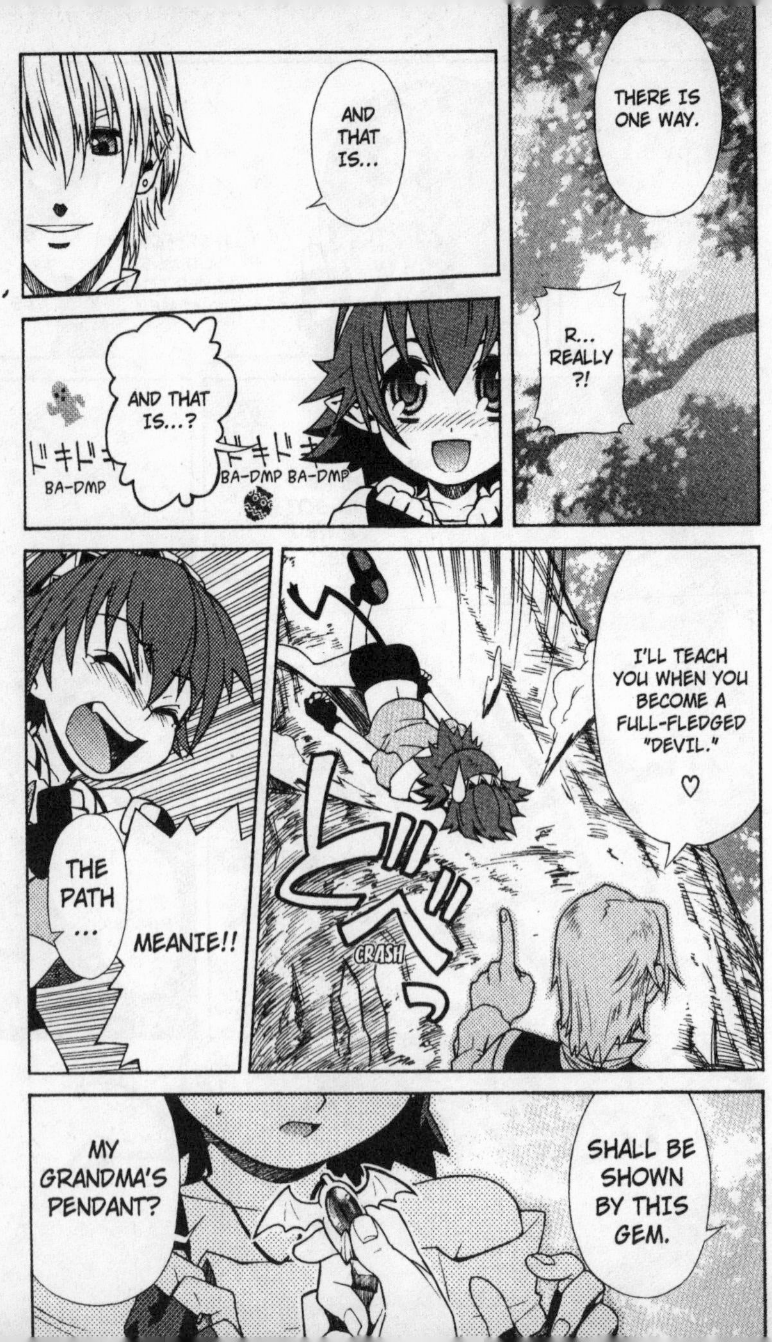
THERE IS ONE WAY.
R... REALLY?!
AND THAT IS...
AND THAT IS...?
ドキドキ
BA-DMP BA-DMP
ドキドキ
BA-DMP
I'LL TEACH YOU WHEN YOU BECOME A FULL-FLEDGED "DEVIL." ♡
CRASH
MEANIE!!
THE PATH...
SHALL BE SHOWN BY THIS GEM.
MY GRANDMA'S PENDANT?

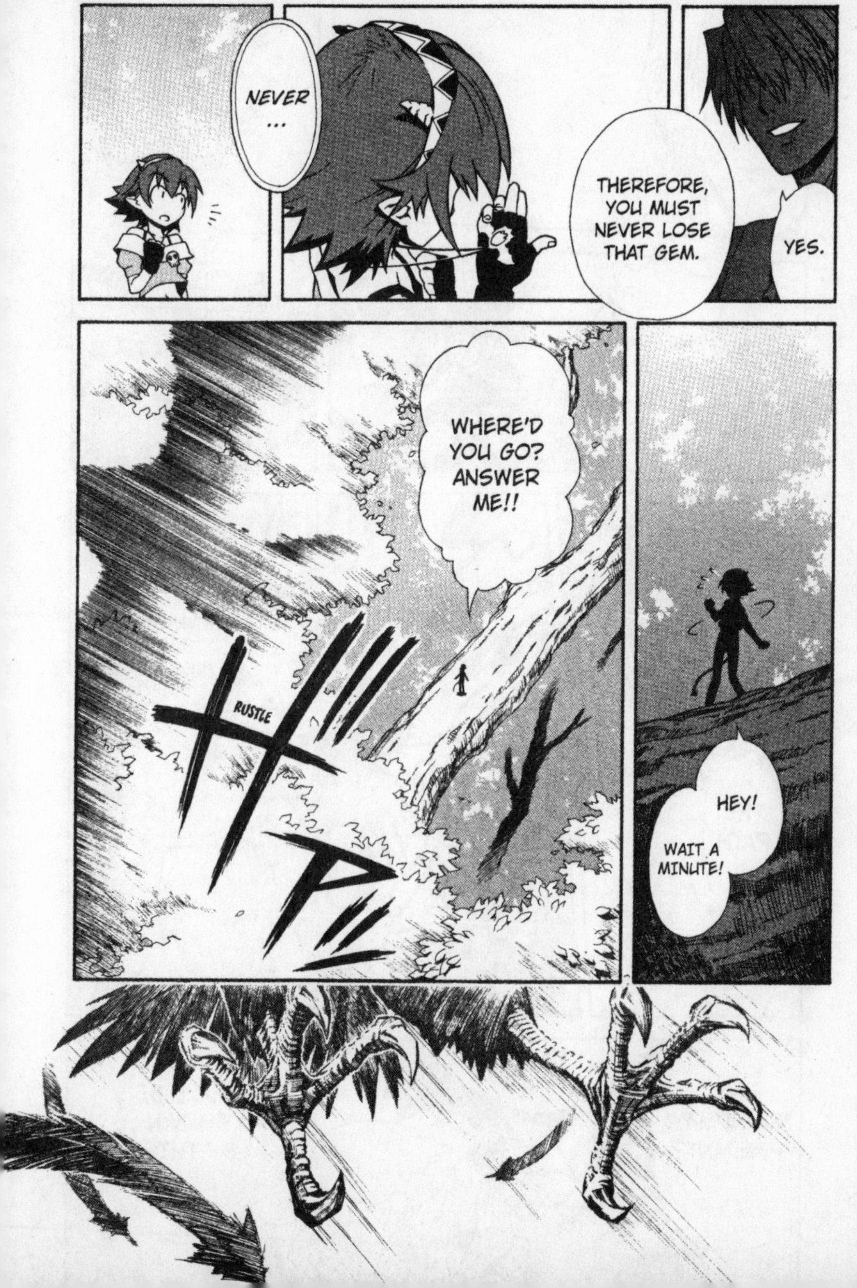
THEREFORE, YOU MUST NEVER LOSE THAT GEM.
YES.
NEVER ...
HEY!
WAIT A MINUTE!
WHERE'D YOU GO? ANSWER ME!!
RUSTLE

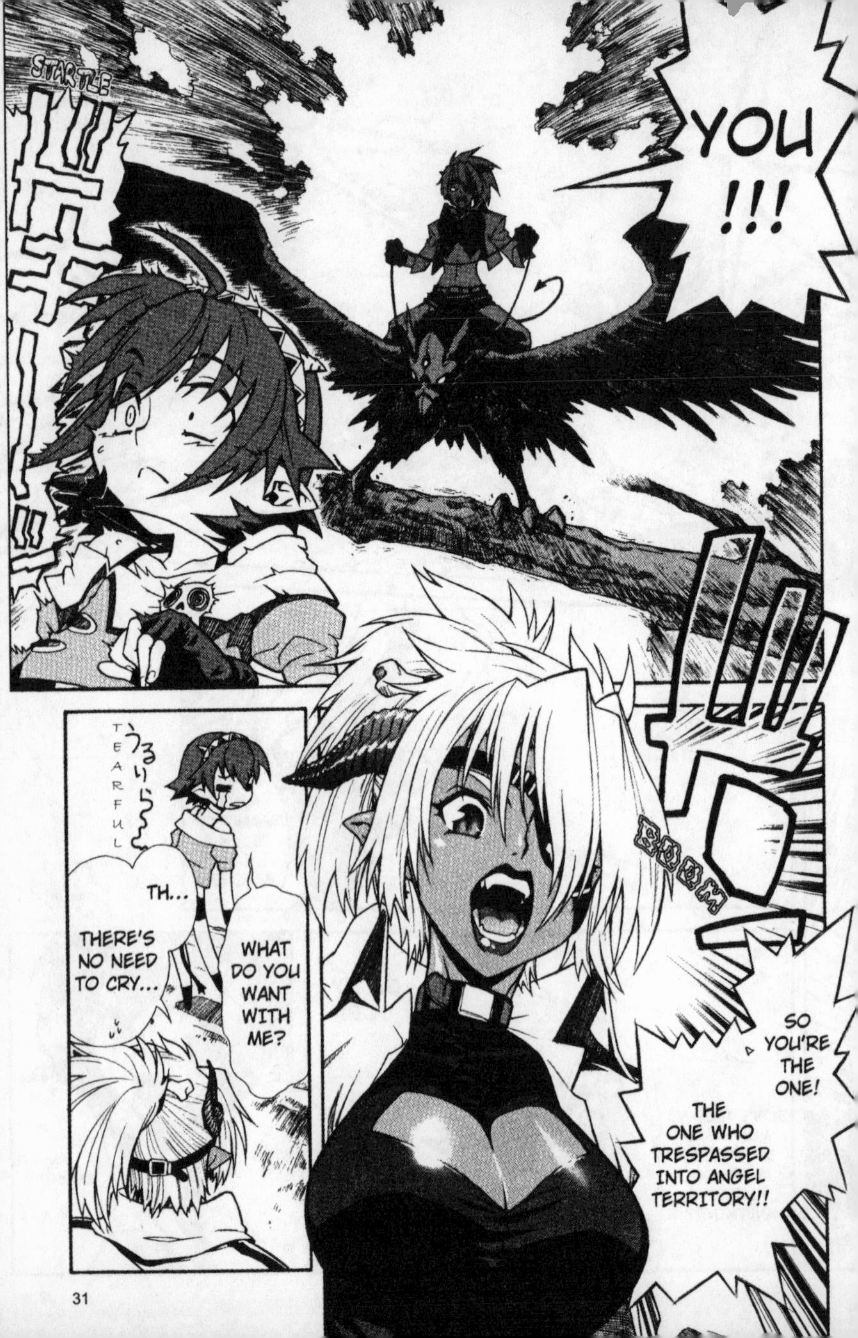
YOU !!!
STARTLE
BOOM
SO YOU'RE THE ONE!
THE ONE WHO TRESPASSED INTO ANGEL TERRITORY!!
TEARFUL
WHAT DO YOU WANT WITH ME?
TH...
THERE'S NO NEED TO CRY...

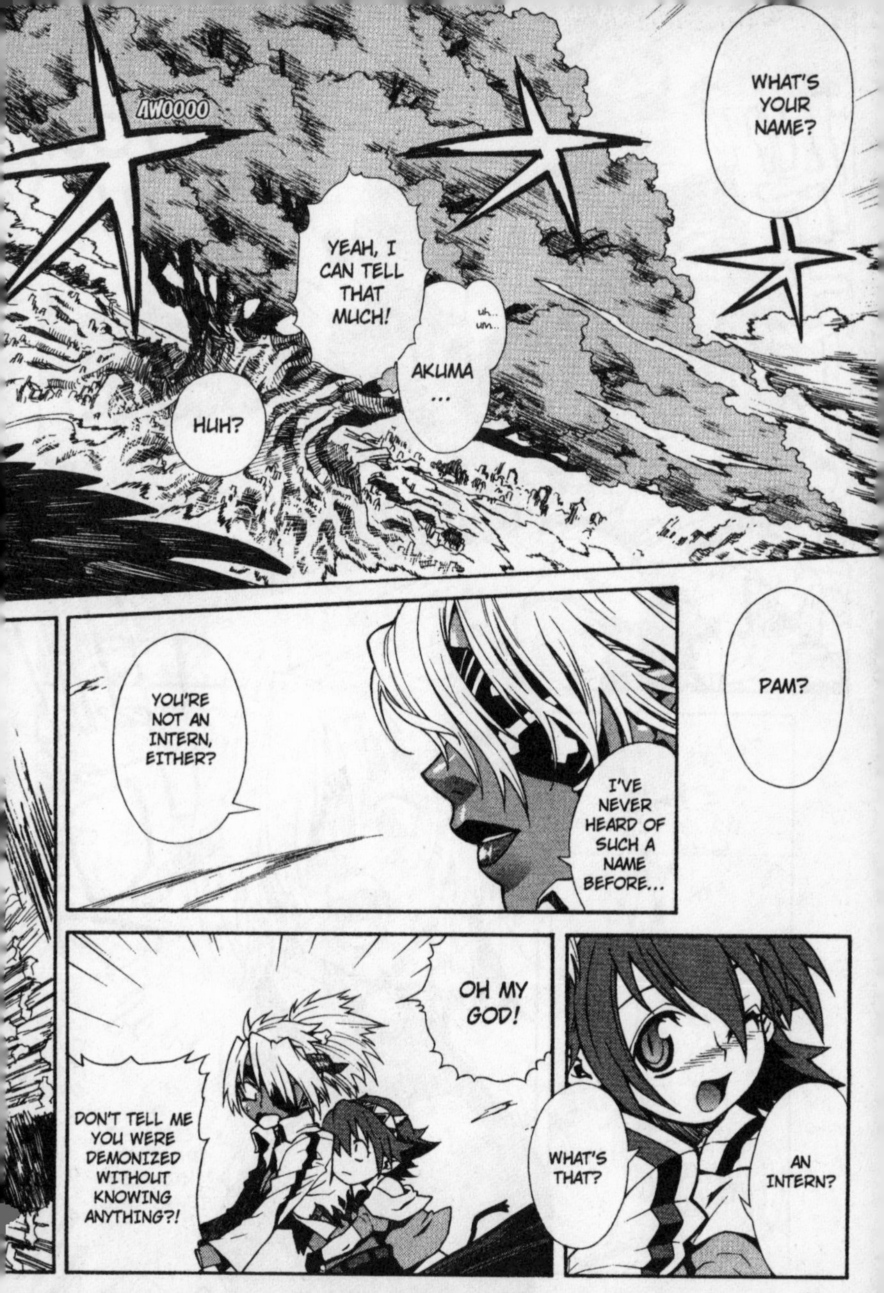
WHAT'S YOUR NAME?
AWOOOO
uh... um...
AKUMA ...
YEAH, I CAN TELL THAT MUCH!
HUH?
PAM?
I'VE NEVER HEARD OF SUCH A NAME BEFORE...
YOU'RE NOT AN INTERN, EITHER?
AN INTERN?
WHAT'S THAT?
OH MY GOD!
DON'T TELL ME YOU WERE DEMONIZED WITHOUT KNOWING ANYTHING?!

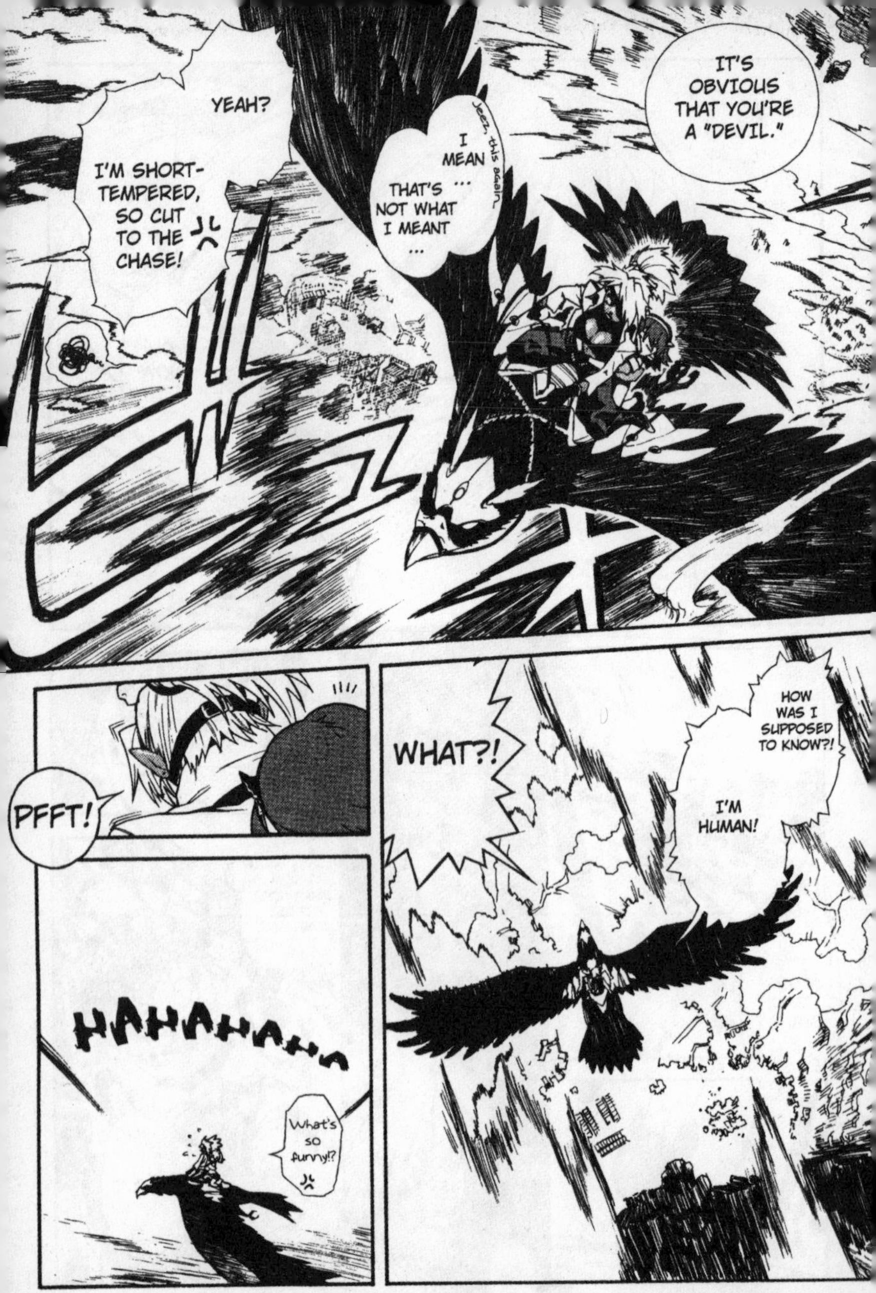
IT'S OBVIOUS THAT YOU'RE A "DEVIL."
I MEAN ... THAT'S NOT WHAT I MEANT ...
Jeez, this again.
YEAH?
I'M SHORT-TEMPERED, SO CUT TO THE CHASE!
HOW WAS I SUPPOSED TO KNOW?!
I'M HUMAN!
WHAT?!
PFFT!
HAHAHAHA
What's so funny!?

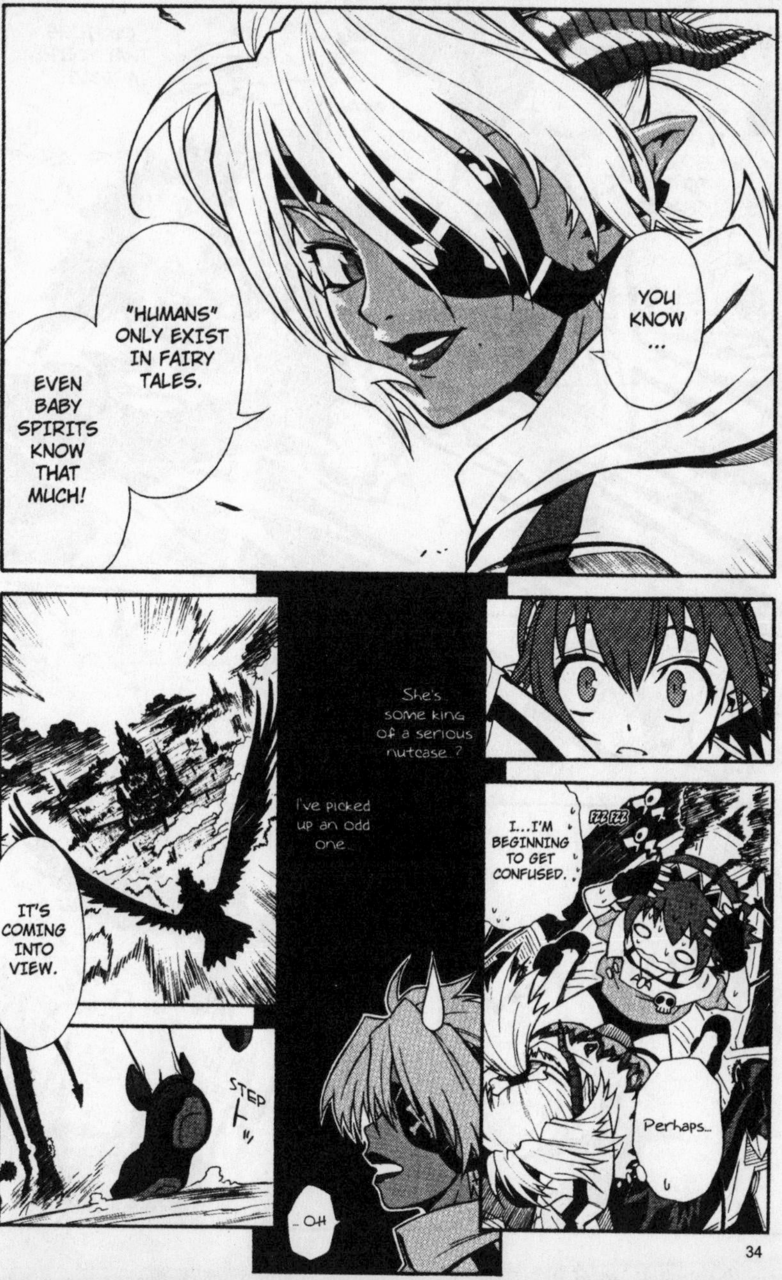

YOU KNOW ...
"HUMANS" ONLY EXIST IN FAIRY TALES.
EVEN BABY SPIRITS KNOW THAT MUCH!
She's some king of a serious nutcase..?
I've picked up an odd one...
I...I'M BEGINNING TO GET CONFUSED.
FZZ FZZ
Perhaps...
...OH
IT'S COMING INTO VIEW.
STEP

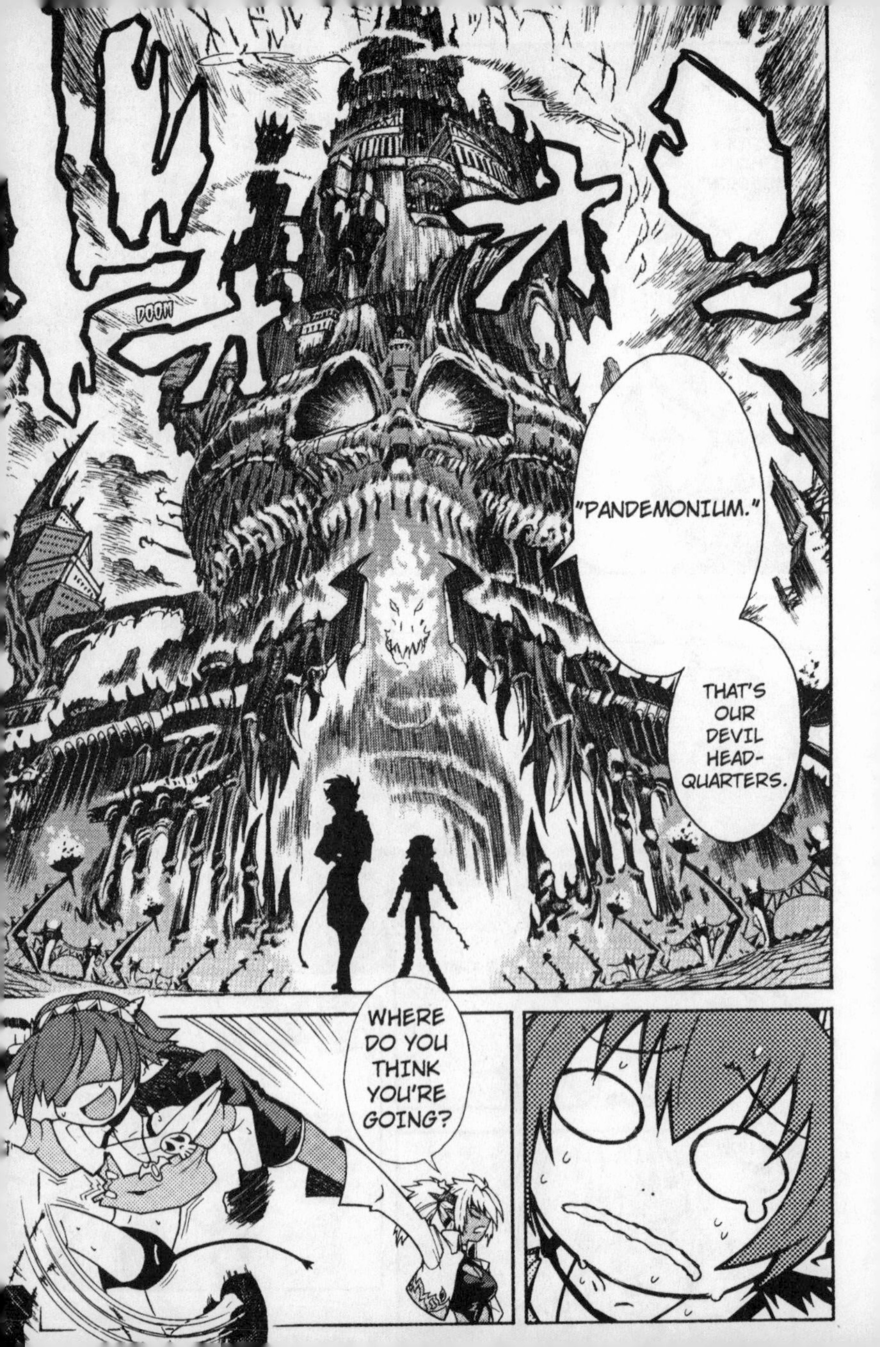
"PANDEMONIUM."
THAT'S OUR DEVIL HEAD-QUARTERS.
DOOM
WHERE DO YOU THINK YOU'RE GOING?

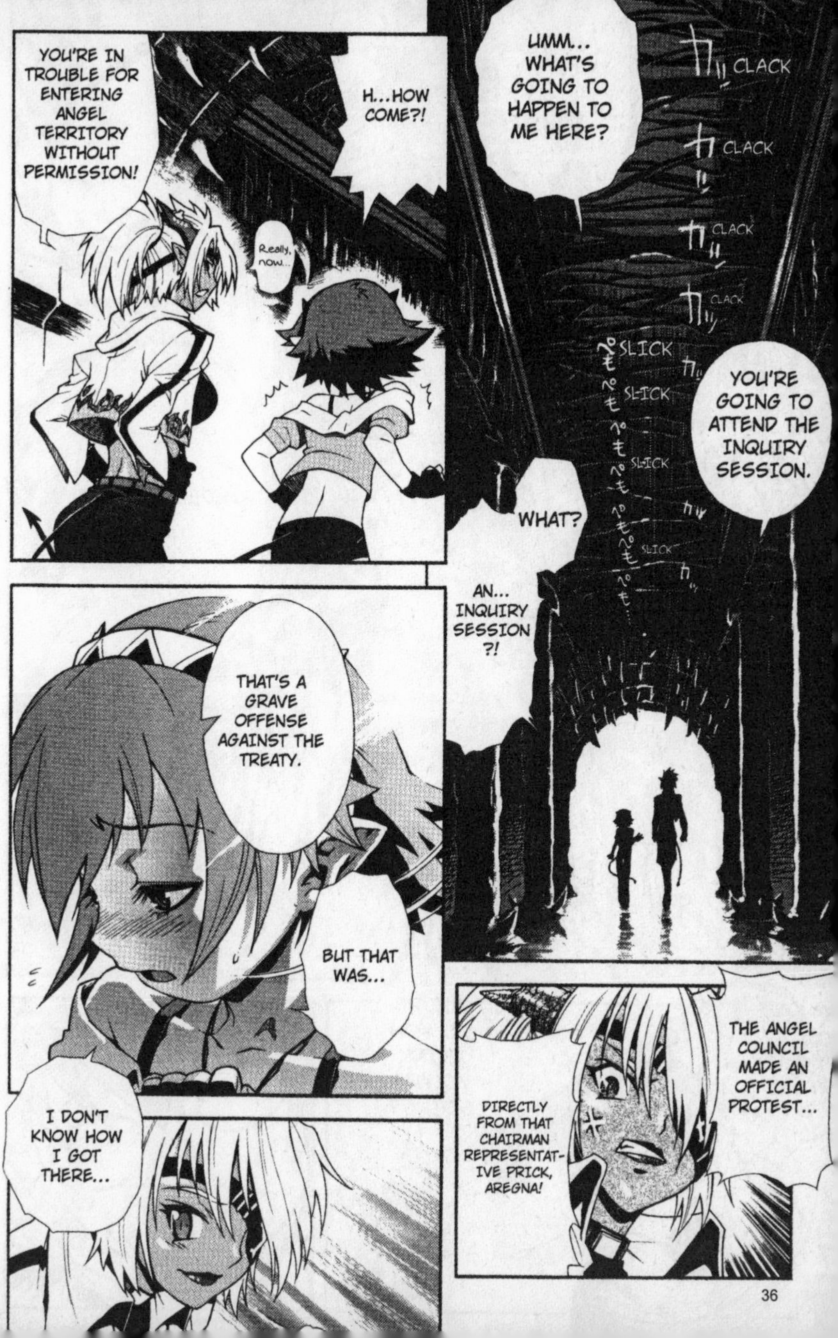
UMM... WHAT'S GOING TO HAPPEN TO ME HERE?
CLACK
CLACK
CLACK
CLACK
SLICK
SLICK
SLICK
SLICK
YOU'RE GOING TO ATTEND THE INQUIRY SESSION.
WHAT?
AN... INQUIRY SESSION?!
YOU'RE IN TROUBLE FOR ENTERING ANGEL TERRITORY WITHOUT PERMISSION!
H...HOW COME?!
Really, now...
THAT'S A GRAVE OFFENSE AGAINST THE TREATY.
BUT THAT WAS...
I DON'T KNOW HOW I GOT THERE...
THE ANGEL COUNCIL MADE AN OFFICIAL PROTEST...
DIRECTLY FROM THAT CHAIRMAN REPRESENTAT-IVE PRICK, AREGNA!

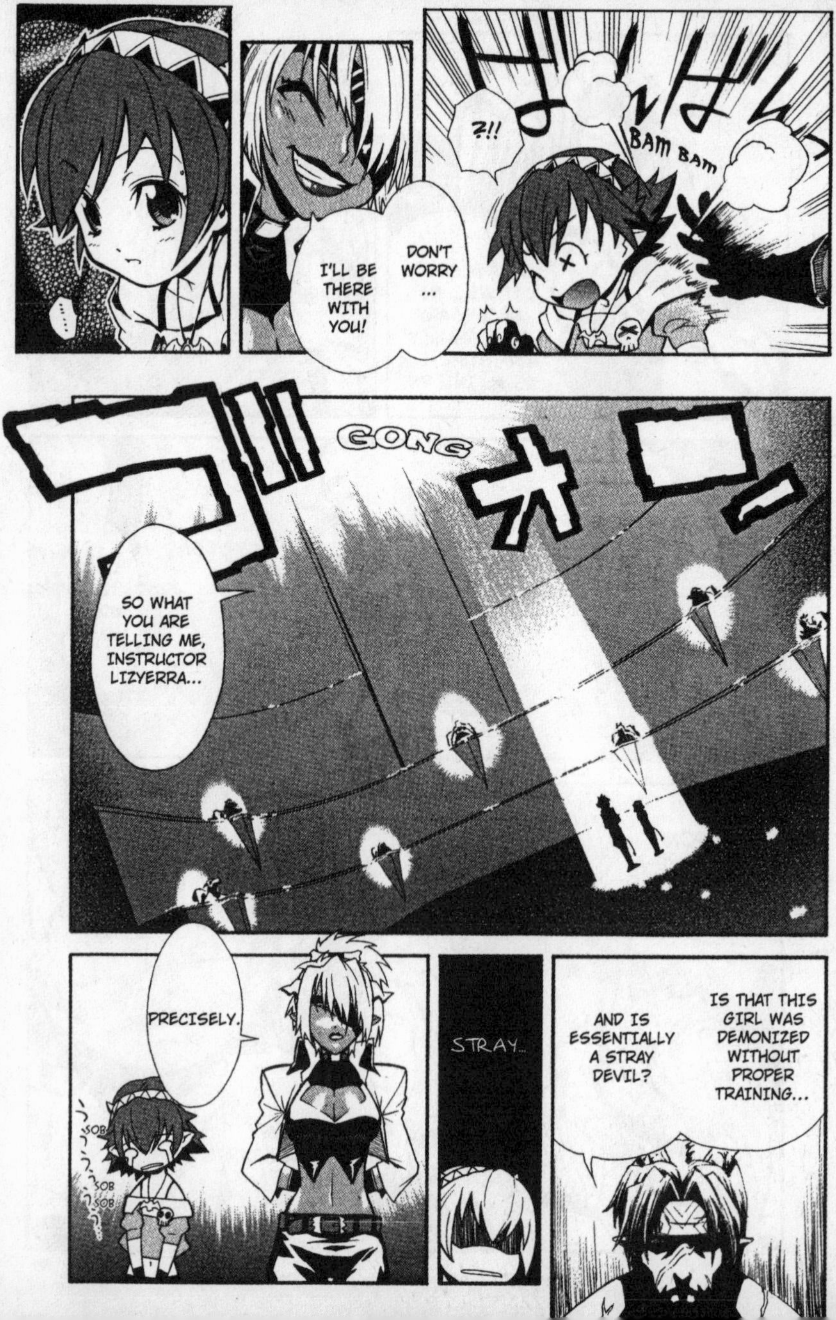
?!!
BAM BAM
DON'T WORRY ...
I'LL BE THERE WITH YOU!
......
GONG
SO WHAT YOU ARE TELLING ME, INSTRUCTOR LIZYERRA...
IS THAT THIS GIRL WAS DEMONIZED WITHOUT PROPER TRAINING...
AND IS ESSENTIALLY A STRAY DEVIL?
STRAY...
PRECISELY.
SOB
SOB
SOB

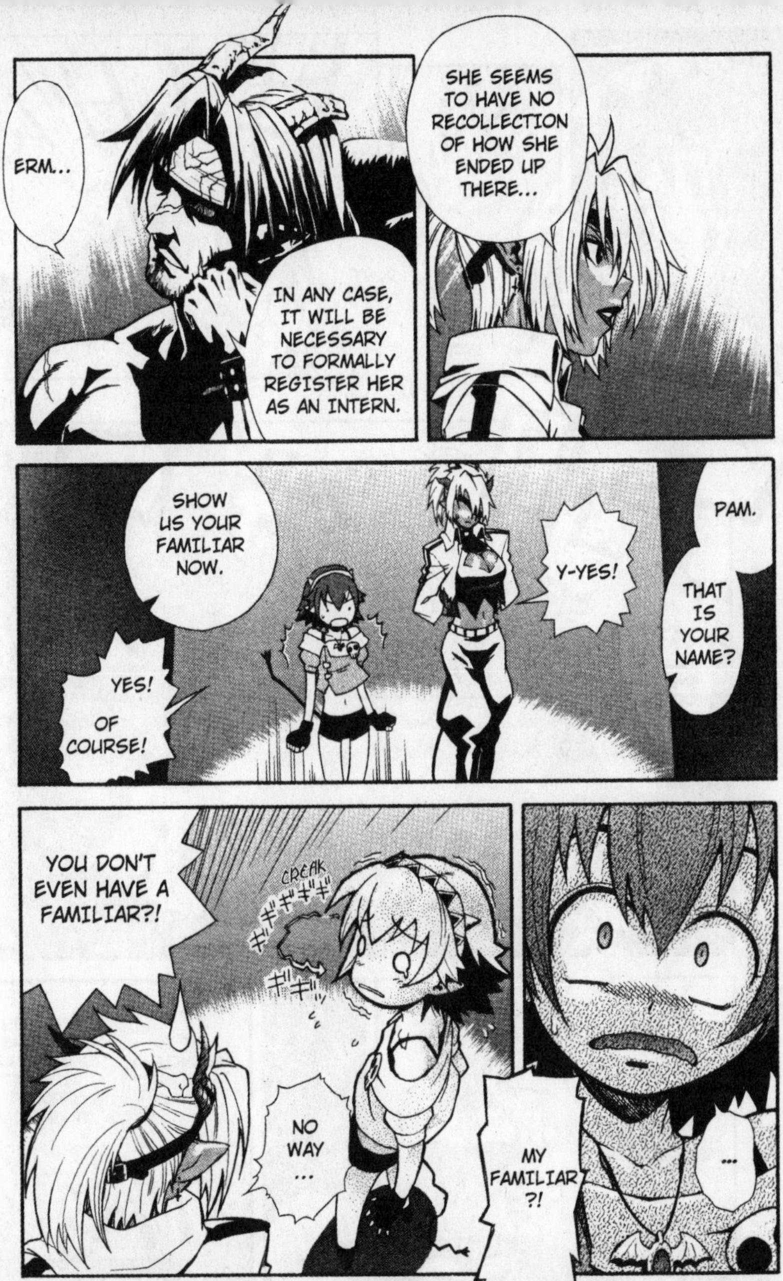

SHE SEEMS TO HAVE NO RECOLLECTION OF HOW SHE ENDED UP THERE...
ERM...
IN ANY CASE, IT WILL BE NECESSARY TO FORMALLY REGISTER HER AS AN INTERN.
PAM.
THAT IS YOUR NAME?
Y-YES!
SHOW US YOUR FAMILIAR NOW.
YES!
OF COURSE!
...
YOU DON'T EVEN HAVE A FAMILIAR?!
CREAK
ギギギギ
ギギッ
NO WAY ...
MY FAMILIAR ?!

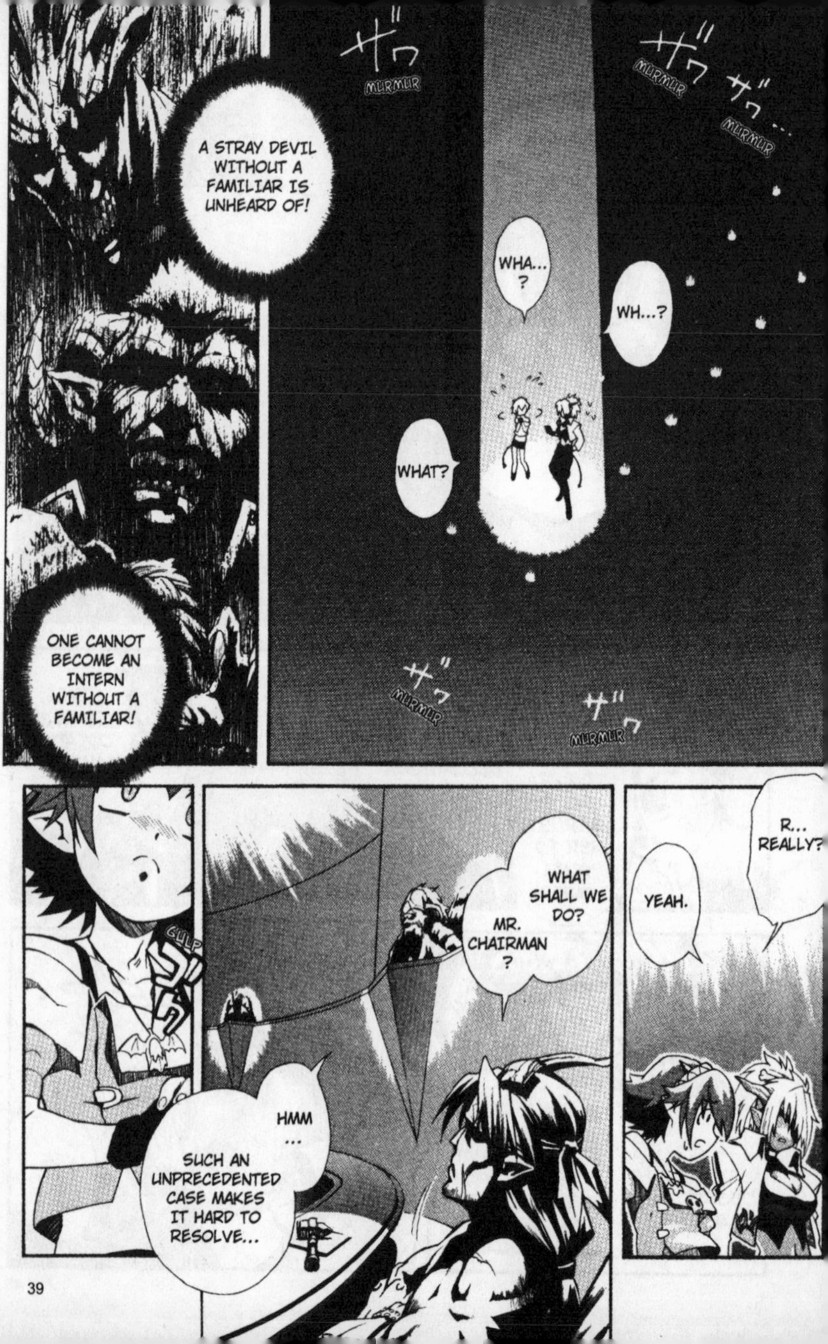
ザワ
MURMUR
ザワ
MURMUR
ザワ…
MURMUR
WHA...?
WH...?
WHAT?
ザワ
MURMUR
ザワ
MURMUR
A STRAY DEVIL WITHOUT A FAMILIAR IS UNHEARD OF!
ONE CANNOT BECOME AN INTERN WITHOUT A FAMILIAR!
R... REALLY?
YEAH.
WHAT SHALL WE DO? MR. CHAIRMAN?
HMM...
SUCH AN UNPRECEDENTED CASE MAKES IT HARD TO RESOLVE...
GULP

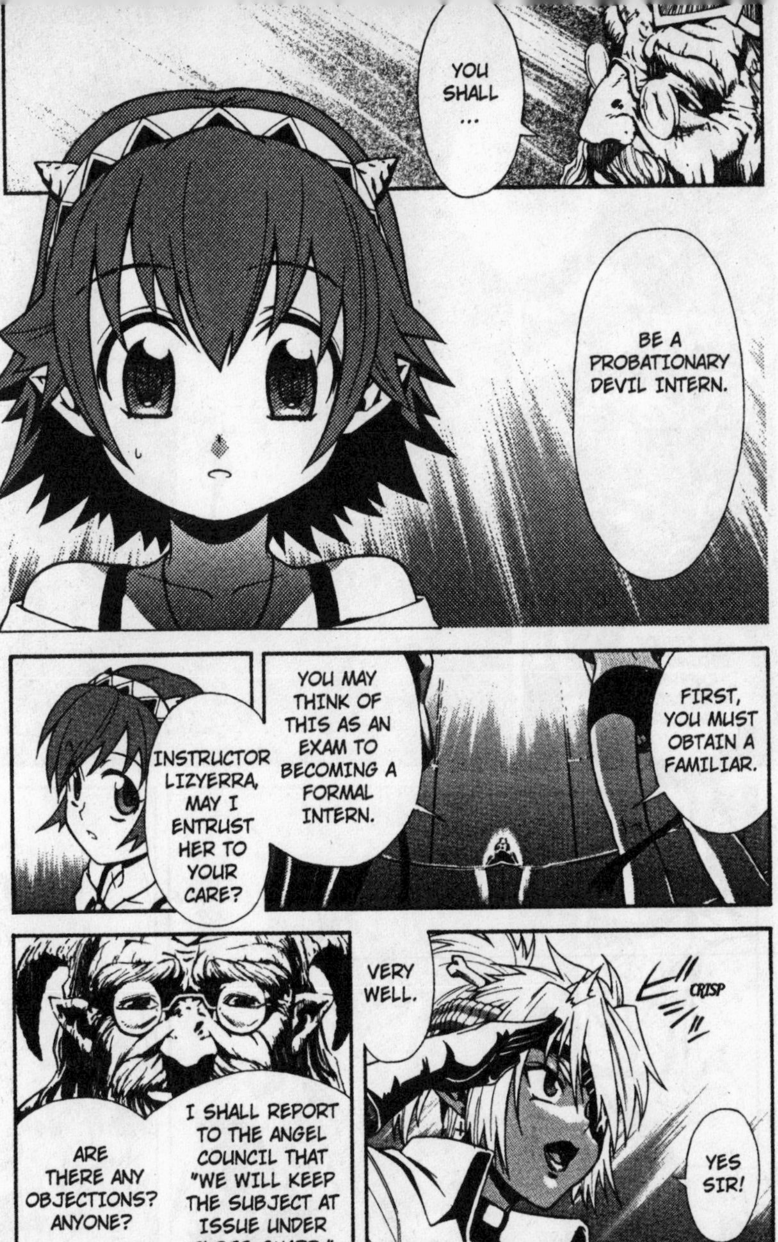
YOU SHALL ...
BE A PROBATIONARY DEVIL INTERN.
FIRST, YOU MUST OBTAIN A FAMILIAR.
YOU MAY THINK OF THIS AS AN EXAM TO BECOMING A FORMAL INTERN.
INSTRUCTOR LIZYERRA, MAY I ENTRUST HER TO YOUR CARE?
CRISP
VERY WELL.
YES SIR!
I SHALL REPORT TO THE ANGEL COUNCIL THAT "WE WILL KEEP THE SUBJECT AT ISSUE UNDER CLOSE GUARD."
ARE THERE ANY OBJECTIONS? ANYONE?

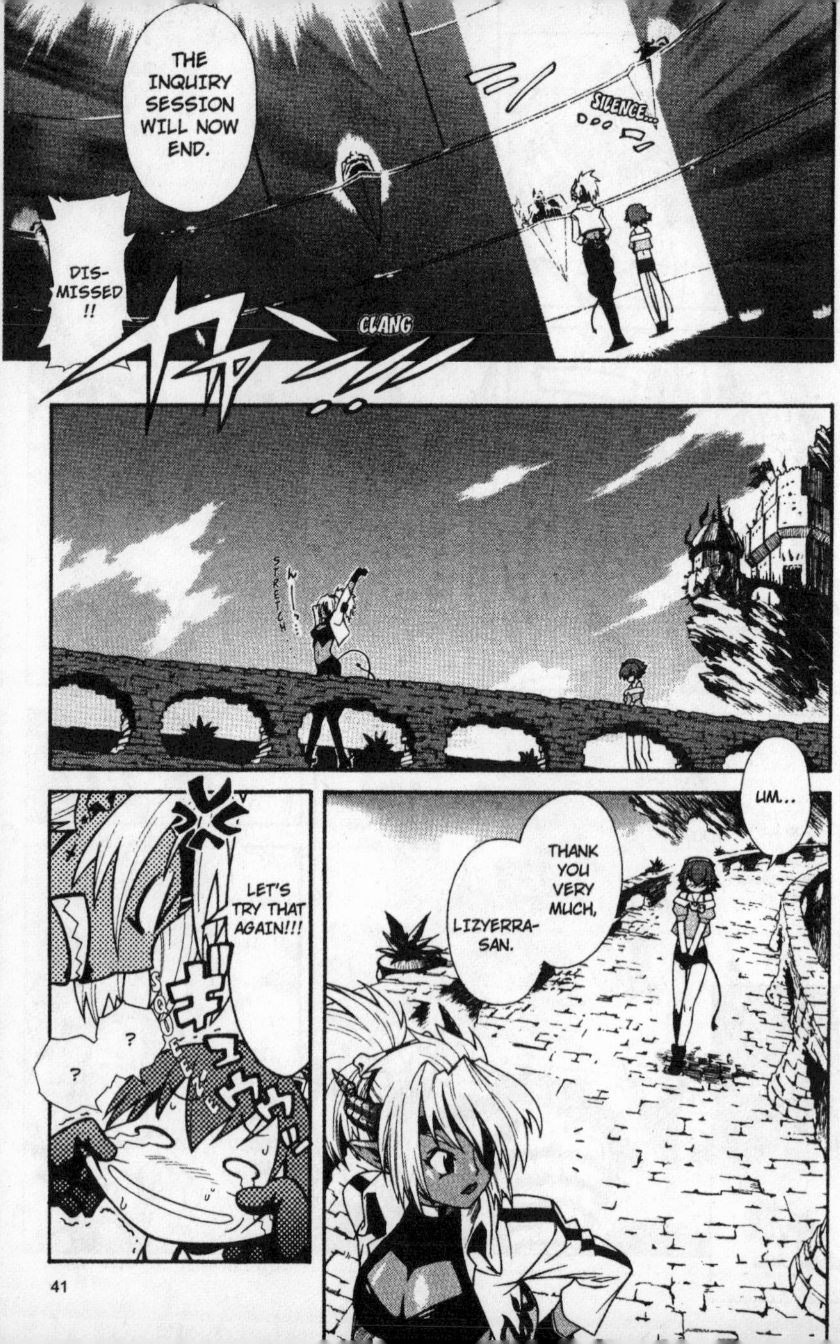
SILENCE...
THE INQUIRY SESSION WILL NOW END.
DIS-MISSED!!
CLANG
STRETCH
UM...
THANK YOU VERY MUCH, LIZYERRA-SAN.
LET'S TRY THAT AGAIN!!!
SQUEEZE
?
?

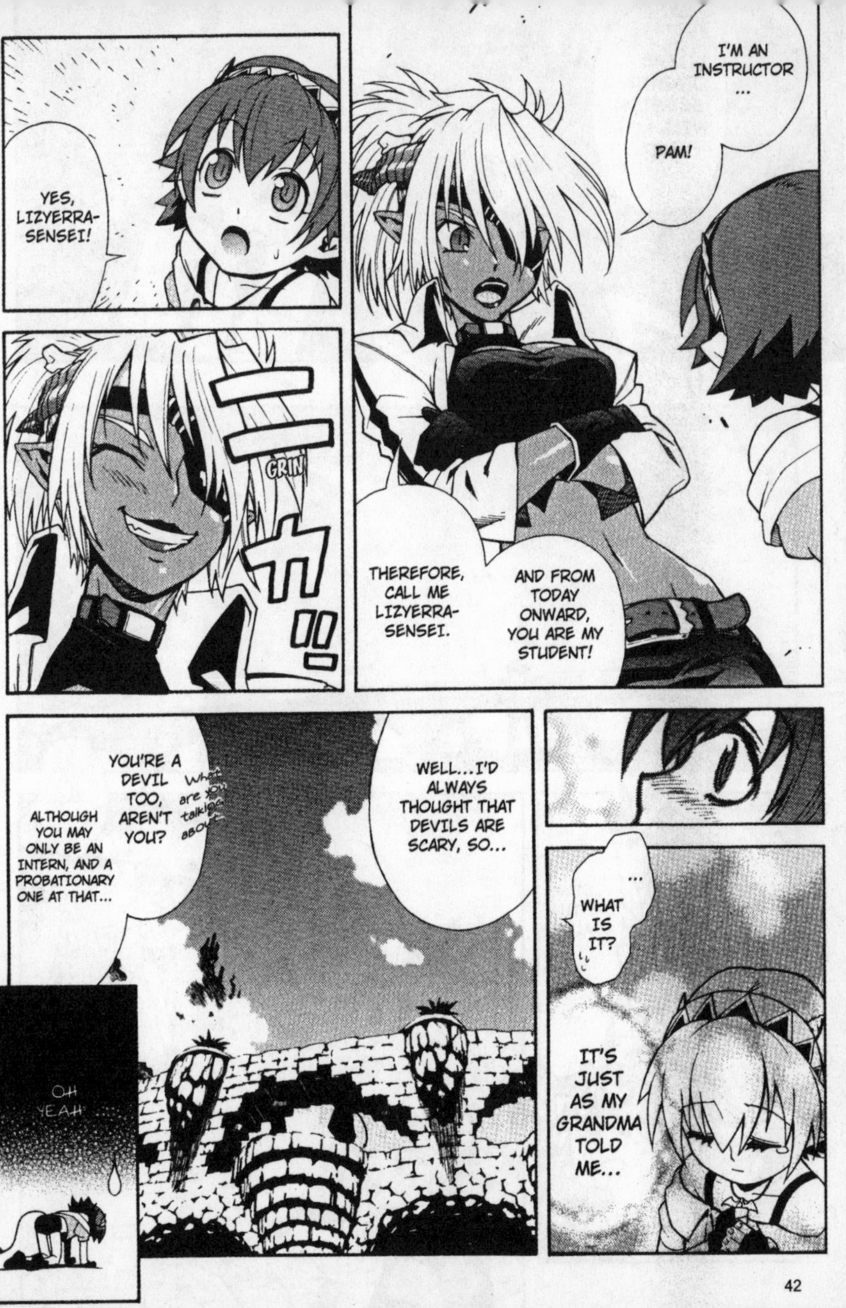
I'M AN INSTRUCTOR ...
PAM!
AND FROM TODAY ONWARD, YOU ARE MY STUDENT!
THEREFORE, CALL ME LIZYERRA-SENSEI.
YES, LIZYERRA-SENSEI!
GRIN
... WHAT IS IT?
IT'S JUST AS MY GRANDMA TOLD ME...
WELL...I'D ALWAYS THOUGHT THAT DEVILS ARE SCARY, SO...
YOU'RE A DEVIL TOO, AREN'T YOU?
What are you talking about
ALTHOUGH YOU MAY ONLY BE AN INTERN, AND A PROBATIONARY ONE AT THAT...
OH YEAH

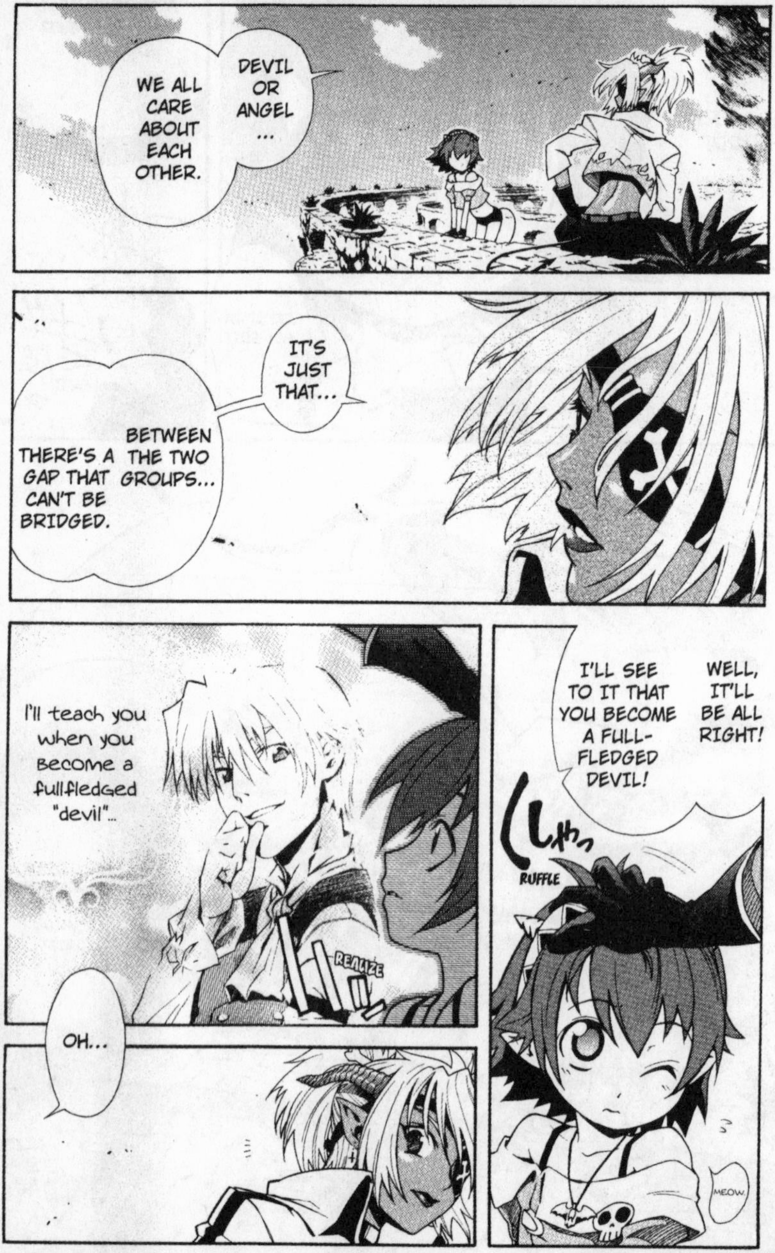
DEVIL OR ANGEL...
WE ALL CARE ABOUT EACH OTHER.
IT'S JUST THAT...
BETWEEN THE TWO GROUPS... THERE'S A GAP THAT CAN'T BE BRIDGED.
WELL, IT'LL BE ALL RIGHT!
I'LL SEE TO IT THAT YOU BECOME A FULL-FLEDGED DEVIL!
しゃっ
RUFFLE
MEOW.
I'll teach you when you become a fullfledged "devil"...
REALIZE
OH...

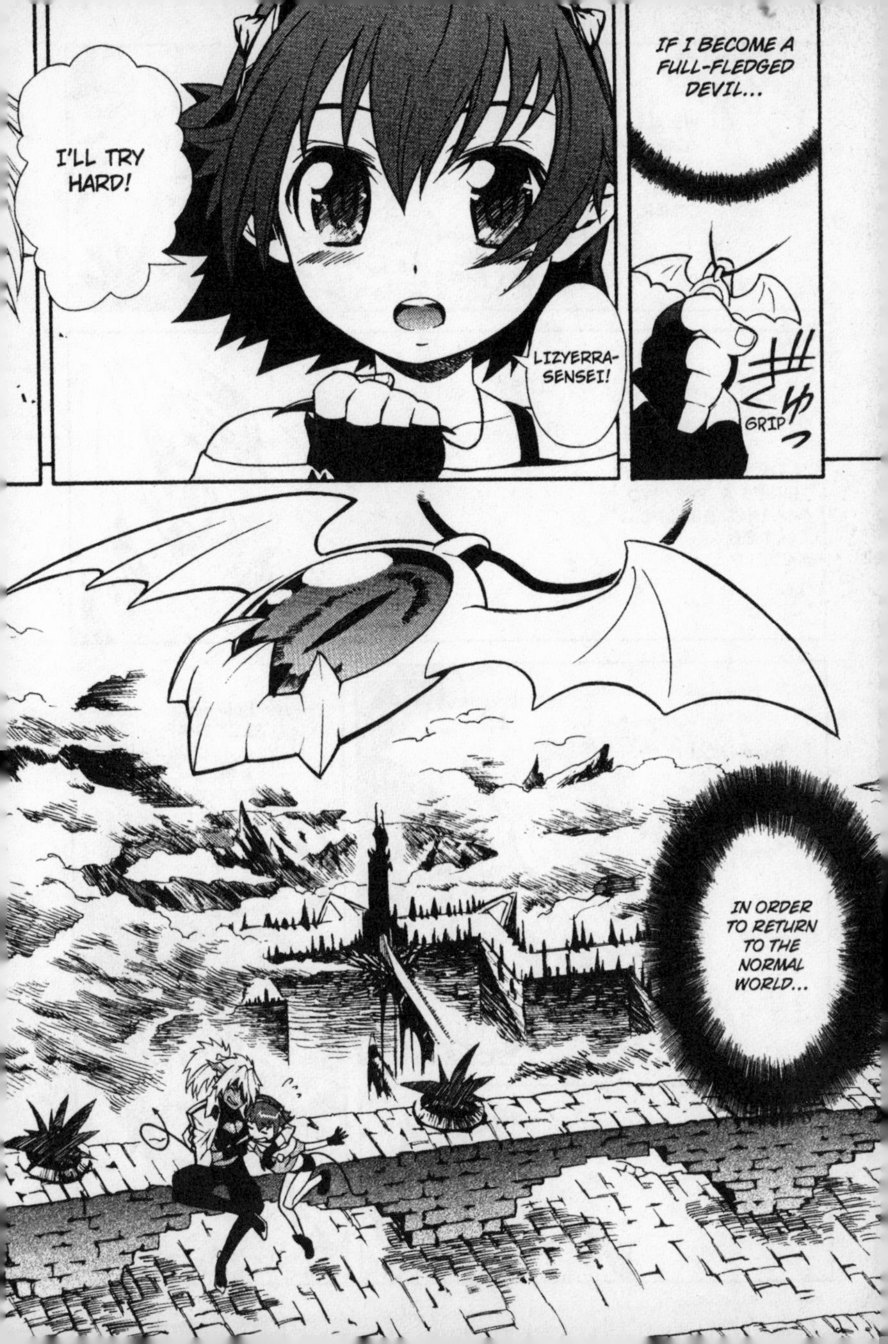
IF I BECOME A FULL-FLEDGED DEVIL...
ぎゅっ
GRIP
LIZYERRA-SENSEI!
I'LL TRY HARD!
IN ORDER TO RETURN TO THE NORMAL WORLD...

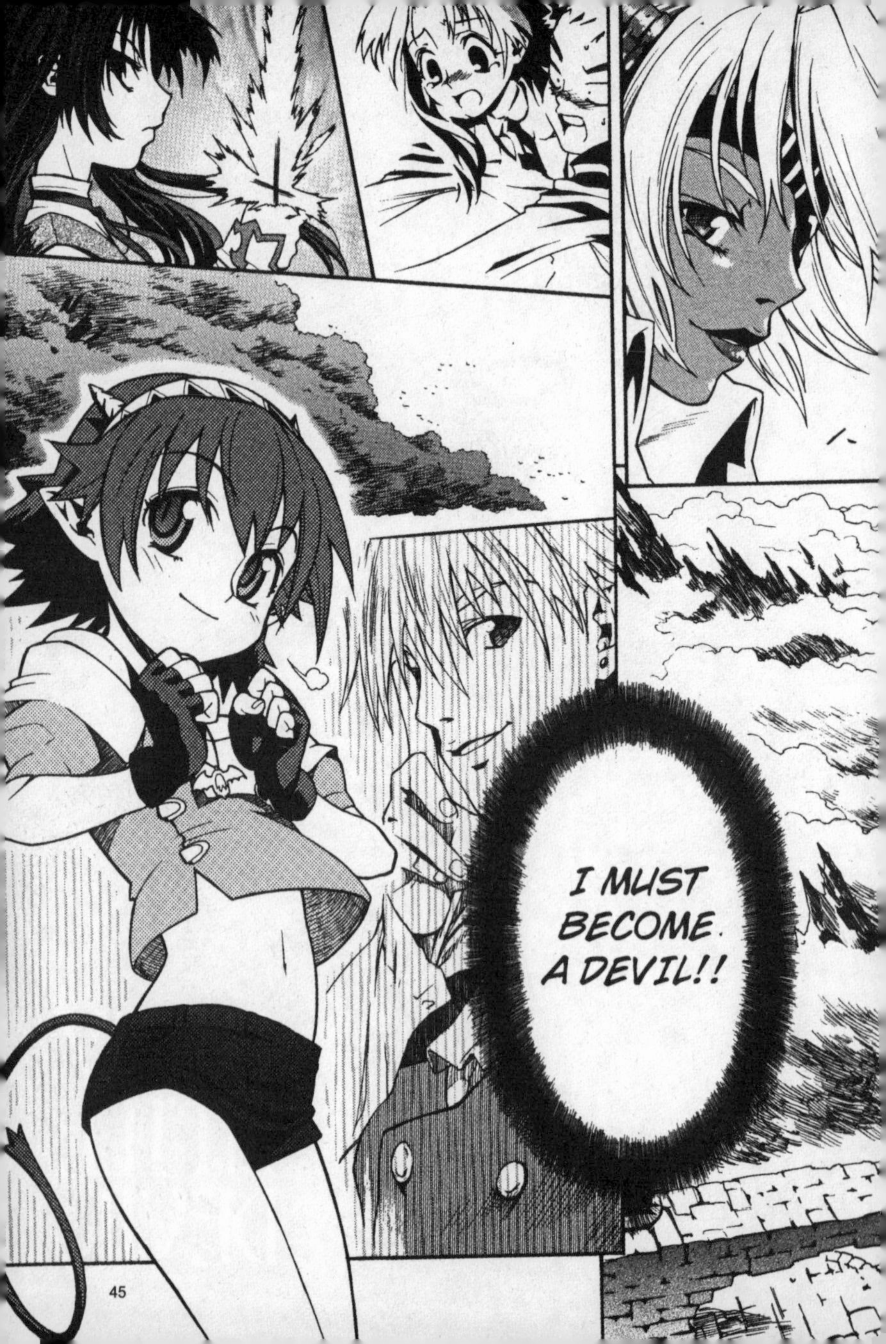
I MUST BECOME A DEVIL!!

STRAY
LITTLE
DEVIL*

ACT.02 PAM, THE DEVIL, AND THE STOLEN PENDANT

Cat Walking

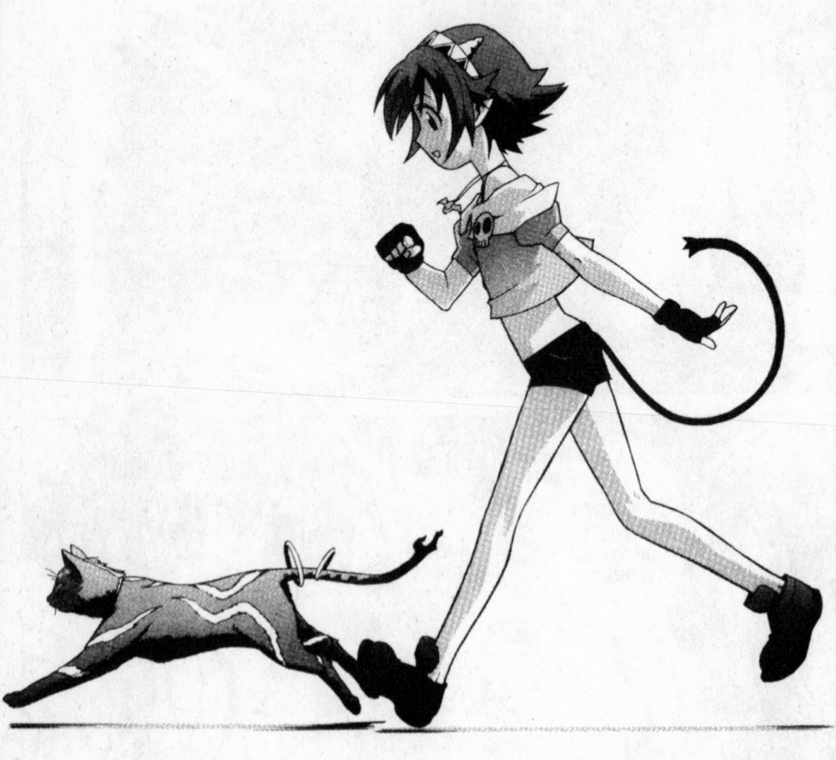

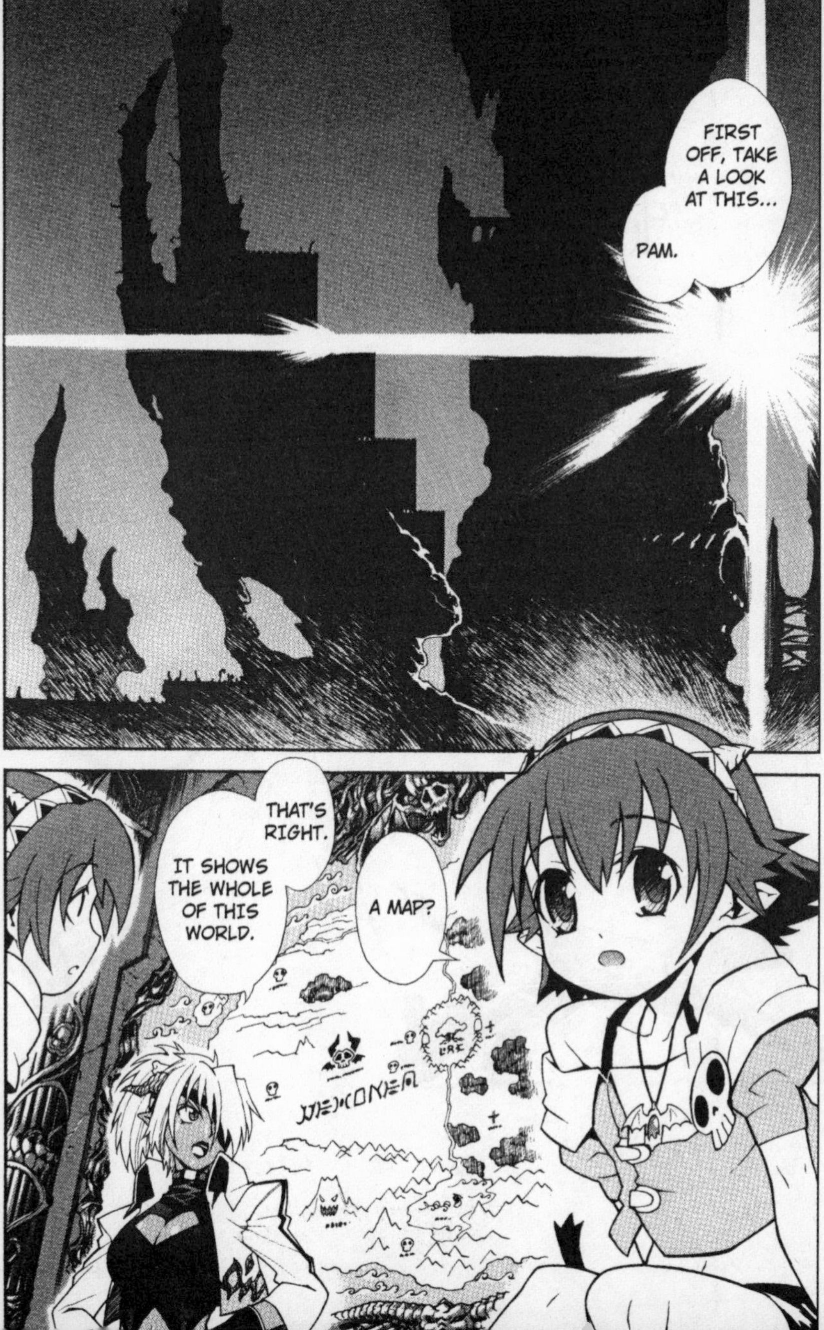
FIRST OFF, TAKE A LOOK AT THIS...
PAM.
A MAP?
THAT'S RIGHT.
IT SHOWS THE WHOLE OF THIS WORLD.

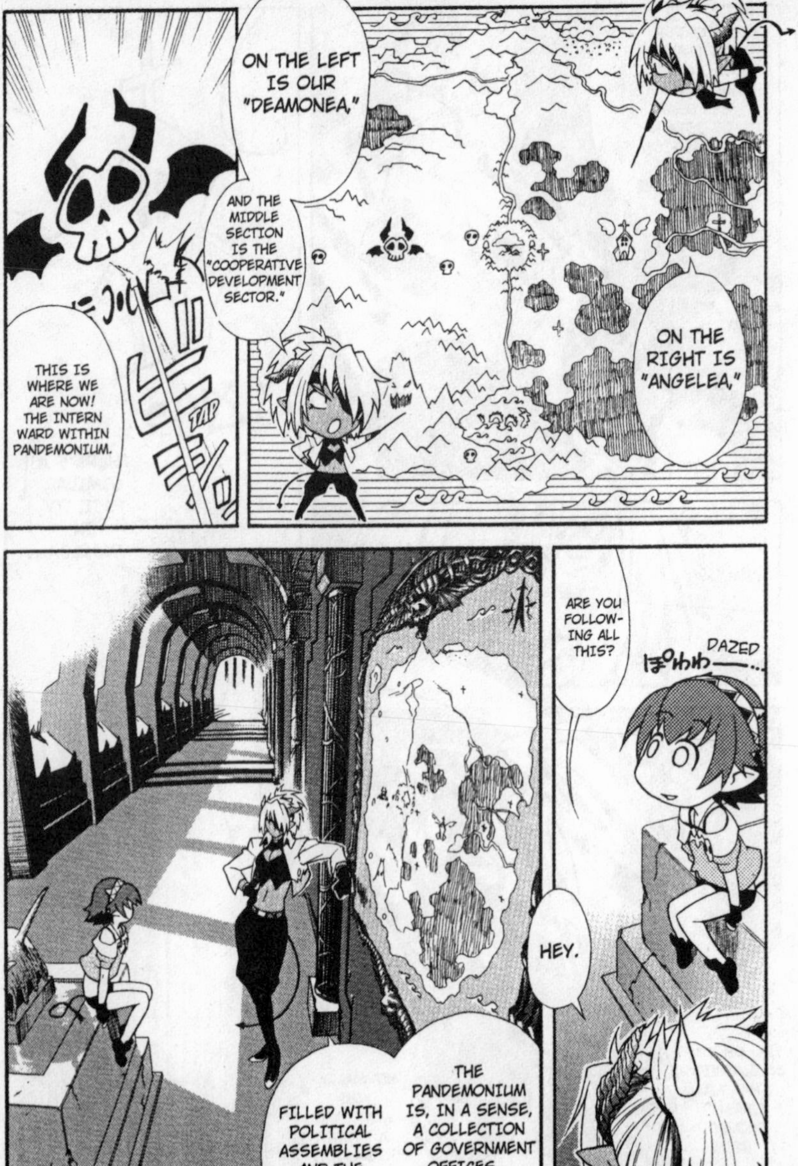
ON THE LEFT IS OUR "DEAMONEA,"
ON THE RIGHT IS "ANGELEA,"
AND THE MIDDLE SECTION IS THE "COOPERATIVE DEVELOPMENT SECTOR."
THIS IS WHERE WE ARE NOW! THE INTERN WARD WITHIN PANDEMONIUM.
TAP
DAZED
ARE YOU FOLLOWING ALL THIS?
HEY.
THE PANDEMONIUM IS, IN A SENSE, A COLLECTION OF GOVERNMENT OFFICES...
FILLED WITH POLITICAL ASSEMBLIES AND THE LIKE.

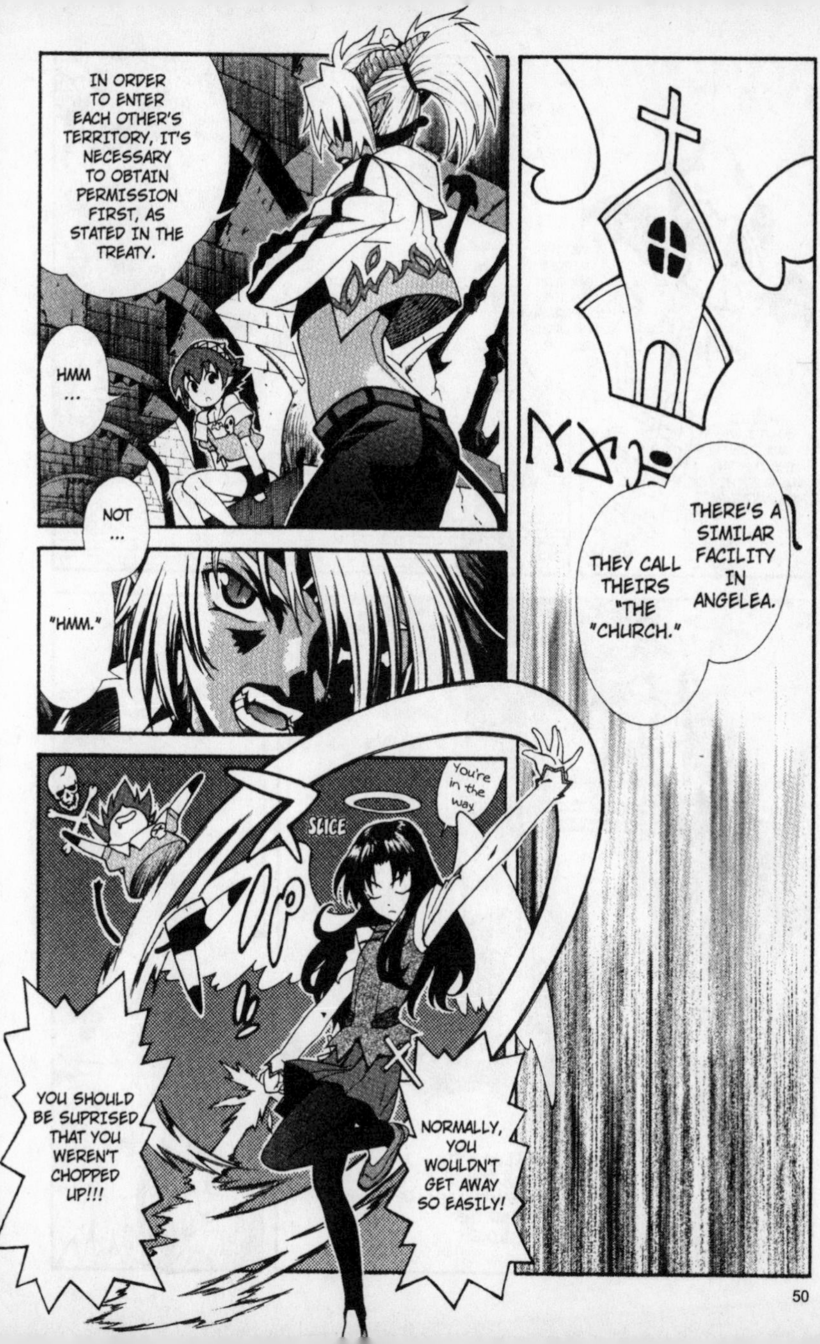
THERE'S A SIMILAR FACILITY IN ANGELEA.
THEY CALL THEIRS "THE "CHURCH."
IN ORDER TO ENTER EACH OTHER'S TERRITORY, IT'S NECESSARY TO OBTAIN PERMISSION FIRST, AS STATED IN THE TREATY.
HMM ...
NOT ...
"HMM."
You're in the way.
SLICE
NORMALLY, YOU WOULDN'T GET AWAY SO EASILY!
YOU SHOULD BE SUPRISED THAT YOU WEREN'T CHOPPED UP!!!

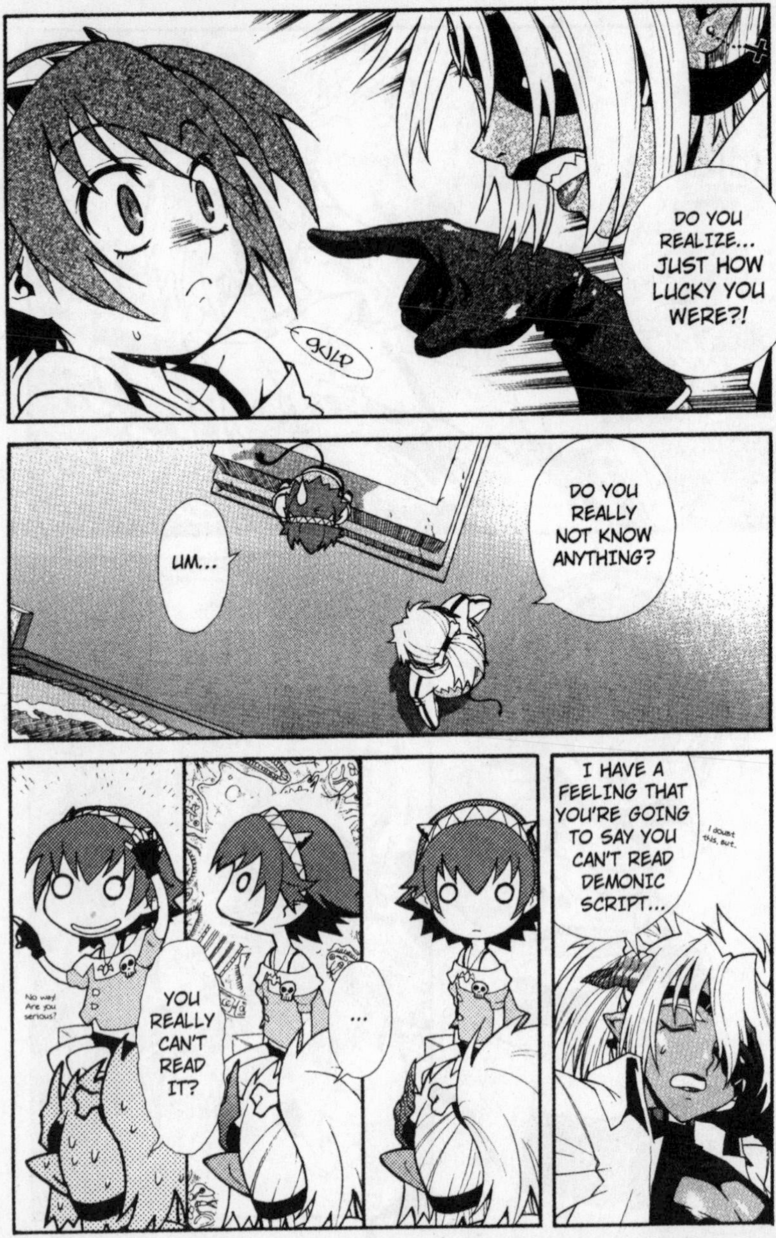
DO YOU REALIZE... JUST HOW LUCKY YOU WERE?!
GULP
DO YOU REALLY NOT KNOW ANYTHING?
UM...
I HAVE A FEELING THAT YOU'RE GOING TO SAY YOU CAN'T READ DEMONIC SCRIPT...
I doubt this, but.
...
YOU REALLY CAN'T READ IT?
No way. Are you serious?

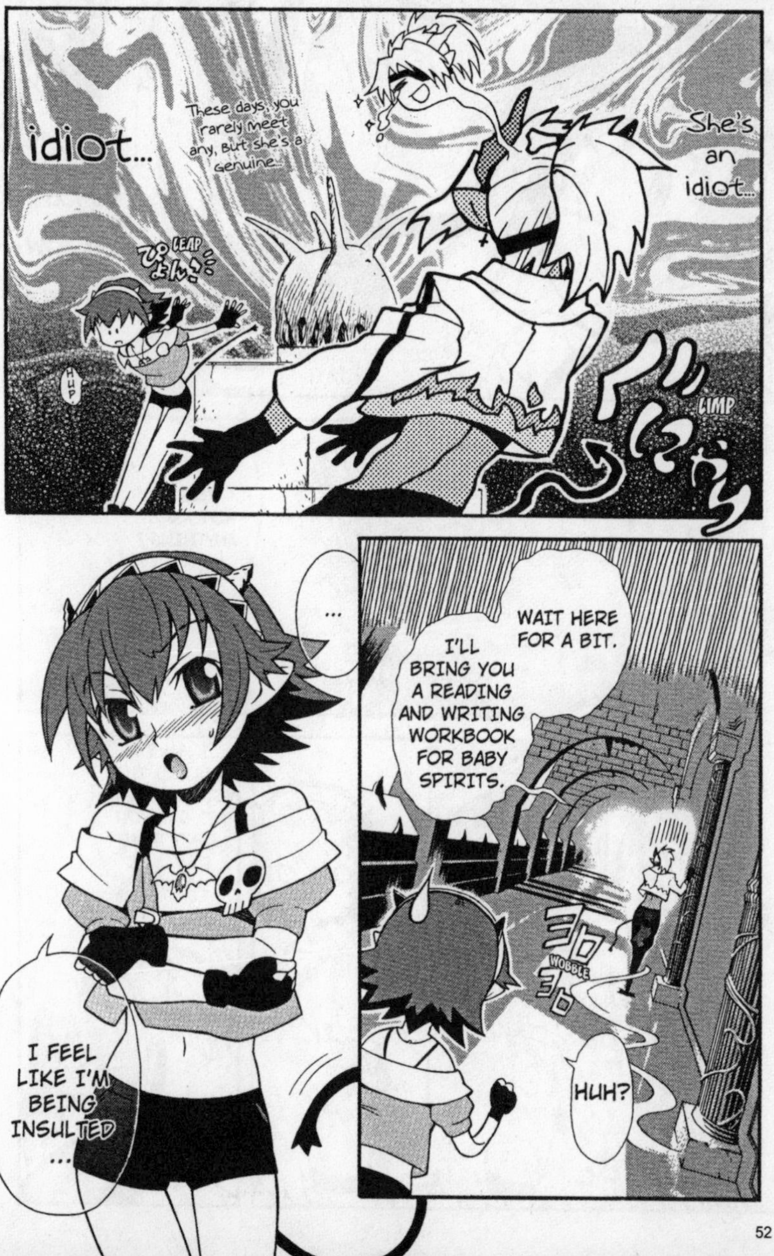
She's an idiot...
These days, you rarely meet any, but she's a genuine...
idiot...
LEAP
HUP
LIMP
WAIT HERE FOR A BIT.
I'LL BRING YOU A READING AND WRITING WORKBOOK FOR BABY SPIRITS.
WOBBLE
HUH?
...
I FEEL LIKE I'M BEING INSULTED...

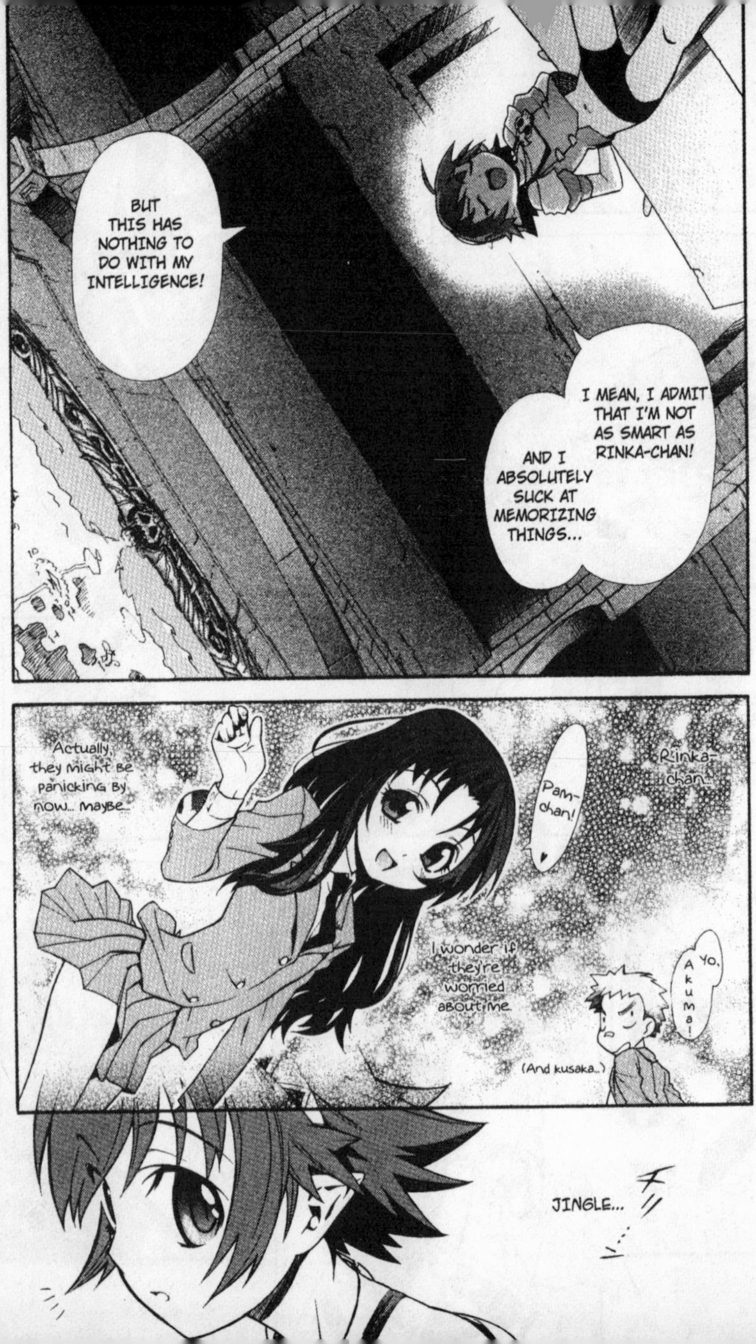
I MEAN, I ADMIT THAT I'M NOT AS SMART AS RINKA-CHAN!
AND I ABSOLUTELY SUCK AT MEMORIZING THINGS...
BUT THIS HAS NOTHING TO DO WITH MY INTELLIGENCE!
Rinka-chan...
Pam-chan!
Yo, Akuma!
(And kusaka...)
I wonder if they're worried about me.
Actually, they might be panicking by now... maybe...
JINGLE...

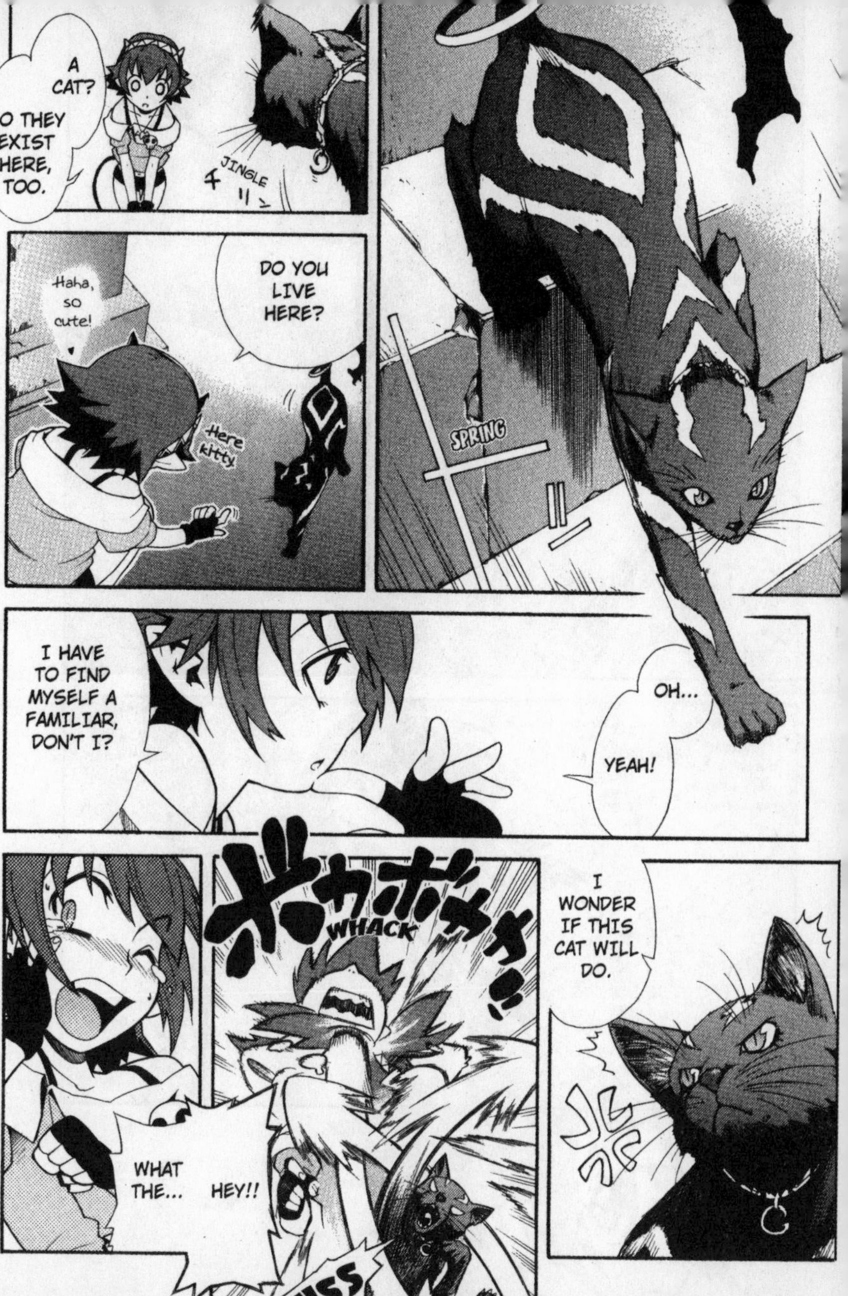
SPRING
A CAT?
SO THEY EXIST HERE, TOO.
JINGLE
DO YOU LIVE HERE?
Haha, so cute!
Here kitty
OH...
YEAH!
I HAVE TO FIND MYSELF A FAMILIAR, DON'T I?
I WONDER IF THIS CAT WILL DO.
WHACK
HEY!!
HISS
WHAT THE...

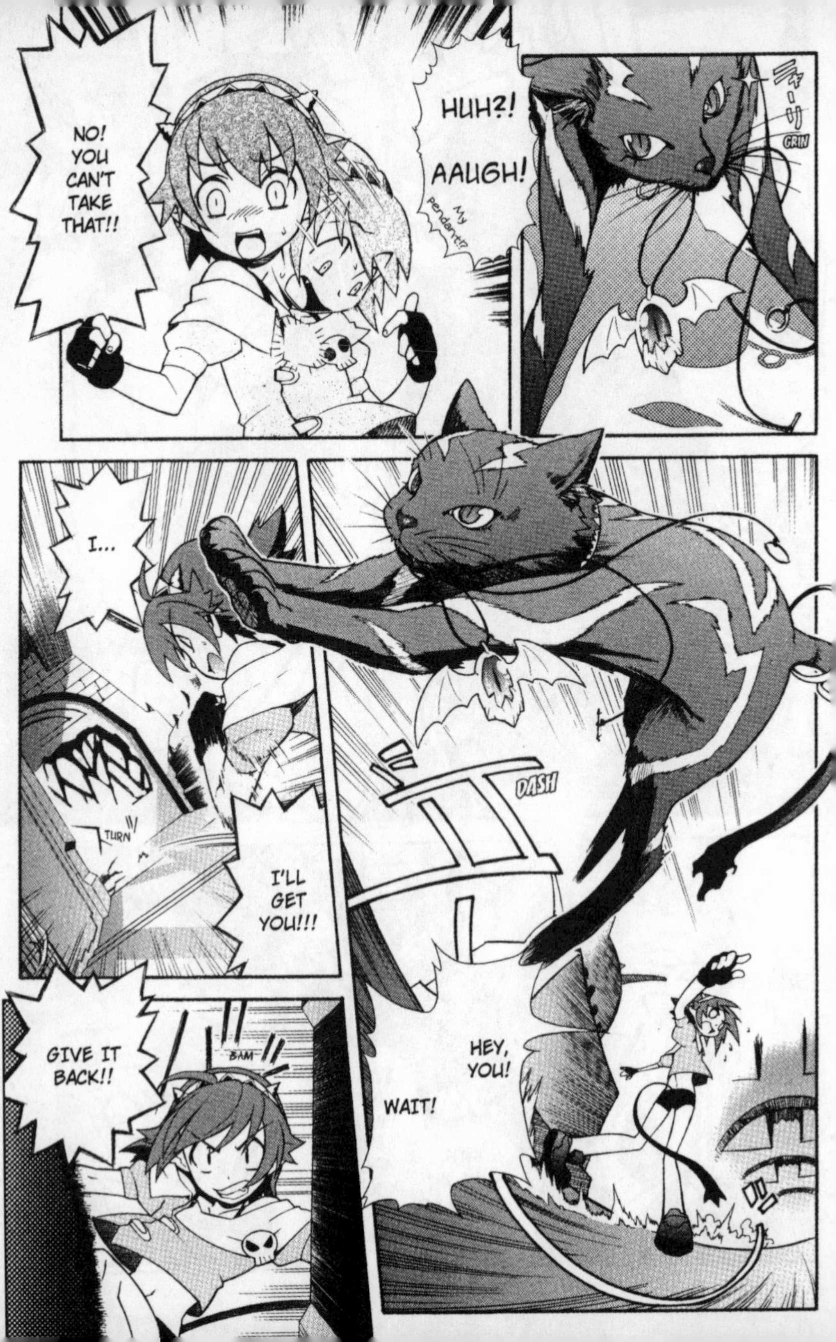

GRIN
HUH?!
AAUGH!
My pendant!?
NO! YOU CAN'T TAKE THAT!!
DASH
I...
TURN
I'LL GET YOU!!!
HEY, YOU!
WAIT!
BAM
GIVE IT BACK!!

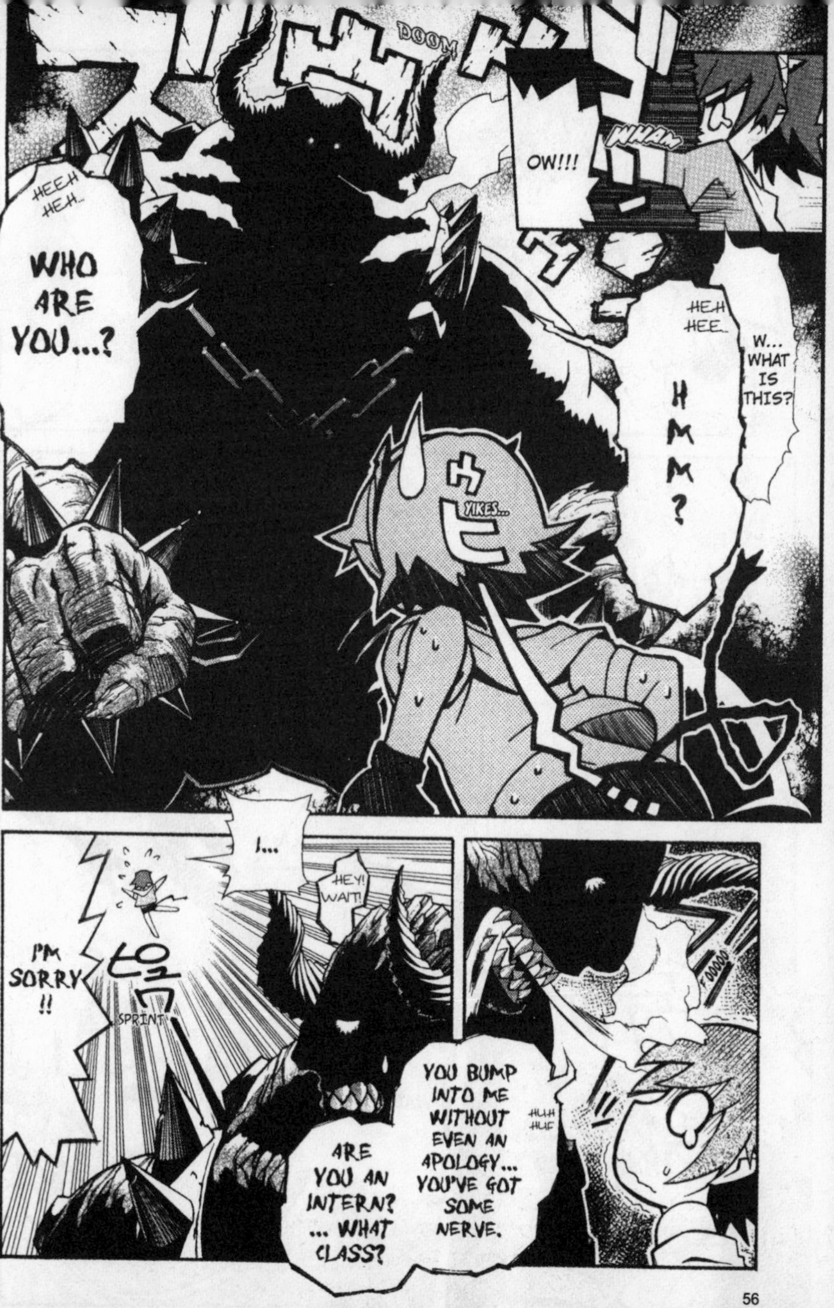
DOOM
WHAM
OW!!!
HEH HEE..
W... WHAT IS THIS?
HMM?
YIKES...
HEEH HEH..
WHO ARE YOU...?
FOOOOO
HUH HUF
YOU BUMP INTO ME WITHOUT EVEN AN APOLOGY... YOU'VE GOT SOME NERVE.
ARE YOU AN INTERN? ... WHAT CLASS?
I...
HEY! WAIT!
I'M SORRY!!
SPRINT

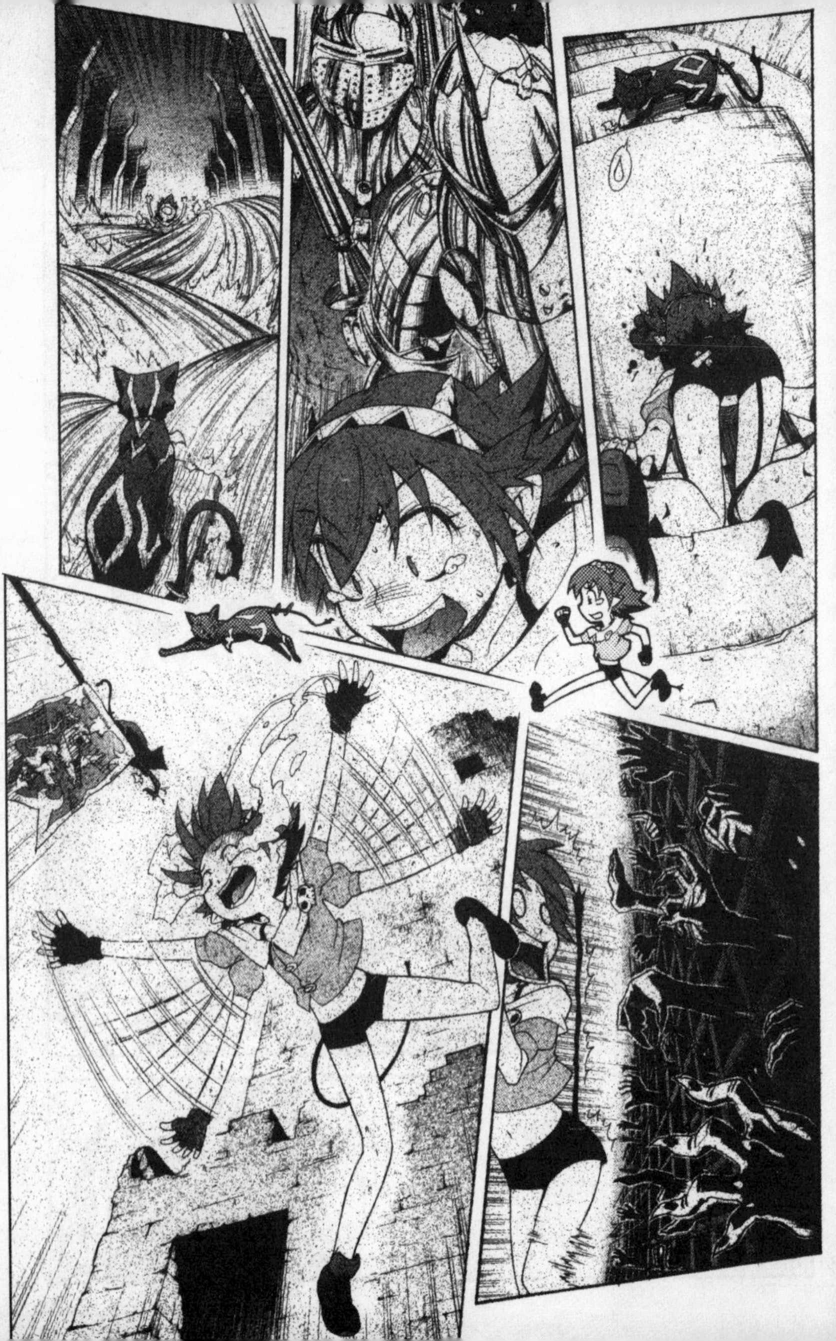

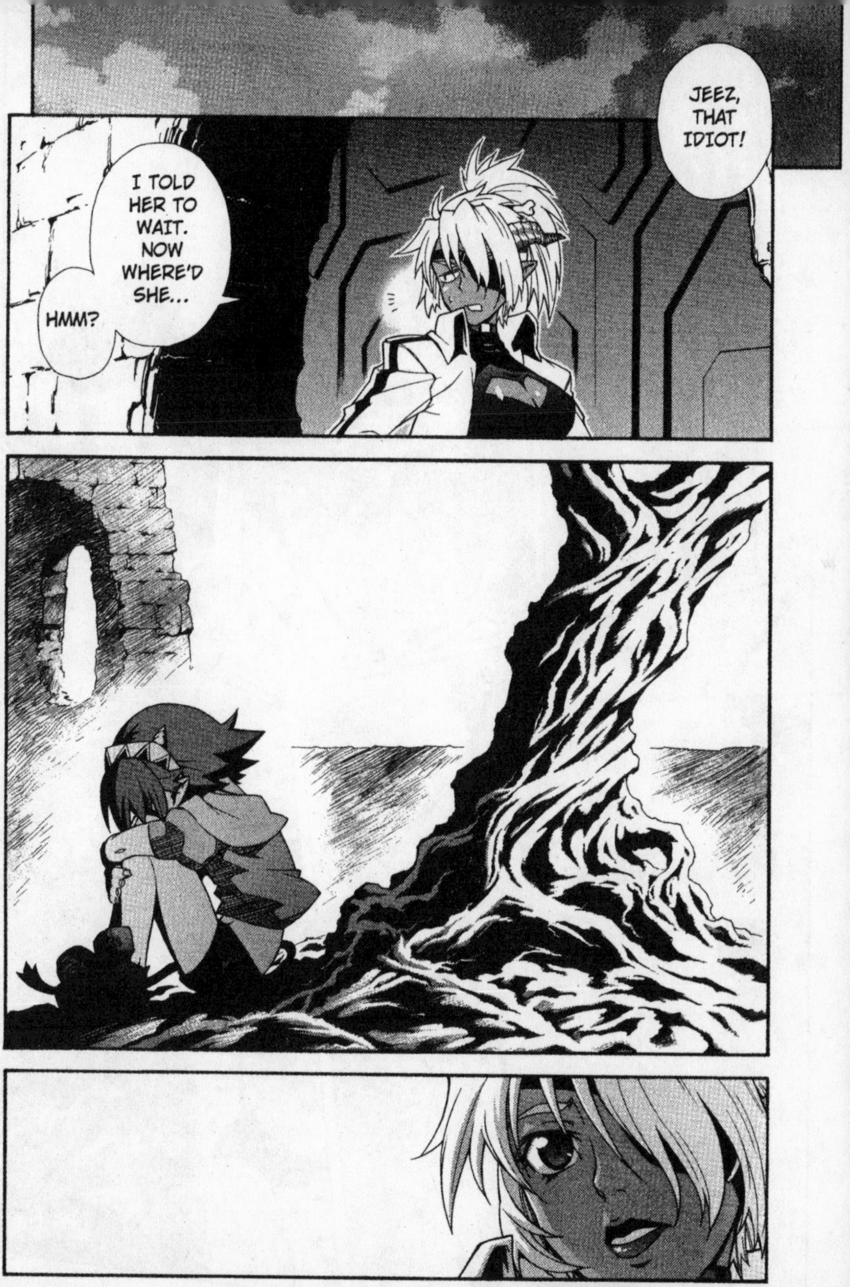
JEEZ, THAT IDIOT!
I TOLD HER TO WAIT. NOW WHERE'D SHE...
HMM?

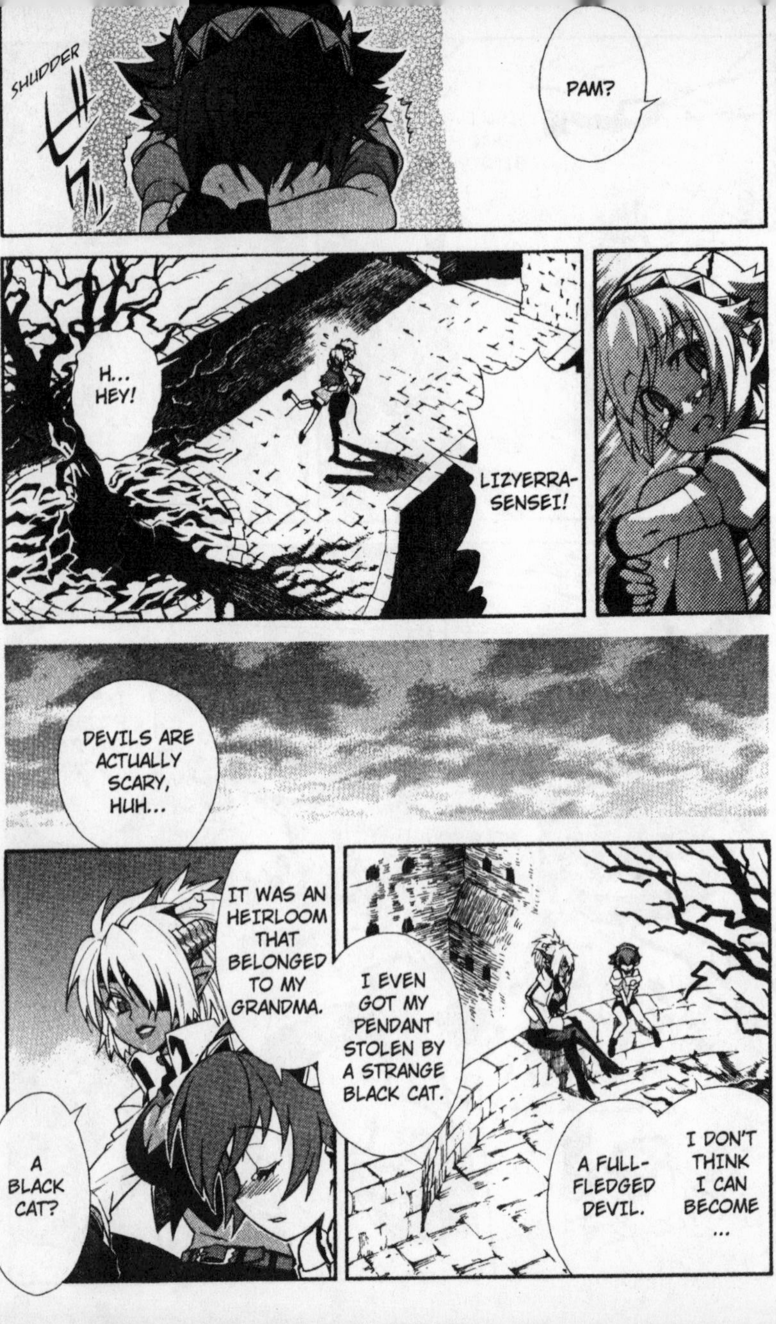
PAM?
SHUDDER
LIZYERRA-SENSEI!
H... HEY!
DEVILS ARE ACTUALLY SCARY, HUH...
I DON'T THINK I CAN BECOME ...
A FULL-FLEDGED DEVIL.
I EVEN GOT MY PENDANT STOLEN BY A STRANGE BLACK CAT.
IT WAS AN HEIRLOOM THAT BELONGED TO MY GRANDMA.
A BLACK CAT?

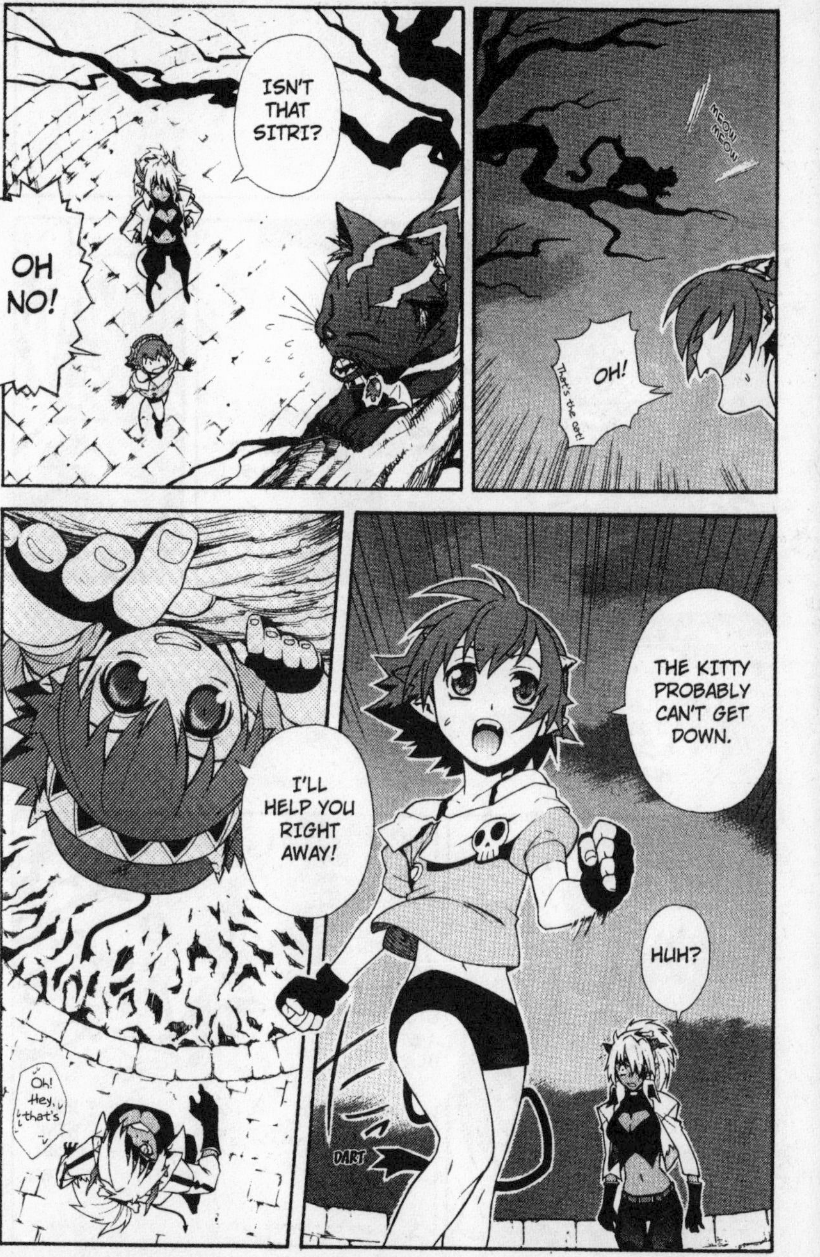
MEOW MEOW
OH!
That's the cat!
ISN'T THAT SITRI?
OH NO!
THE KITTY PROBABLY CAN'T GET DOWN.
HUH?
DART
I'LL HELP YOU RIGHT AWAY!
Oh! Hey, that's ...

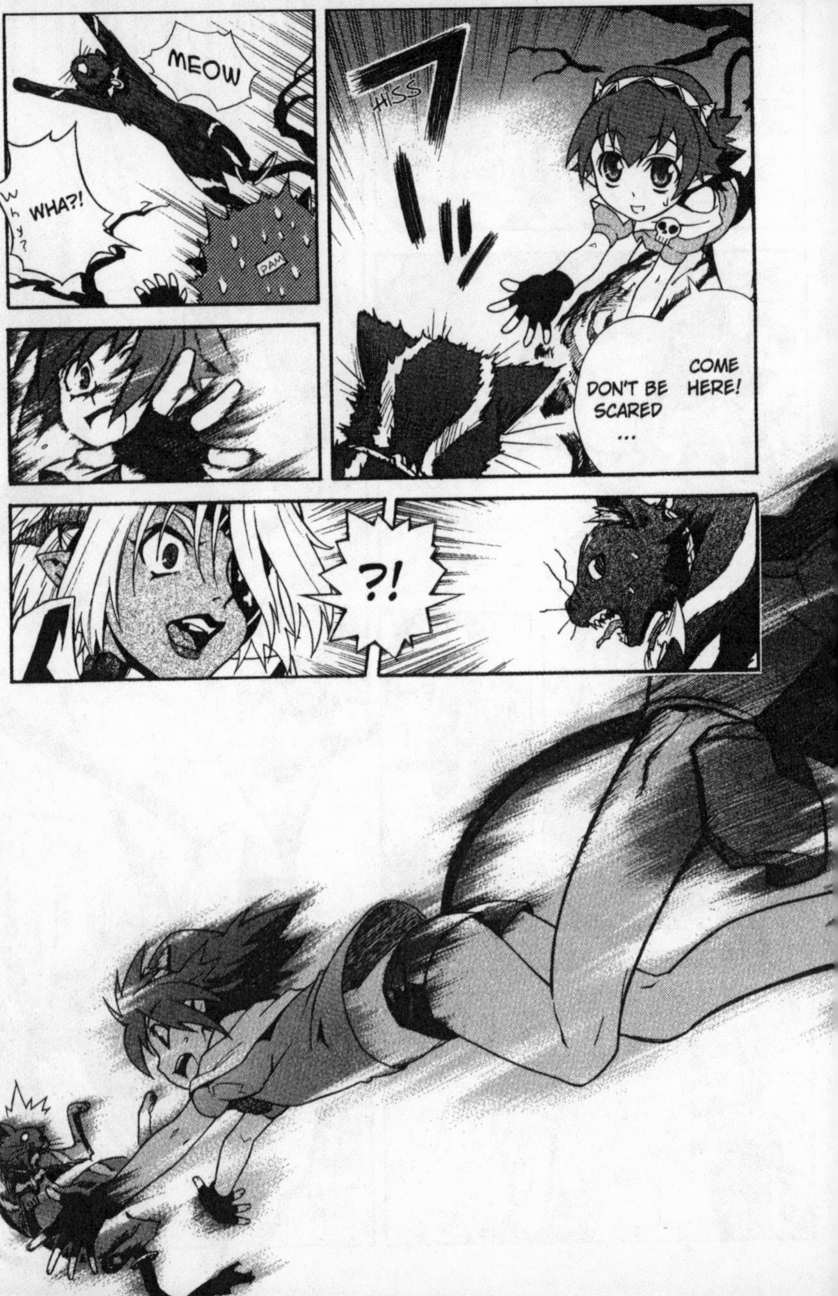
HISS
COME HERE!
DON'T BE SCARED ...
MEOW
WHA?!
Why?
PAM
?!

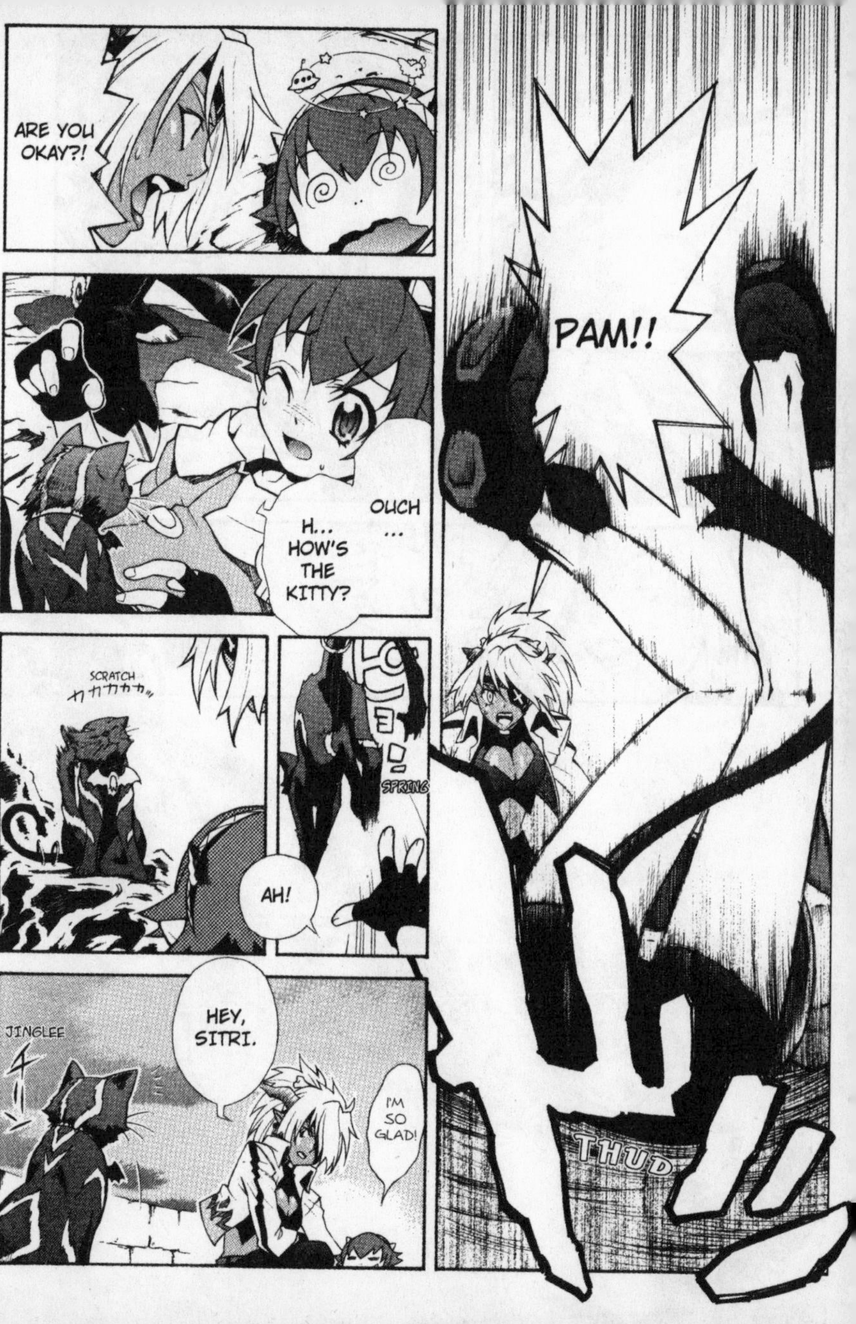
PAM!!
THUD
ARE YOU OKAY?!
OUCH ...
H... HOW'S THE KITTY?
SPRING
AH!
SCRATCH
I'M SO GLAD!
HEY, SITRI.
JINGLEE

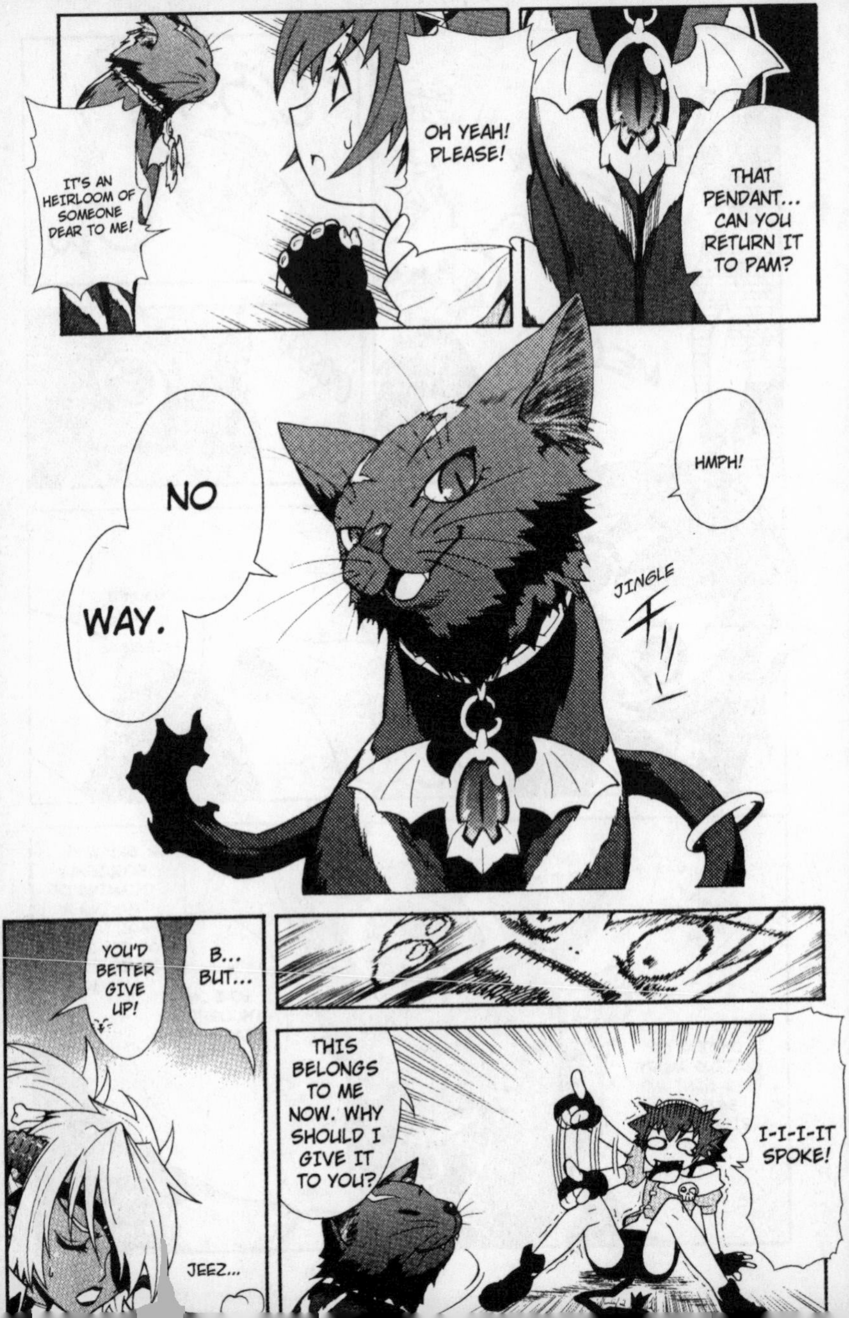
THAT PENDANT... CAN YOU RETURN IT TO PAM?
OH YEAH! PLEASE!
IT'S AN HEIRLOOM OF SOMEONE DEAR TO ME!
HMPH!
JINGLE
NO WAY.
I-I-I-IT SPOKE!
THIS BELONGS TO ME NOW. WHY SHOULD I GIVE IT TO YOU?
B... BUT...
YOU'D BETTER GIVE UP!
JEEZ...

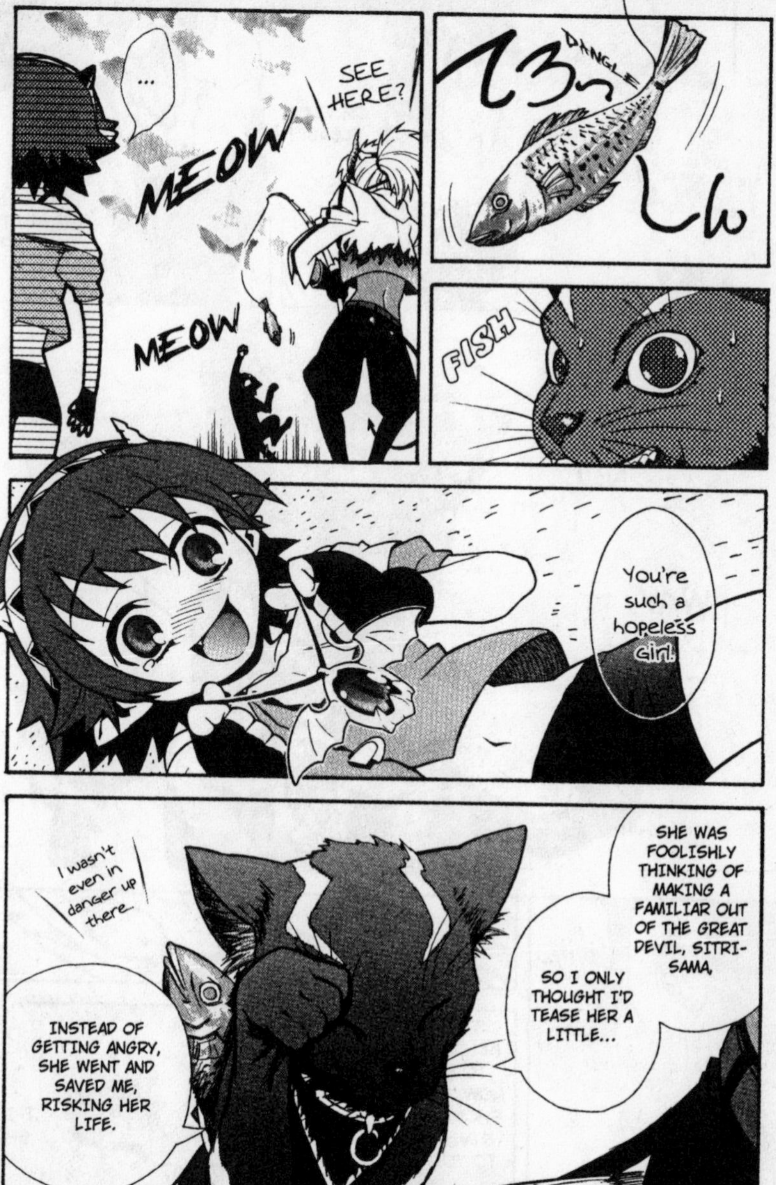
DANGLE
FISH
...
SEE HERE?
MEOW
MEOW
You're such a hopeless girl.
SHE WAS FOOLISHLY THINKING OF MAKING A FAMILIAR OUT OF THE GREAT DEVIL, SITRI-SAMA,
SO I ONLY THOUGHT I'D TEASE HER A LITTLE...
I wasn't even in danger up there.
INSTEAD OF GETTING ANGRY, SHE WENT AND SAVED ME, RISKING HER LIFE.

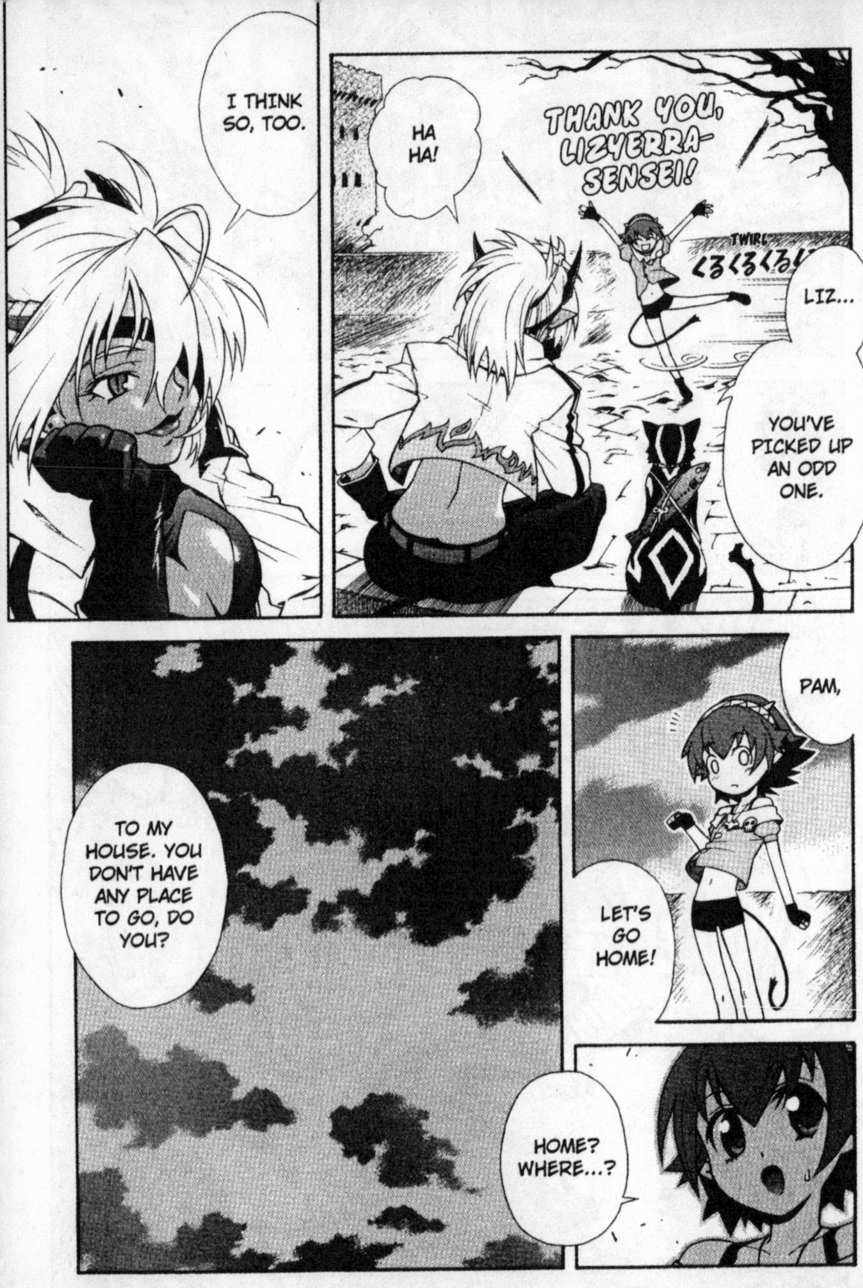
THANK YOU, LIZYERRA-SENSEI!
HA HA!
TWIRL
くるくるくる!!
LIZ...
YOU'VE PICKED UP AN ODD ONE.
I THINK SO, TOO.
PAM,
LET'S GO HOME!
HOME? WHERE...?
TO MY HOUSE. YOU DON'T HAVE ANY PLACE TO GO, DO YOU?

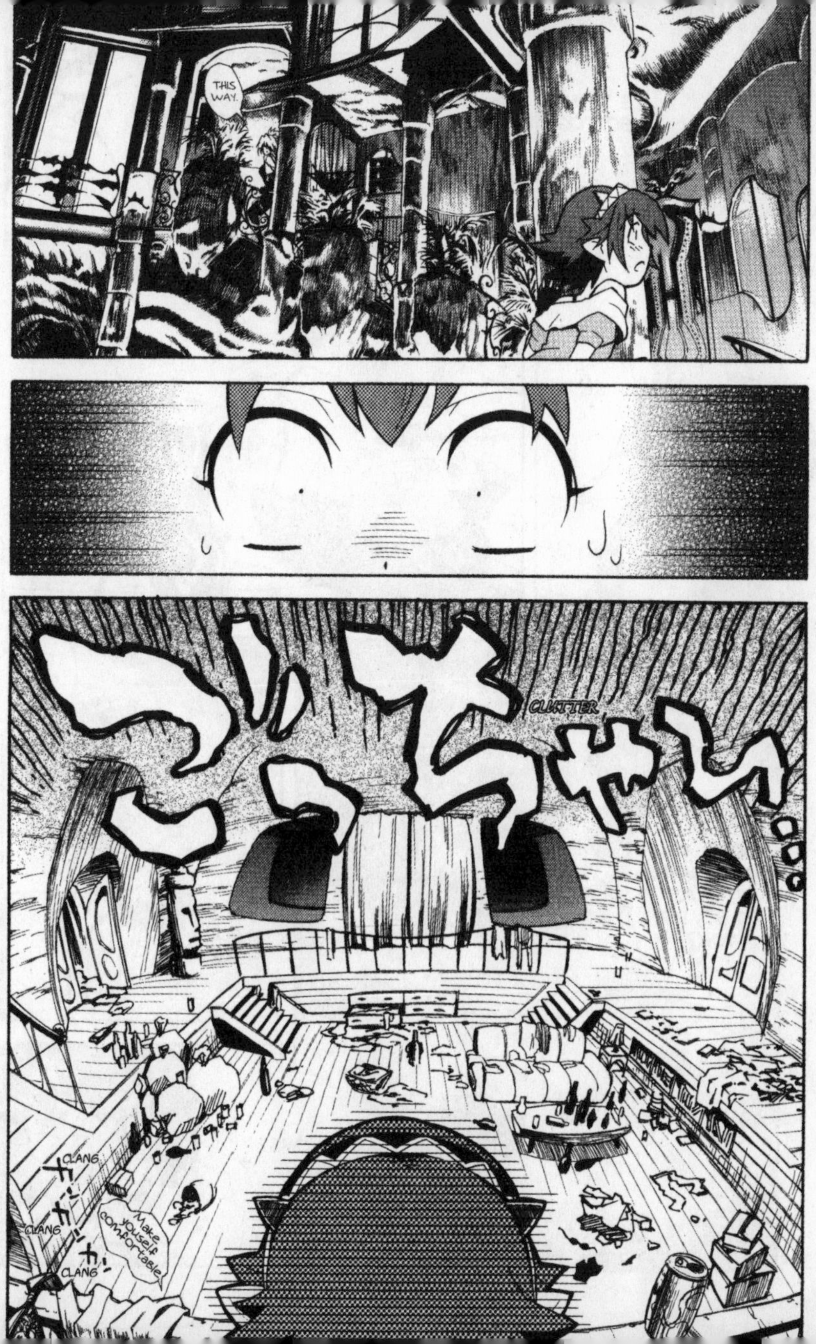
THIS WAY.
CLATTER
CLANG
CLANG
CLANG
Make youself comfortable

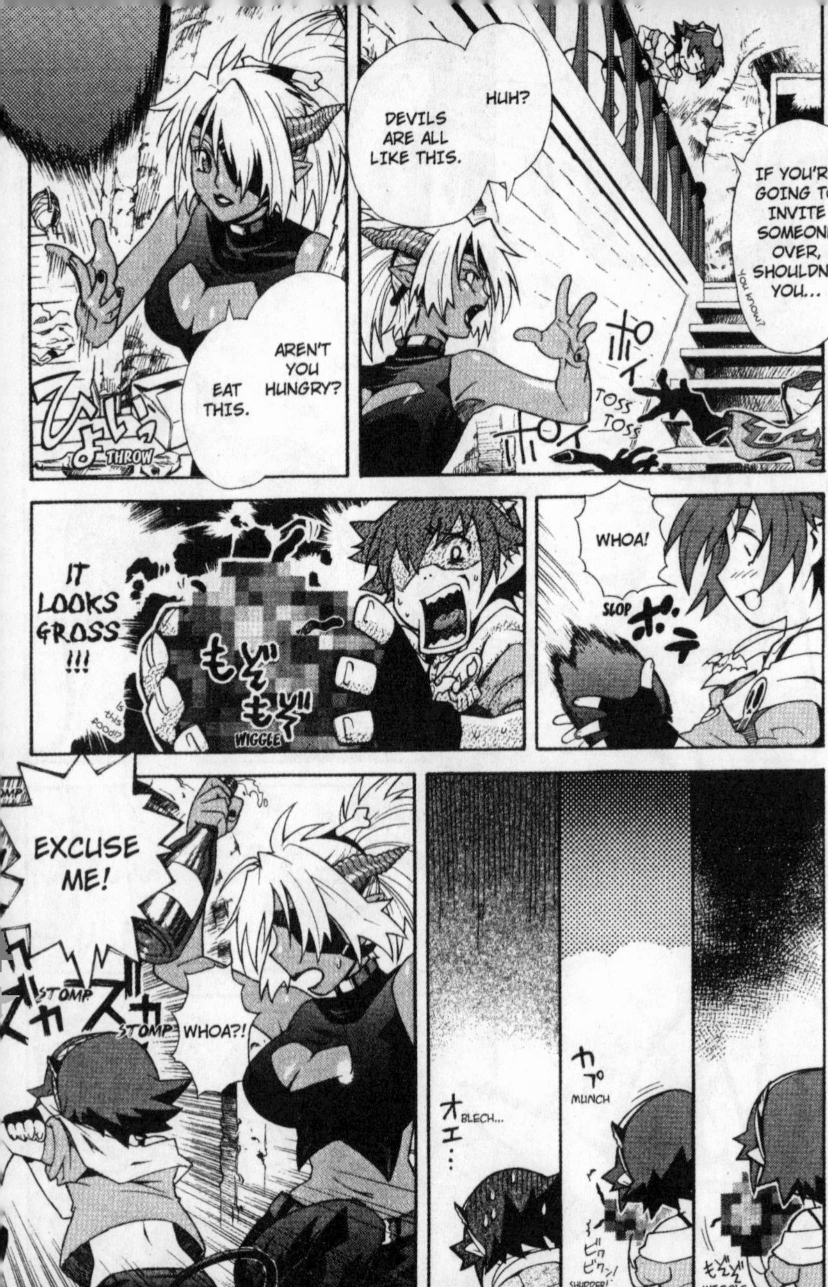
IF YOU'RE GOING TO INVITE SOMEONE OVER, SHOULDN'T YOU...
YOU KNOW?
HUH?
DEVILS ARE ALL LIKE THIS.
ポイ
TOSS
TOSS
ポイ
AREN'T YOU HUNGRY?
EAT THIS.
ひょいっ
THROW
WHOA!
ボテ
SLOP
IT LOOKS GROSS!!!
Is this food!?
もぞもぞ
WIGGLE
もぞ
WIGGLE
カプ
MUNCH
ビクッビクン!
SHUDDER!
オエ…
BLECH...
EXCUSE ME!
ズカズカ
STOMP
STOMP
WHOA?!

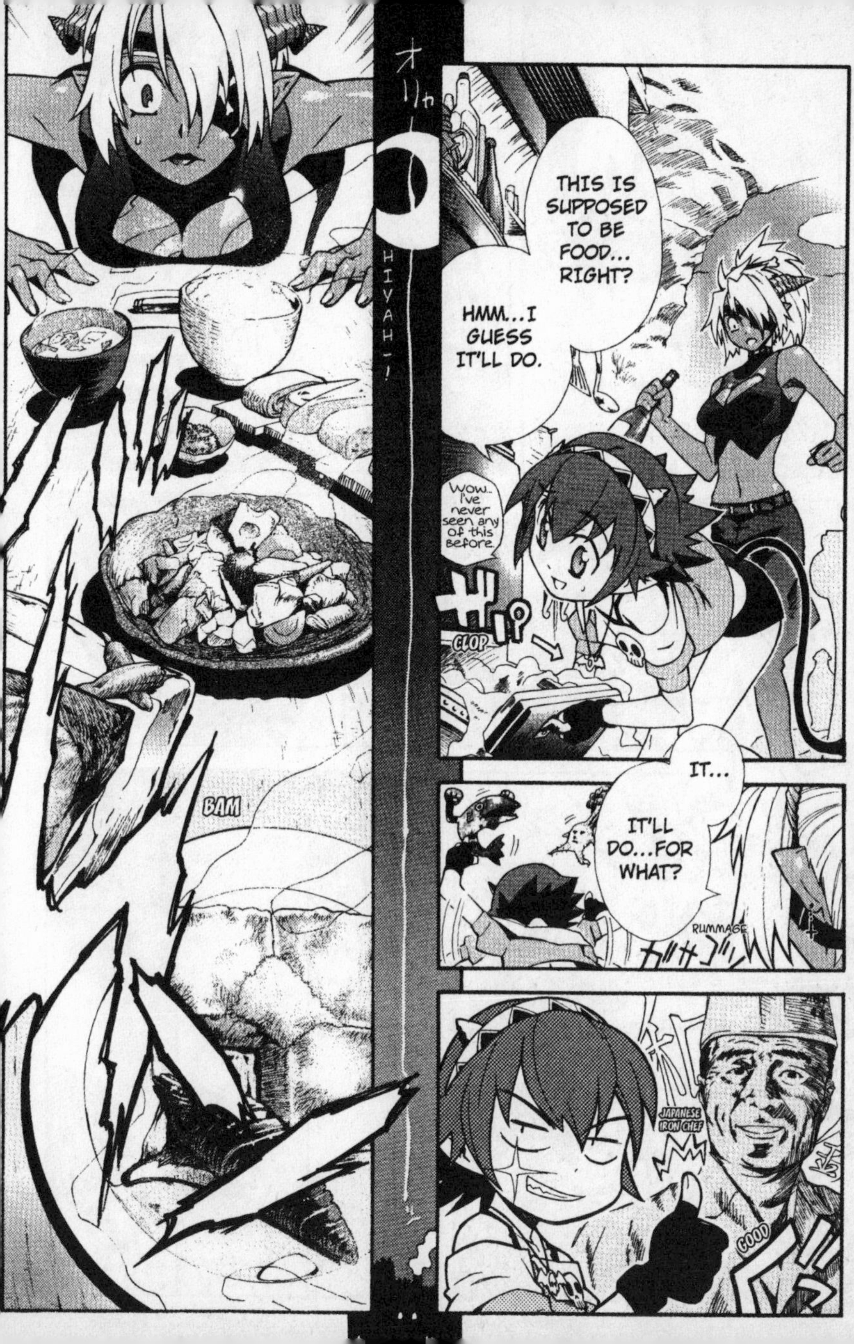
THIS IS SUPPOSED TO BE FOOD... RIGHT?
HMM...I GUESS IT'LL DO.
Wow.. I've never seen any of this before.
CLOP
IT...
IT'LL DO...FOR WHAT?
RUMMAGE
JAPANESE IRON CHEF
GOOD
オリャー！
HIYAH—!
BAM

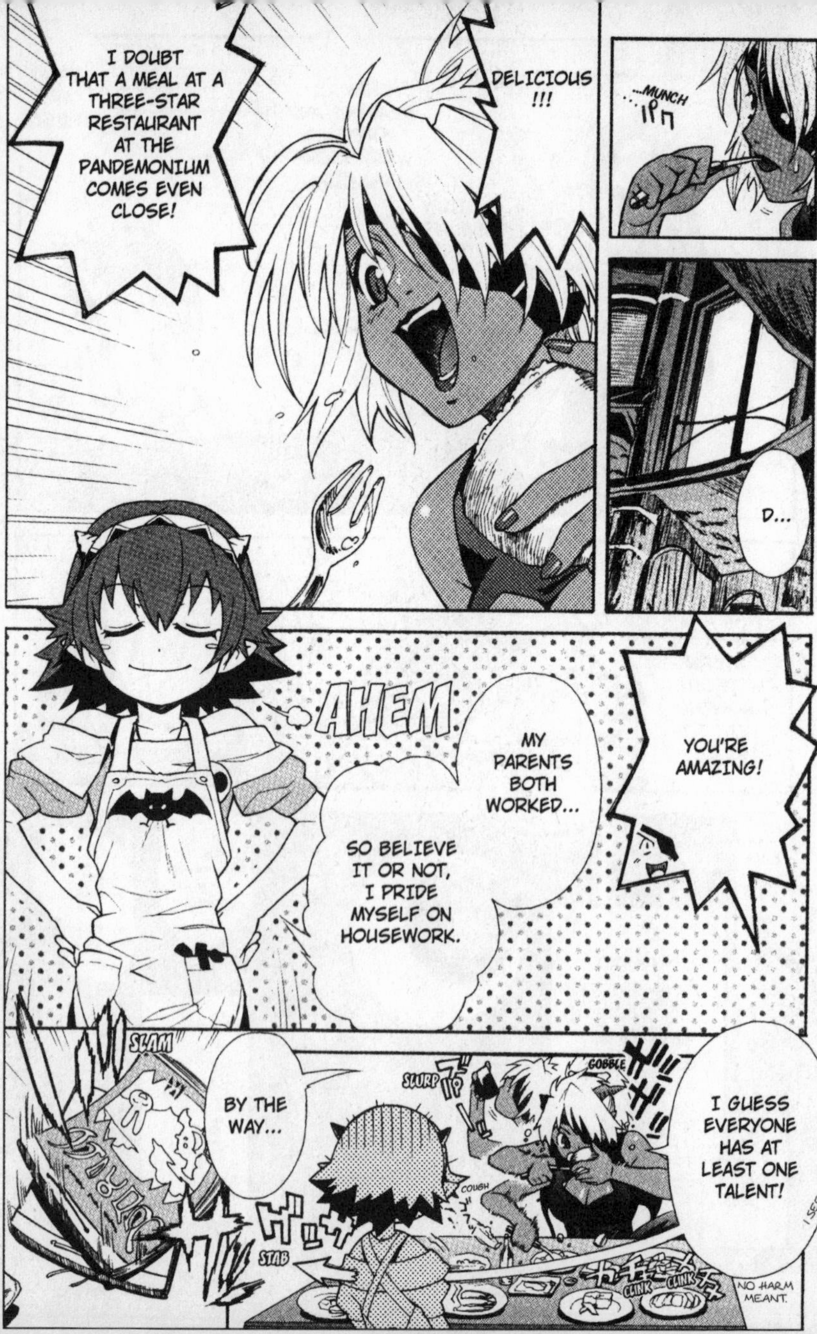
...MUNCH
D...
DELICIOUS!!!
I DOUBT THAT A MEAL AT A THREE-STAR RESTAURANT AT THE PANDEMONIUM COMES EVEN CLOSE!
YOU'RE AMAZING!
MY PARENTS BOTH WORKED...
AHEM
SO BELIEVE IT OR NOT, I PRIDE MYSELF ON HOUSEWORK.
I GUESS EVERYONE HAS AT LEAST ONE TALENT!
I SEE.
NO HARM MEANT.
GOBBLE
SLURP
COUGH
CLINK CLINK
BY THE WAY...
SLAM
STAB

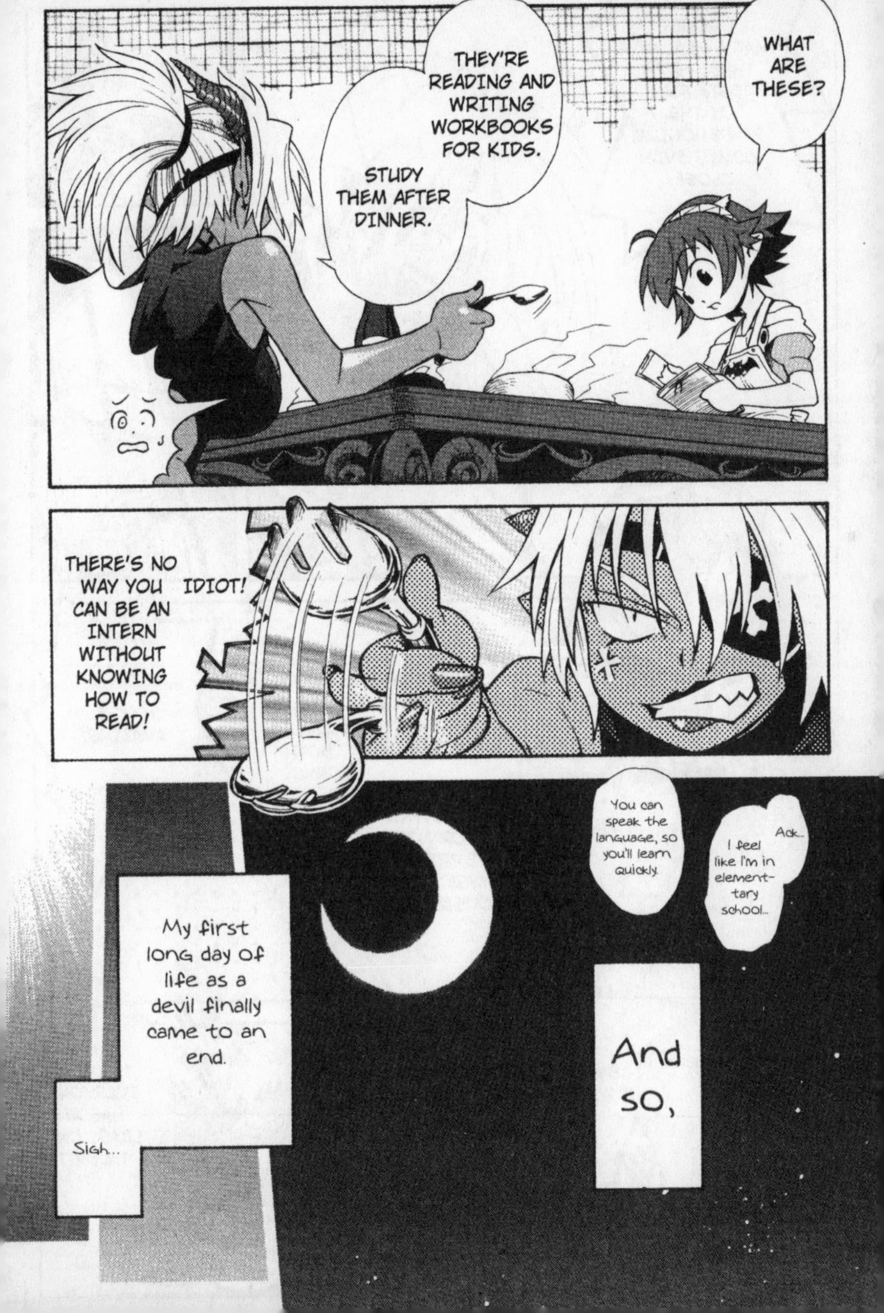
WHAT ARE THESE?
THEY'RE READING AND WRITING WORKBOOKS FOR KIDS.
STUDY THEM AFTER DINNER.
IDIOT!
THERE'S NO WAY YOU CAN BE AN INTERN WITHOUT KNOWING HOW TO READ!
Ack...
I feel like I'm in elementary school...
You can speak the language, so you'll learn quickly.
And so,
My first long day of life as a devil finally came to an end.
Sigh...

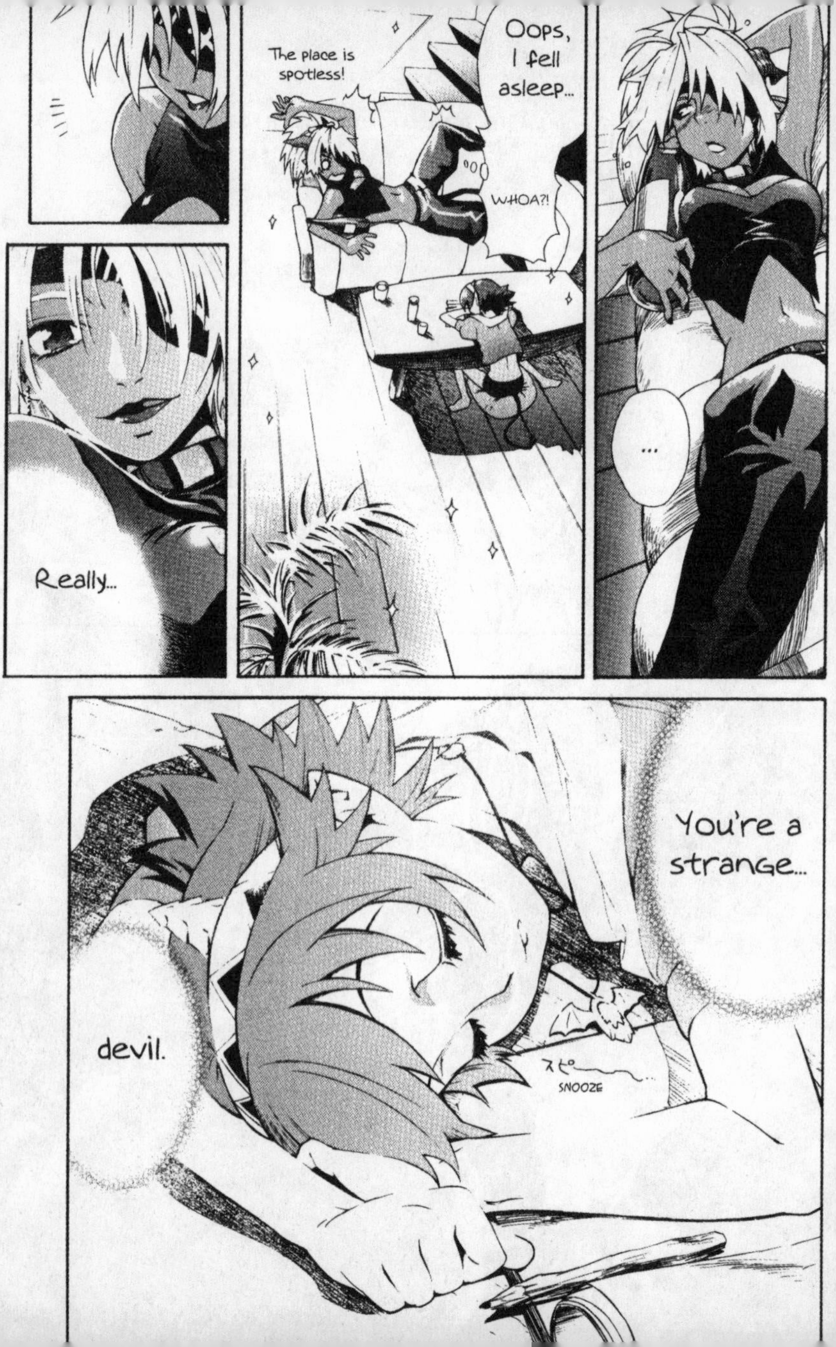
...
Oops, I fell asleep...
The place is spotless!
WHOA?!
Really...
You're a strange...
devil.
スピー...
SNOOZE

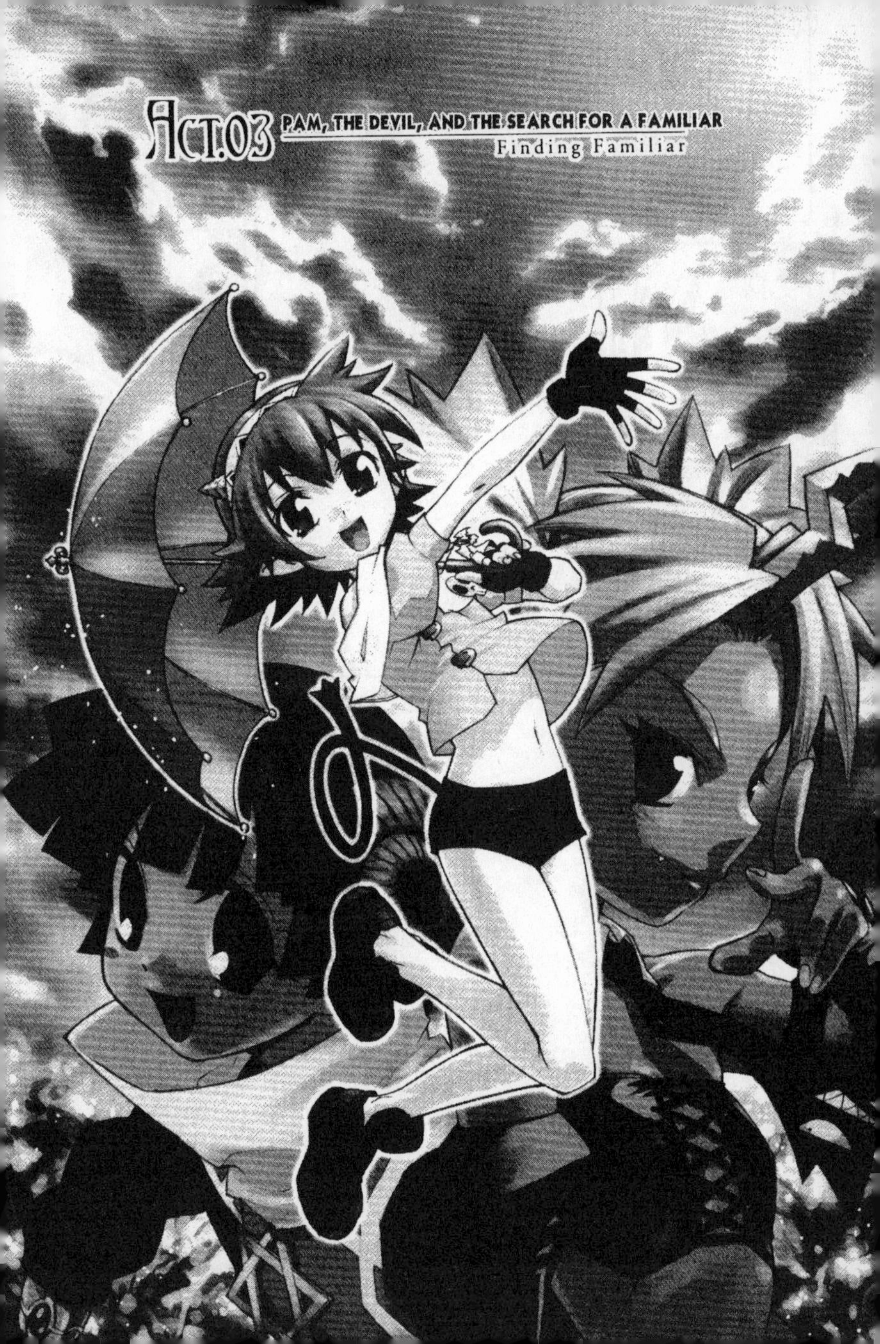
ACT.03 PAM, THE DEVIL, AND THE SEARCH FOR A FAMILIAR
Finding Familiar

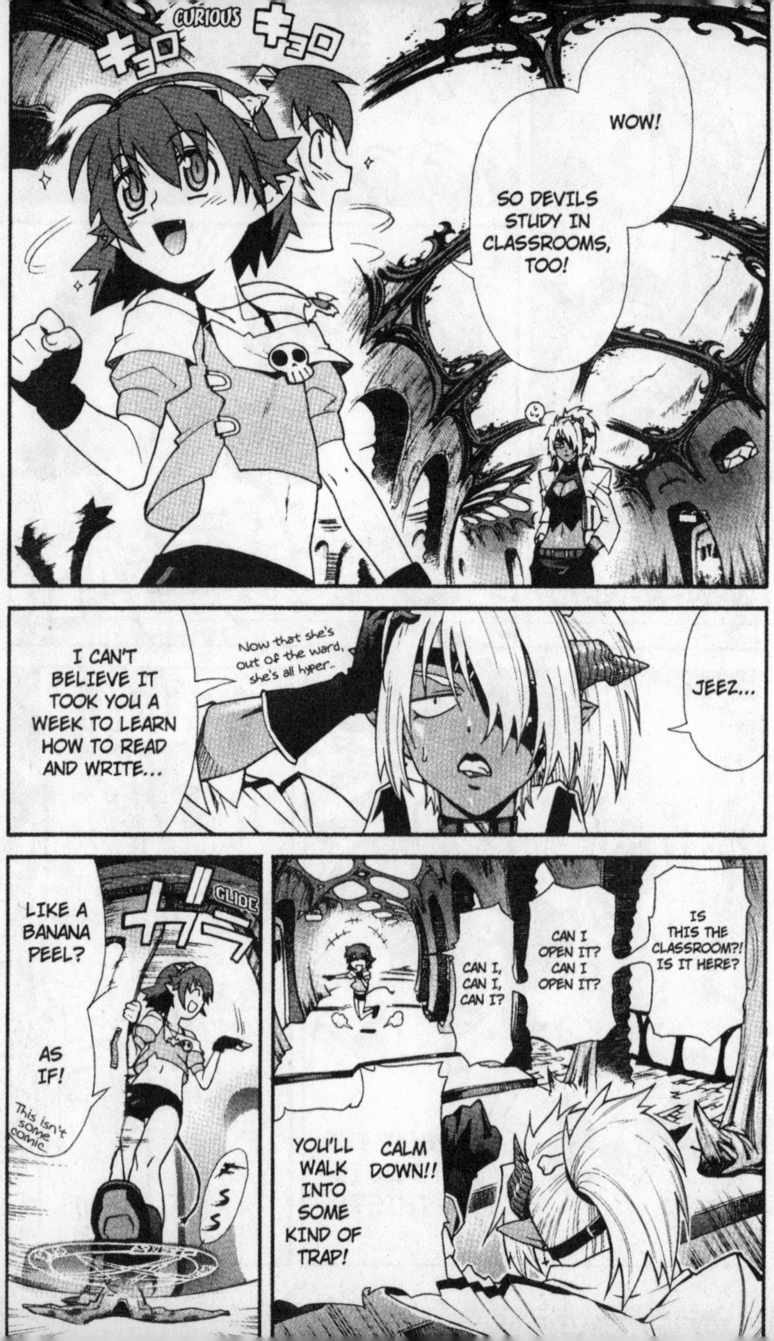

CURIOUS
キョロ
キョロ
WOW!
SO DEVILS STUDY IN CLASSROOMS, TOO!
JEEZ...
Now that she's out of the ward, she's all hyper..
I CAN'T BELIEVE IT TOOK YOU A WEEK TO LEARN HOW TO READ AND WRITE...
IS THIS THE CLASSROOM?! IS IT HERE?
CAN I OPEN IT? CAN I OPEN IT?
CAN I, CAN I, CAN I?
CALM DOWN!!
YOU'LL WALK INTO SOME KIND OF TRAP!
GLIDE
ガラ
LIKE A BANANA PEEL?
AS IF!
This isn't some comic

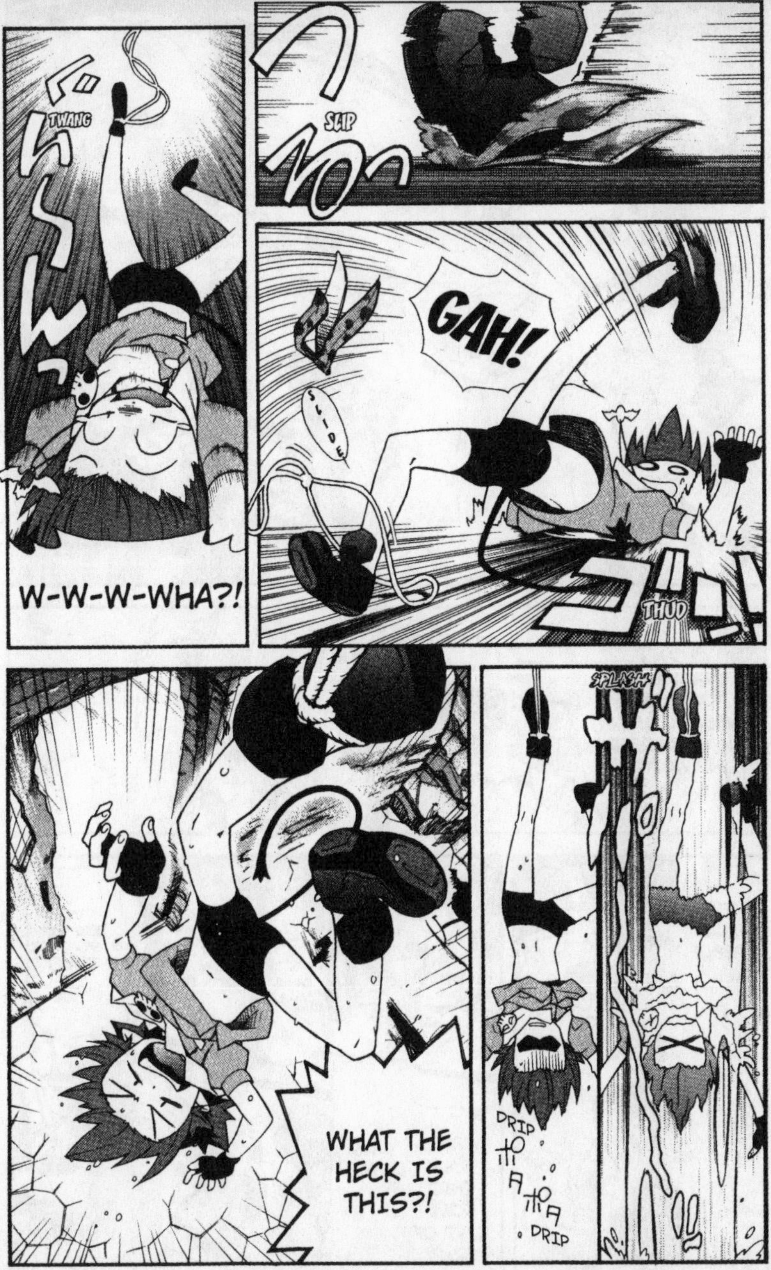
SLIP
GAH!
SLIDE
THUD
TWANG
W-W-W-WHA?!
SPLASH
DRIP
DRIP
WHAT THE HECK IS THIS?!

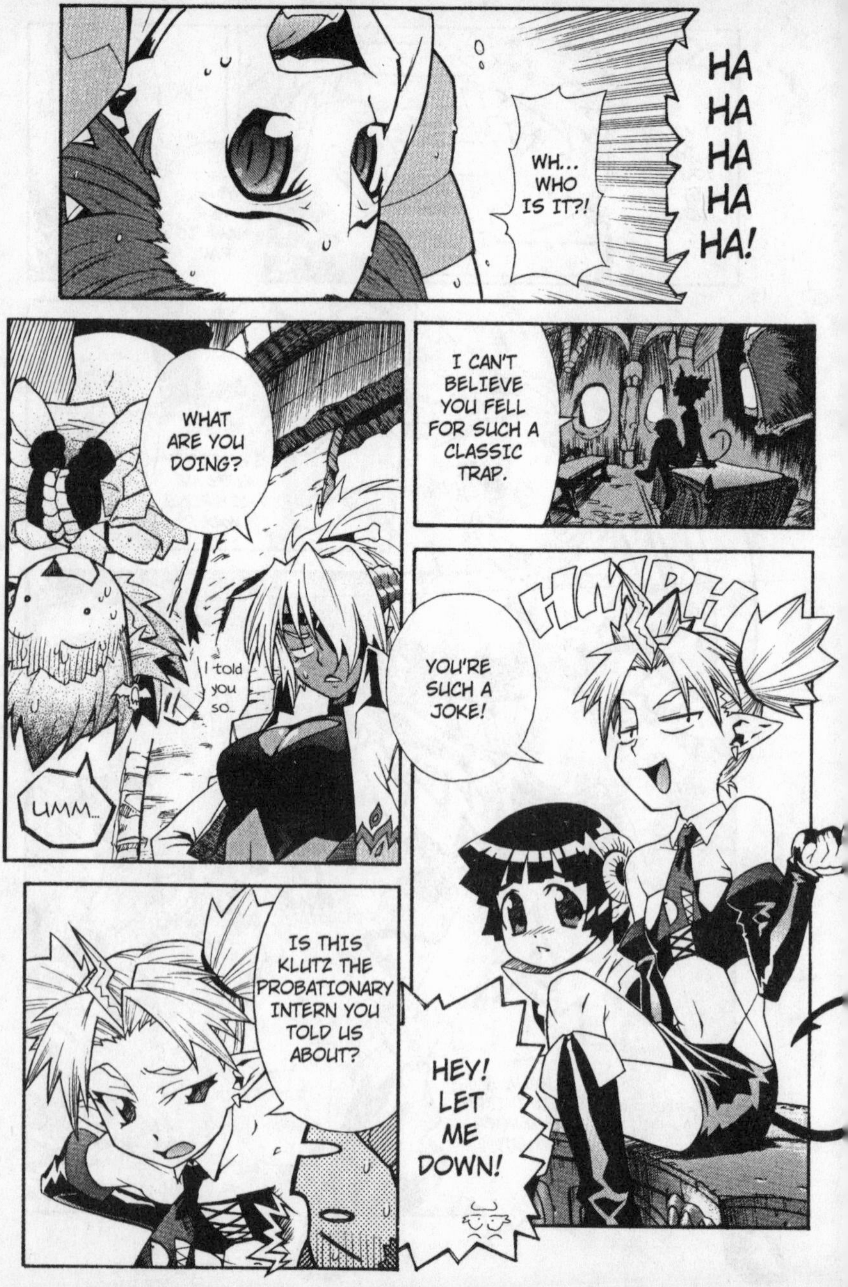
HA HA HA HA HA!
WH... WHO IS IT?!
I CAN'T BELIEVE YOU FELL FOR SUCH A CLASSIC TRAP.
HMPH
YOU'RE SUCH A JOKE!
HEY! LET ME DOWN!
WHAT ARE YOU DOING?
I told you so...
UMM...
IS THIS KLUTZ THE PROBATIONARY INTERN YOU TOLD US ABOUT?

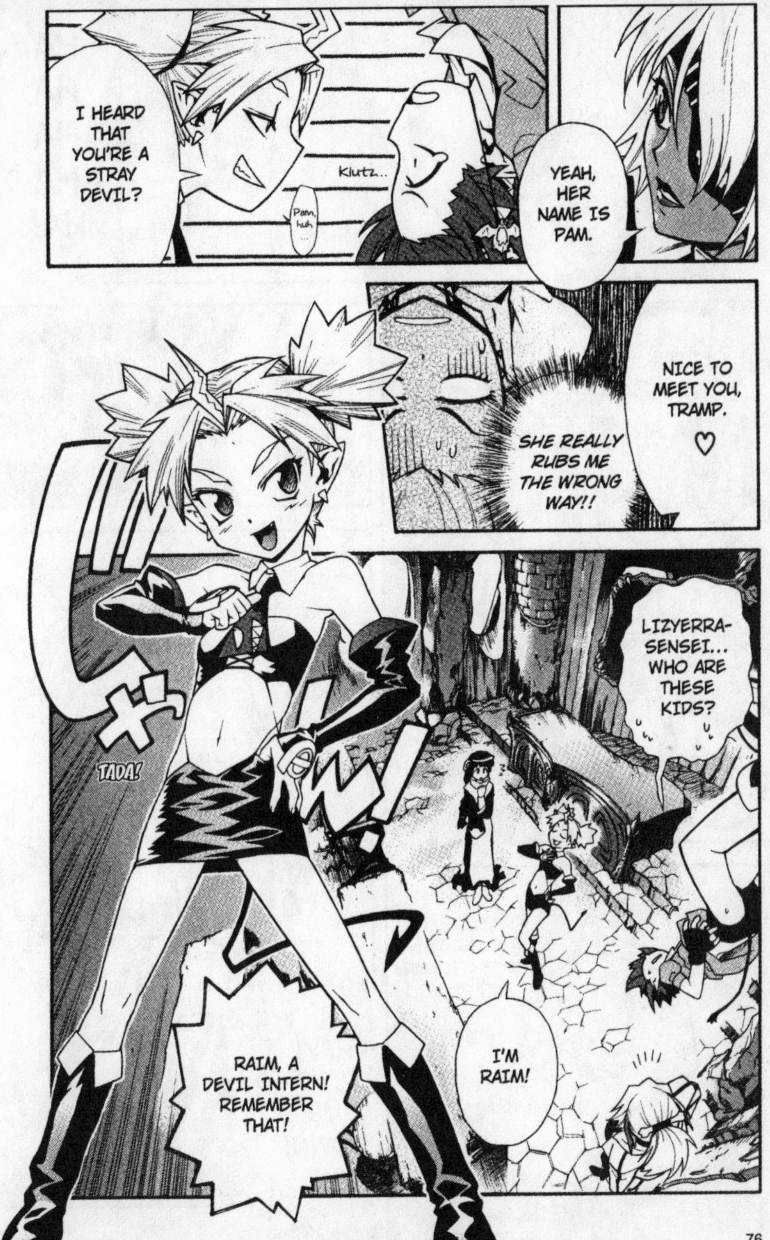
YEAH, HER NAME IS PAM.
I HEARD THAT YOU'RE A STRAY DEVIL?
Klutz...
Pam, huh...
NICE TO MEET YOU, TRAMP. ♡
SHE REALLY RUBS ME THE WRONG WAY!!
LIZYERRA-SENSEI... WHO ARE THESE KIDS?
I'M RAIM!
RAIM, A DEVIL INTERN! REMEMBER THAT!
TADA!

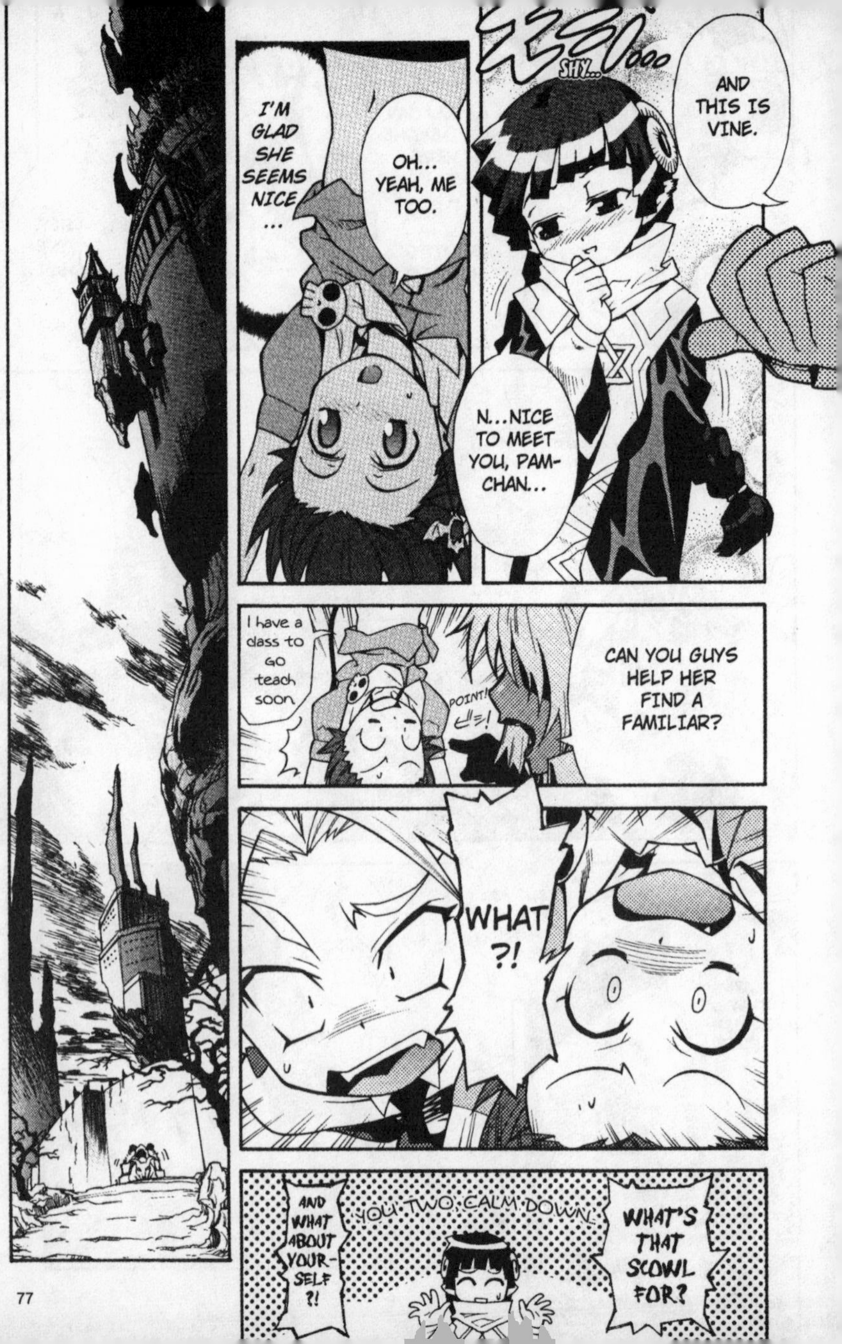
SHY...
AND THIS IS VINE.
N...NICE TO MEET YOU, PAM-CHAN...
I'M GLAD SHE SEEMS NICE...
OH... YEAH, ME TOO.
CAN YOU GUYS HELP HER FIND A FAMILIAR?
POINT!
I have a class to go teach soon.
WHAT?!
WHAT'S THAT SCOWL FOR?
YOU TWO, CALM DOWN.
AND WHAT ABOUT YOURSELF?!

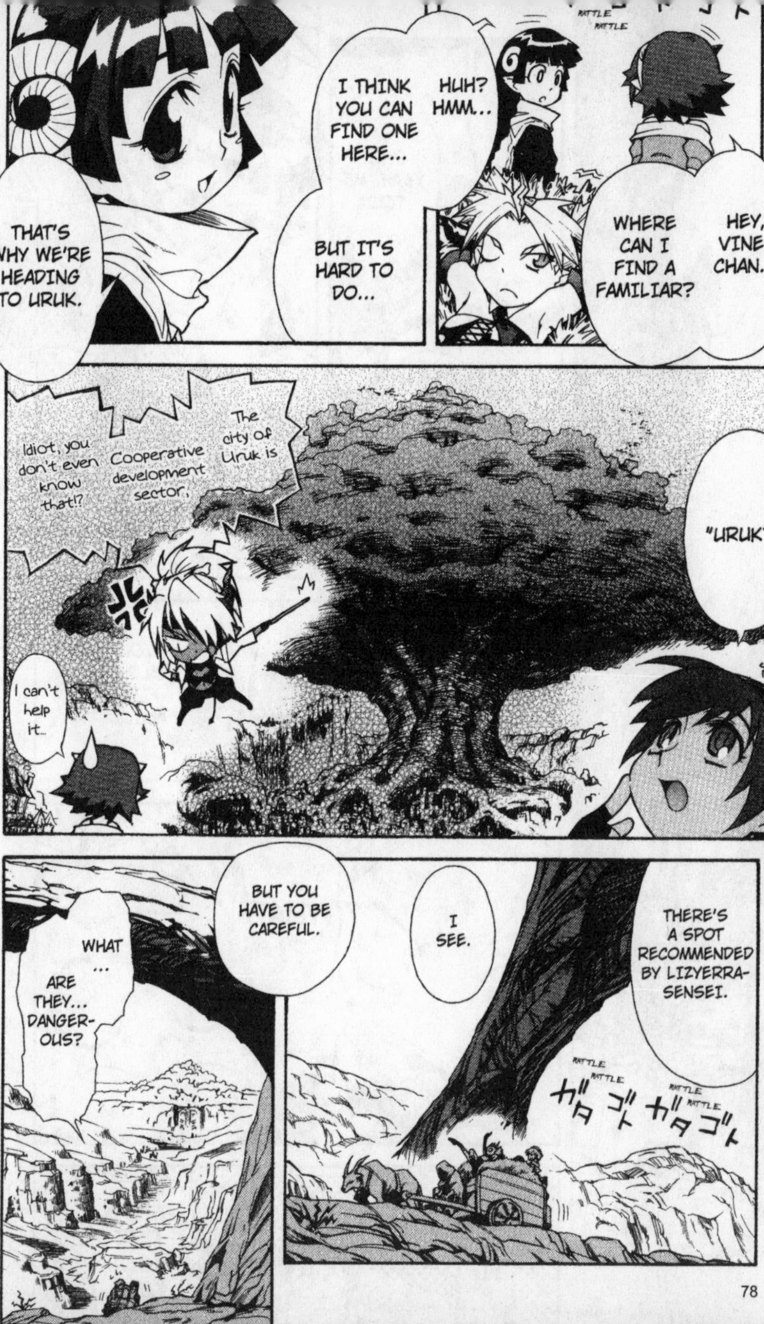
RATTLE RATTLE
HEY, VINE-CHAN...
WHERE CAN I FIND A FAMILIAR?
HUH? HMM...
I THINK YOU CAN FIND ONE HERE...
BUT IT'S HARD TO DO...
THAT'S WHY WE'RE HEADING TO URUK.
"URUK?"
The city of Uruk is
Cooperative development sector,
Idiot, you don't even know that!?
I can't help it...
THERE'S A SPOT RECOMMENDED BY LIZYERRA-SENSEI.
RATTLE RATTLE
ガタゴト
RATTLE RATTLE
ガタゴト
I SEE.
BUT YOU HAVE TO BE CAREFUL.
WHAT ... ARE THEY... DANGEROUS?

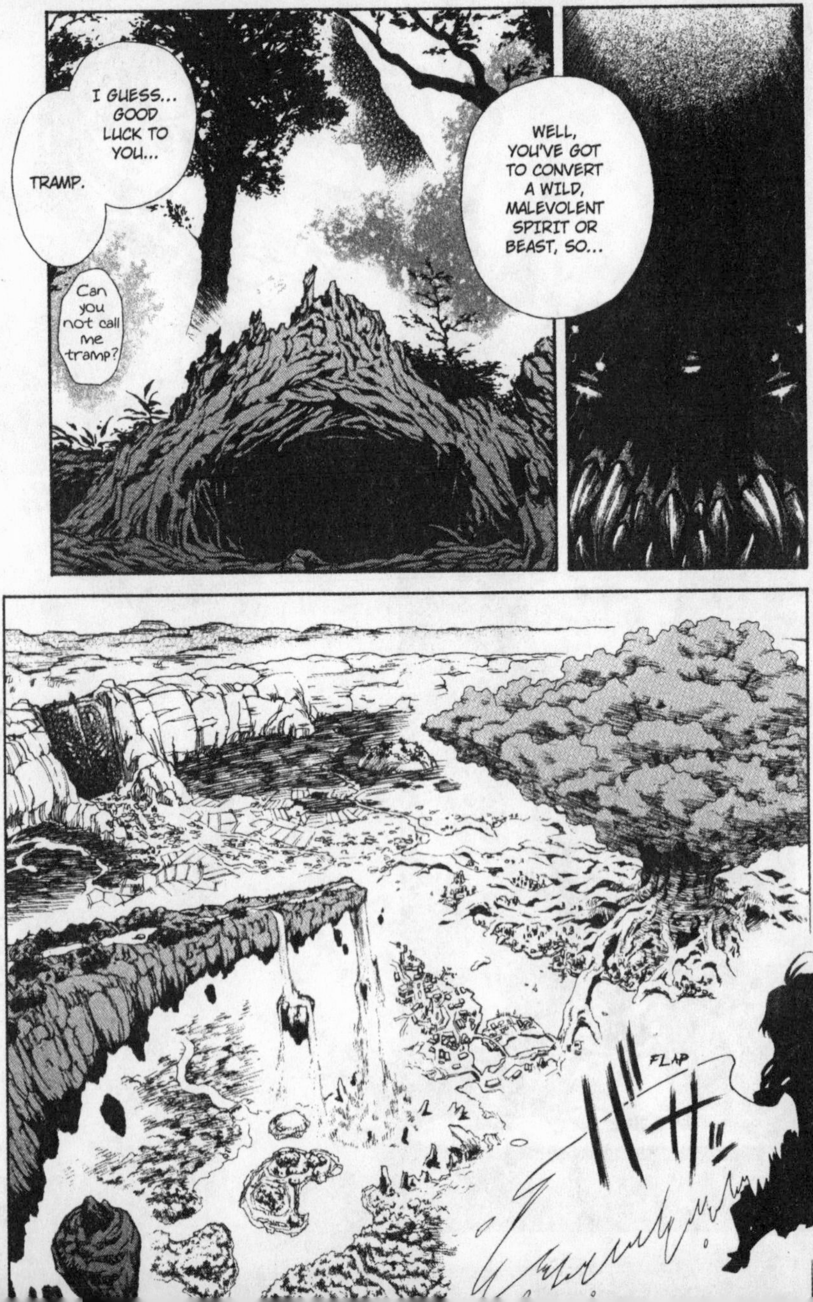
WELL, YOU'VE GOT TO CONVERT A WILD, MALEVOLENT SPIRIT OR BEAST, SO...
I GUESS... GOOD LUCK TO YOU...
TRAMP.
Can you not call me tramp?
FLAP

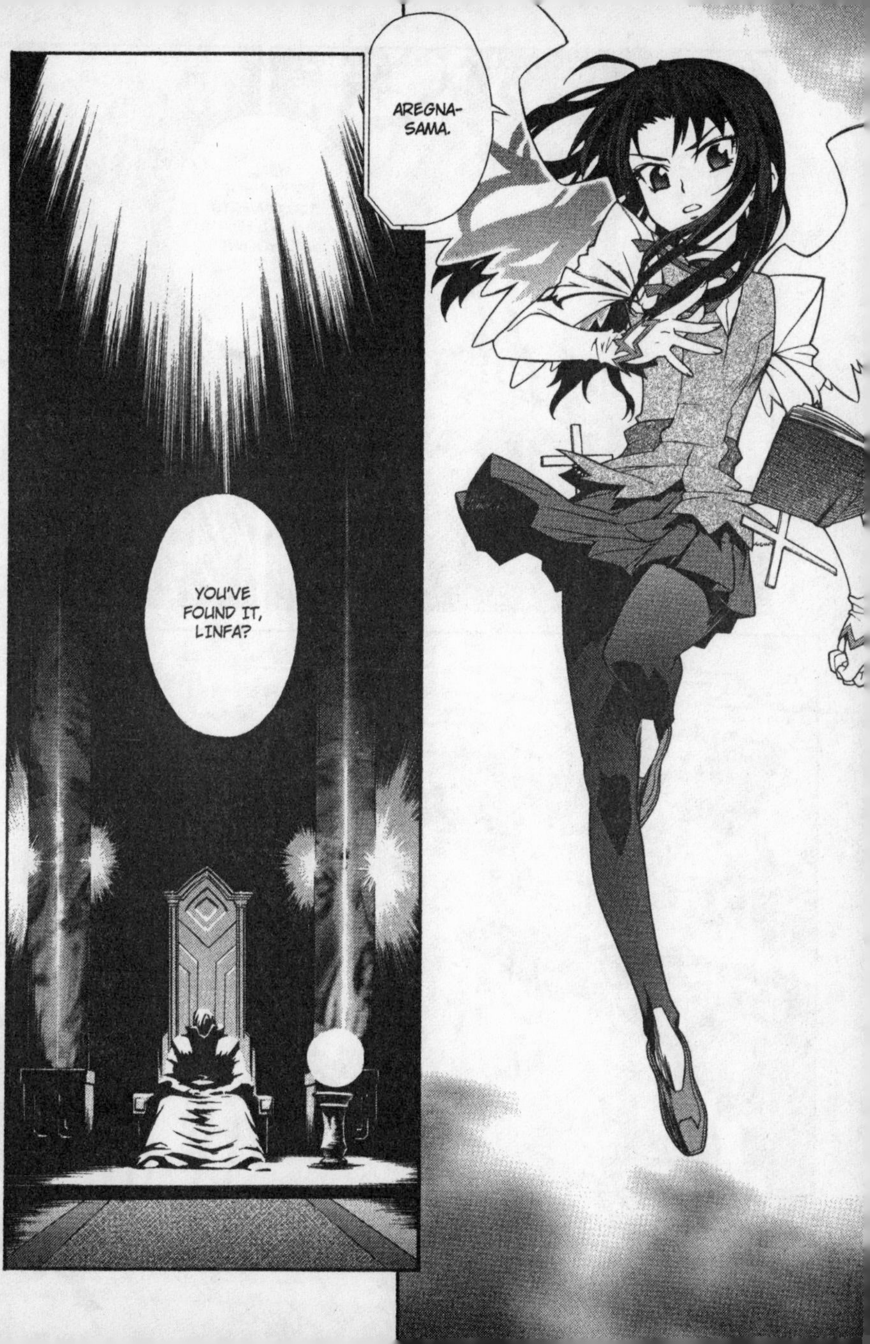
AREGNA-SAMA.
YOU'VE FOUND IT, LINFA?

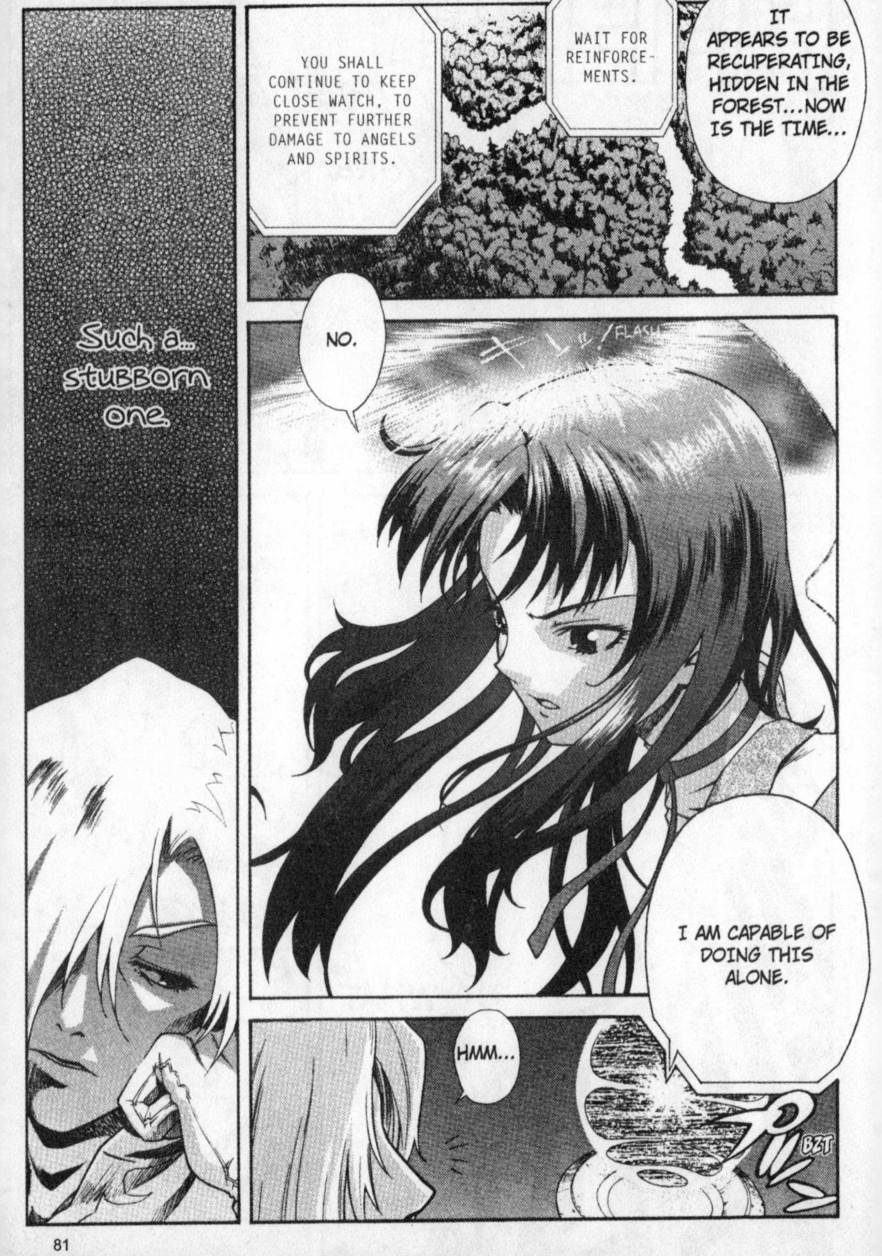
IT APPEARS TO BE RECUPERATING, HIDDEN IN THE FOREST...NOW IS THE TIME...
WAIT FOR REINFORCEMENTS.
YOU SHALL CONTINUE TO KEEP CLOSE WATCH, TO PREVENT FURTHER DAMAGE TO ANGELS AND SPIRITS.
FLASH
NO.
I AM CAPABLE OF DOING THIS ALONE.
BZT
HMM...
Such a... stubborn one.

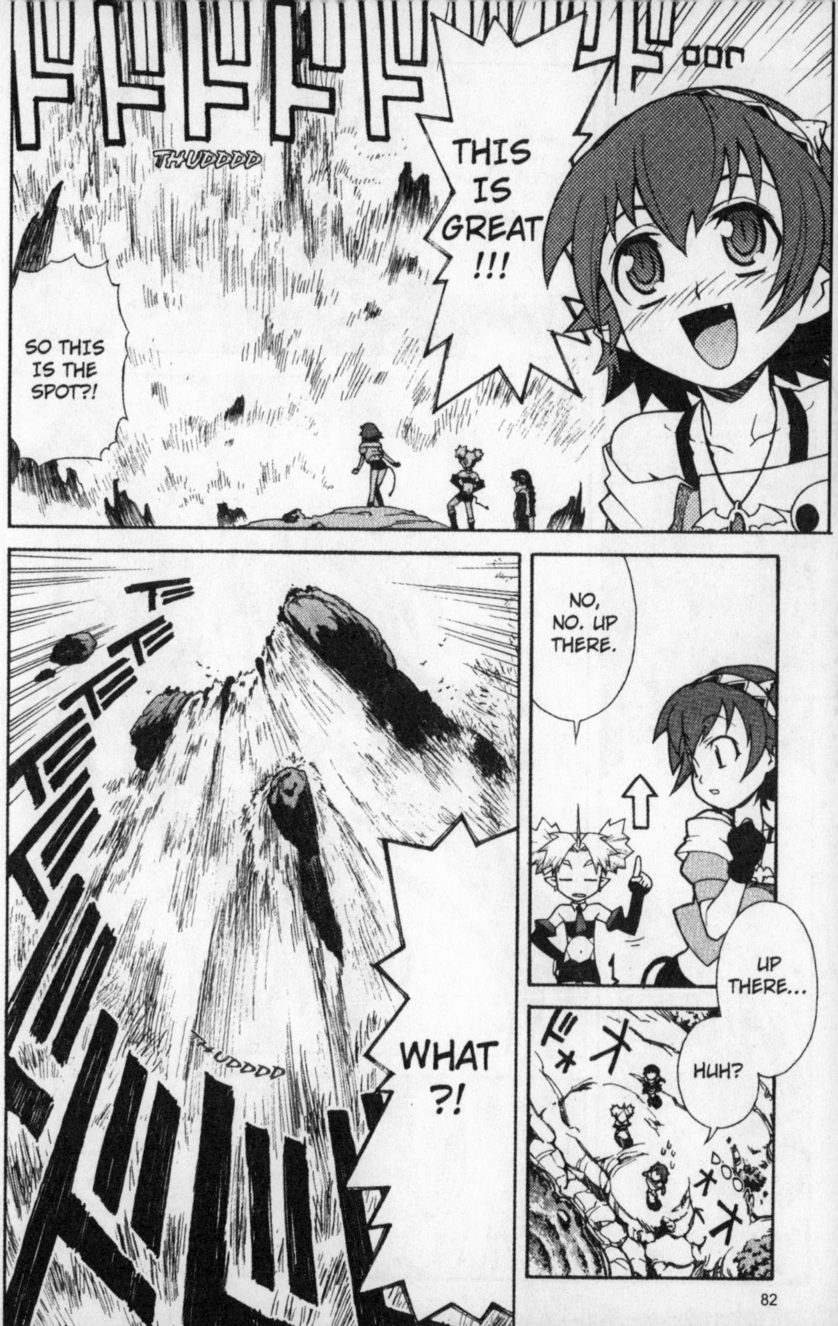

THIS IS GREAT !!!
THUDDDD
SO THIS IS THE SPOT?!
NO, NO. UP THERE.
UP THERE...
HUH?
WHAT ?!
THUDDDD

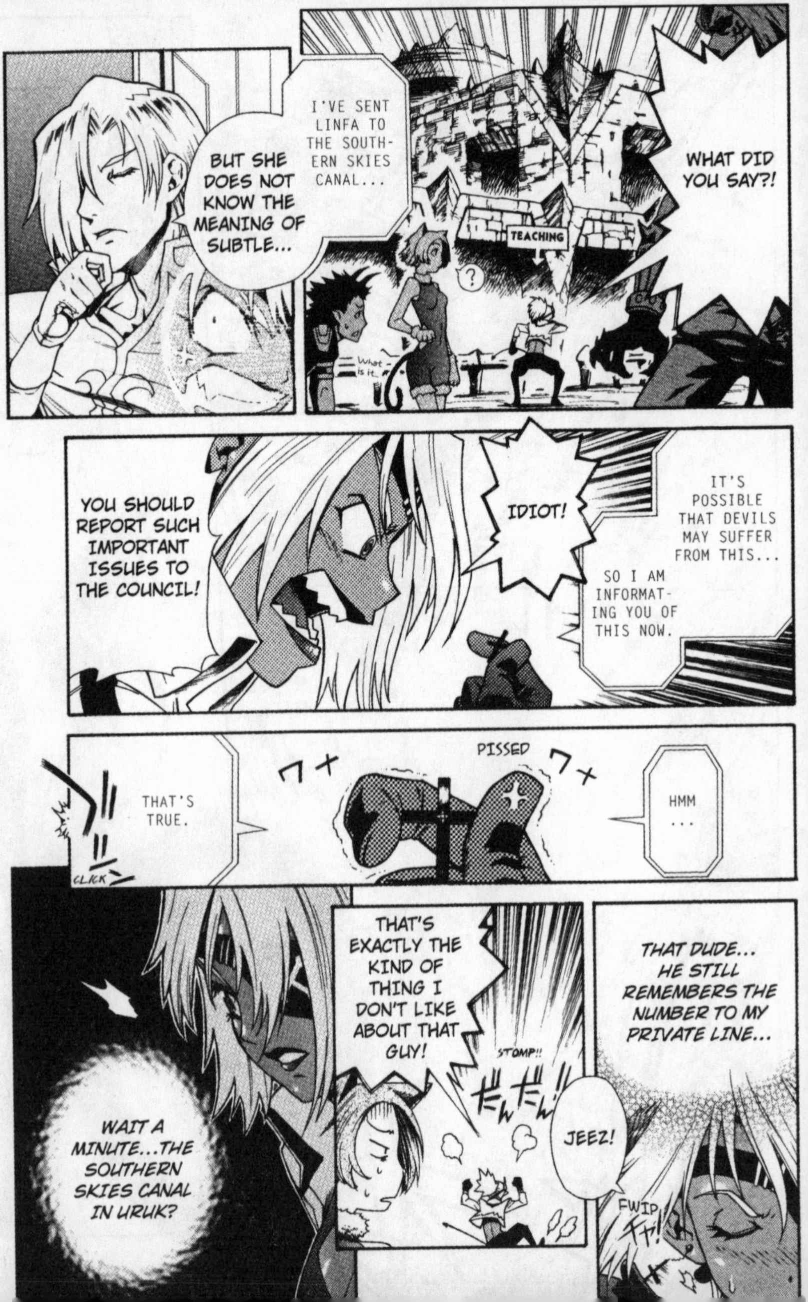
WHAT DID YOU SAY?!
TEACHING
?
What is it
I'VE SENT LINFA TO THE SOUTHERN SKIES CANAL...
BUT SHE DOES NOT KNOW THE MEANING OF SUBTLE...
IT'S POSSIBLE THAT DEVILS MAY SUFFER FROM THIS...
SO I AM INFORMATING YOU OF THIS NOW.
IDIOT!
YOU SHOULD REPORT SUCH IMPORTANT ISSUES TO THE COUNCIL!
HMM ...
PISSED
THAT'S TRUE.
CLICK
THAT DUDE... HE STILL REMEMBERS THE NUMBER TO MY PRIVATE LINE...
FWIP
THAT'S EXACTLY THE KIND OF THING I DON'T LIKE ABOUT THAT GUY!
STOMP!!
JEEZ!
WAIT A MINUTE...THE SOUTHERN SKIES CANAL IN URUK?

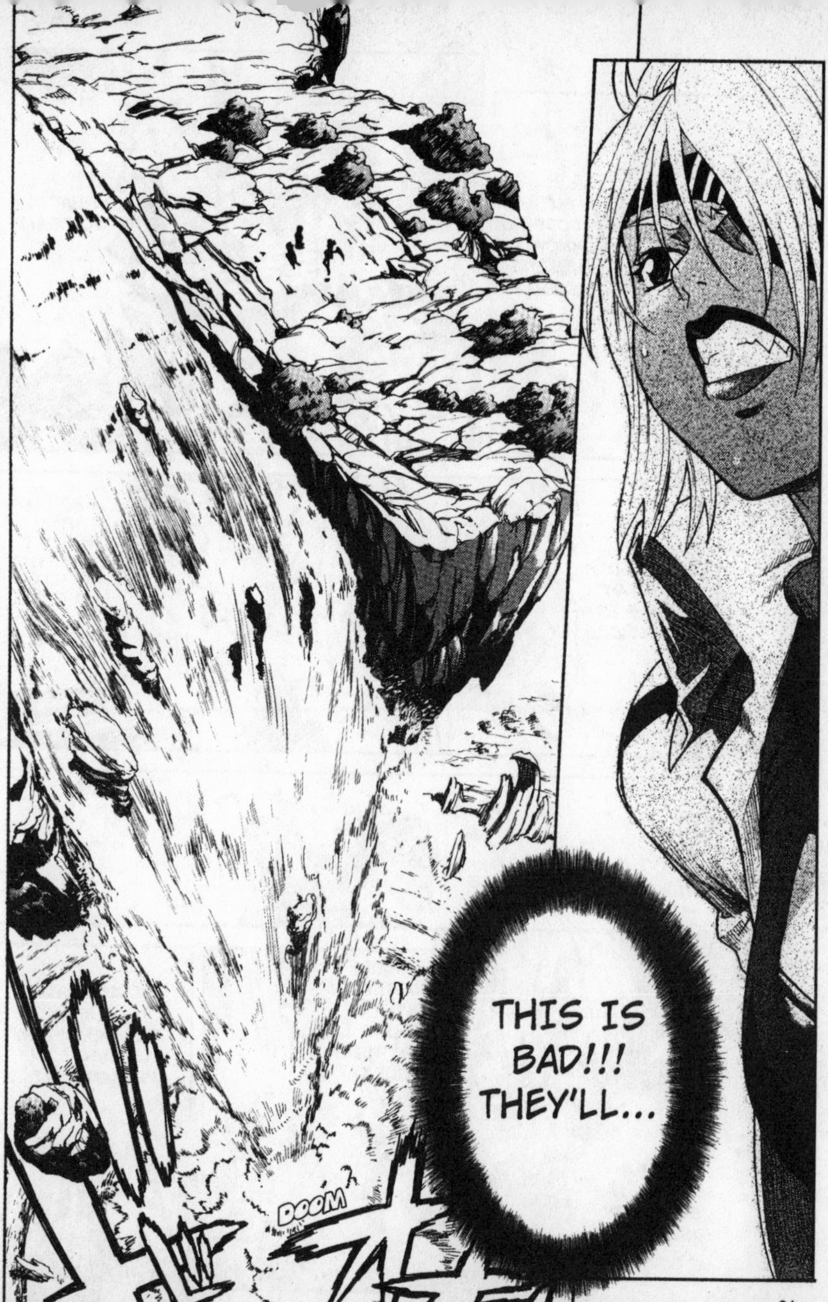
THIS IS BAD!!! THEY'LL...
DOOM

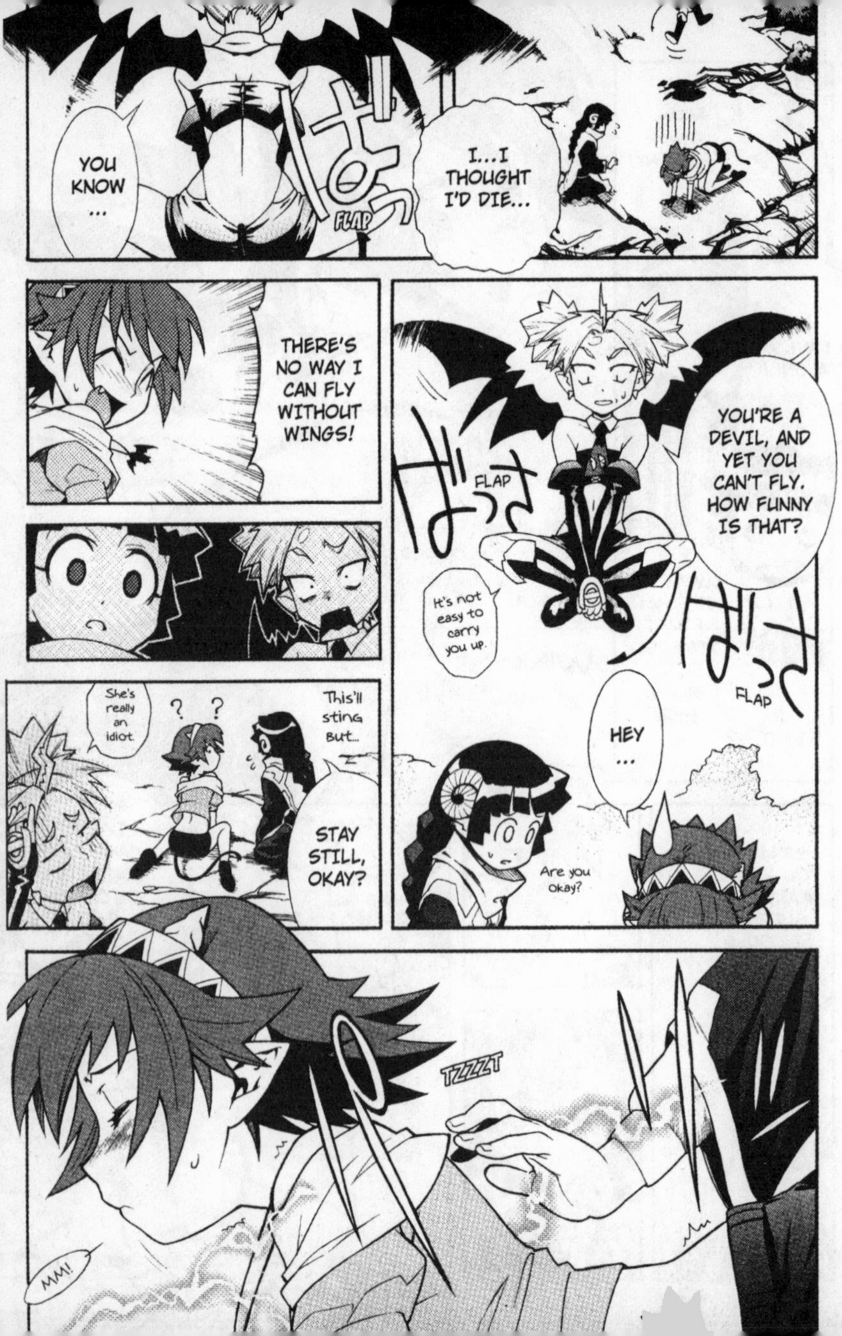

I...I THOUGHT I'D DIE...
ばっ
FLAP
YOU KNOW ...
YOU'RE A DEVIL, AND YET YOU CAN'T FLY. HOW FUNNY IS THAT?
ばっさ
FLAP
It's not easy to carry you up.
ばっさ
FLAP
THERE'S NO WAY I CAN FLY WITHOUT WINGS!
HEY ...
Are you okay?
This'll sting but...
STAY STILL, OKAY?
? ?
She's really an idiot.
TZZZT
MM!

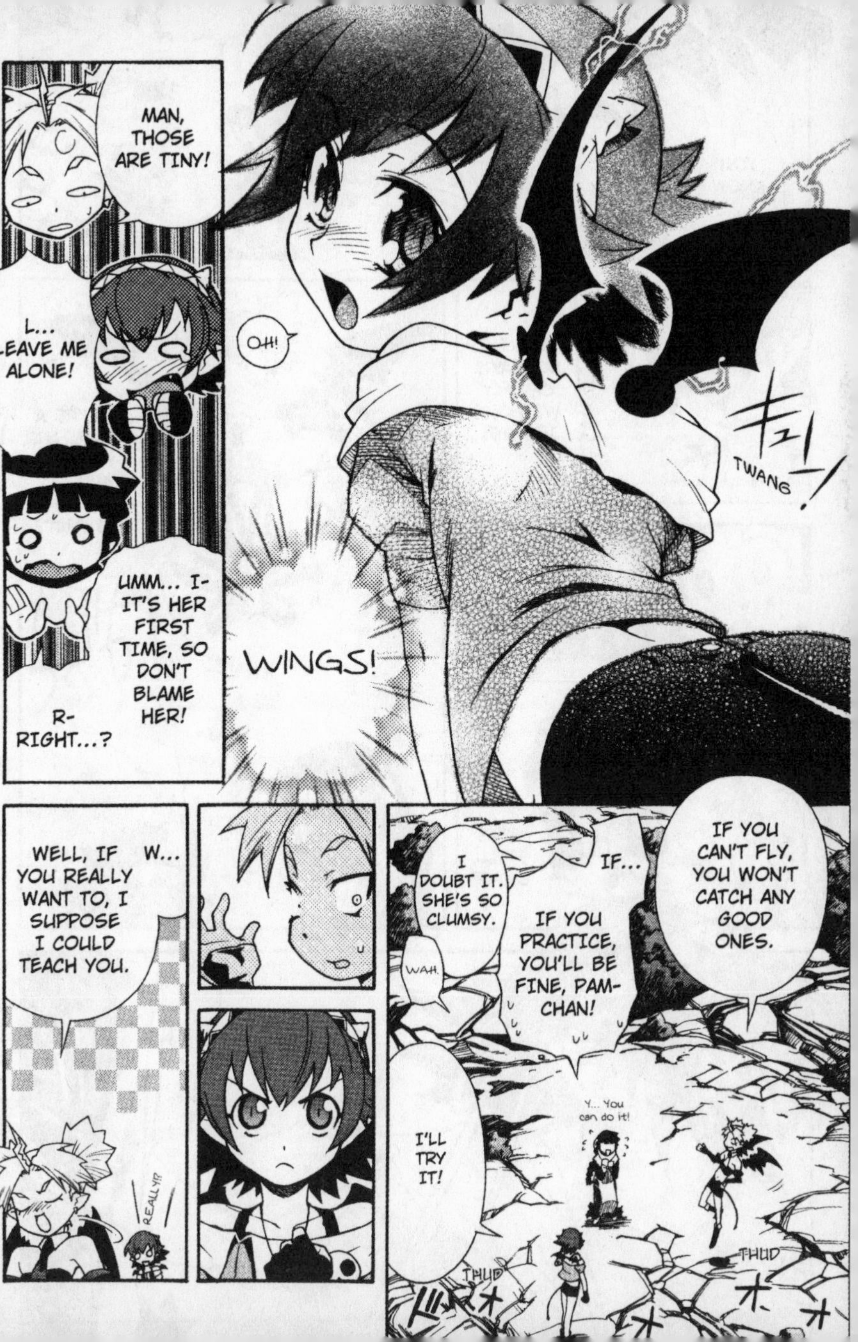
OH!
TWANG
WINGS!
MAN, THOSE ARE TINY!
L... LEAVE ME ALONE!
UMM... I- IT'S HER FIRST TIME, SO DON'T BLAME HER!
R- RIGHT...?
IF YOU CAN'T FLY, YOU WON'T CATCH ANY GOOD ONES.
IF...
IF YOU PRACTICE, YOU'LL BE FINE, PAM-CHAN!
I DOUBT IT. SHE'S SO CLUMSY.
WAH.
Y... You can do it!
I'LL TRY IT!
THUD
THUD
W...
WELL, IF YOU REALLY WANT TO, I SUPPOSE I COULD TEACH YOU.
REALLY!?

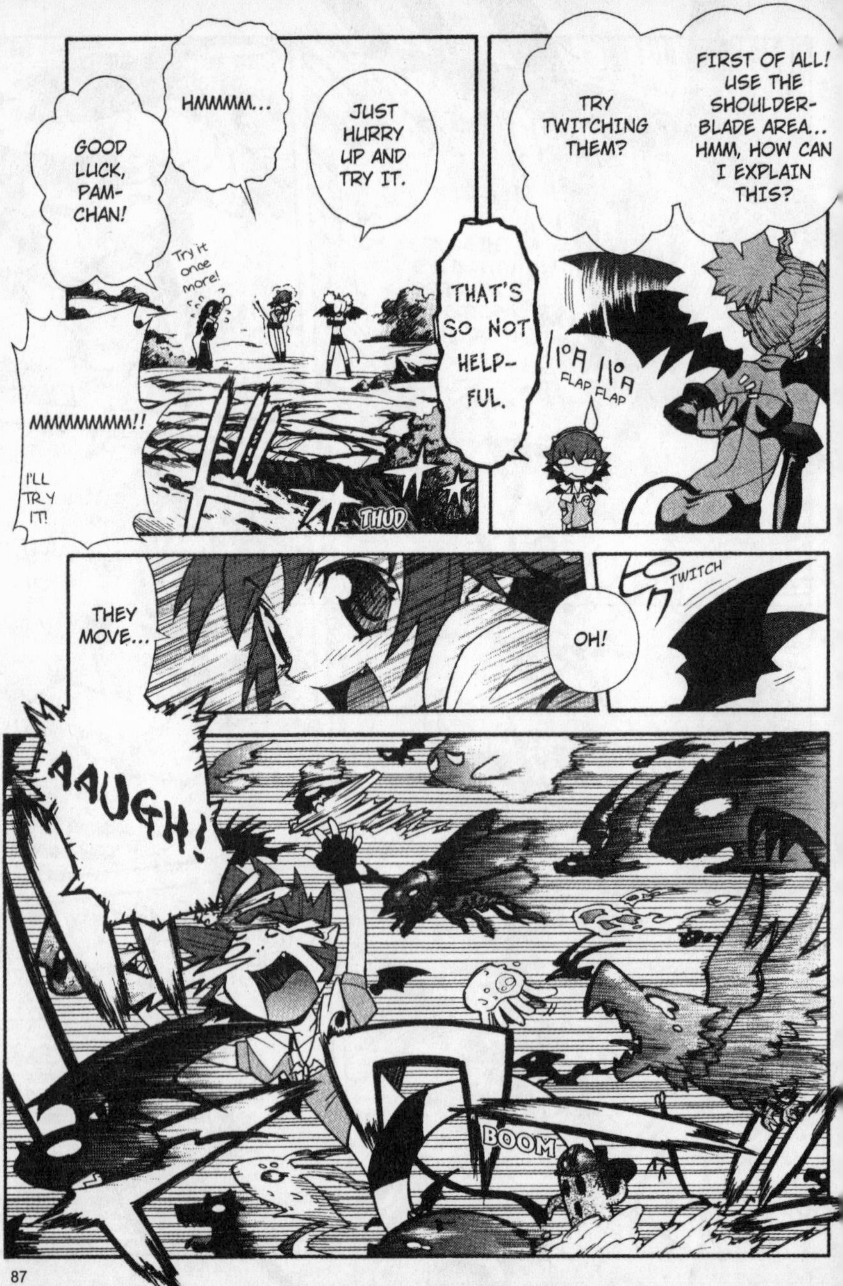
FIRST OF ALL! USE THE SHOULDER-BLADE AREA... HMM, HOW CAN I EXPLAIN THIS?
TRY TWITCHING THEM?
FLAP FLAP
THAT'S SO NOT HELP-FUL.
JUST HURRY UP AND TRY IT.
HMMMMM...
GOOD LUCK, PAM-CHAN!
Try it once more!
MMMMMMMMM!!
I'LL TRY IT!
THUD
TWITCH
OH!
THEY MOVE...
AAUGH!
BOOM

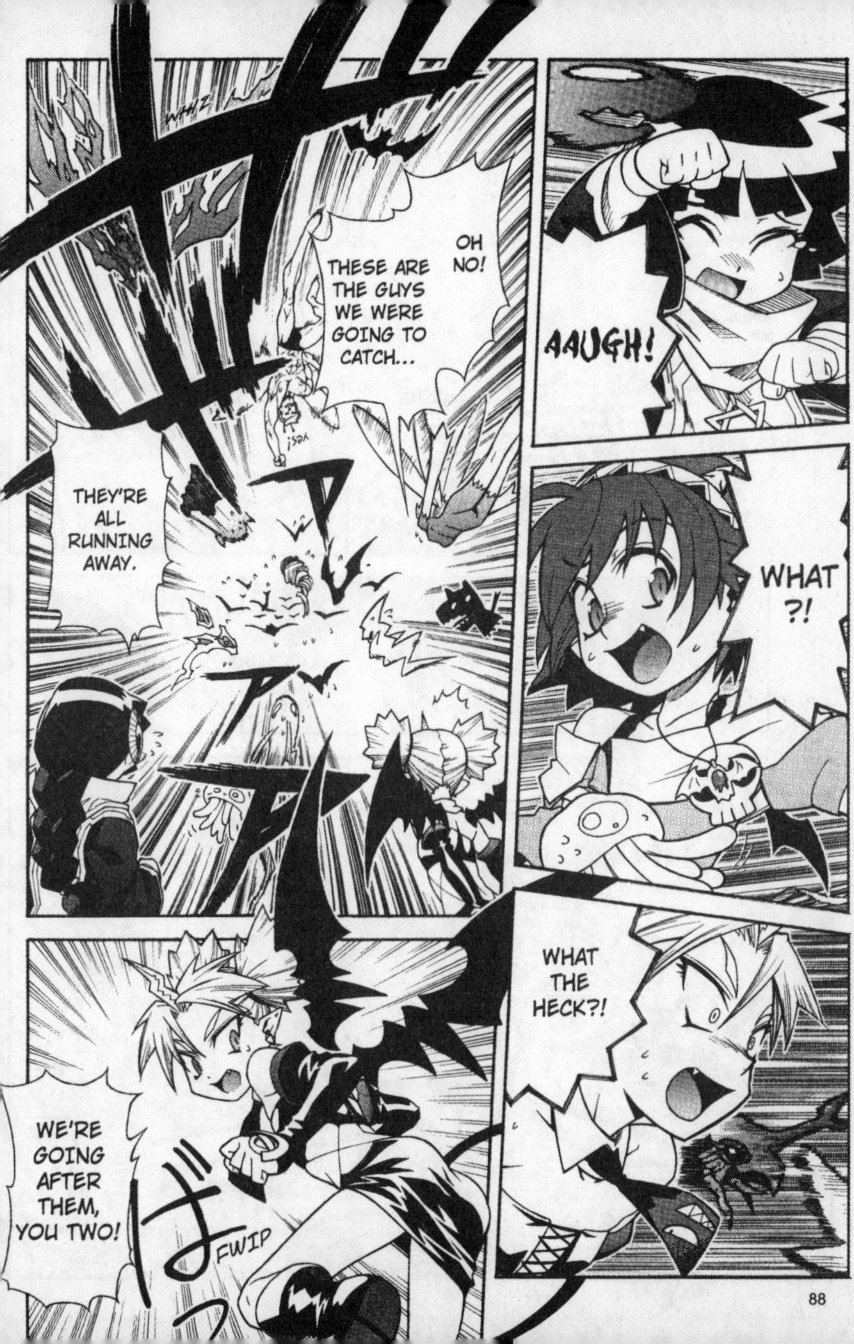
AAUGH!
WHAT ?!
WHIZ
OH NO!
THESE ARE THE GUYS WE WERE GOING TO CATCH...
THEY'RE ALL RUNNING AWAY.
WHAT THE HECK?!
WE'RE GOING AFTER THEM, YOU TWO!
FWIP

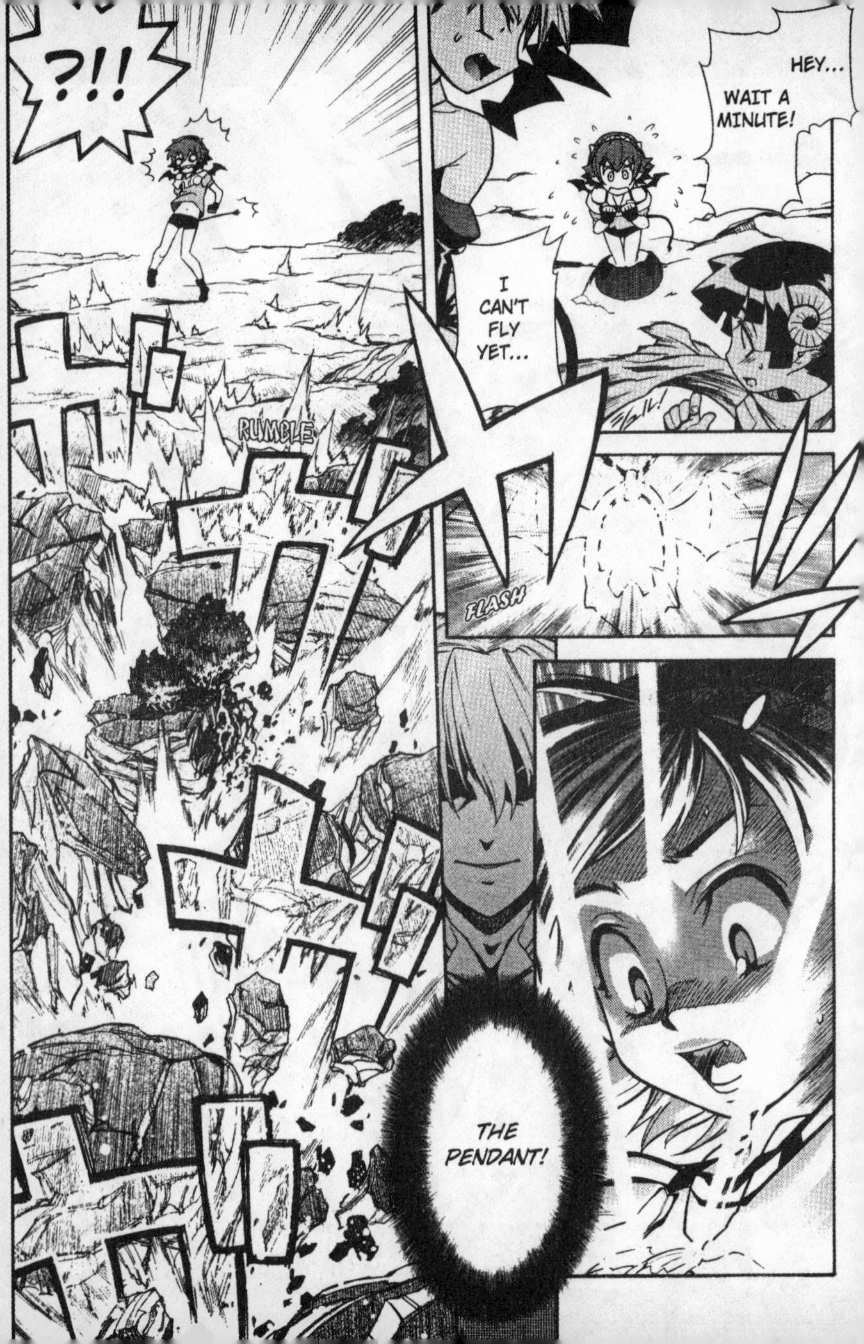

HEY...
WAIT A MINUTE!
I CAN'T FLY YET...
FLASH
THE PENDANT!
?!!
RUMBLE

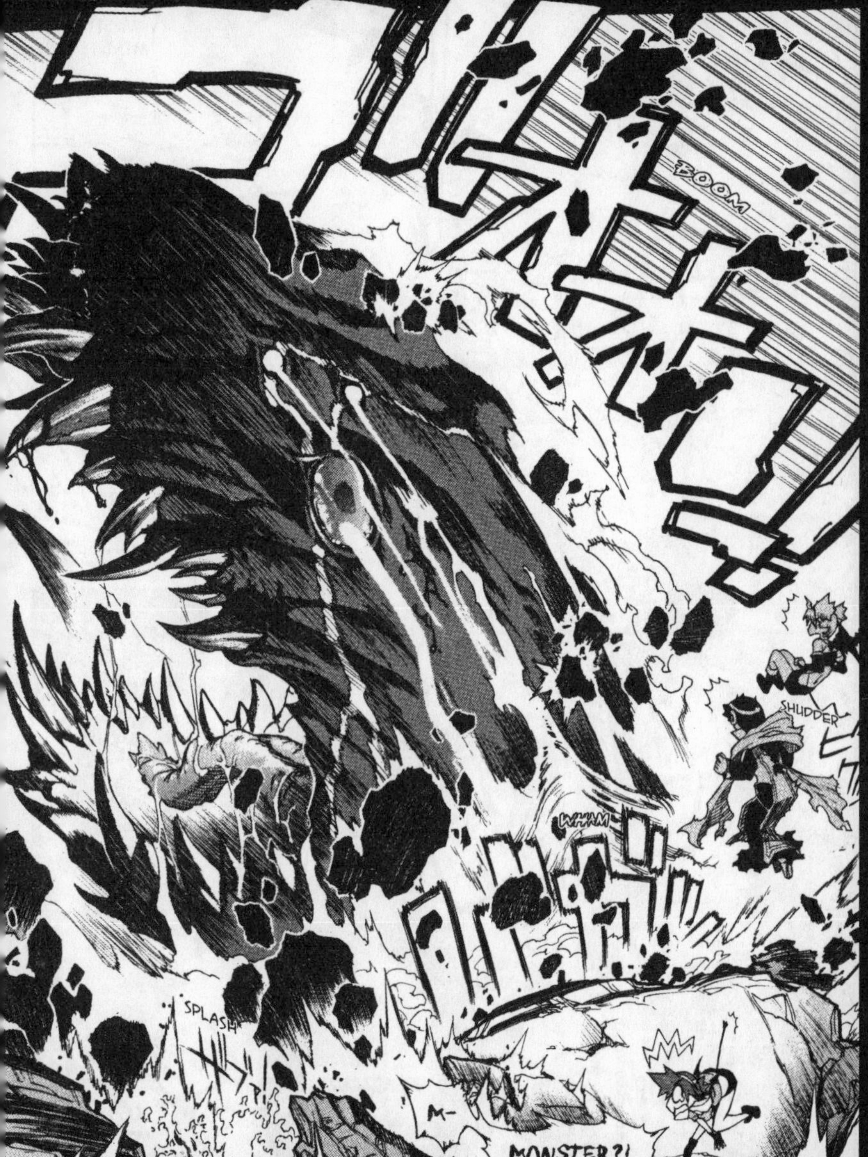
BOOM
SHUDDER
WHAM
SPLASH
M-
MONSTER?!

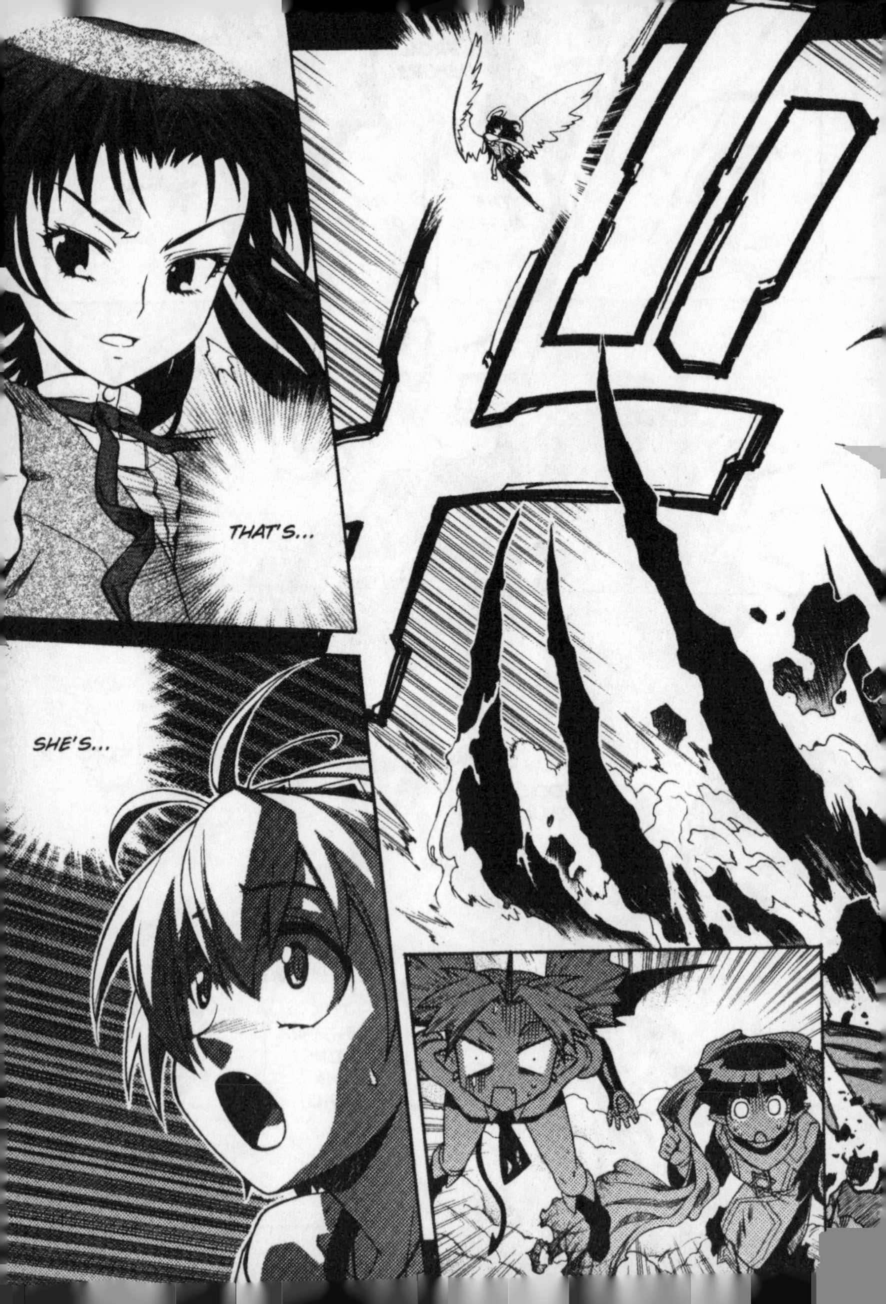
THAT'S...
SHE'S...

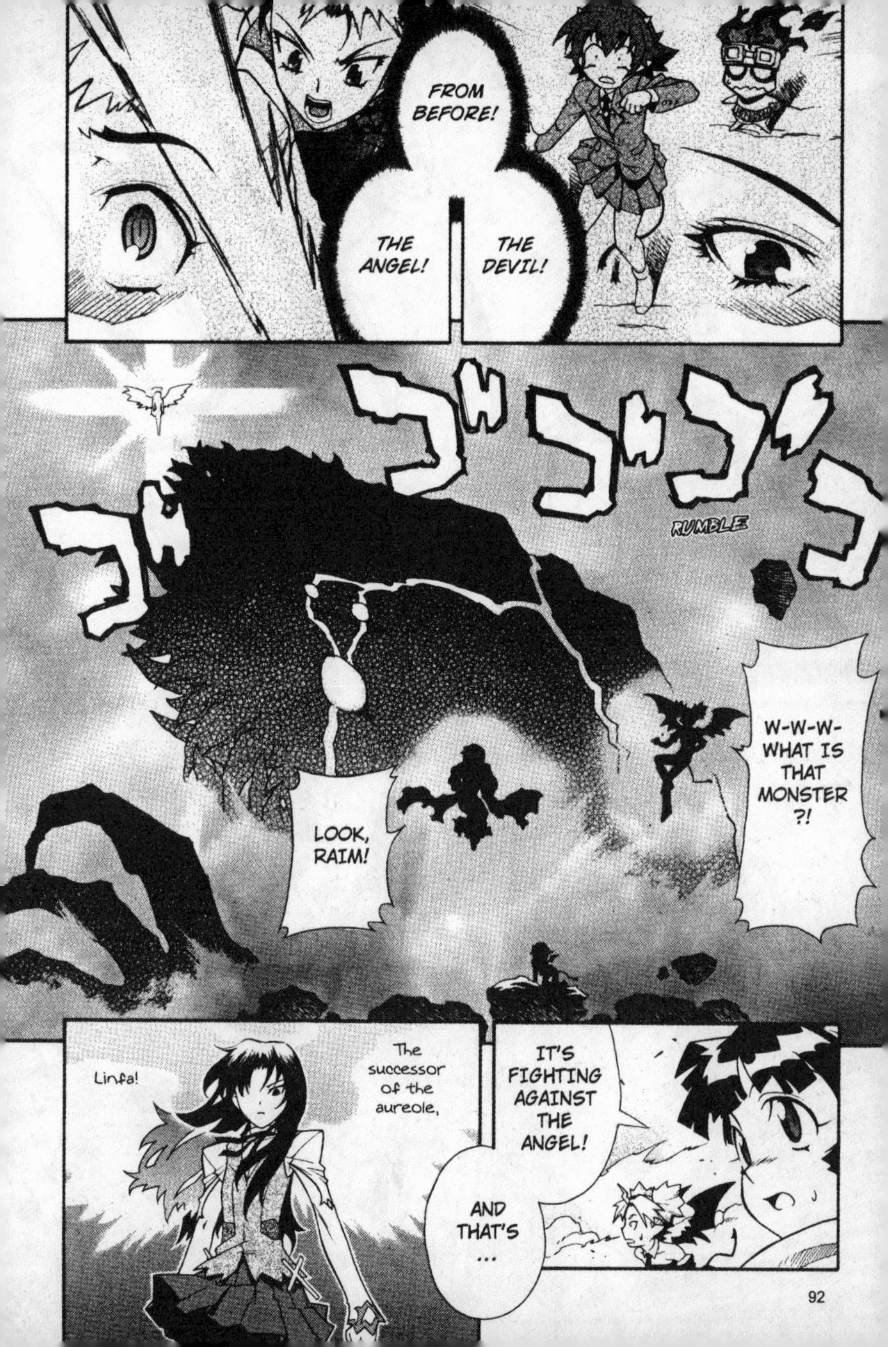
FROM BEFORE!
THE DEVIL!
THE ANGEL!
ゴゴゴゴゴ
RUMBLE
W-W-W-WHAT IS THAT MONSTER?!
LOOK, RAIM!
IT'S FIGHTING AGAINST THE ANGEL!
AND THAT'S ...
The successor of the aureole,
Linfa!

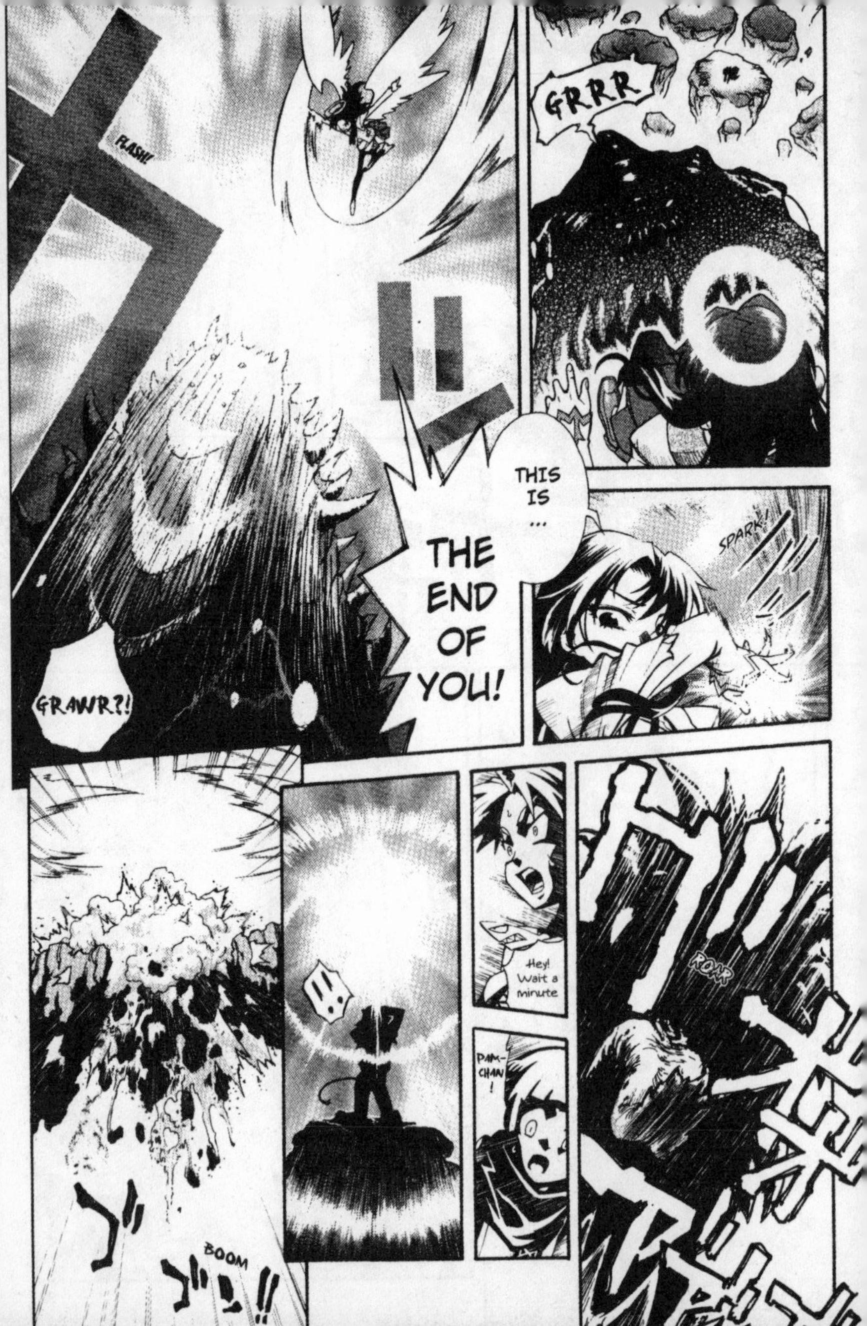
GRRR
SPARK!
THIS IS ... THE END OF YOU!
FLASH!
GRAWR?!
ROAR
Hey! Wait a minute
PAM-CHAN!
!!
BOOM

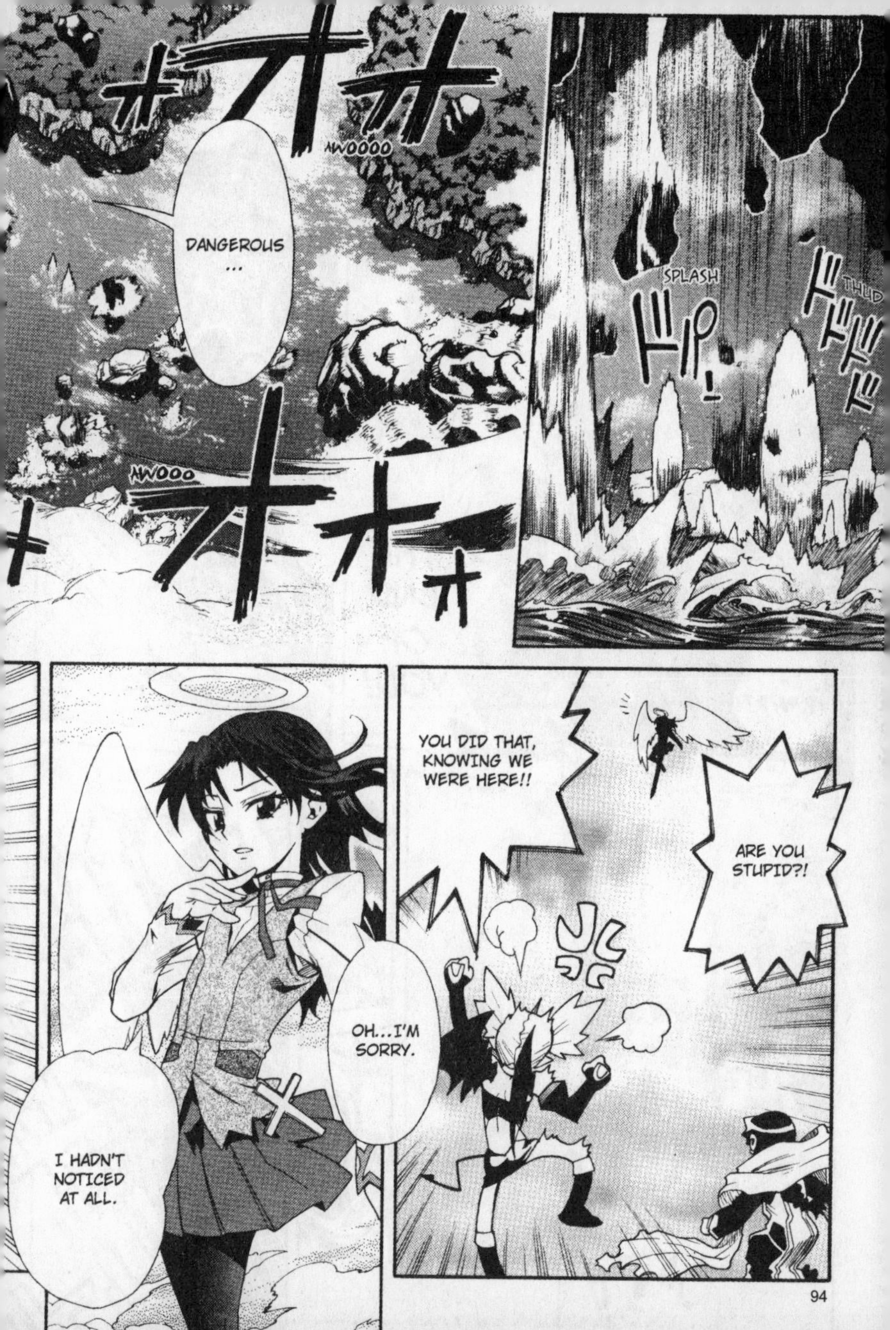
THUD
ドドドド
SPLASH
ドパ!
AWOOOO
DANGEROUS...
AWOOO
YOU DID THAT, KNOWING WE WERE HERE!!
ARE YOU STUPID?!
OH...I'M SORRY.
I HADN'T NOTICED AT ALL.

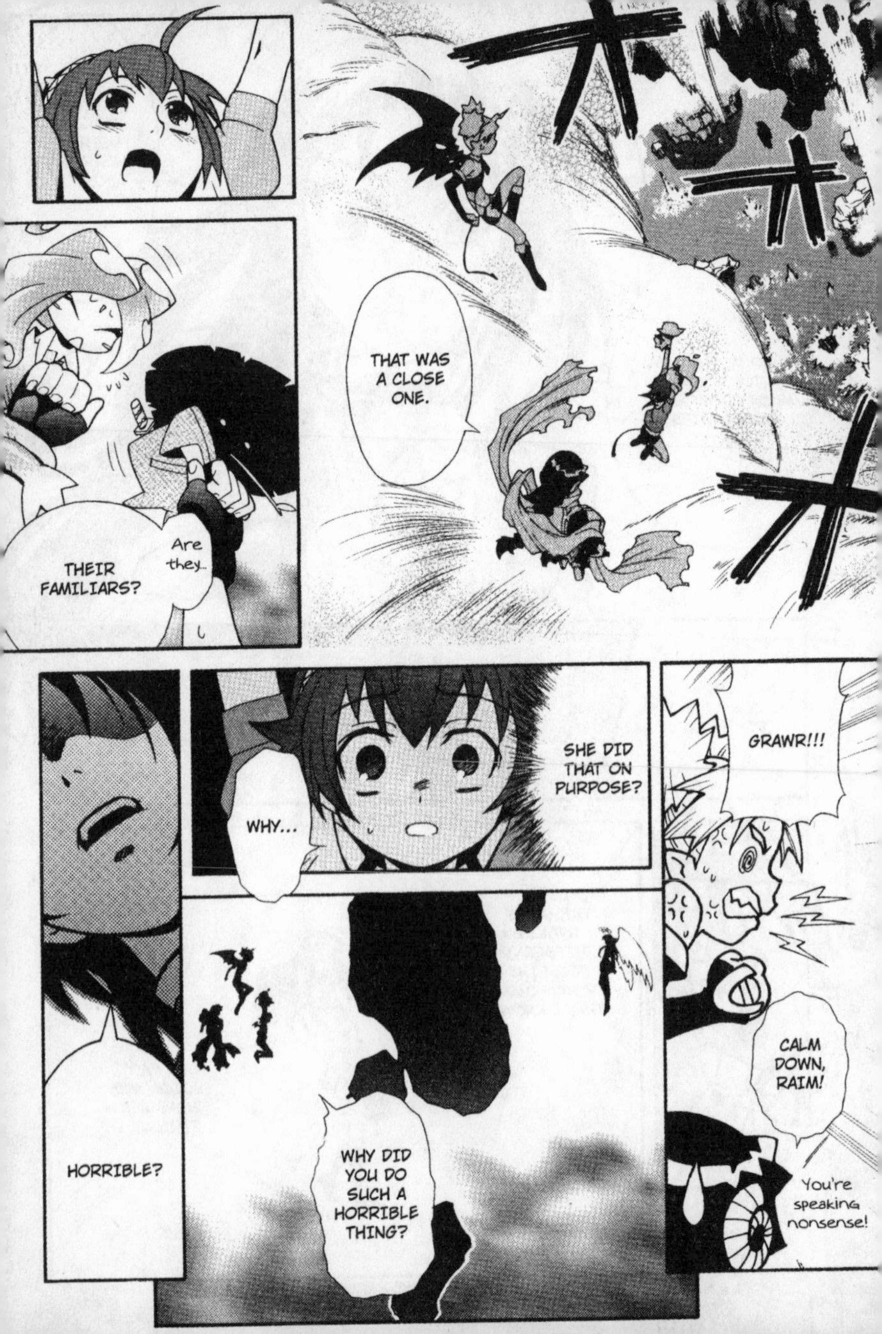

THAT WAS A CLOSE ONE.
Are they...
THEIR FAMILIARS?
GRAWR!!!
CALM DOWN, RAIM!
You're speaking nonsense!
SHE DID THAT ON PURPOSE?
WHY...
WHY DID YOU DO SUCH A HORRIBLE THING?
HORRIBLE?

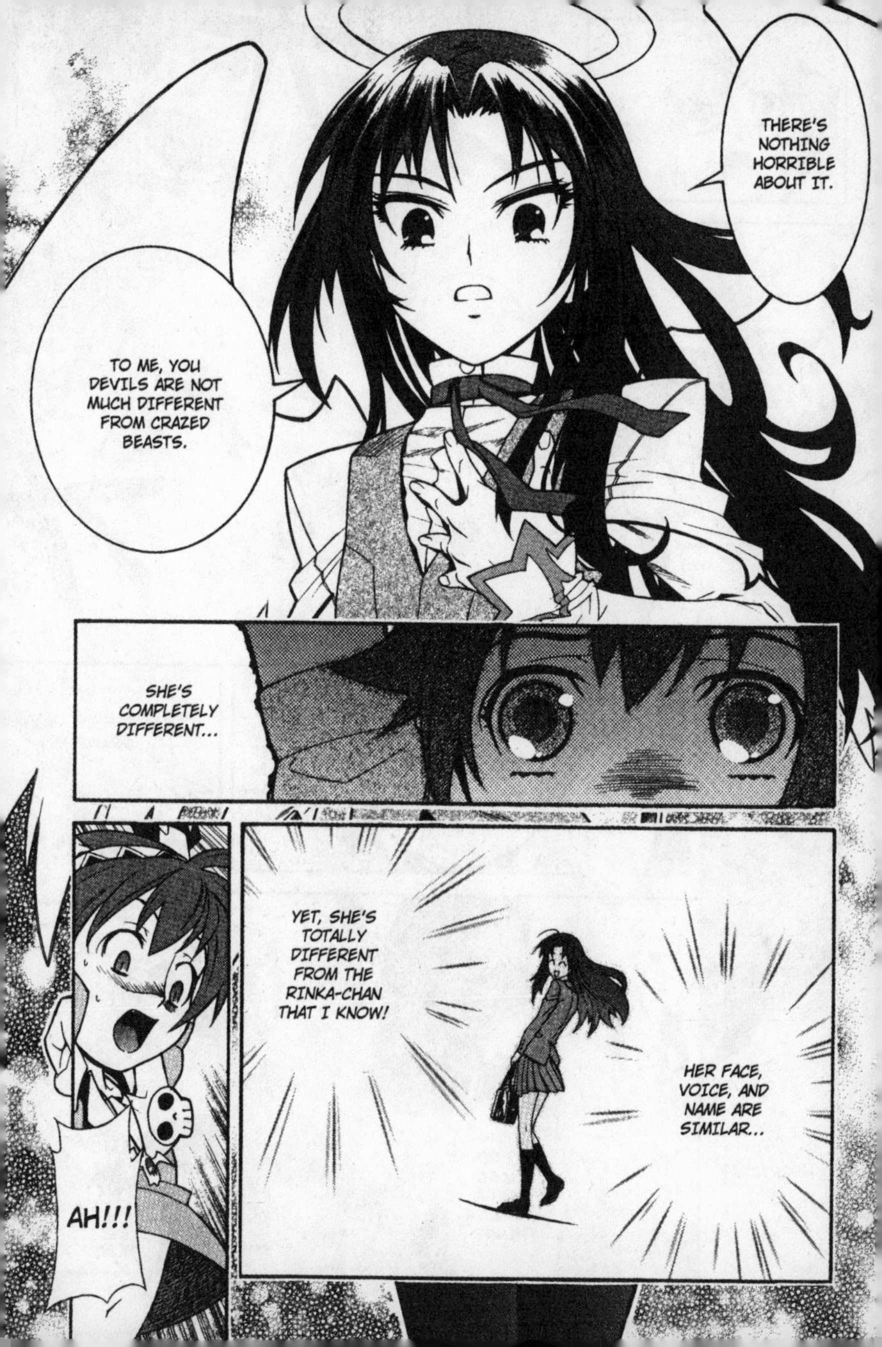

THERE'S NOTHING HORRIBLE ABOUT IT.
TO ME, YOU DEVILS ARE NOT MUCH DIFFERENT FROM CRAZED BEASTS.
SHE'S COMPLETELY DIFFERENT...
HER FACE, VOICE, AND NAME ARE SIMILAR...
YET, SHE'S TOTALLY DIFFERENT FROM THE RINKA-CHAN THAT I KNOW!
AH!!!

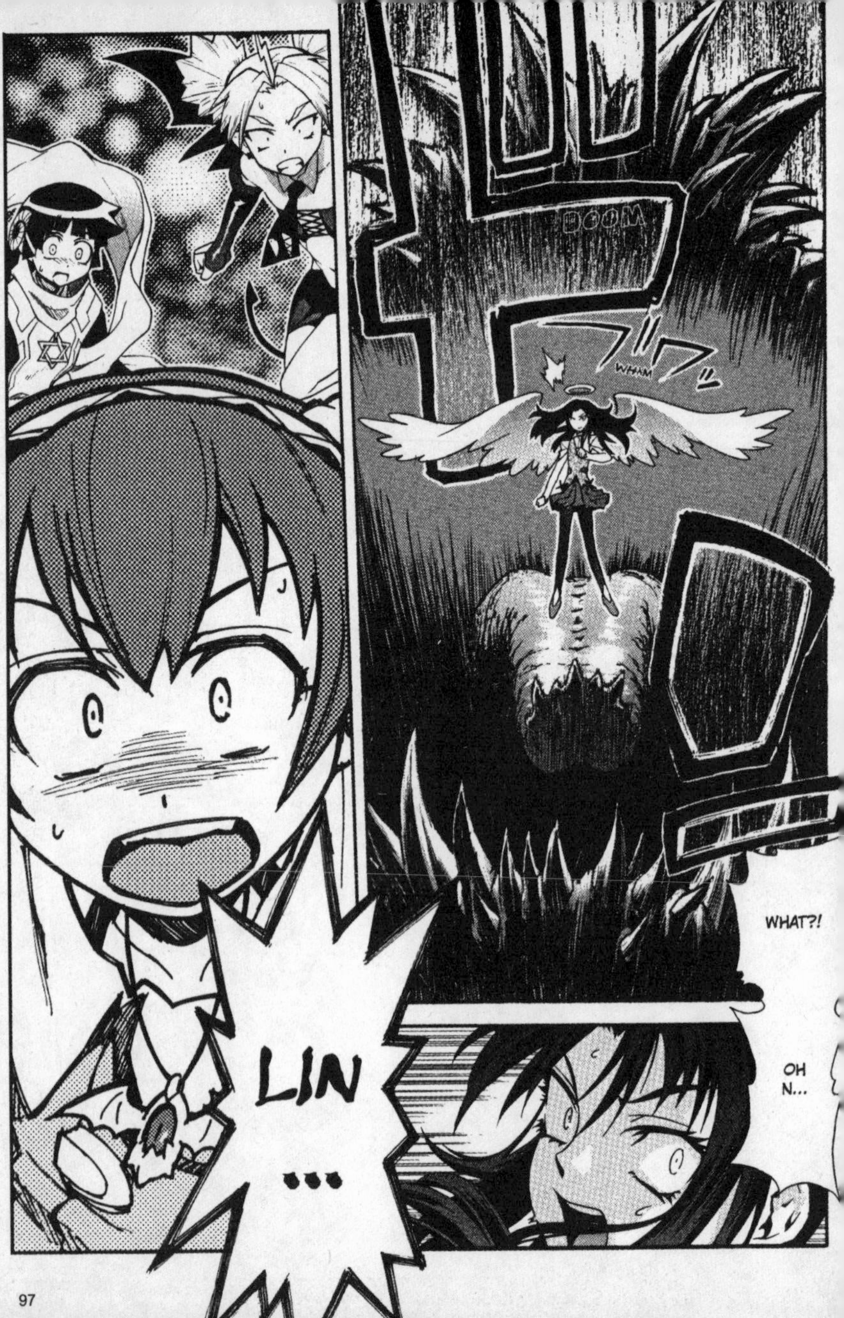
DOOM
WHAM
WHAT?!
OH N...
LIN ...

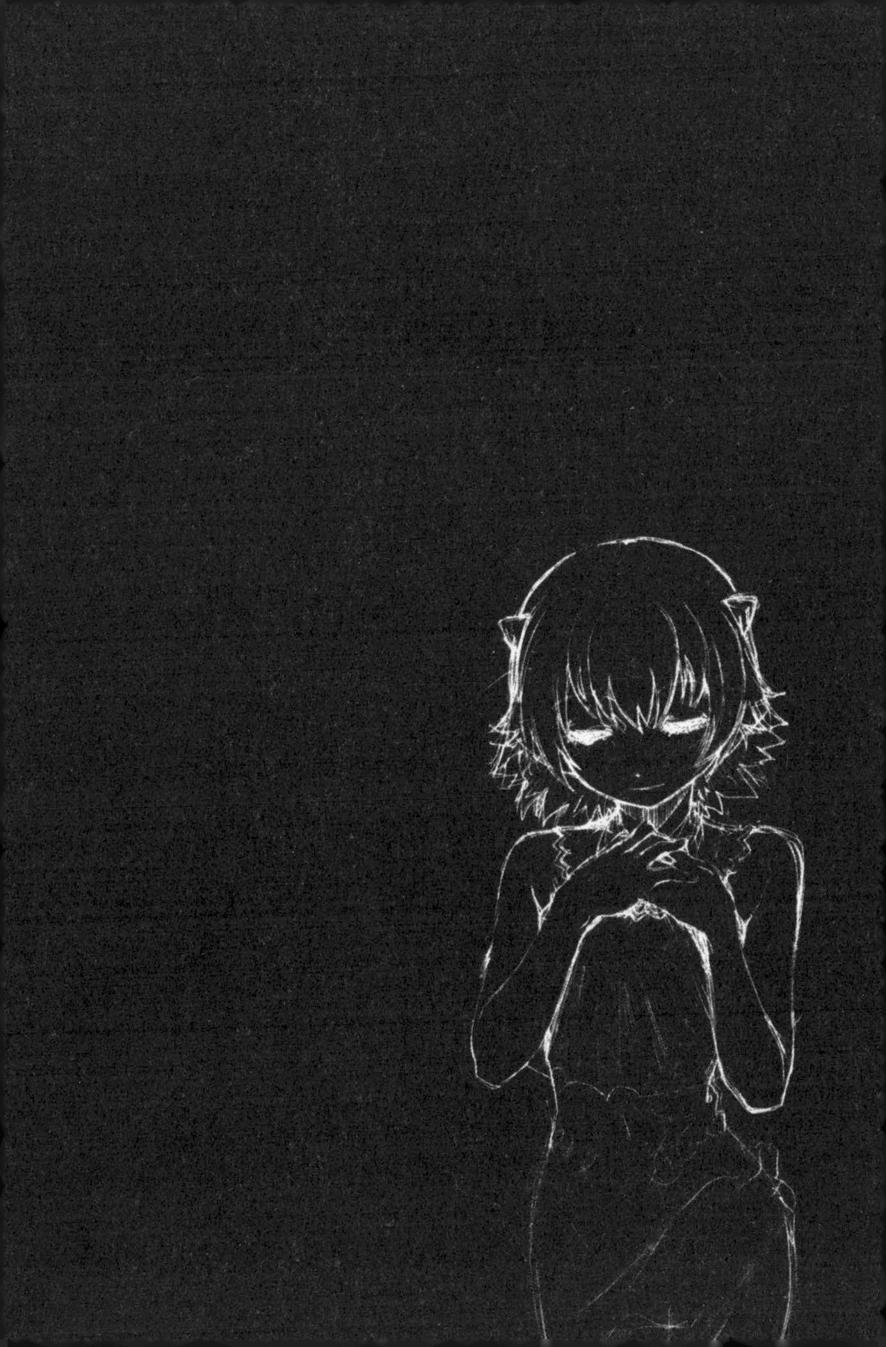

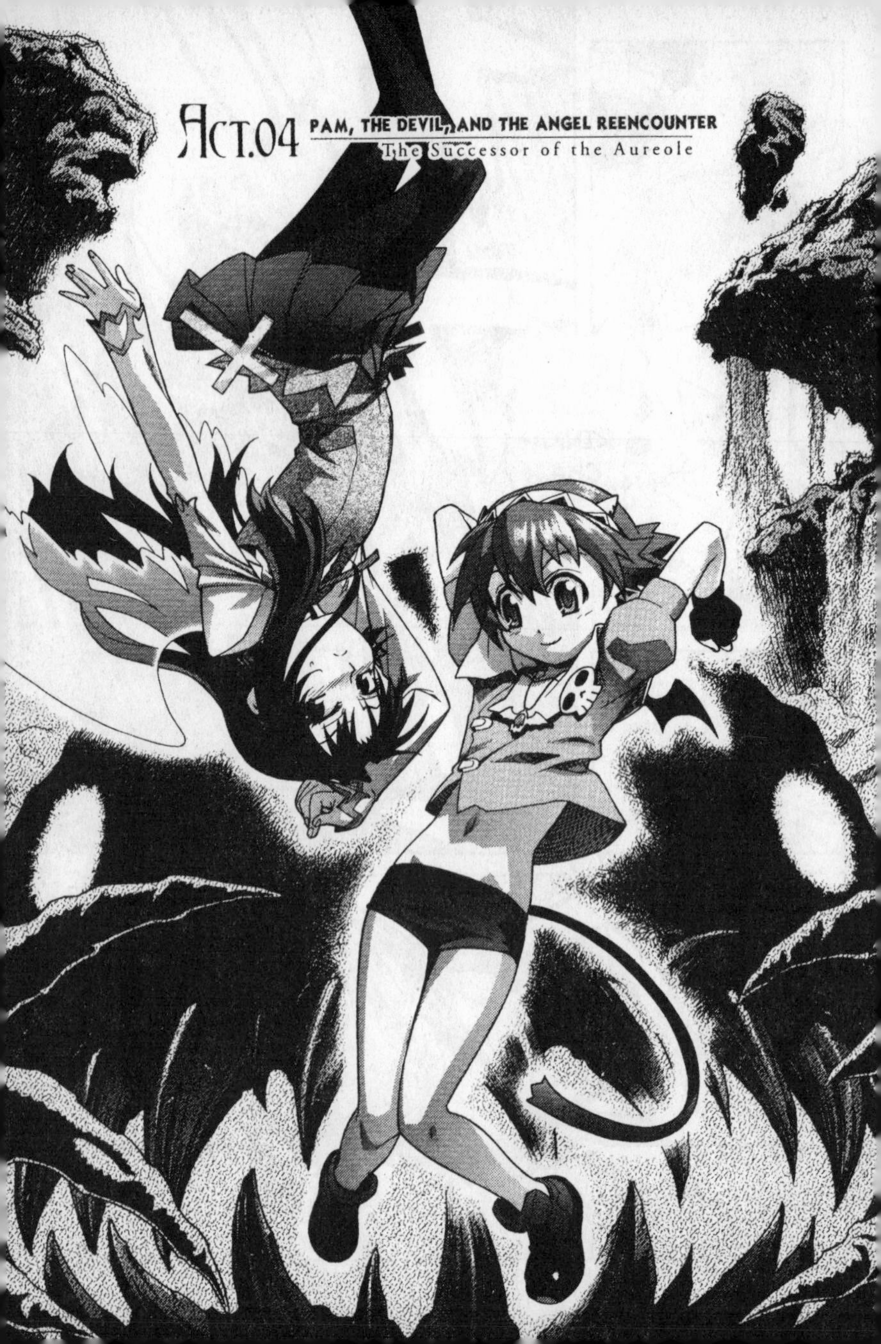
ACT.04
PAM, THE DEVIL, AND THE ANGEL REENCOUNTER
The Successor of the Aureole

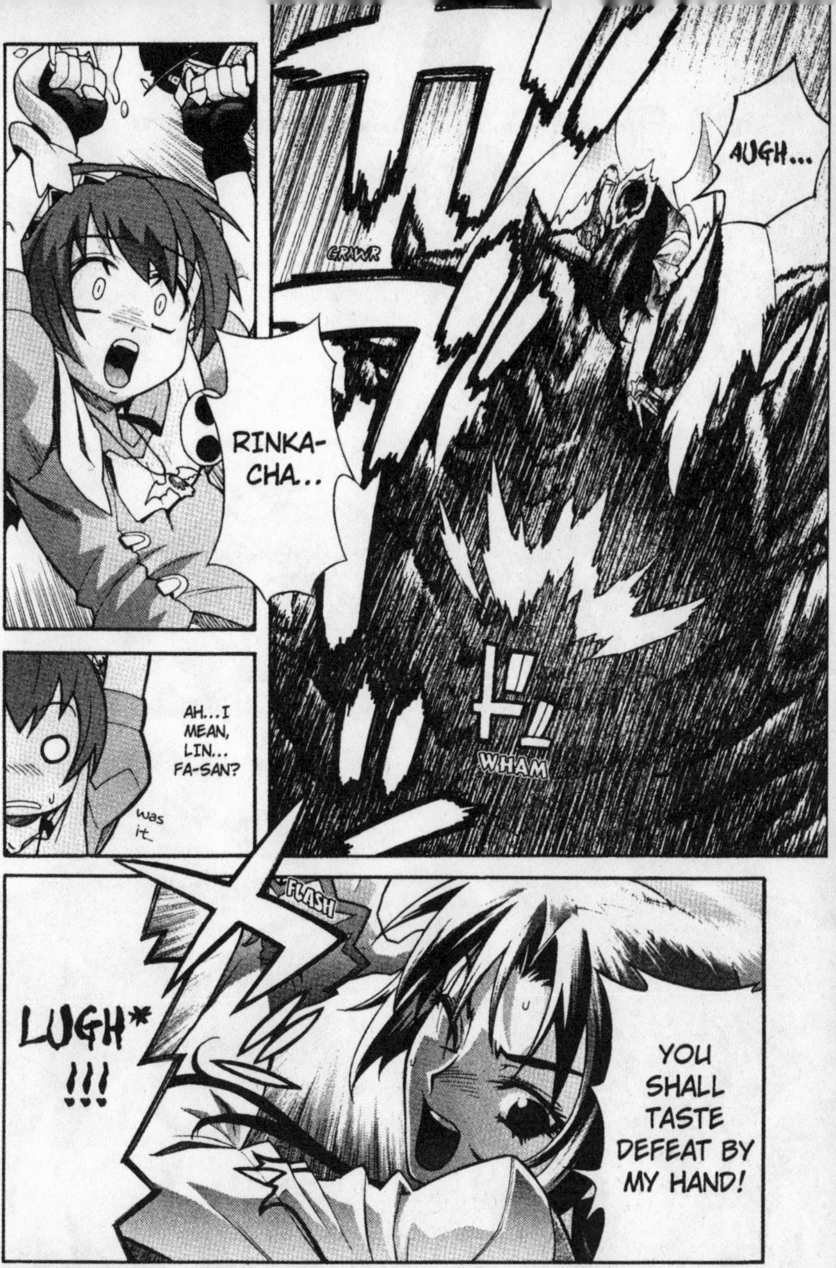
AUGH...
GRAWR
WHAM
RINKA-CHA...
AH...I MEAN, LIN... FA-SAN?
was it..
FLASH
YOU SHALL TASTE DEFEAT BY MY HAND!
LUGH* !!!

*LUGH IS A SPELL FOR LIGHT.

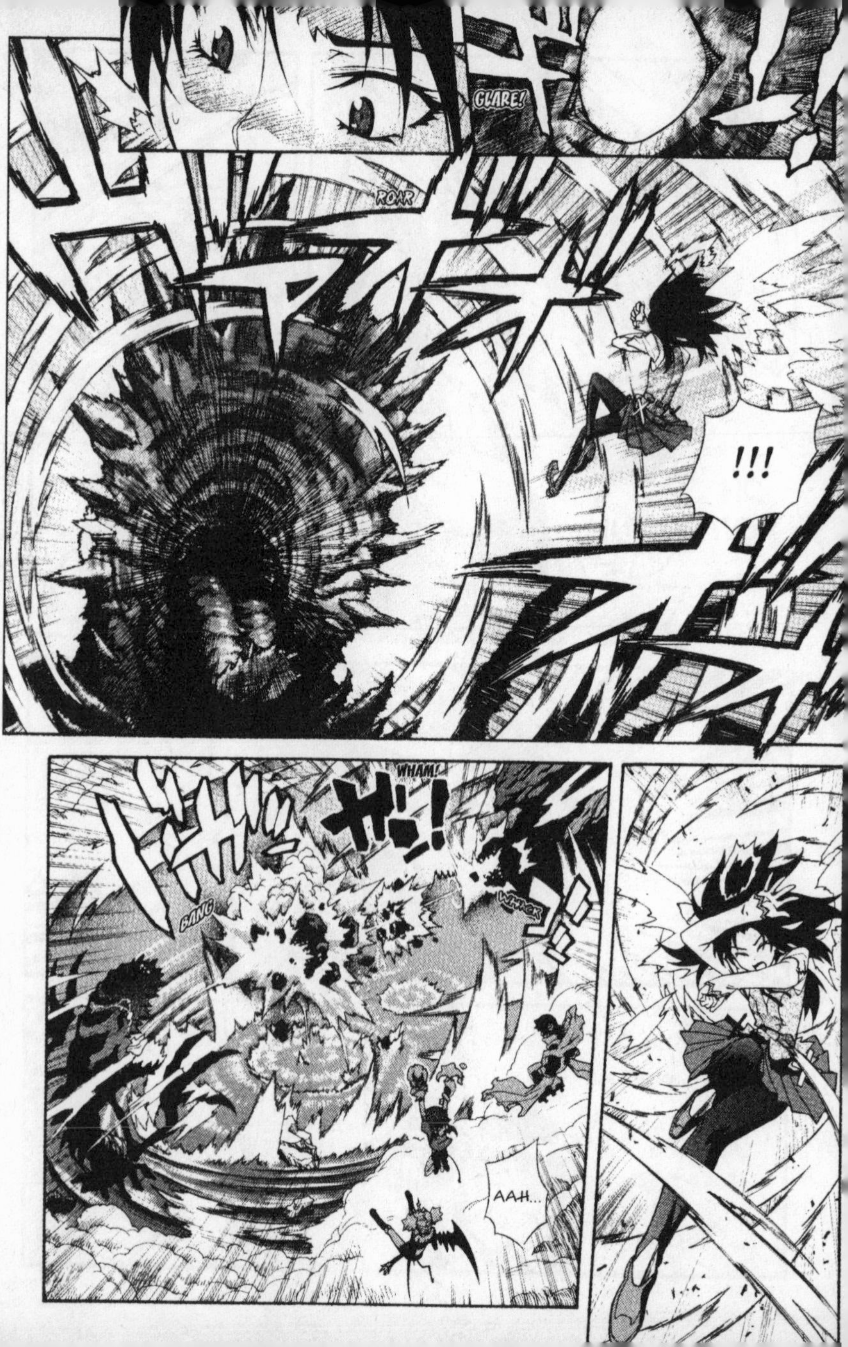
GLARE!
ROAR
!!!
WHAM!
WHACK
BANG
AAH...

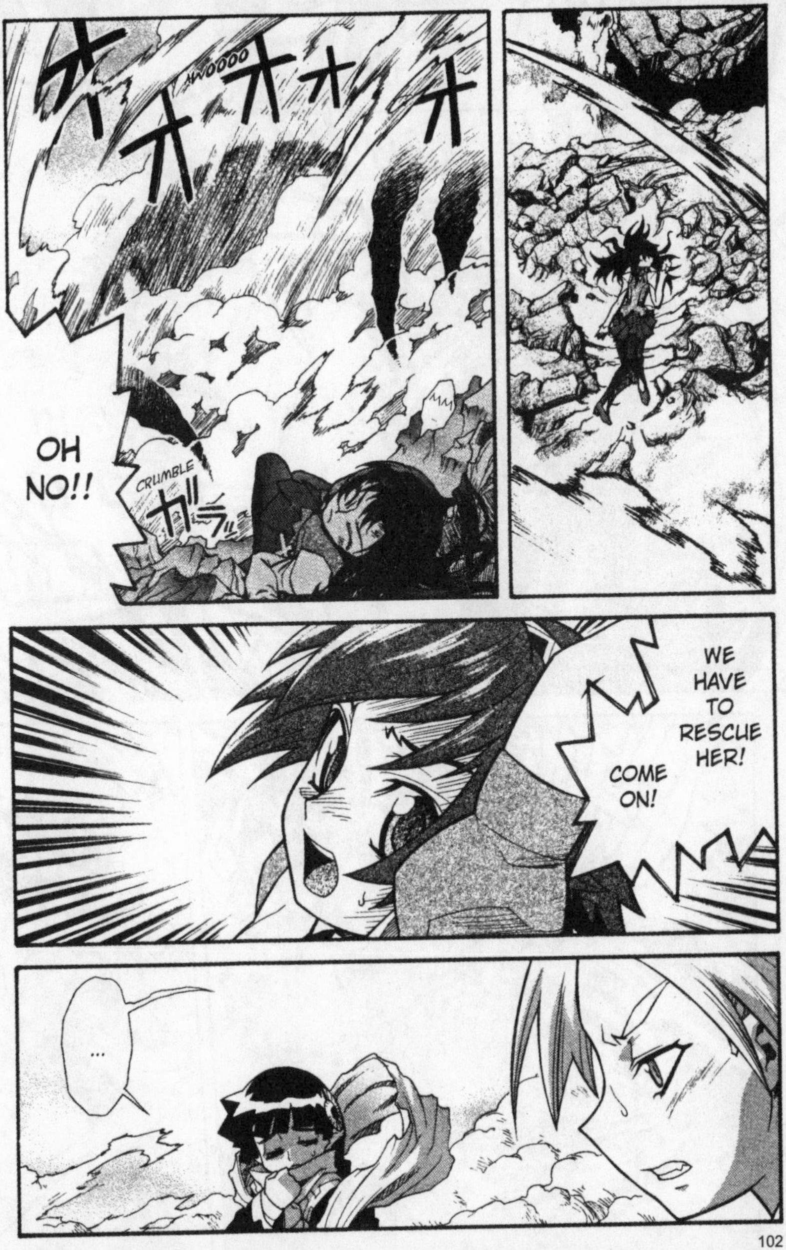
AWOOOO
CRUMBLE
OH NO!!
WE HAVE TO RESCUE HER!
COME ON!
...

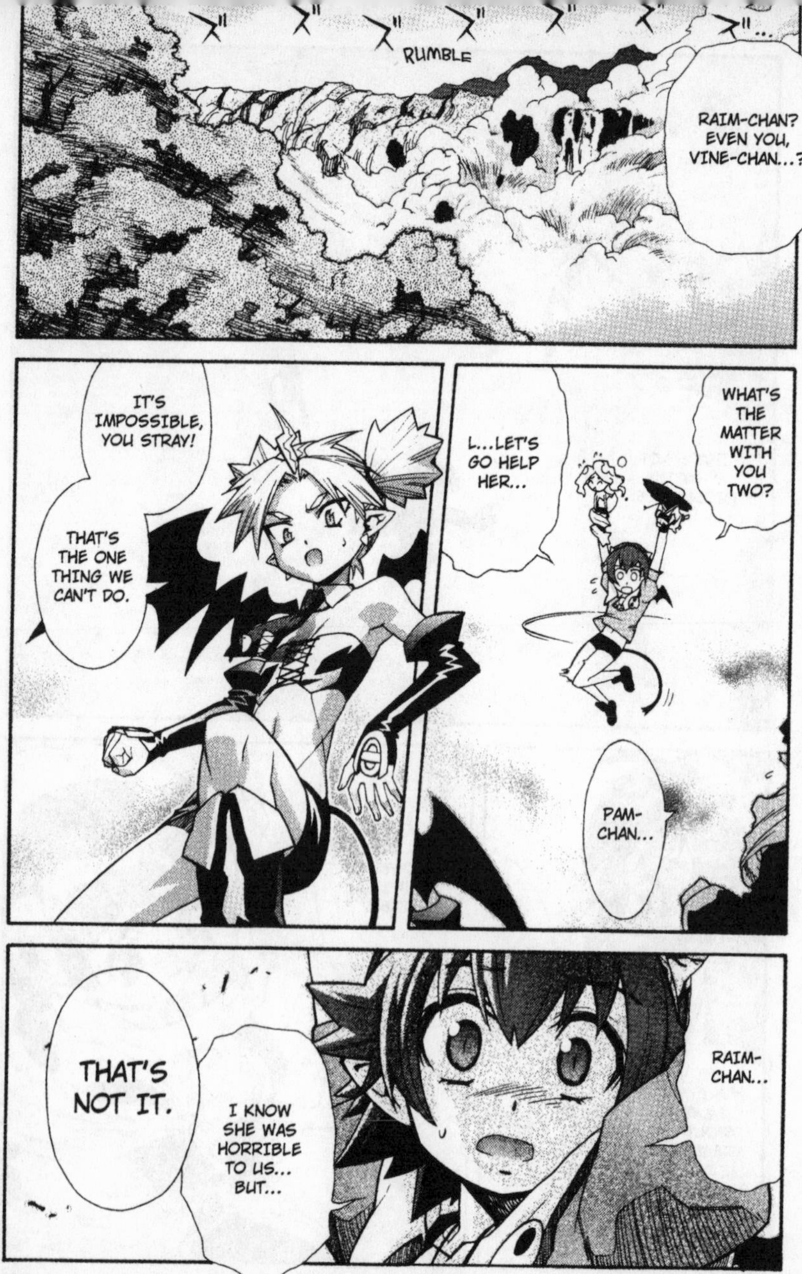

ズズズズズズズ...
RUMBLE
RAIM-CHAN? EVEN YOU, VINE-CHAN...?
WHAT'S THE MATTER WITH YOU TWO?
L...LET'S GO HELP HER...
PAM-CHAN...
IT'S IMPOSSIBLE, YOU STRAY!
THAT'S THE ONE THING WE CAN'T DO.
RAIM-CHAN...
I KNOW SHE WAS HORRIBLE TO US... BUT...
THAT'S NOT IT.

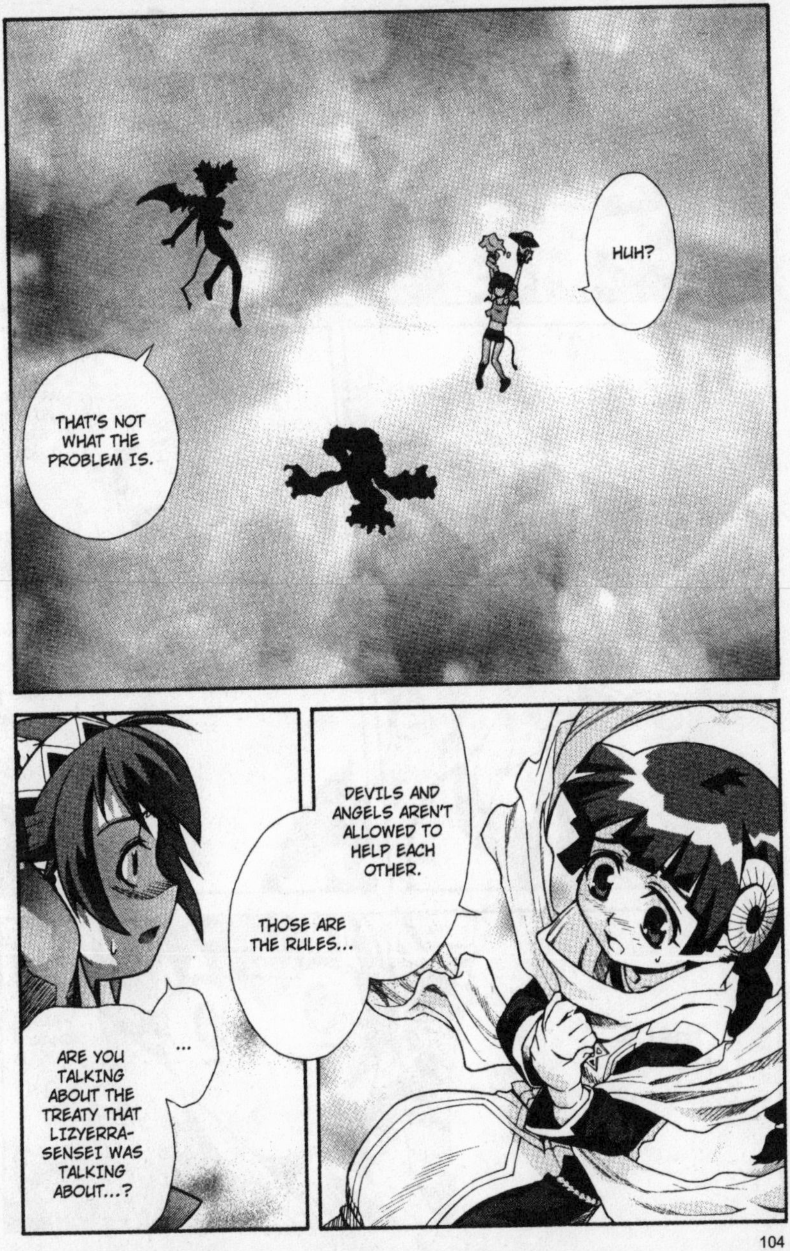
HUH?
THAT'S NOT WHAT THE PROBLEM IS.
DEVILS AND ANGELS AREN'T ALLOWED TO HELP EACH OTHER.
THOSE ARE THE RULES...
...
ARE YOU TALKING ABOUT THE TREATY THAT LIZYERRA-SENSEI WAS TALKING ABOUT...?

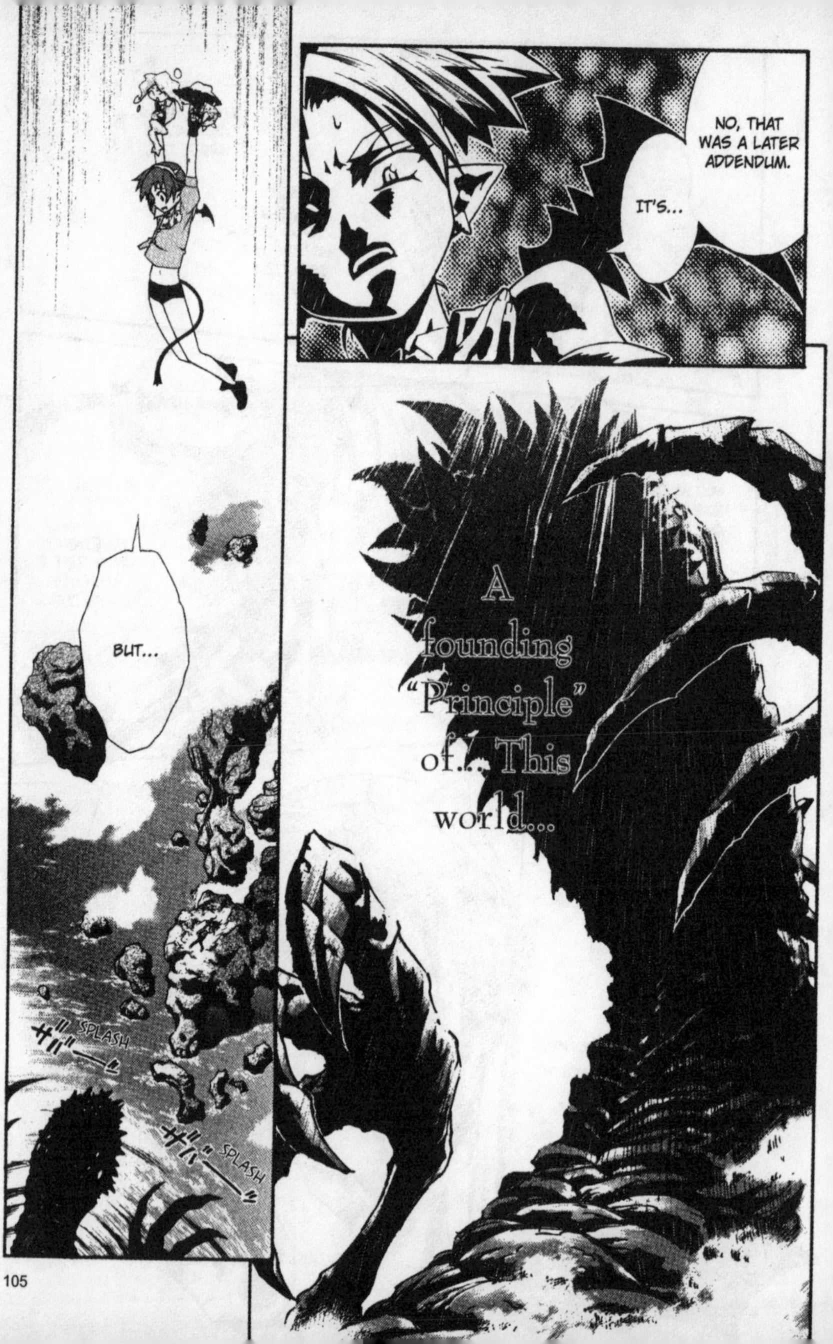
NO, THAT WAS A LATER ADDENDUM.
IT'S...
A founding "Principle" of... This world...
BUT...
SPLASH
SPLASH

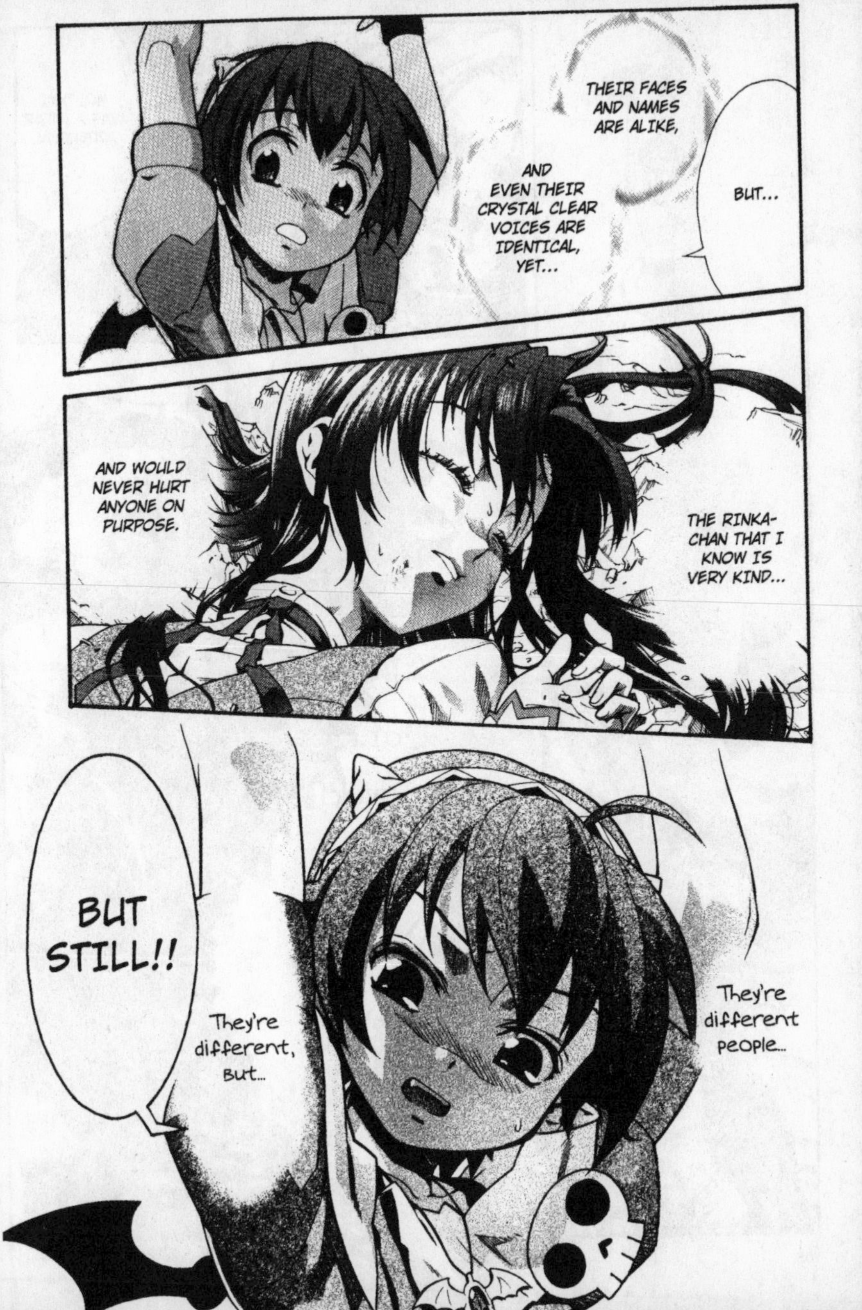

THEIR FACES AND NAMES ARE ALIKE,
AND EVEN THEIR CRYSTAL CLEAR VOICES ARE IDENTICAL, YET...
BUT...
THE RINKA-CHAN THAT I KNOW IS VERY KIND...
AND WOULD NEVER HURT ANYONE ON PURPOSE.
They're different people...
They're different, but...
BUT STILL!!

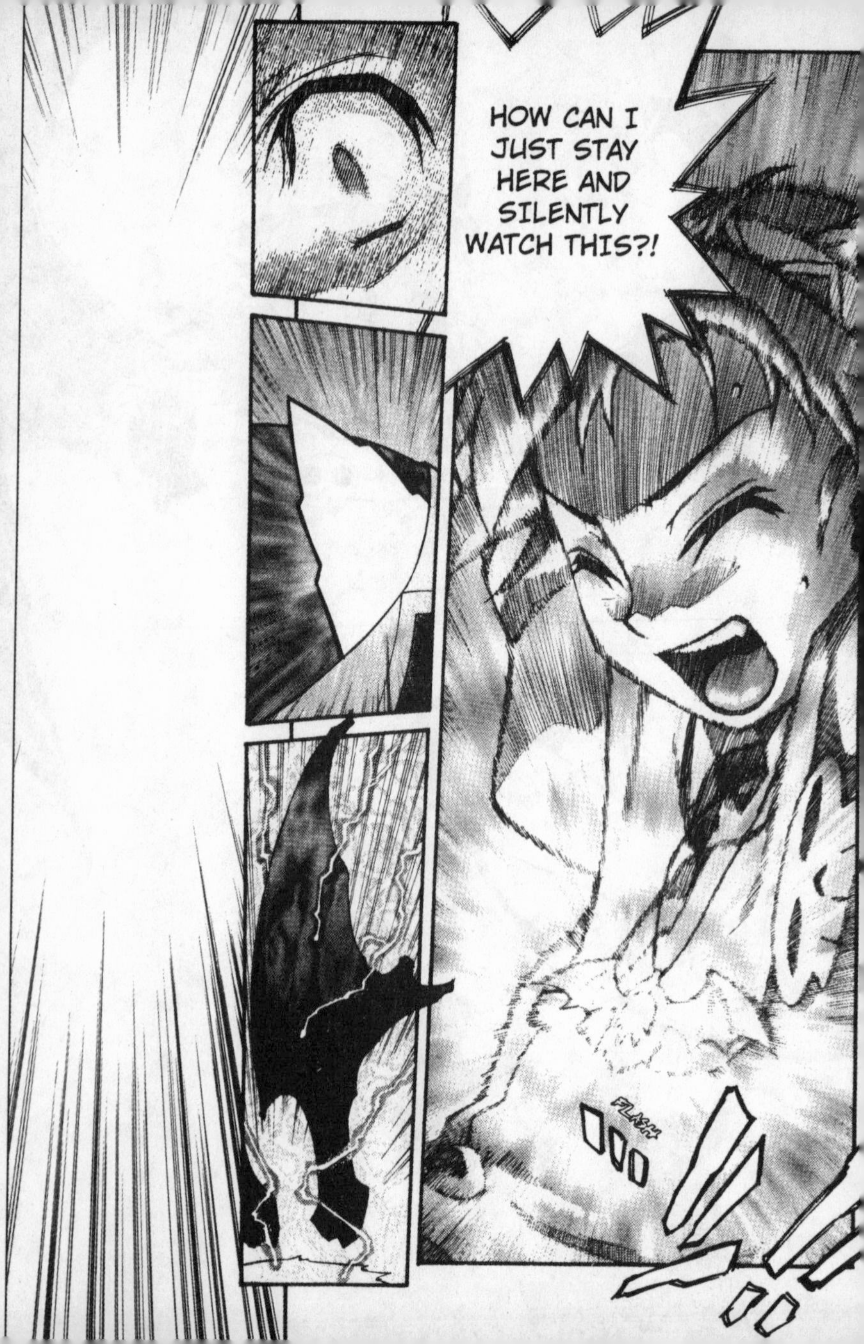
HOW CAN I JUST STAY HERE AND SILENTLY WATCH THIS?!
FLASH

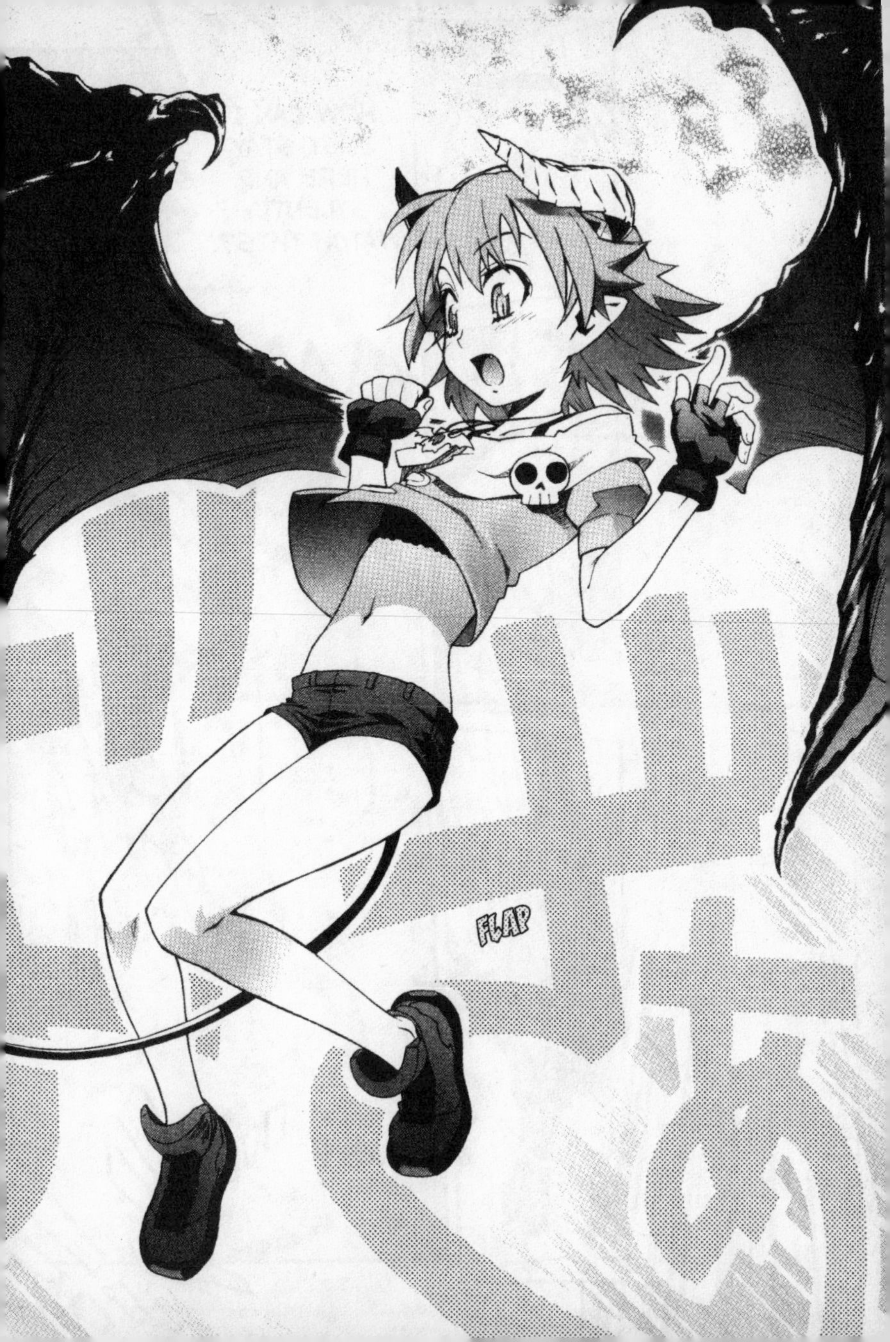
FLAP

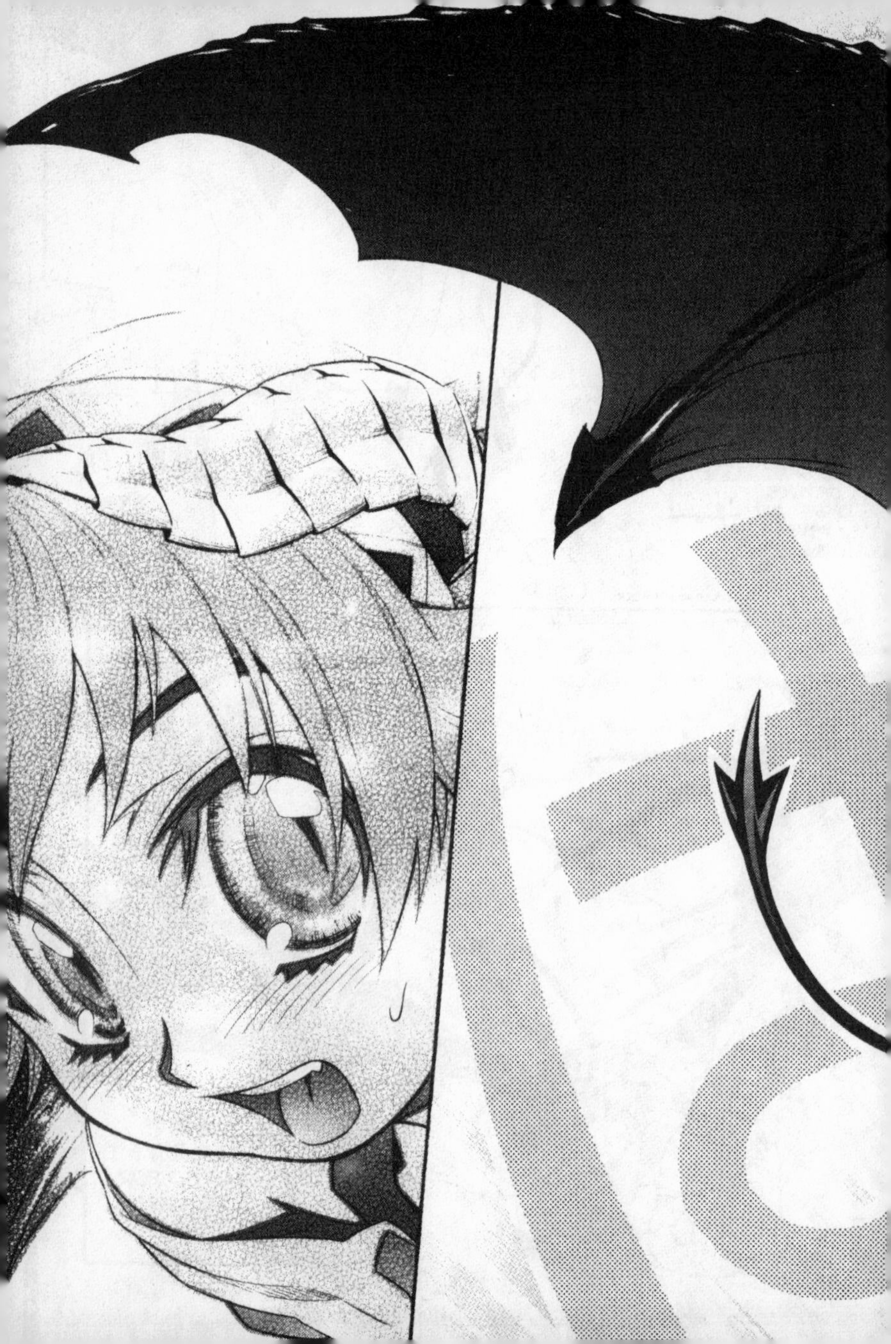

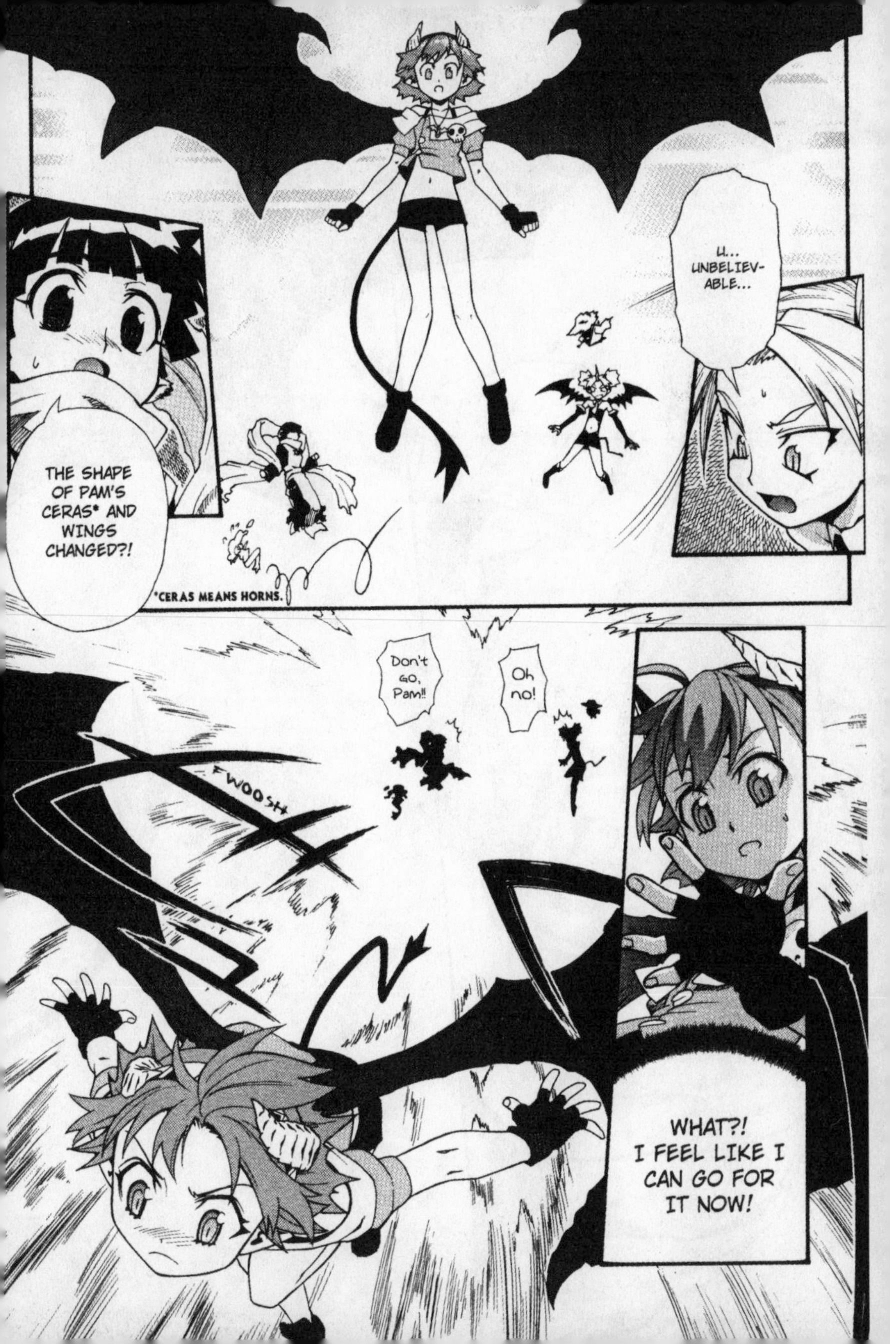
U... UNBELIEVABLE...
THE SHAPE OF PAM'S CERAS* AND WINGS CHANGED?!
*CERAS MEANS HORNS.
Oh no!
Don't go, Pam!!
FWOOSH
WHAT?! I FEEL LIKE I CAN GO FOR IT NOW!

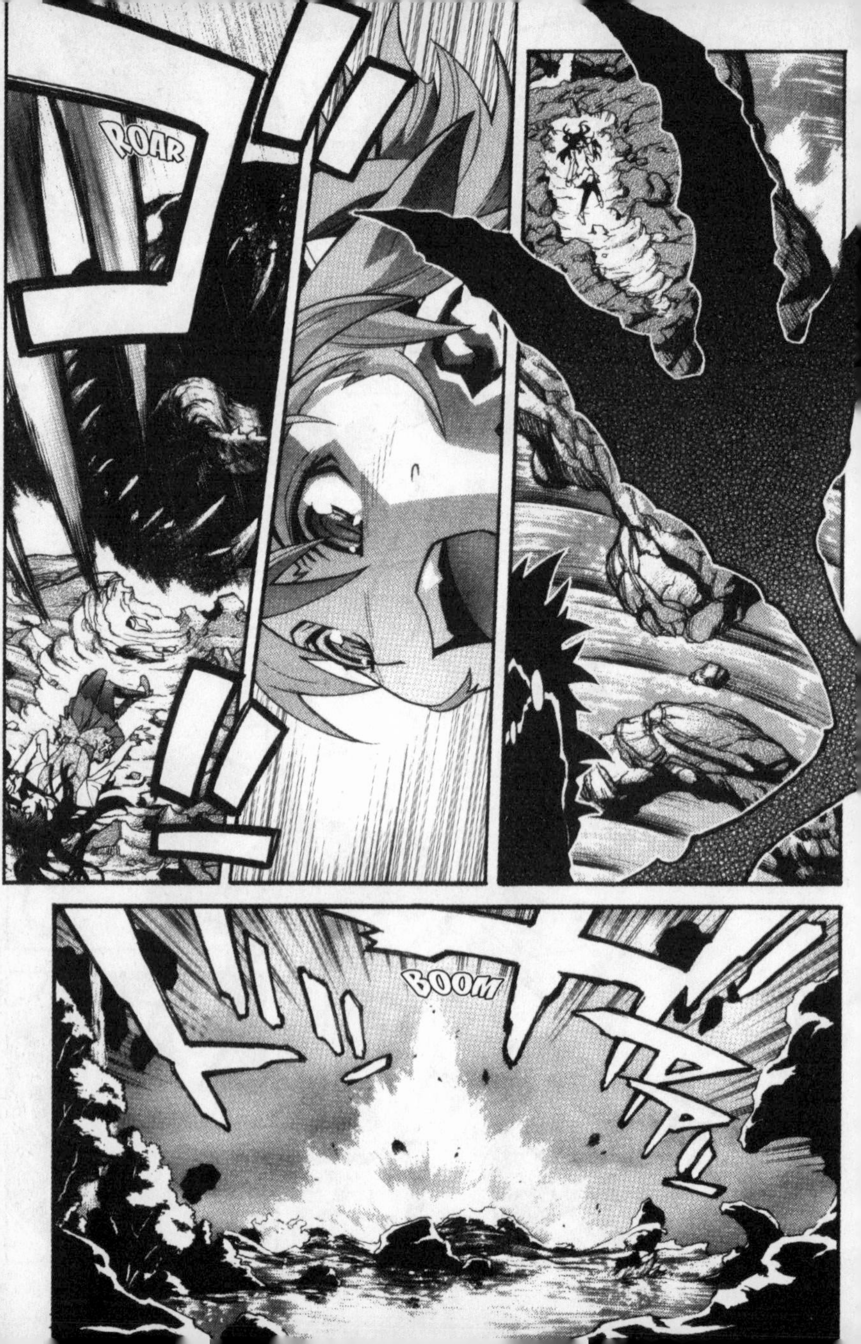
ROAR
BOOM

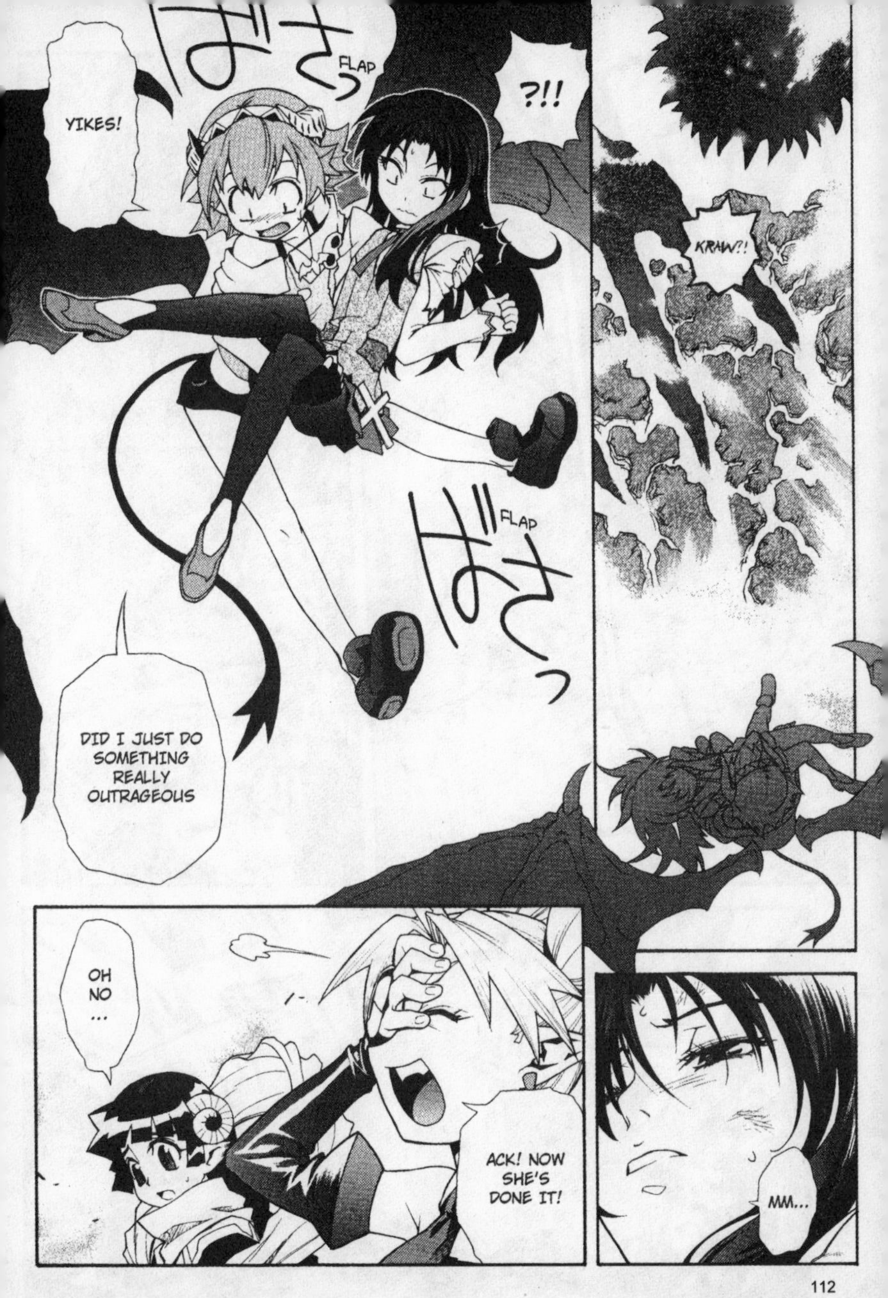
KRAW?!
?!!
ばさっ
FLAP
YIKES!
ばさっ
FLAP
DID I JUST DO SOMETHING REALLY OUTRAGEOUS
MM...
ACK! NOW SHE'S DONE IT!
OH NO ...

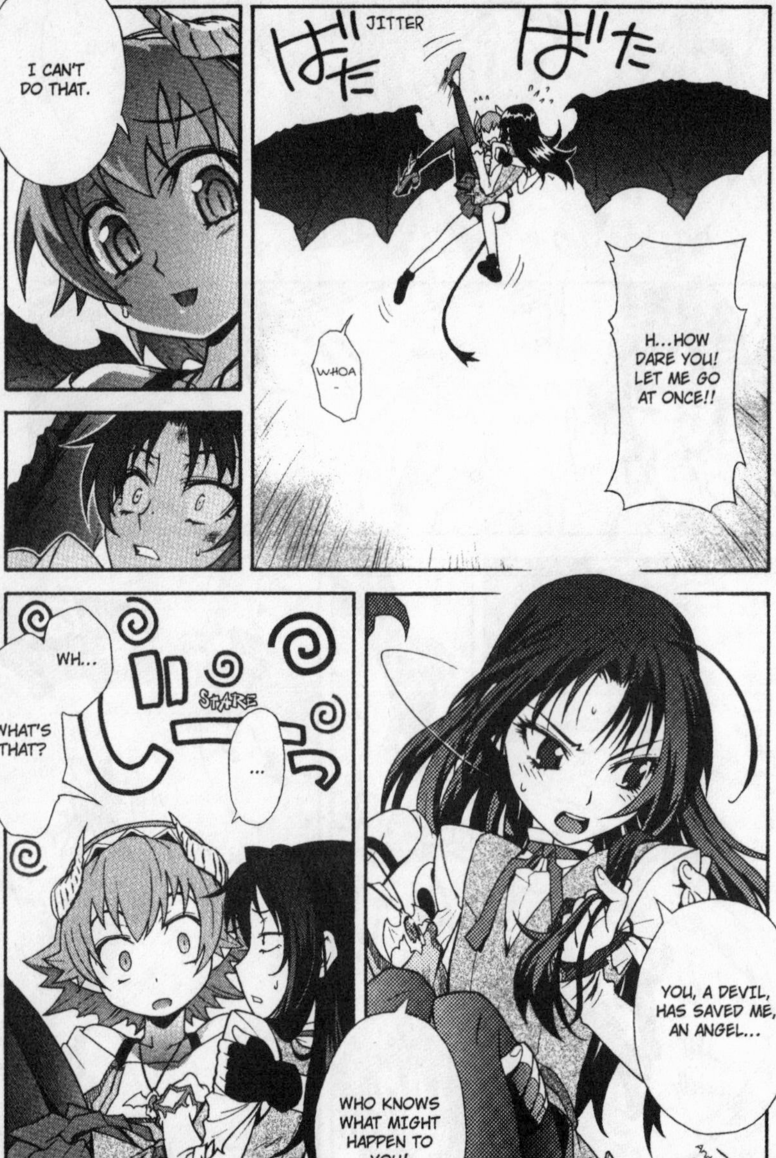
ばた
JITTER
ばた
WHOA
H...HOW DARE YOU! LET ME GO AT ONCE!!
I CAN'T DO THAT.
YOU, A DEVIL, HAS SAVED ME, AN ANGEL...
WHO KNOWS WHAT MIGHT HAPPEN TO YOU!
And I didn't even ask for it!
WH...
WHAT'S THAT?
じーっ
STARE
...

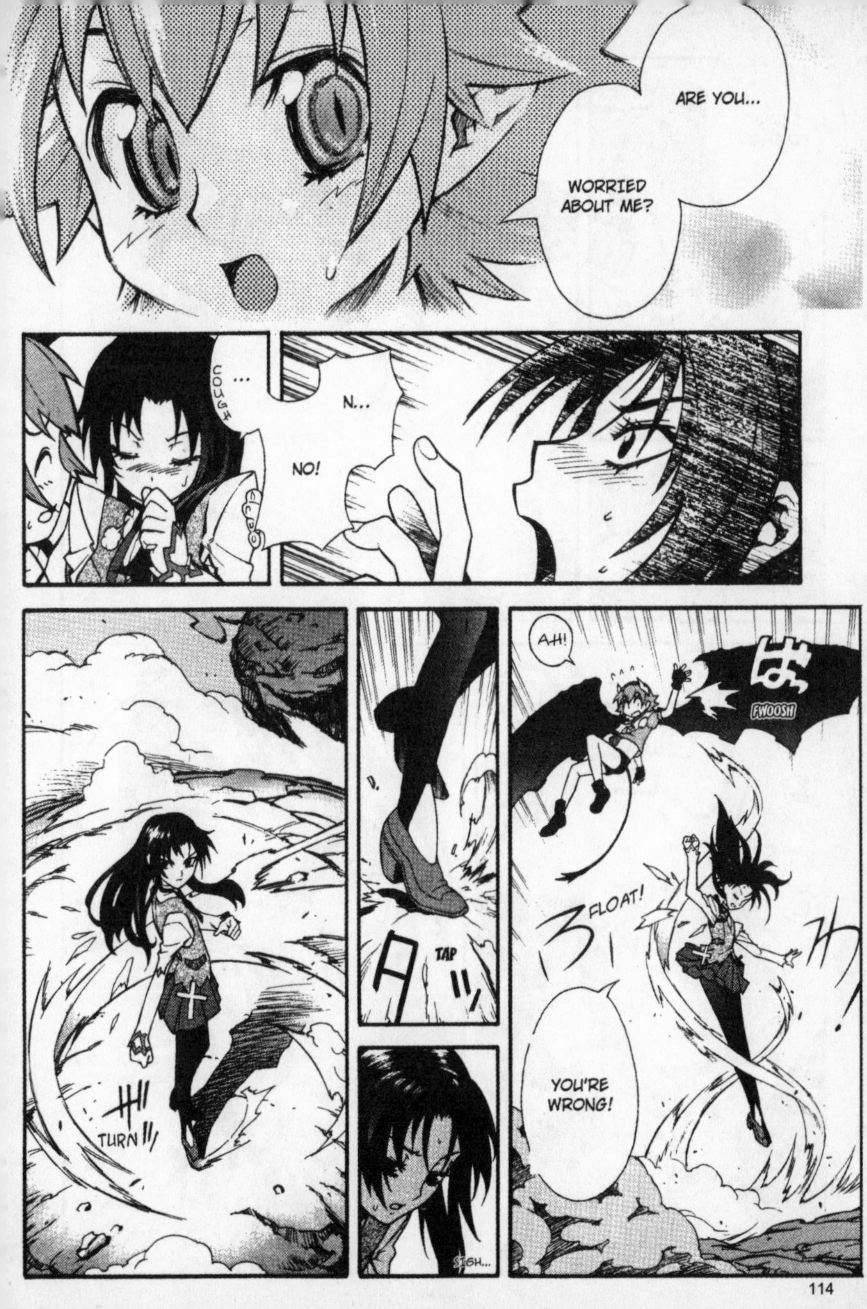
ARE YOU...
WORRIED ABOUT ME?
N...
NO!
...
COUGH
AH!
ぱっ
FWOOSH
FLOAT!
YOU'RE WRONG!
TAP
SIGH...
TURN

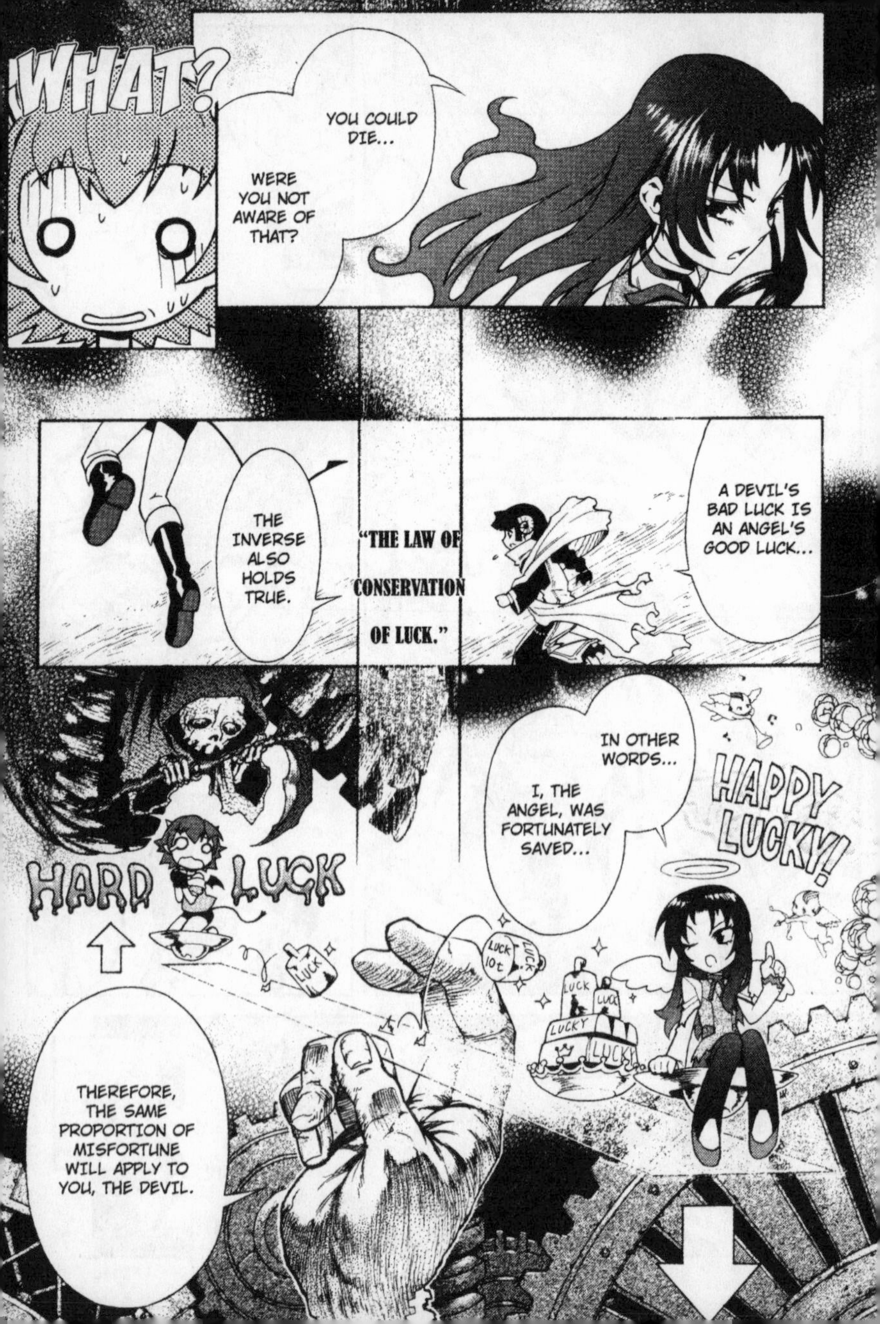
YOU COULD DIE...
WERE YOU NOT AWARE OF THAT?
WHAT?
A DEVIL'S BAD LUCK IS AN ANGEL'S GOOD LUCK...
"THE LAW OF CONSERVATION OF LUCK."
THE INVERSE ALSO HOLDS TRUE.
IN OTHER WORDS...
I, THE ANGEL, WAS FORTUNATELY SAVED...
HAPPY LUCKY!
HARD LUCK
LUCK 10t
LUCK
LUCKY
THEREFORE, THE SAME PROPORTION OF MISFORTUNE WILL APPLY TO YOU, THE DEVIL.

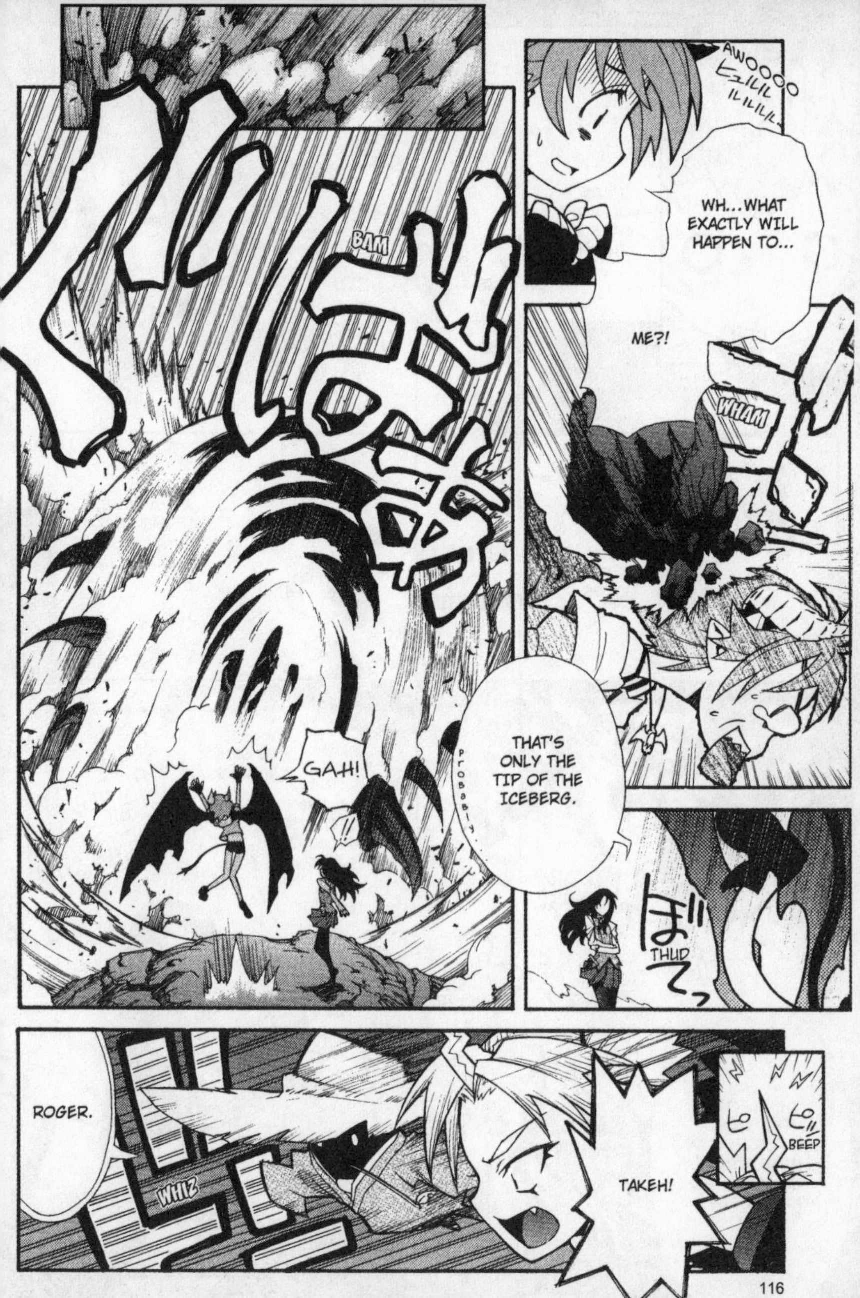
AWOOOO
WH...WHAT EXACTLY WILL HAPPEN TO...
ME?!
WHAM
THUD
ぼてっ
BAM
GAH!
!!
THAT'S ONLY THE TIP OF THE ICEBERG.
probably...
ピピ
BEEP
TAKEH!
WHIZ
ROGER.

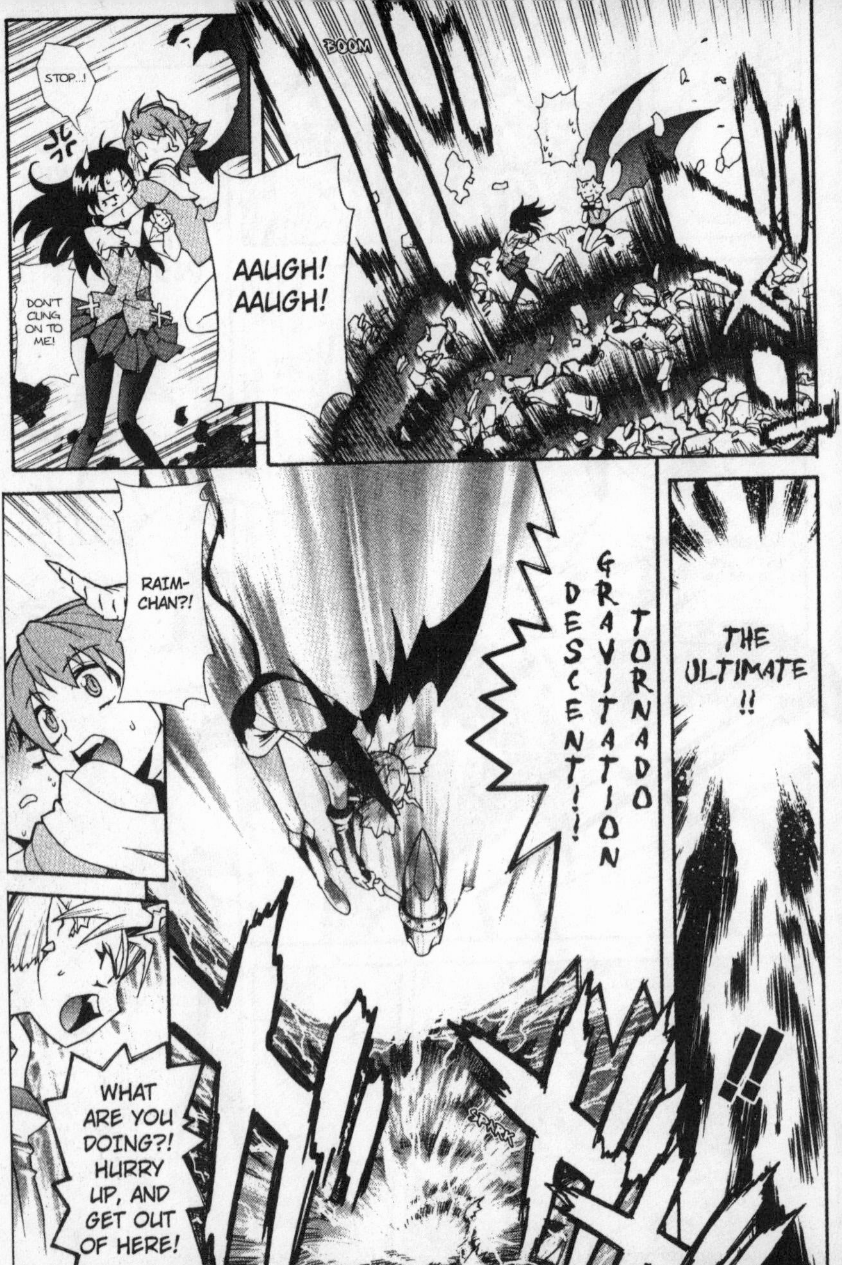
BOOM
STOP...!
AAUGH! AAUGH!
DON'T CLING ON TO ME!
THE ULTIMATE !!
TORNADO GRAVITATION DESCENT!!
!!
SPARK
RAIM-CHAN?!
WHAT ARE YOU DOING?! HURRY UP, AND GET OUT OF HERE!

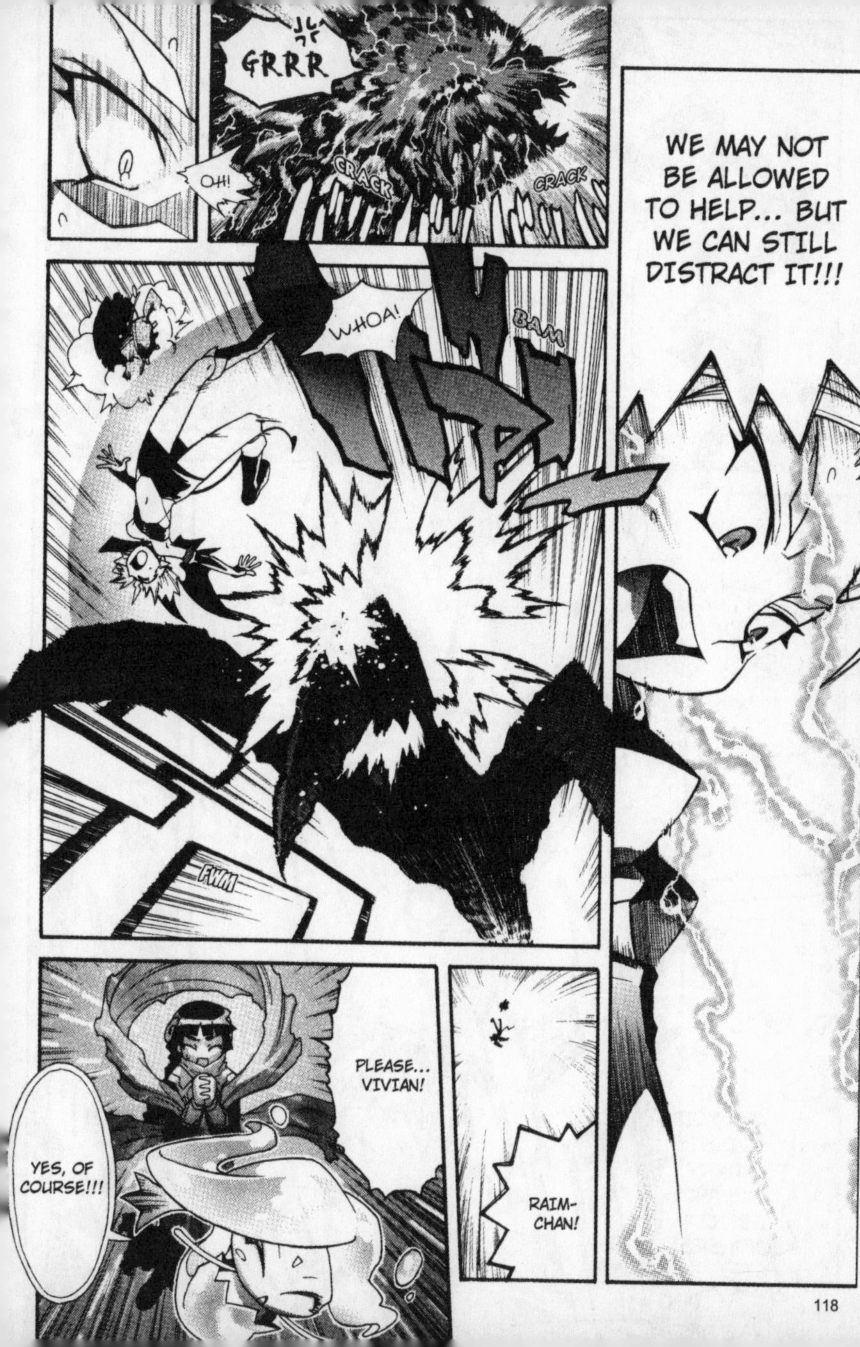
WE MAY NOT BE ALLOWED TO HELP... BUT WE CAN STILL DISTRACT IT!!!
GRRR
CRACK
CRACK
OH!
BAM
WHOA!
FWM
RAIM-CHAN!
PLEASE... VIVIAN!
YES, OF COURSE!!!

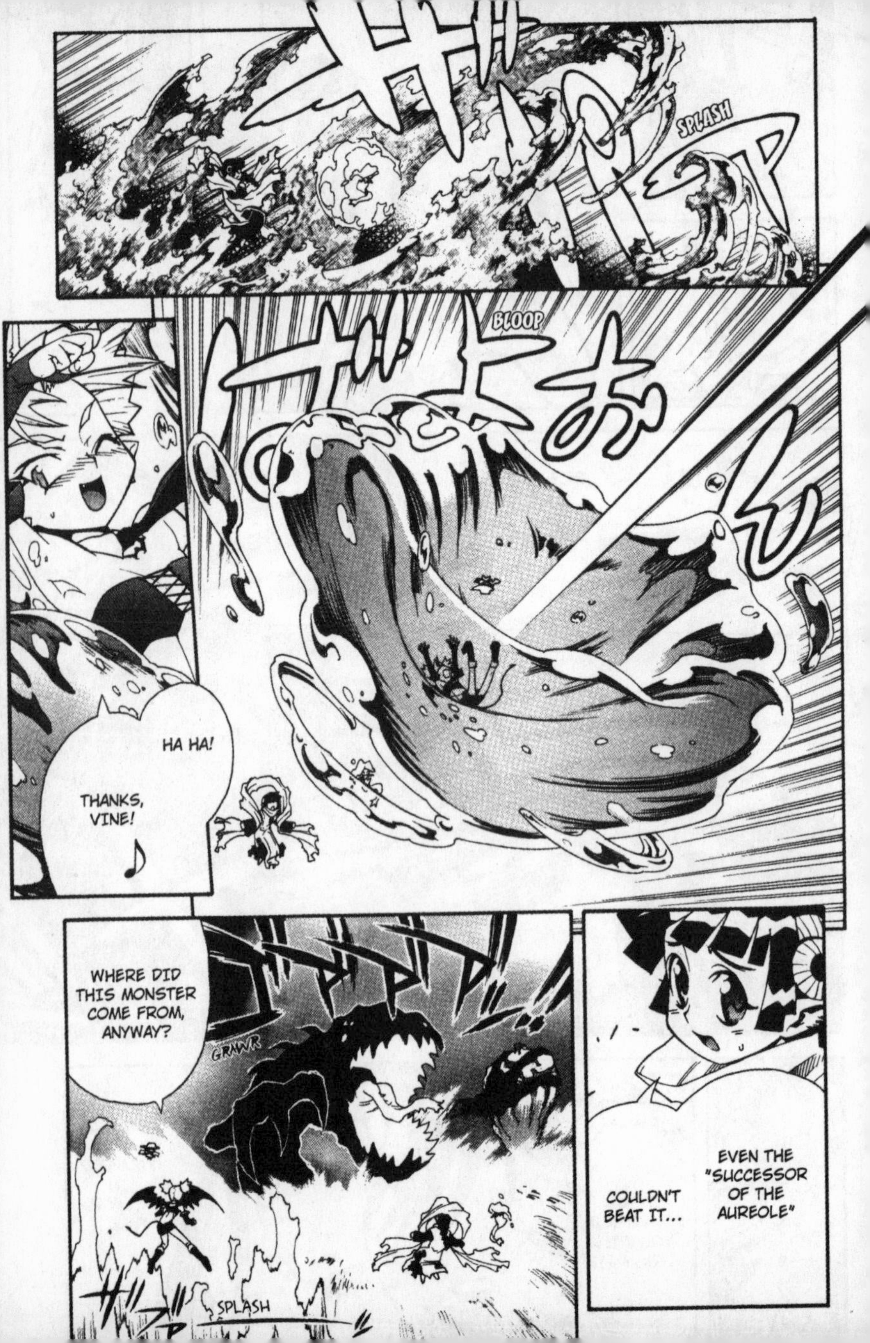
SPLASH
BLOOP
HA HA!
THANKS, VINE! ♪
EVEN THE "SUCCESSOR OF THE AUREOLE"
COULDN'T BEAT IT...
WHERE DID THIS MONSTER COME FROM, ANYWAY?
GRAWR
SPLASH

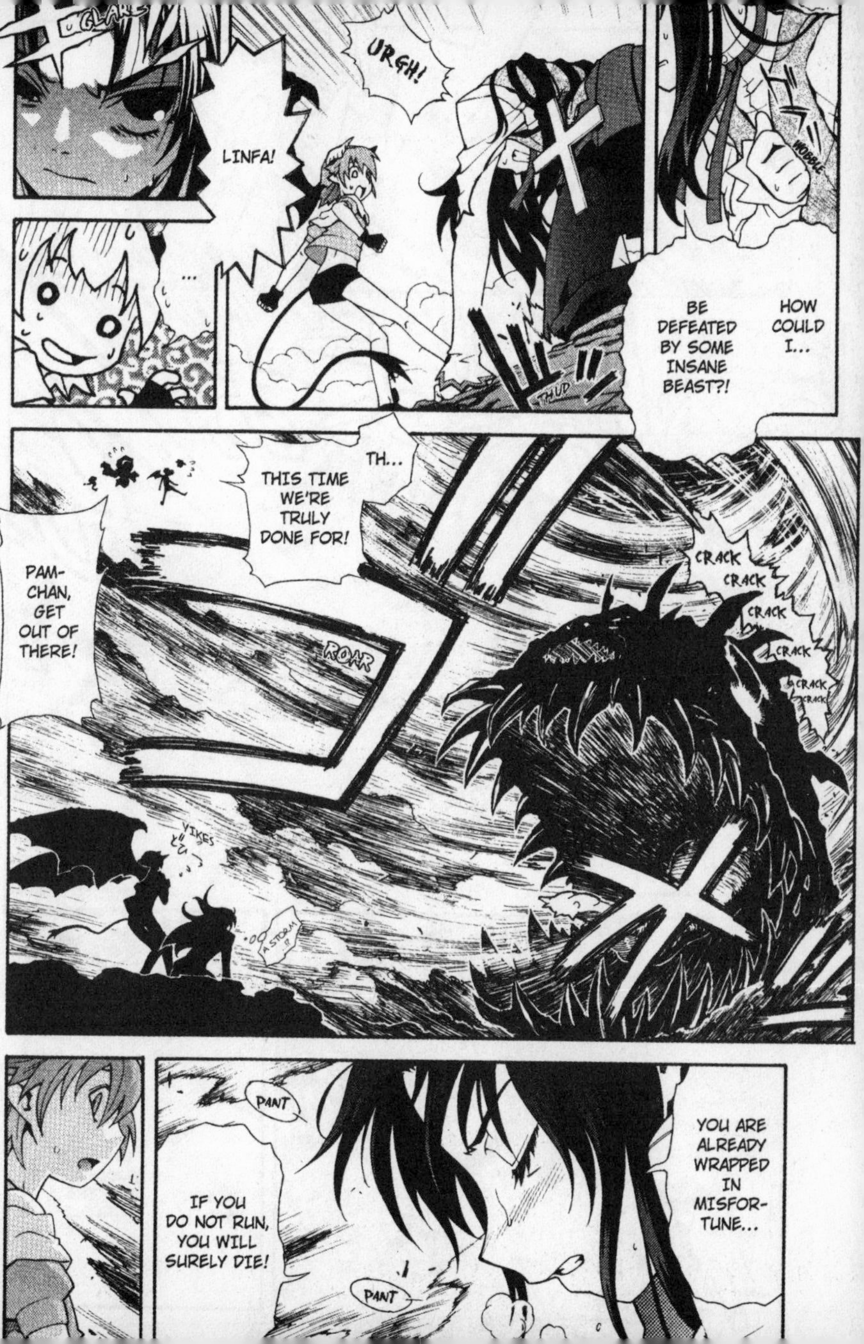
WOBBLE
HOW COULD I...
BE DEFEATED BY SOME INSANE BEAST?!
THUD
URGH!
LINFA!
GLARE
...
CRACK
CRACK
CRACK
CRACK
CRACK
CRACK
TH...
THIS TIME WE'RE TRULY DONE FOR!
ROAR
PAM-CHAN, GET OUT OF THERE!
YIKES
A STORM!?
YOU ARE ALREADY WRAPPED IN MISFORTUNE...
PANT
IF YOU DO NOT RUN, YOU WILL SURELY DIE!
PANT

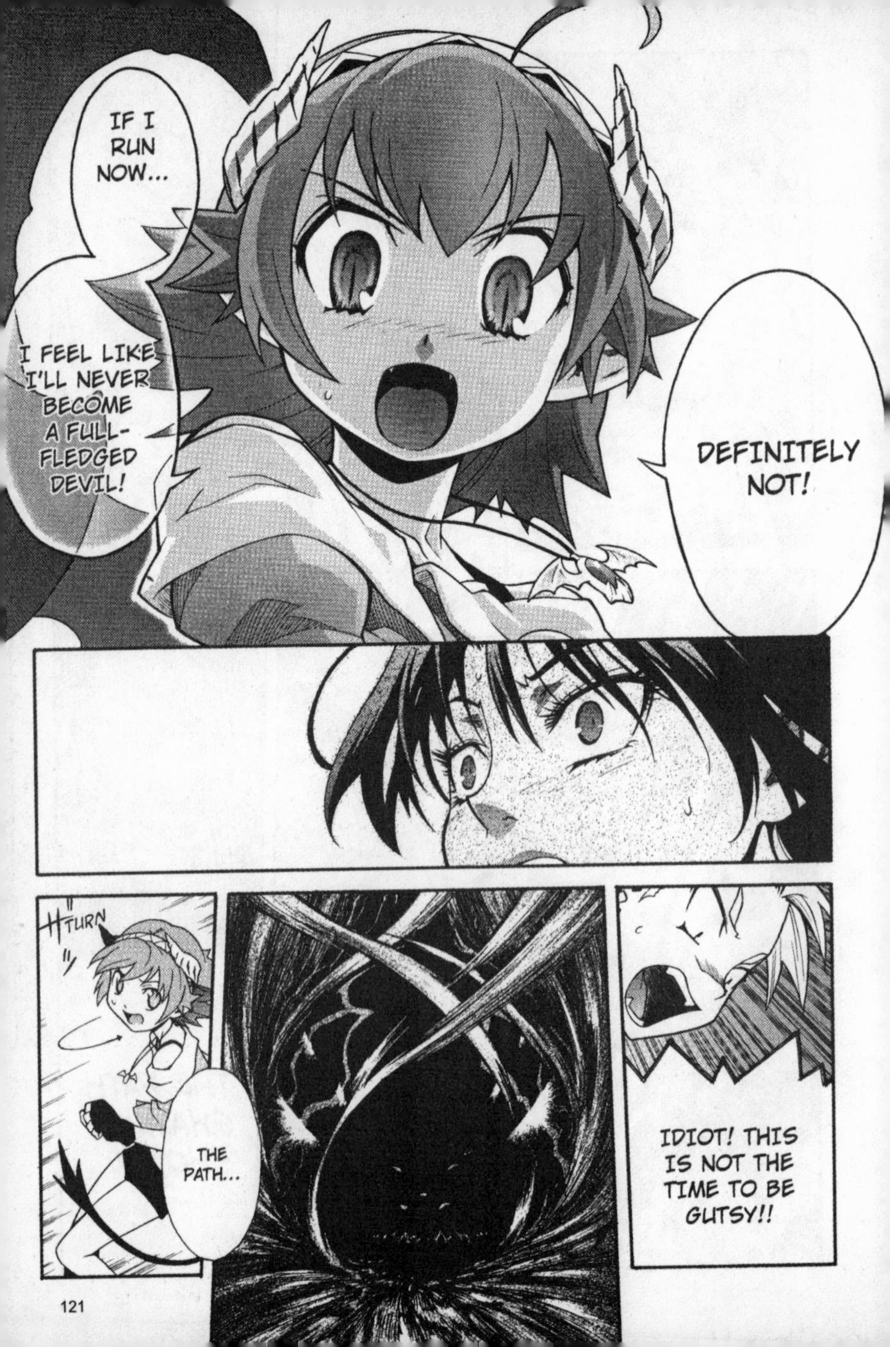
IF I RUN NOW...
I FEEL LIKE I'LL NEVER BECOME A FULL-FLEDGED DEVIL!
DEFINITELY NOT!
IDIOT! THIS IS NOT THE TIME TO BE GUTSY!!
TURN
THE PATH...

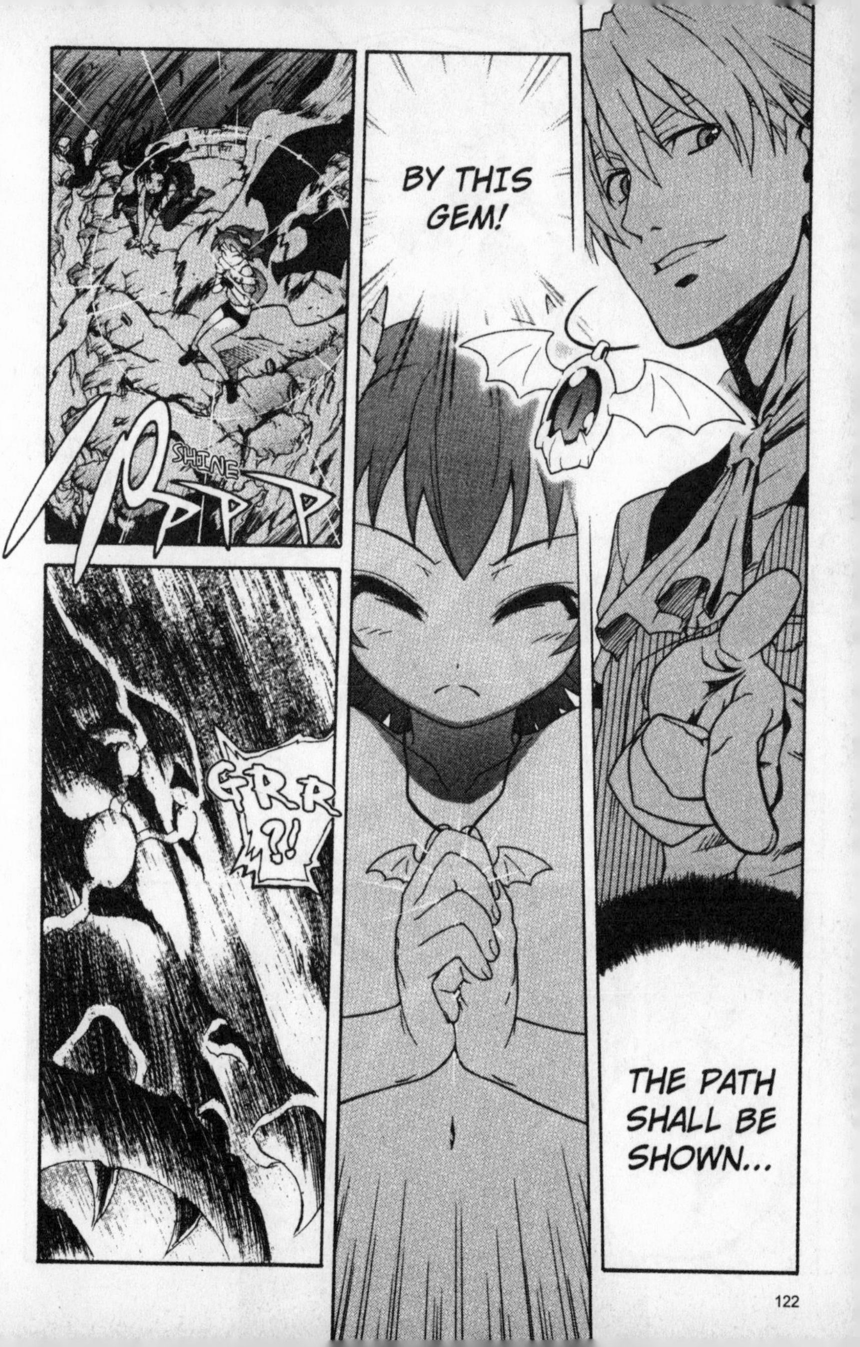

THE PATH SHALL BE SHOWN...
BY THIS GEM!
SHINE
GRR ?!

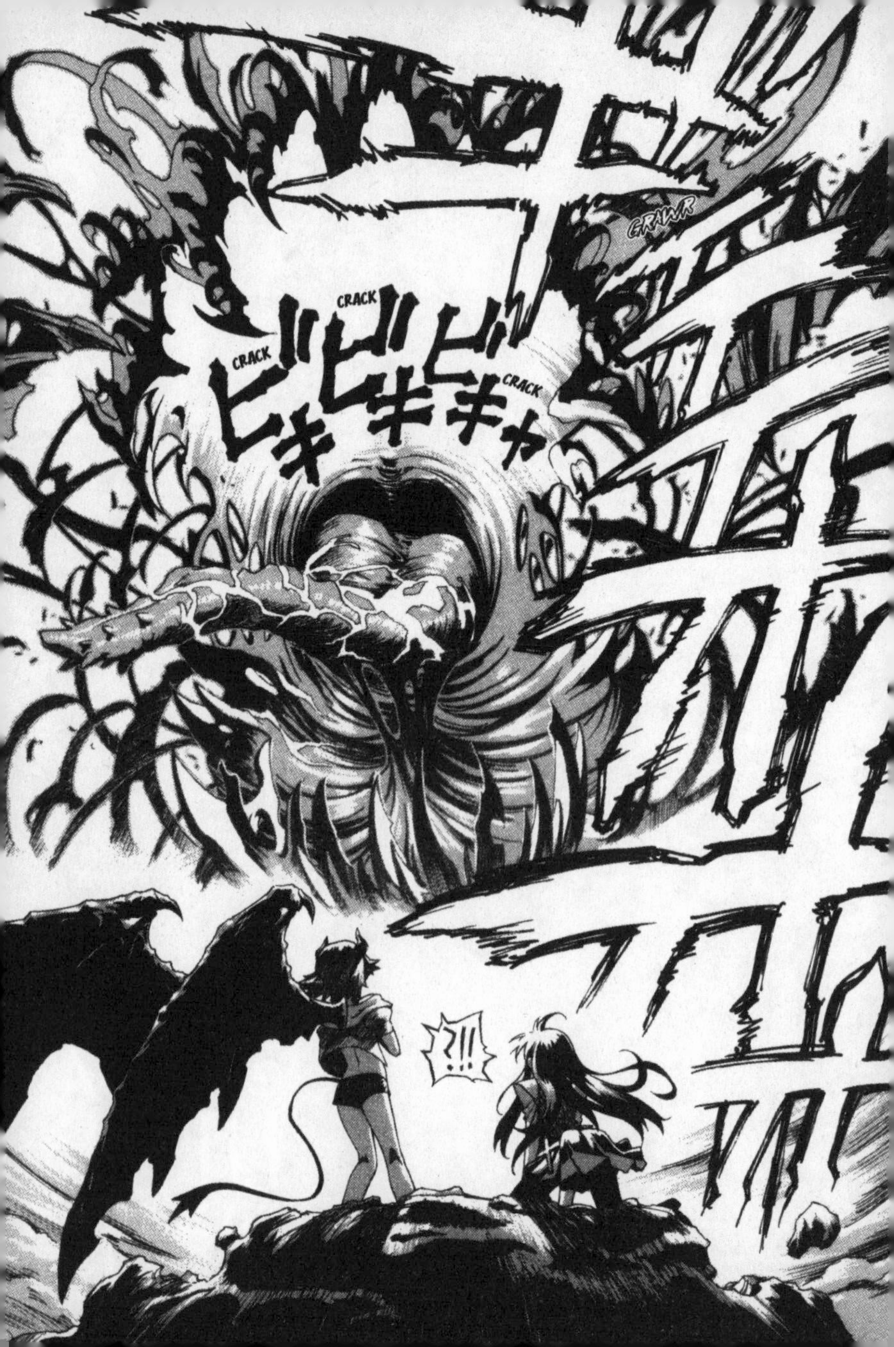
GRAWR
CRACK
CRACK
CRACK
?!!

STRAY
LITTLE
DEVIL*

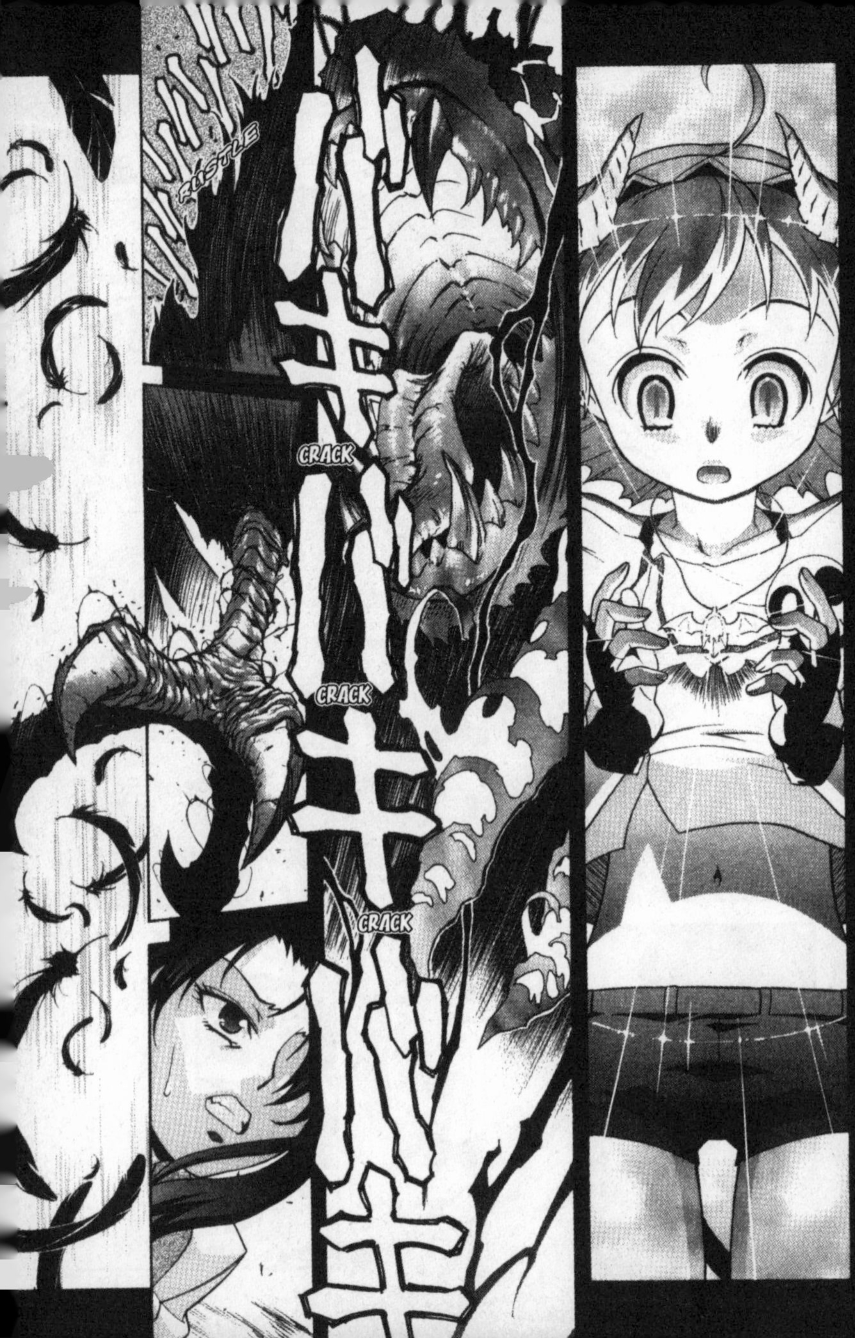
RUSTLE
CRACK
CRACK
CRACK

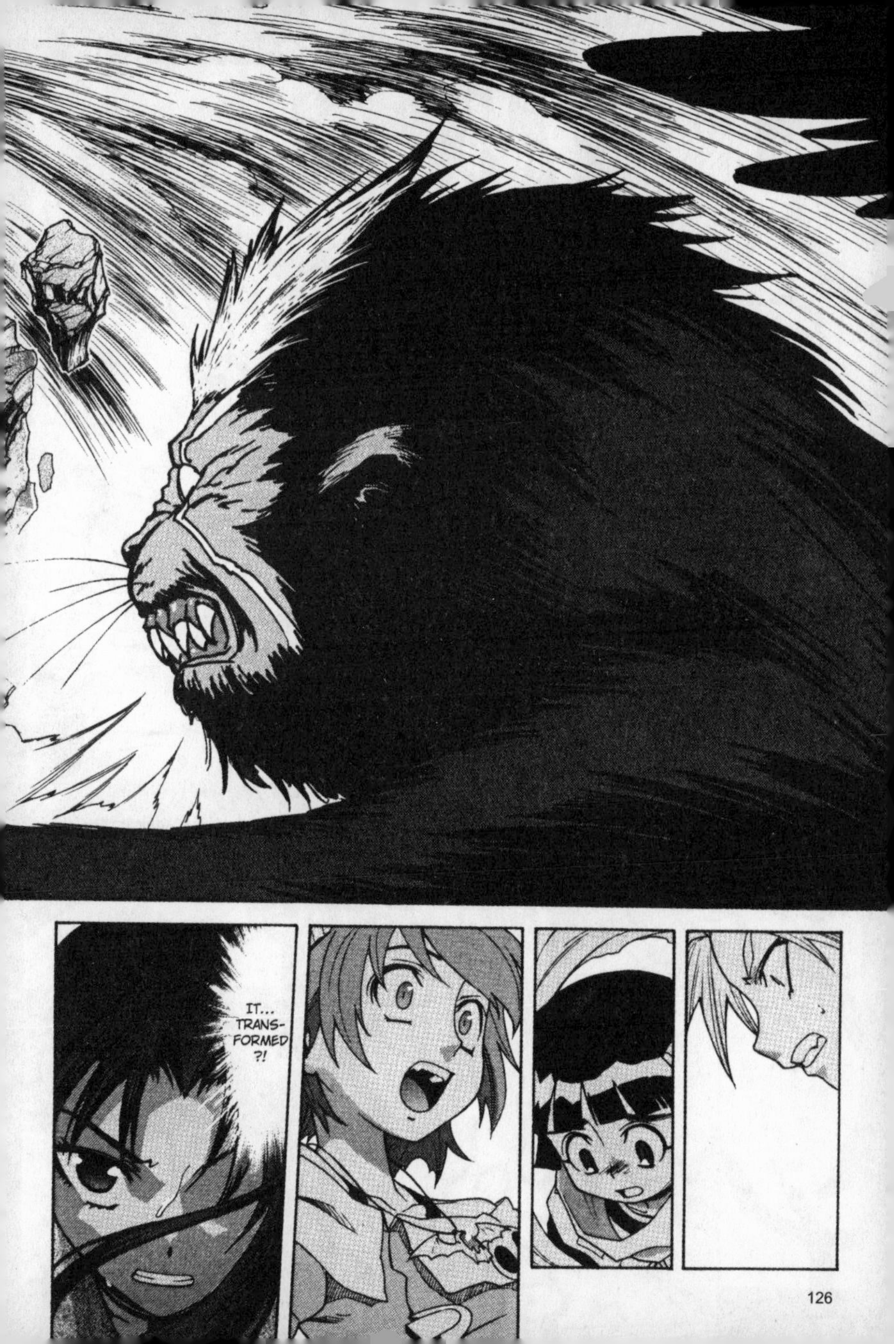
IT... TRANS-FORMED ?!

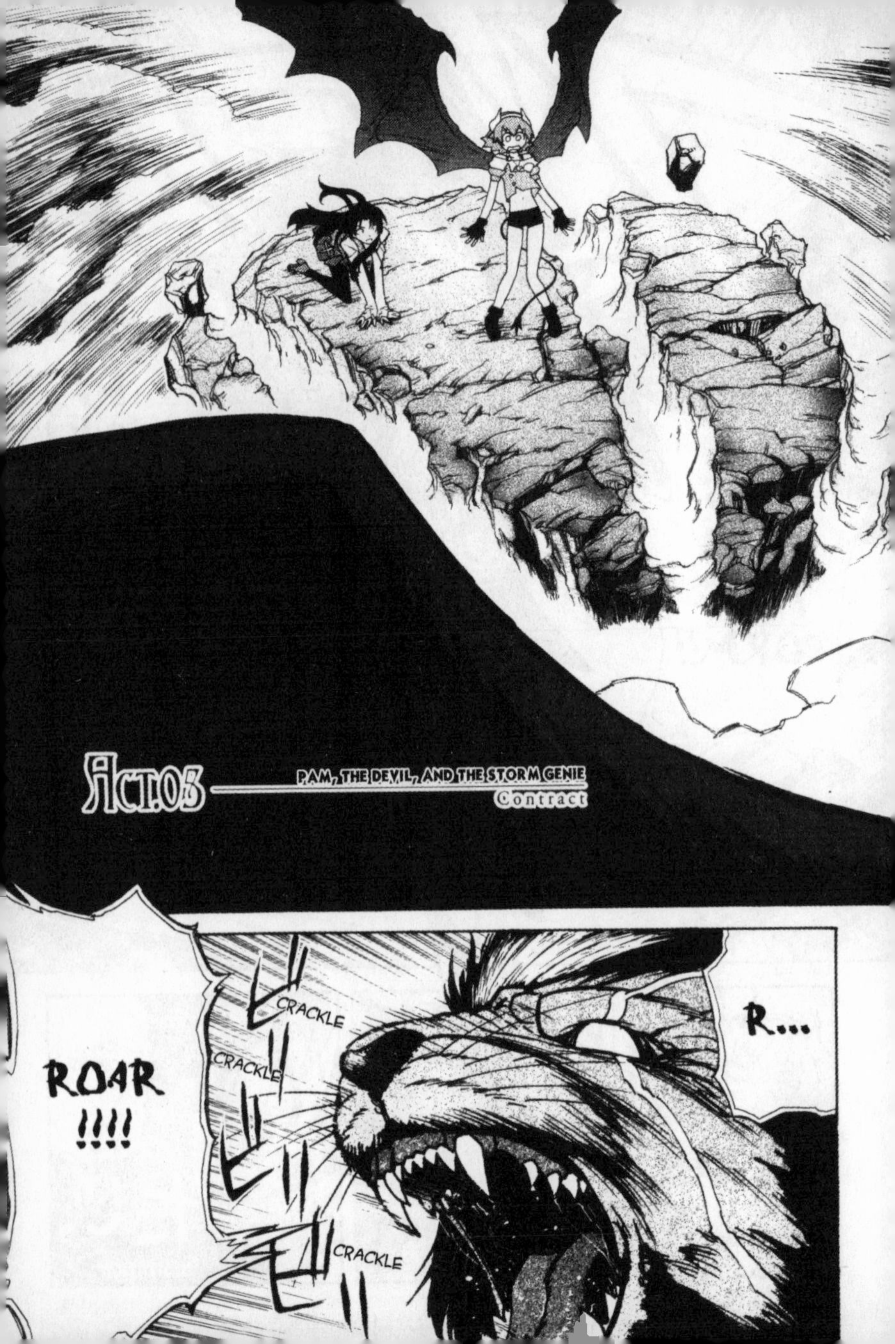
ACT.03
PAM, THE DEVIL, AND THE STORM GENIE
Contract
R...
CRACKLE
CRACKLE
CRACKLE
ROAR !!!!

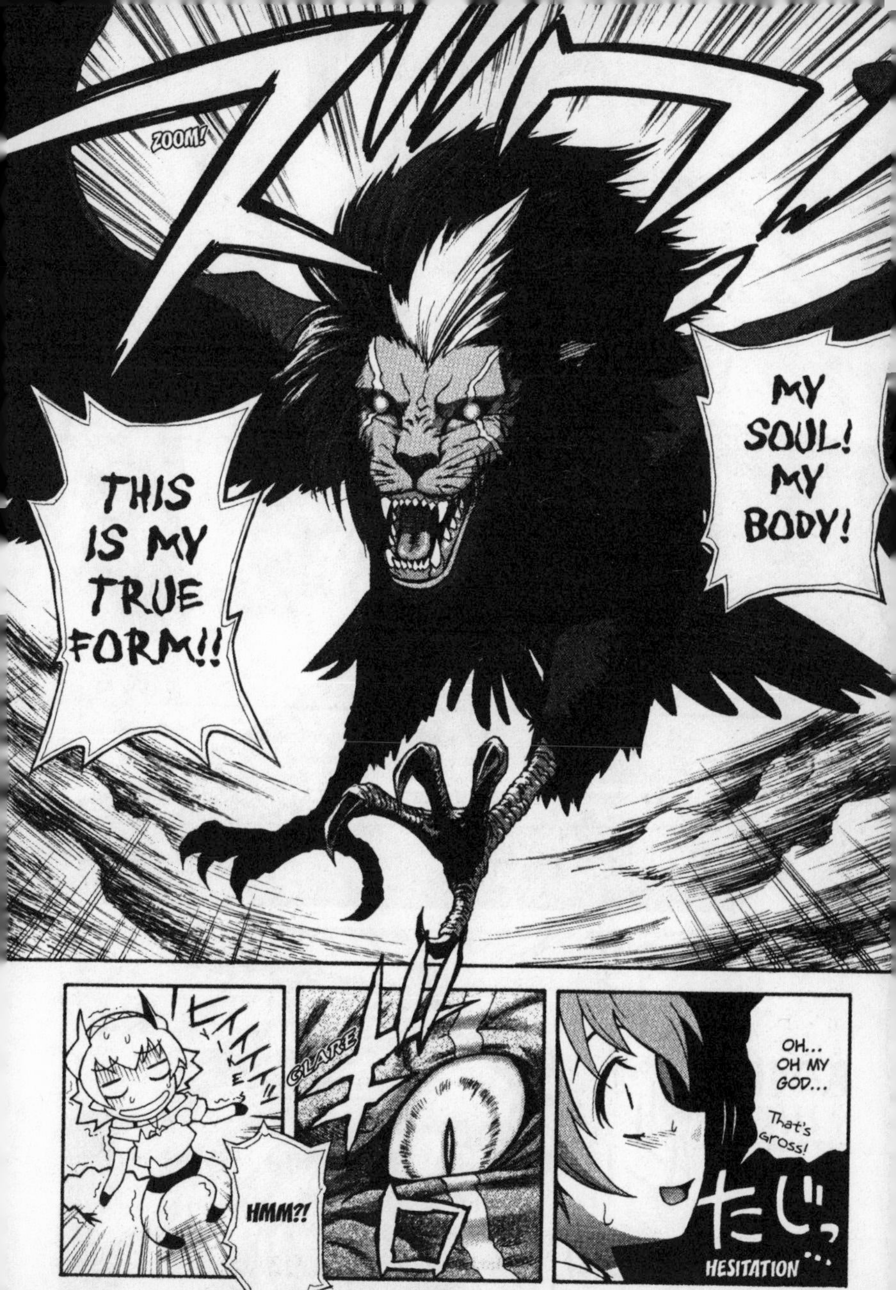
ZOOM!
MY SOUL! MY BODY!
THIS IS MY TRUE FORM!!
OH... OH MY GOD...
That's gross!
たじっ
HESITATION
GLARE
YIKES
HMM?!

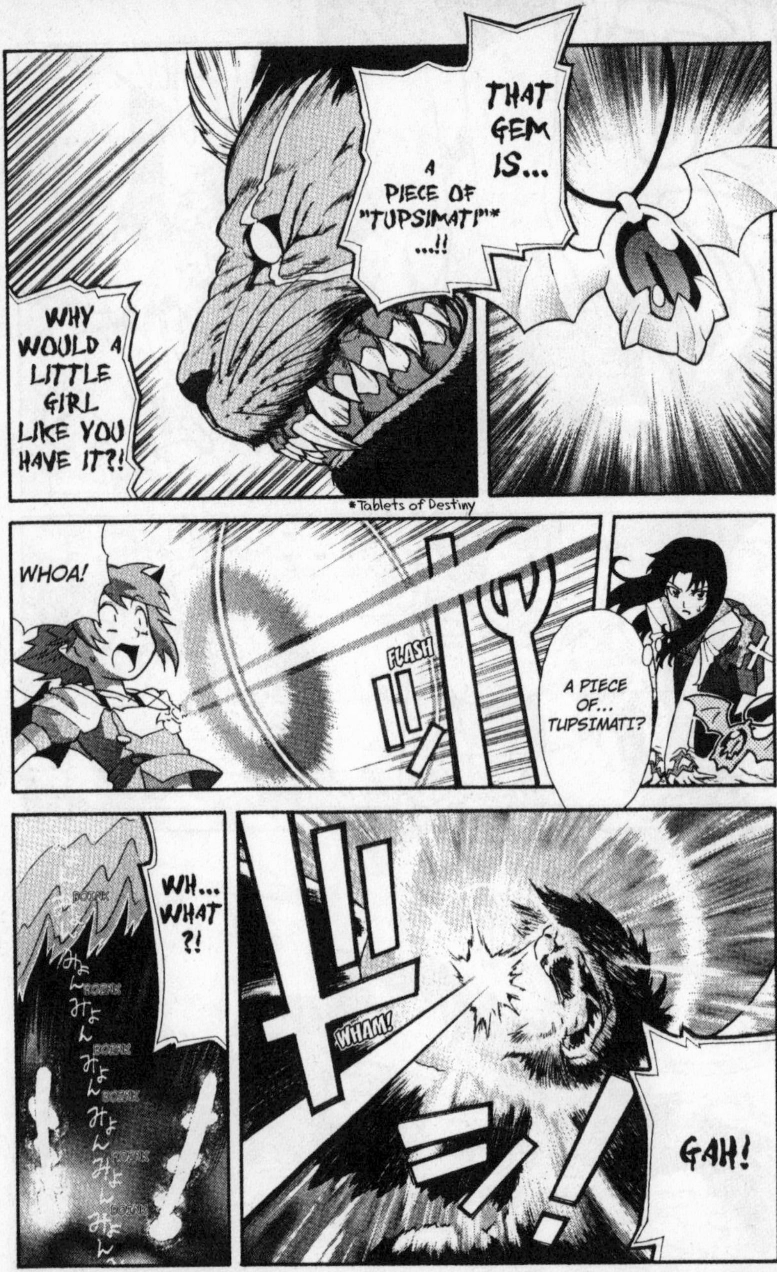
THAT GEM IS...
A PIECE OF "TUPSIMATI"* ...!!
WHY WOULD A LITTLE GIRL LIKE YOU HAVE IT?!
A PIECE OF... TUPSIMATI?
FLASH
WHOA!
WHAM!
GAH!
WH... WHAT ?!
BOINK
BOINK
BOINK
BOINK
BOINK
BOINK

*Tablets of Destiny

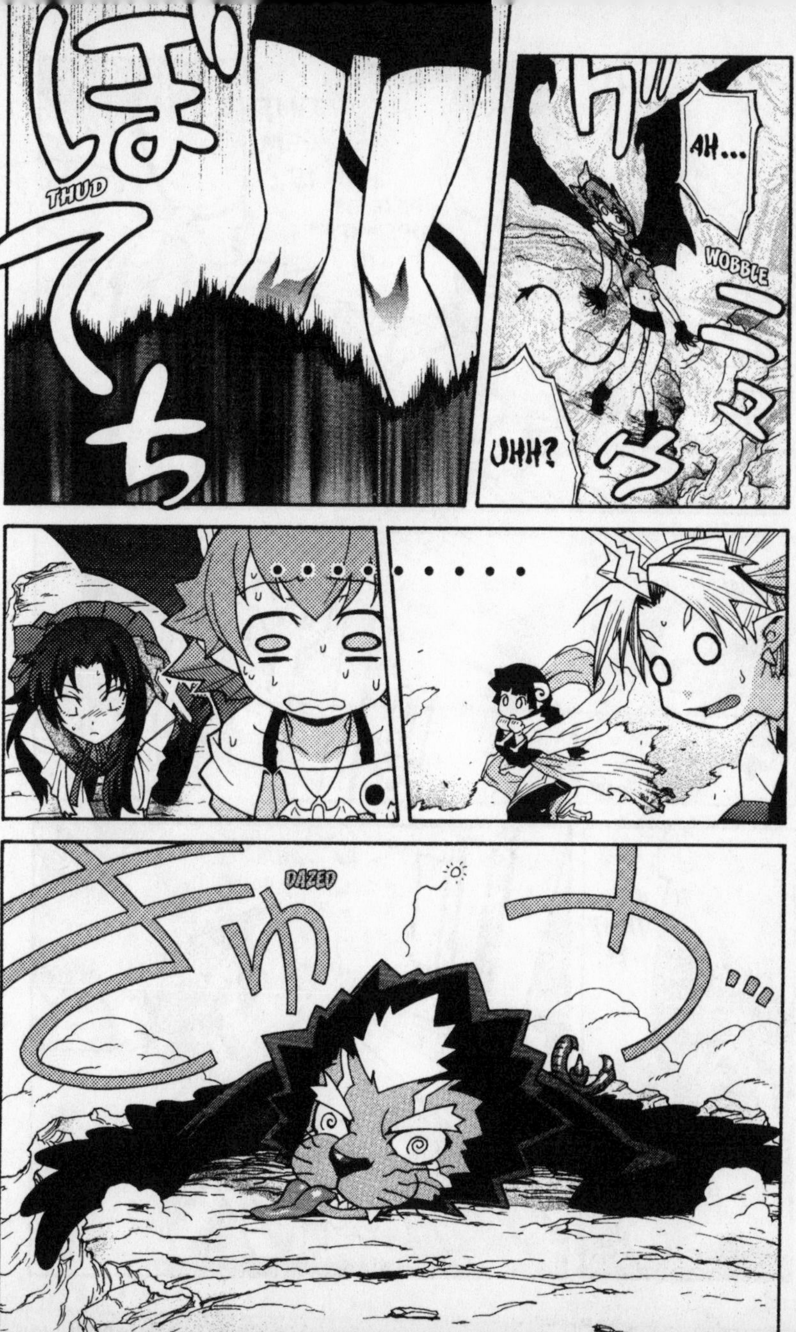
AH...
WOBBLE
UHH?
THUD
....
DAZED

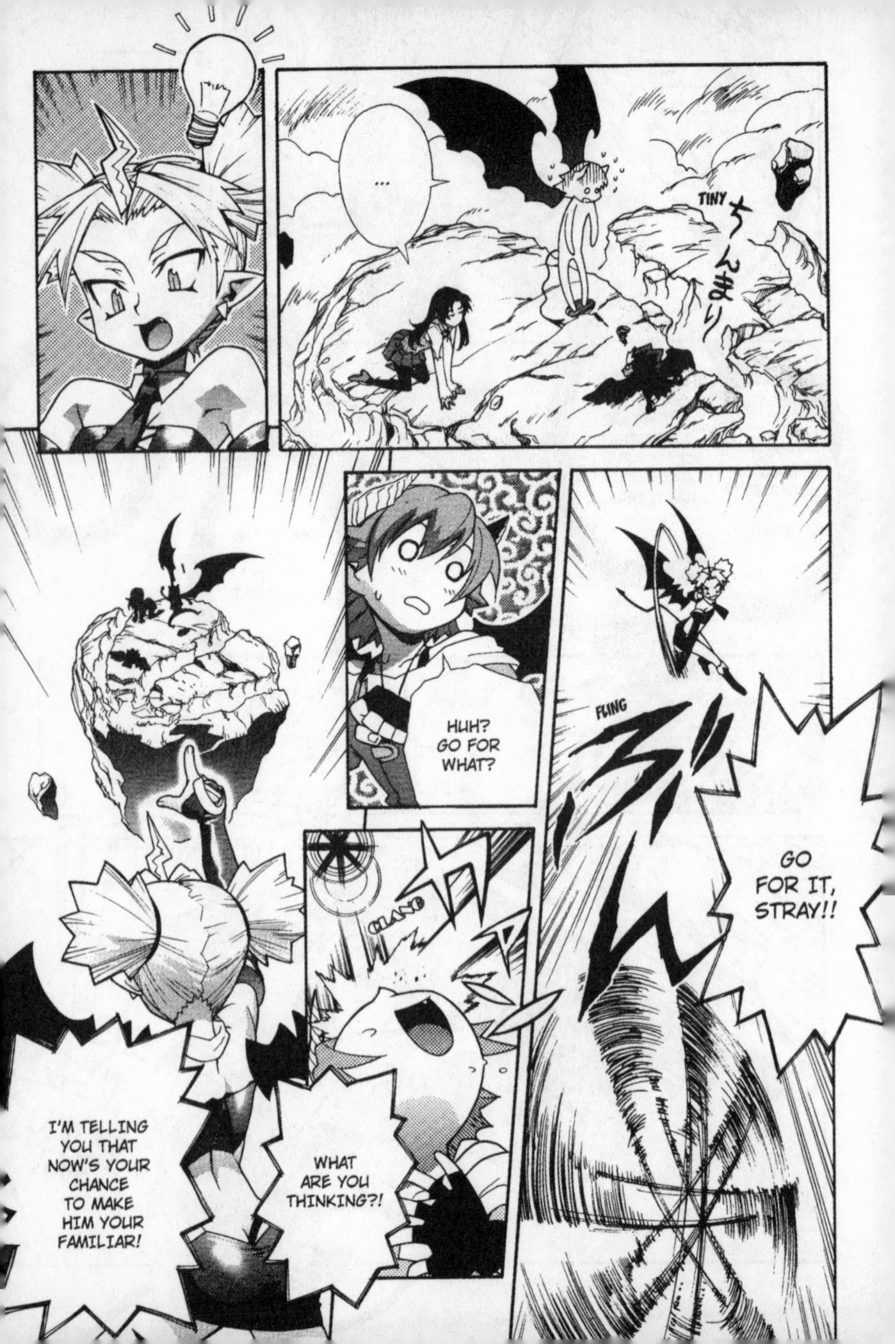
...
TINY
ちんまり
FLING
GO FOR IT, STRAY!!
HUH? GO FOR WHAT?
CLANG
WHAT ARE YOU THINKING?!
I'M TELLING YOU THAT NOW'S YOUR CHANCE TO MAKE HIM YOUR FAMILIAR!

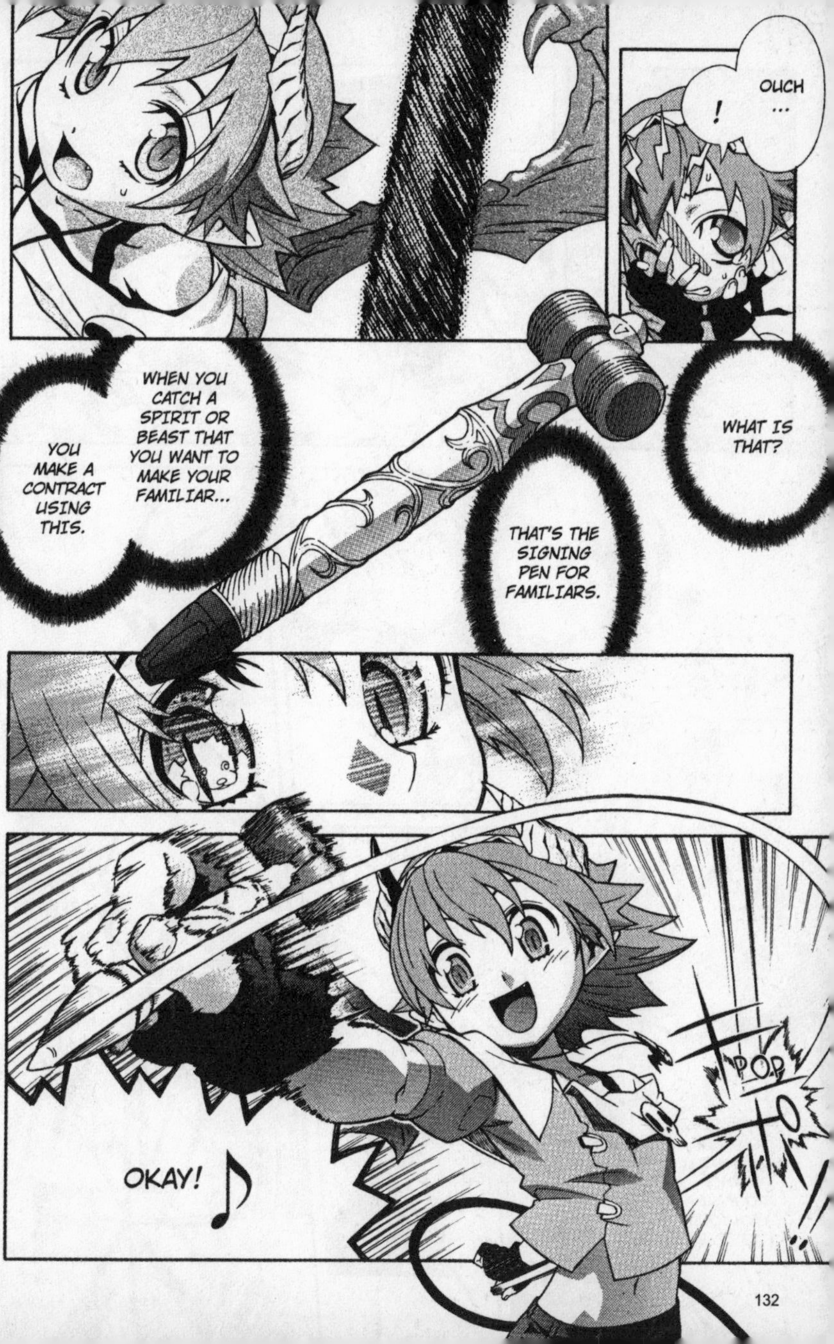
!
OUCH ...
WHAT IS THAT?
THAT'S THE SIGNING PEN FOR FAMILIARS.
WHEN YOU CATCH A SPIRIT OR BEAST THAT YOU WANT TO MAKE YOUR FAMILIAR...
YOU MAKE A CONTRACT USING THIS.
POP
OKAY! ♪

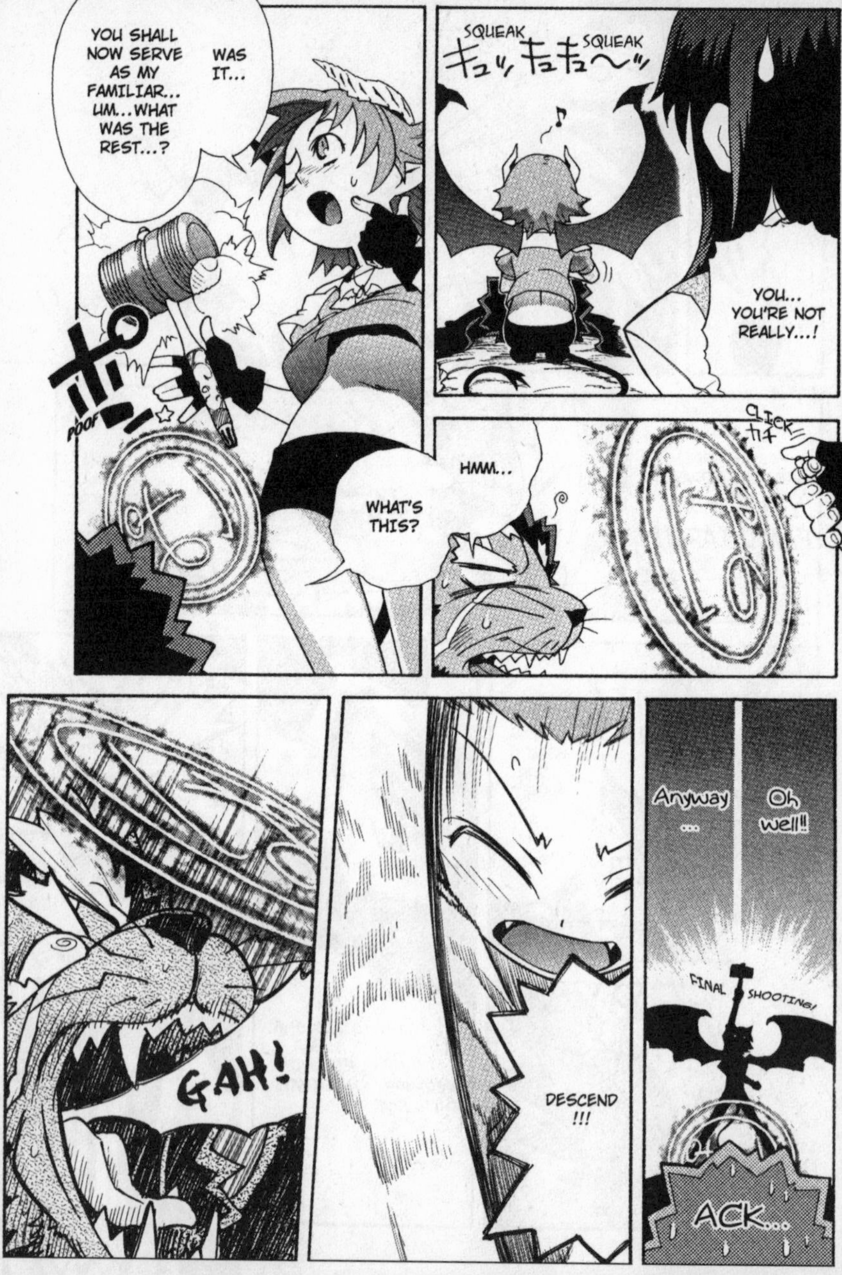

SQUEAK
キュッ
SQUEAK
キュキュ～ッ
YOU... YOU'RE NOT REALLY...!
CLICK
カチ
HMM...
WHAT'S THIS?
YOU SHALL NOW SERVE AS MY FAMILIAR... UM...WHAT WAS THE REST...?
WAS IT...
ポン
POOF
Oh well!!
Anyway ...
FINAL SHOOTING!
ACK...
DESCEND !!!
GAH!

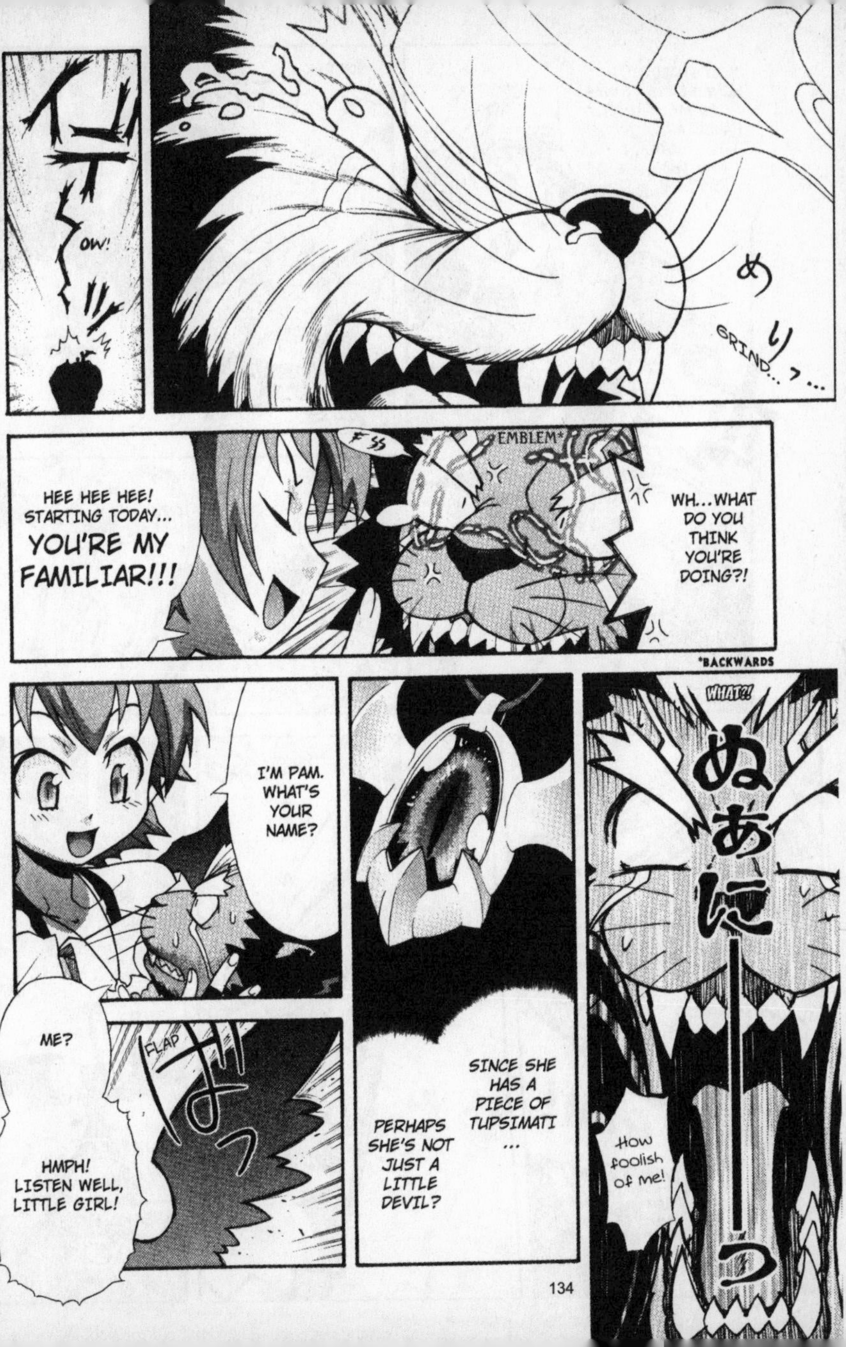
めり
GRIND...っ...
OW!
WH...WHAT DO YOU THINK YOU'RE DOING?!
EMBLEM*
HEE HEE HEE! STARTING TODAY... YOU'RE MY FAMILIAR!!!
*BACKWARDS
WHAT?!
ぬあにーっ
How foolish of me!
SINCE SHE HAS A PIECE OF TUPSIMATI ...
PERHAPS SHE'S NOT JUST A LITTLE DEVIL?
I'M PAM. WHAT'S YOUR NAME?
ME?
FLAP
ばっ
HMPH! LISTEN WELL, LITTLE GIRL!

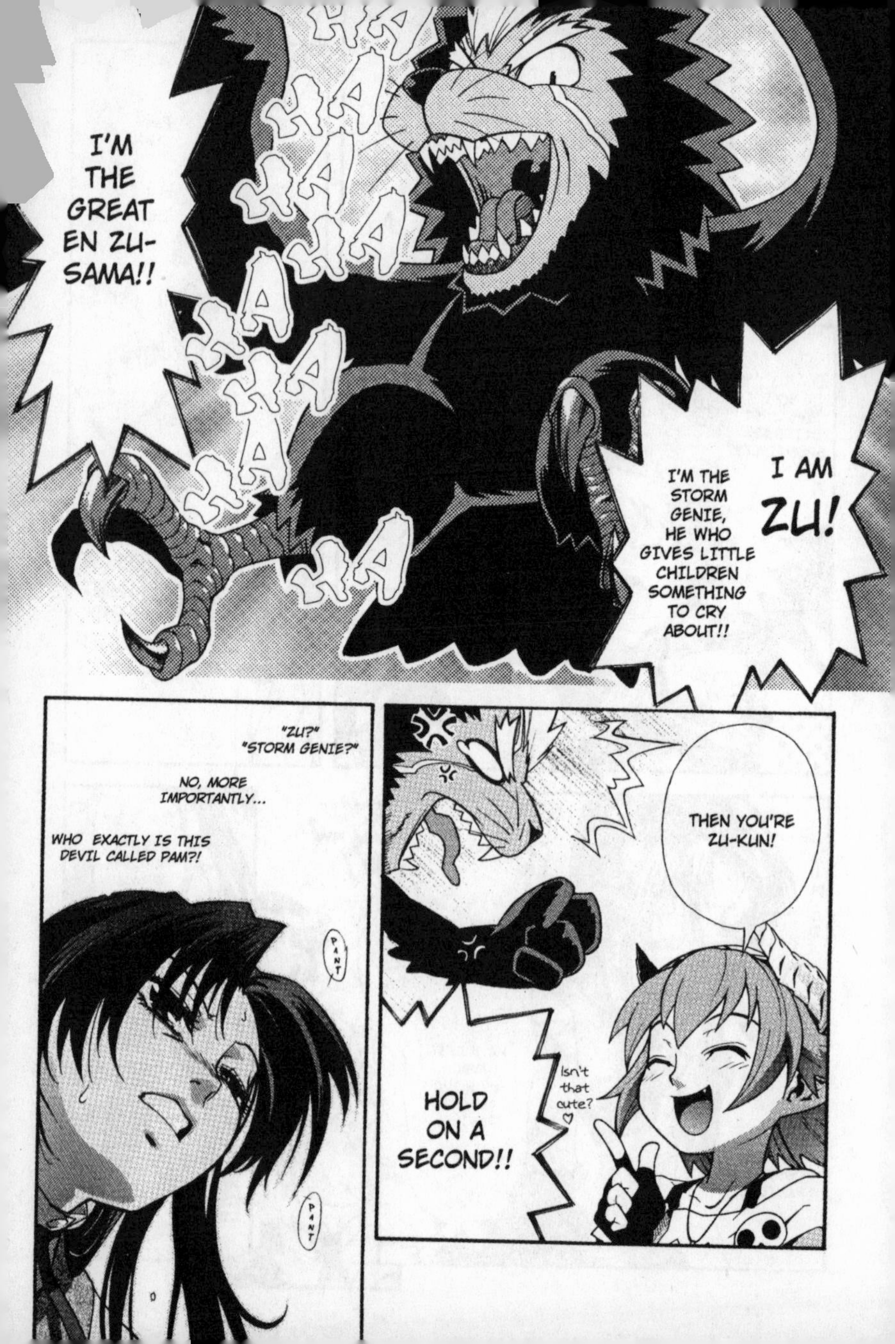

HA HA HA HA HA HA HA HA HA
I'M THE GREAT EN ZU-SAMA!!
I AM ZU!
I'M THE STORM GENIE, HE WHO GIVES LITTLE CHILDREN SOMETHING TO CRY ABOUT!!
THEN YOU'RE ZU-KUN!
Isn't that cute? ♡
HOLD ON A SECOND!!
"ZU?" "STORM GENIE?"
NO, MORE IMPORTANTLY...
WHO EXACTLY IS THIS DEVIL CALLED PAM?!
PANT
PANT

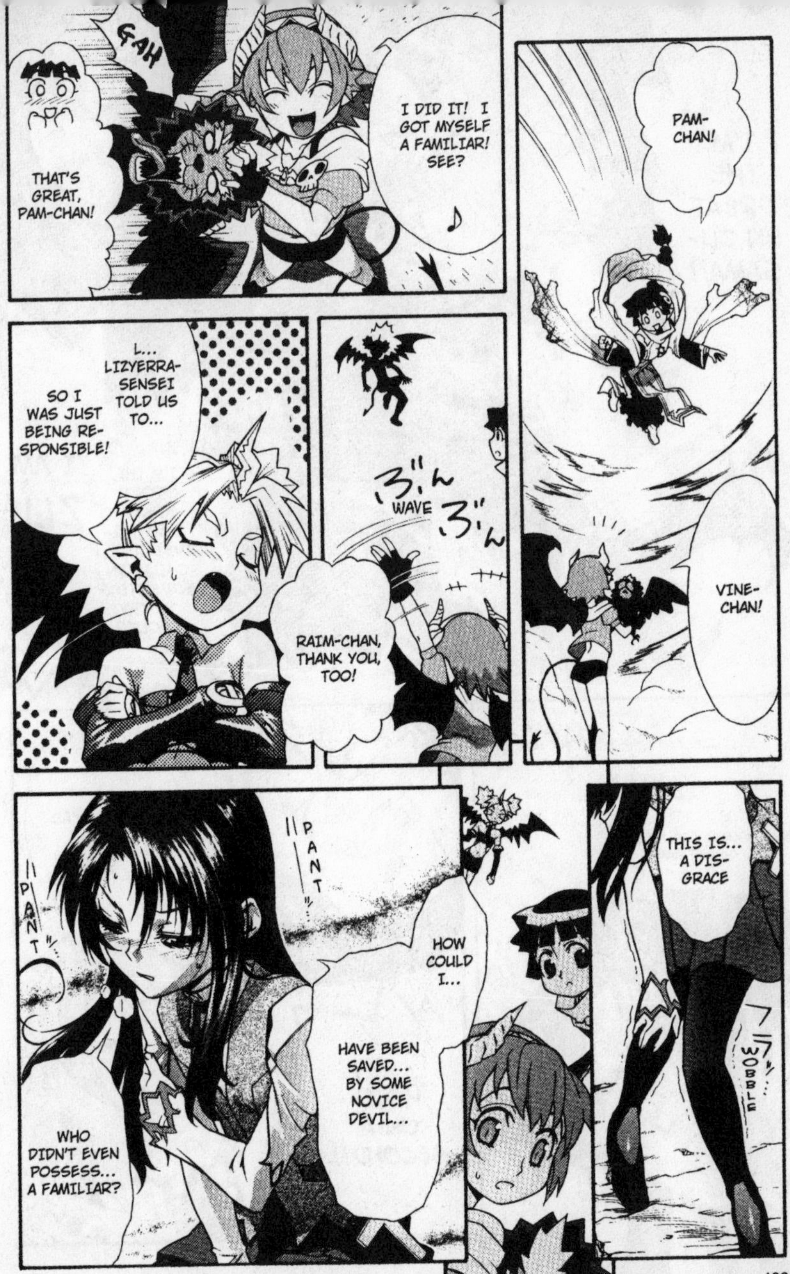
PAM-CHAN!
VINE-CHAN!
I DID IT! I GOT MYSELF A FAMILIAR! SEE? ♪
GAH
THAT'S GREAT, PAM-CHAN!
ぶんぶん
WAVE
RAIM-CHAN, THANK YOU, TOO!
L... LIZYERRA-SENSEI TOLD US TO...
SO I WAS JUST BEING RESPONSIBLE!
THIS IS... A DISGRACE
WOBBLE...
PANT
PANT...
HOW COULD I...
HAVE BEEN SAVED... BY SOME NOVICE DEVIL...
WHO DIDN'T EVEN POSSESS... A FAMILIAR?

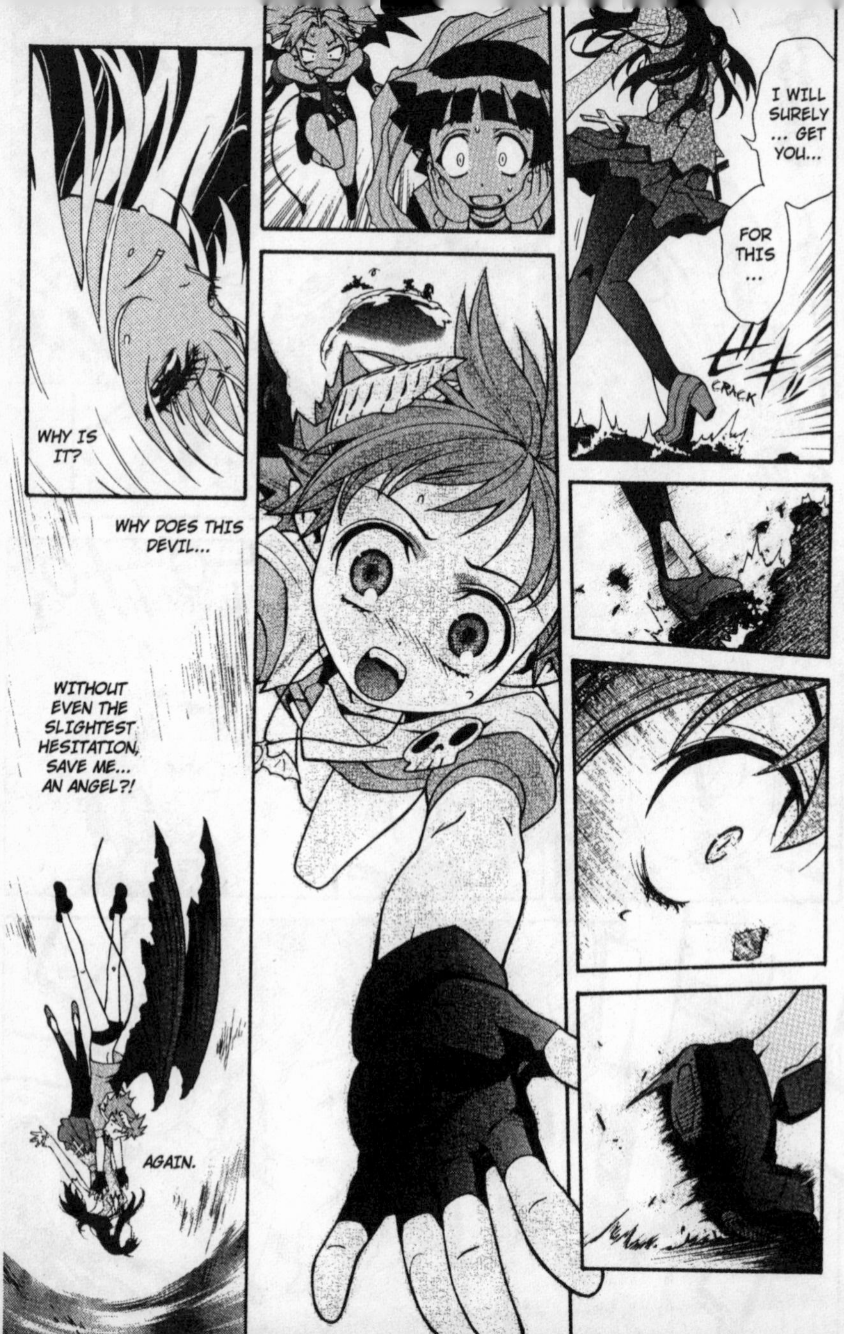
I WILL SURELY ... GET YOU...
FOR THIS ...
CRACK
WHY IS IT?
WHY DOES THIS DEVIL...
WITHOUT EVEN THE SLIGHTEST HESITATION, SAVE ME... AN ANGEL?!
AGAIN.

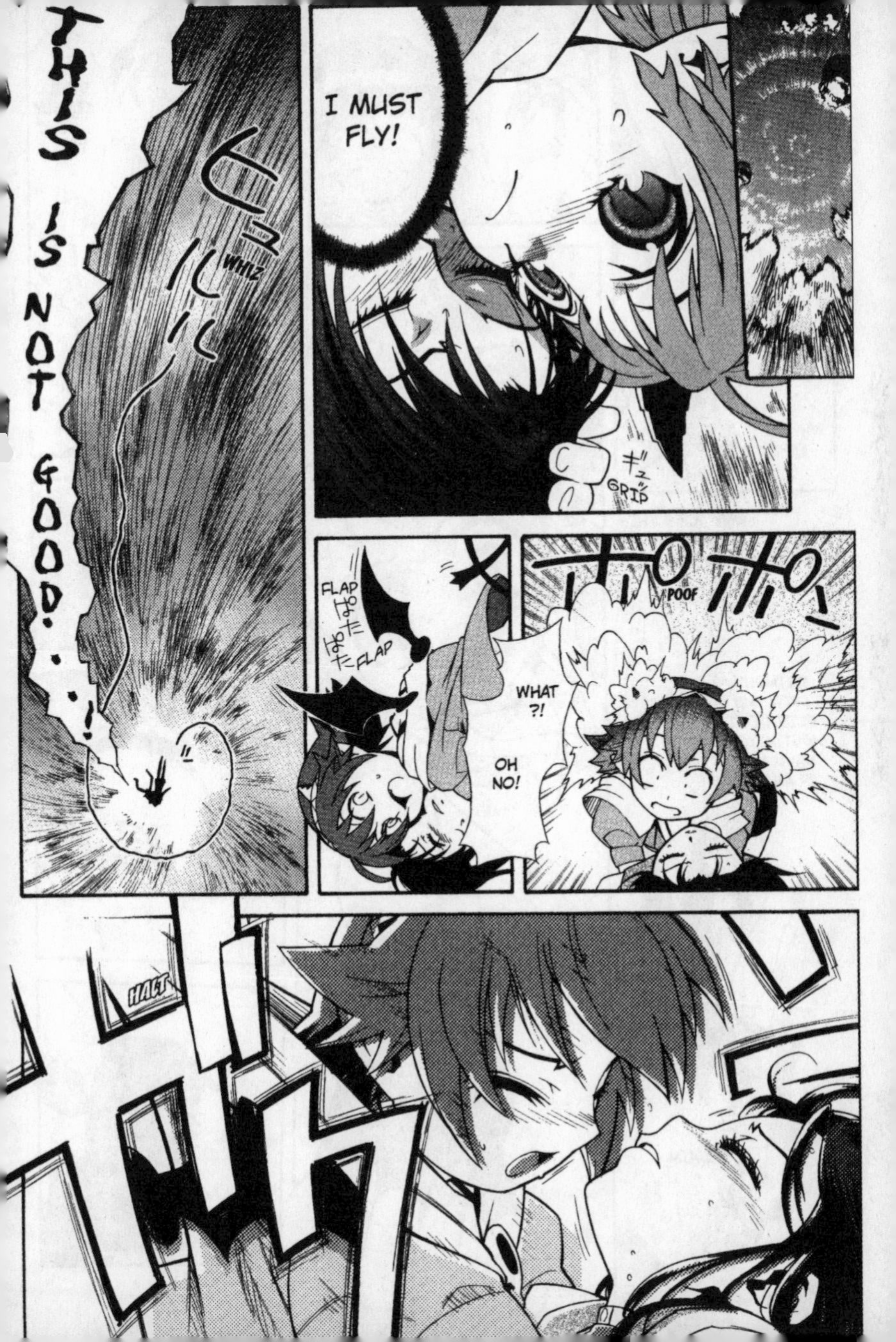

I MUST FLY!
GRIP
POOF
WHAT ?!
OH NO!
FLAP ぱた ぱた FLAP
WHIZ
THIS IS NOT GOOD...!
HALT

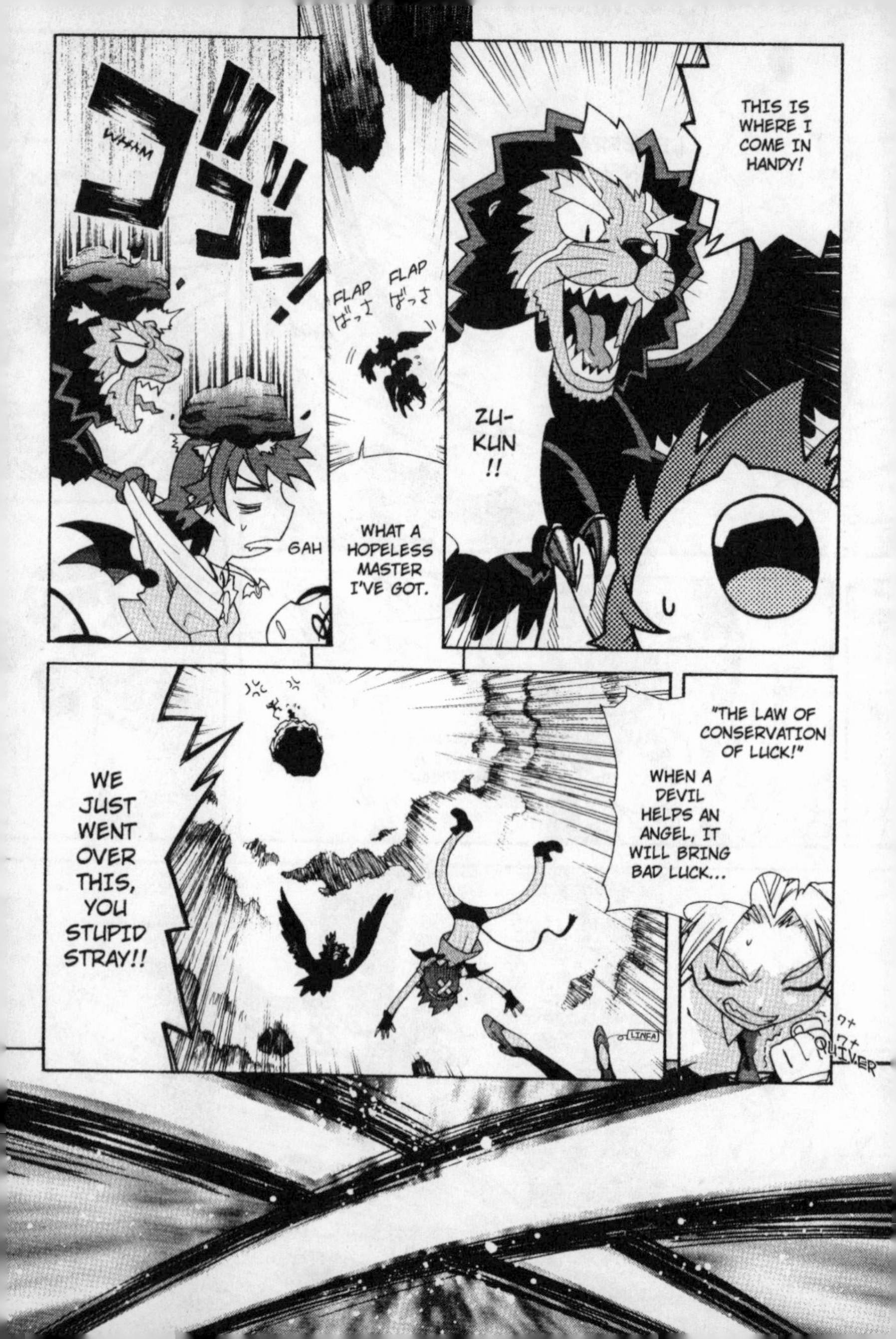
THIS IS WHERE I COME IN HANDY!
ZU-KUN!!
FLAP ばっさ
FLAP ばっさ
WHAT A HOPELESS MASTER I'VE GOT.
WHAM
GAH
"THE LAW OF CONSERVATION OF LUCK!"
WHEN A DEVIL HELPS AN ANGEL, IT WILL BRING BAD LUCK...
QUIVER
WE JUST WENT OVER THIS, YOU STUPID STRAY!!
LINFA

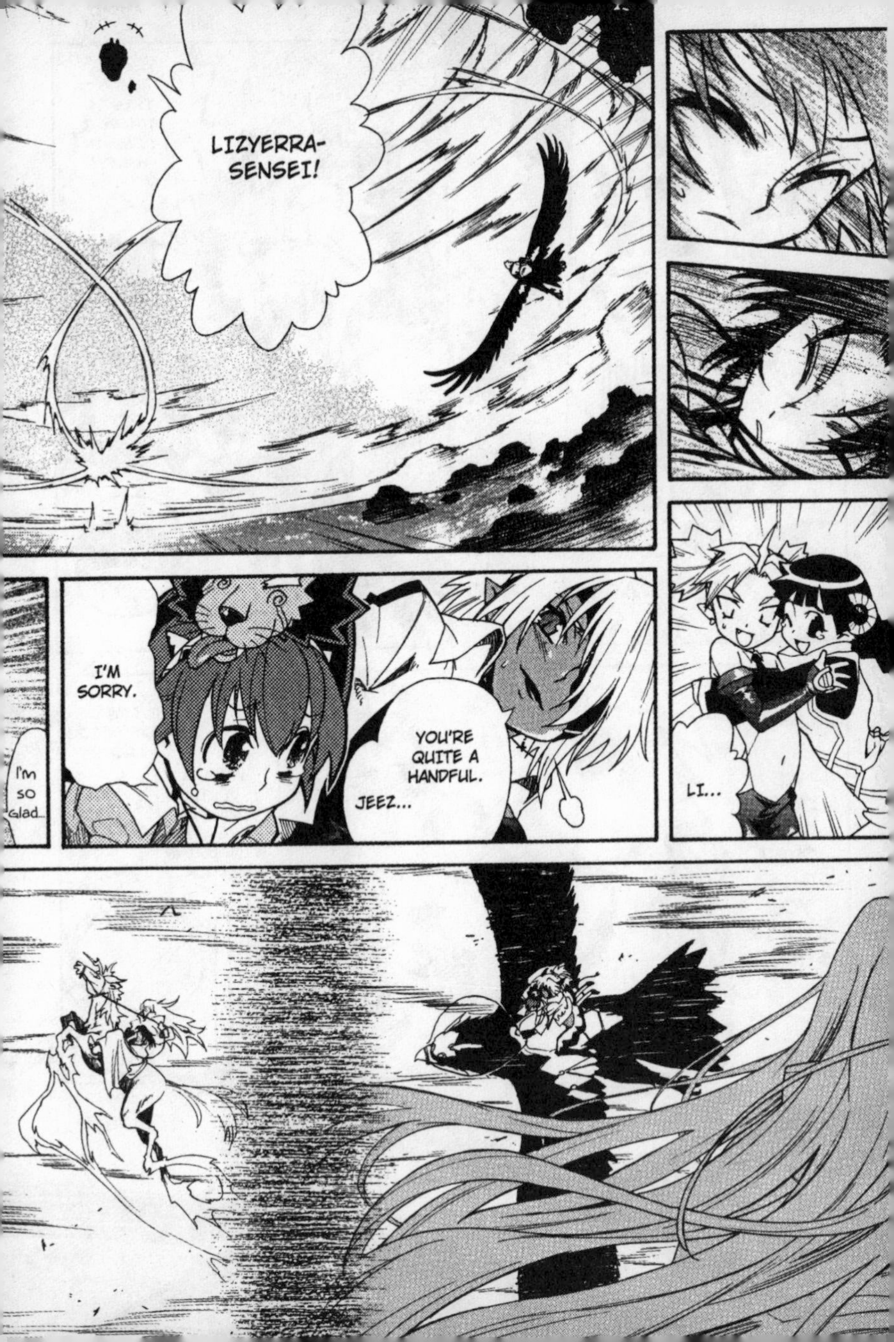
LI...
LIZYERRA-SENSEI!
YOU'RE QUITE A HANDFUL.
JEEZ...
I'M SORRY.
I'm so glad...

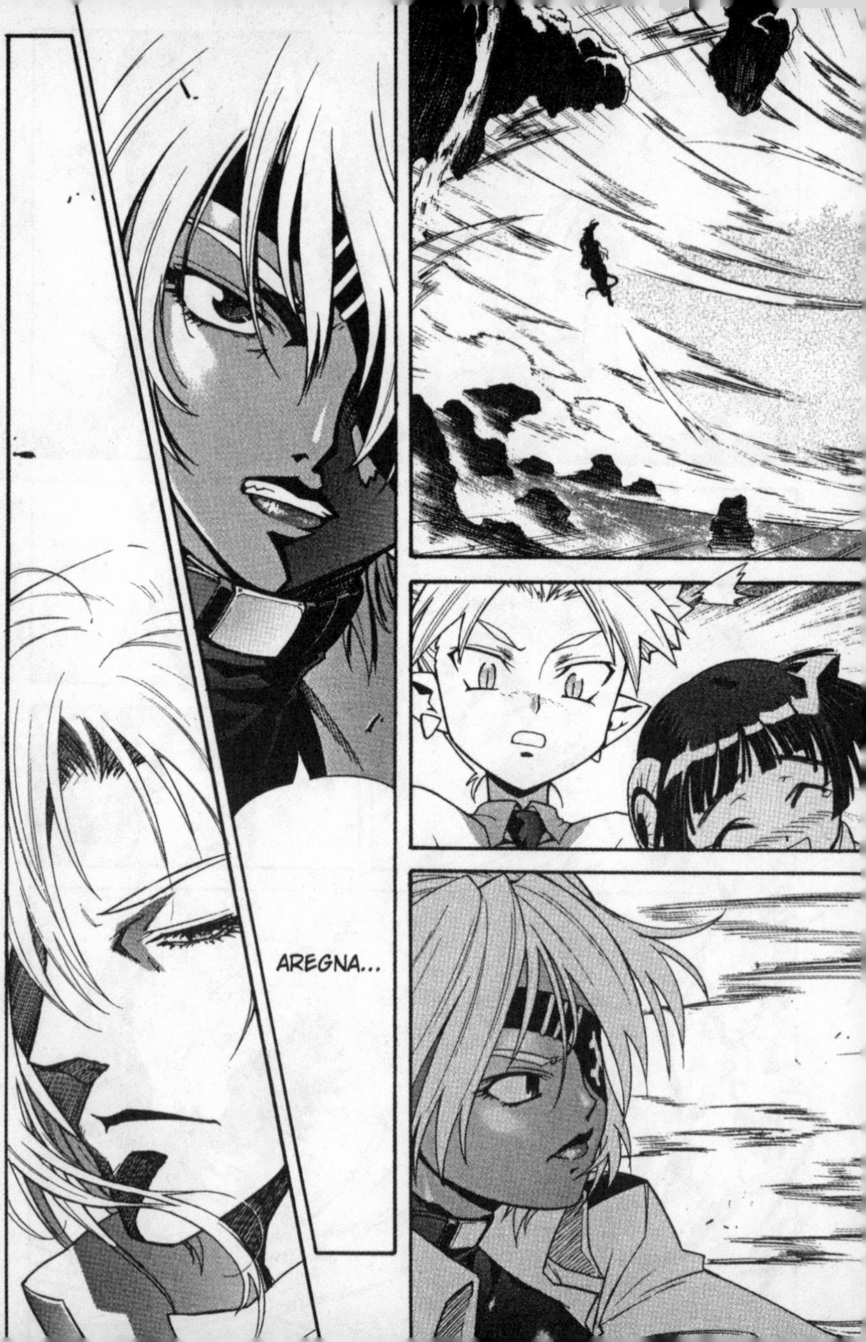
AREGNA...

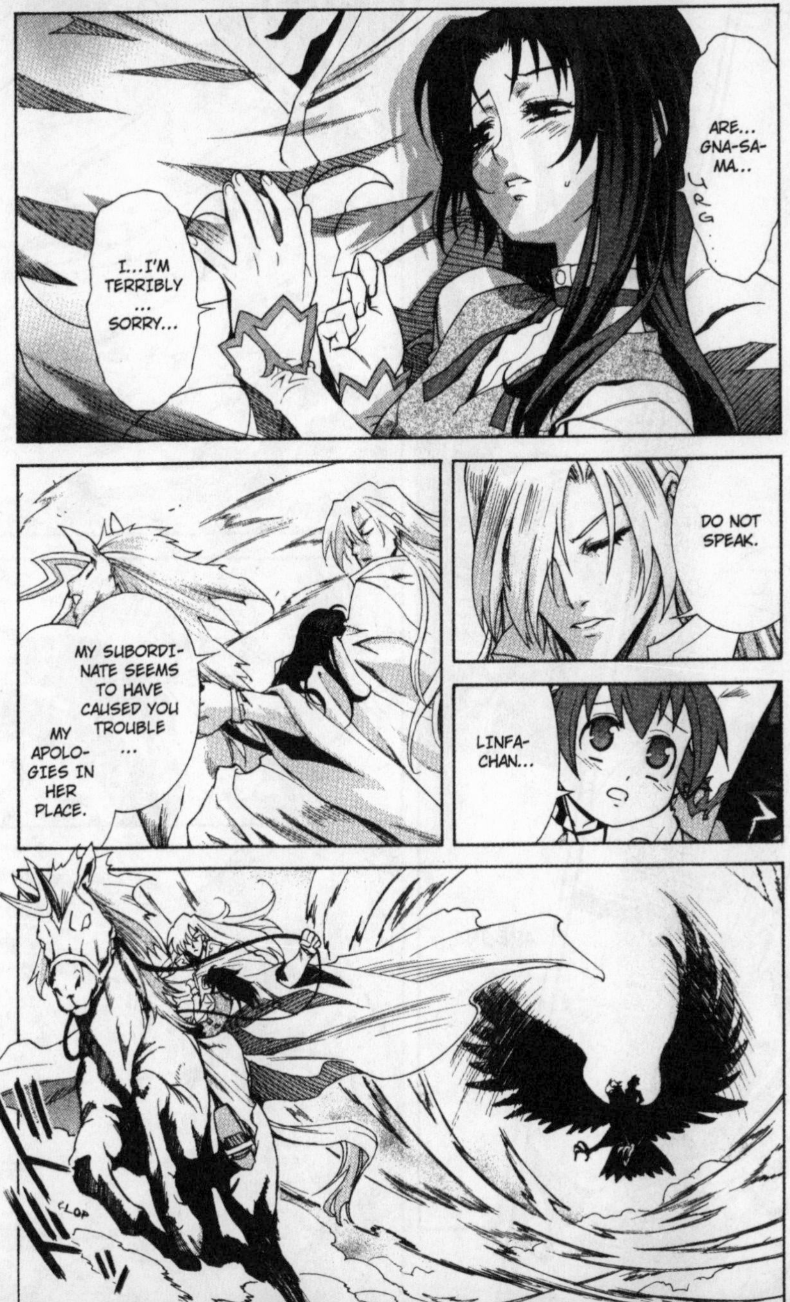
ARE... GNA-SAMA...
URG...
I...I'M TERRIBLY ... SORRY...
DO NOT SPEAK.
LINFA-CHAN...
MY SUBORDINATE SEEMS TO HAVE CAUSED YOU TROUBLE ...
MY APOLOGIES IN HER PLACE.
CLOP

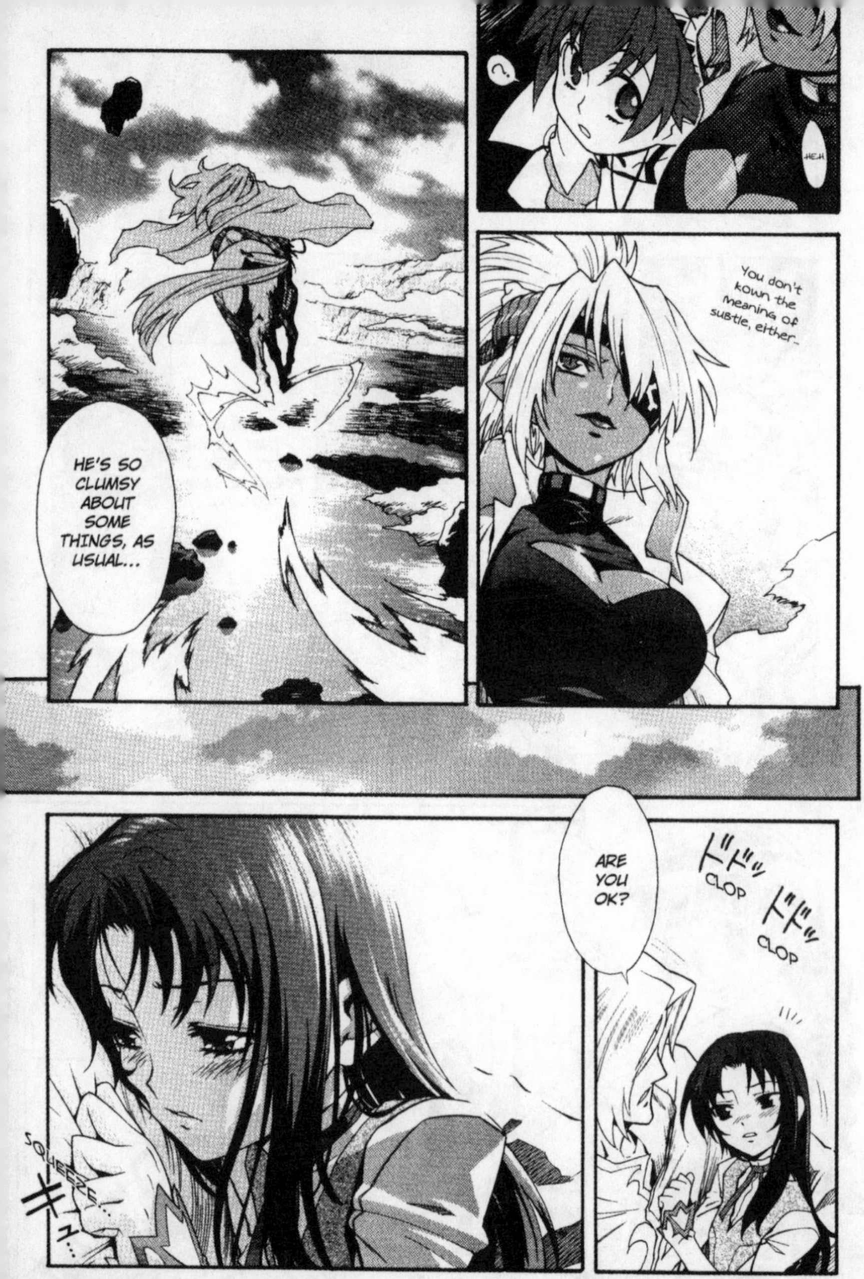
?
HEH
You don't kown the meaning of subtle, either...
HE'S SO CLUMSY ABOUT SOME THINGS, AS USUAL...
ARE YOU OK?
ドドッ
CLOP
ドドッ
CLOP
SQUEEZE...
ギュ...

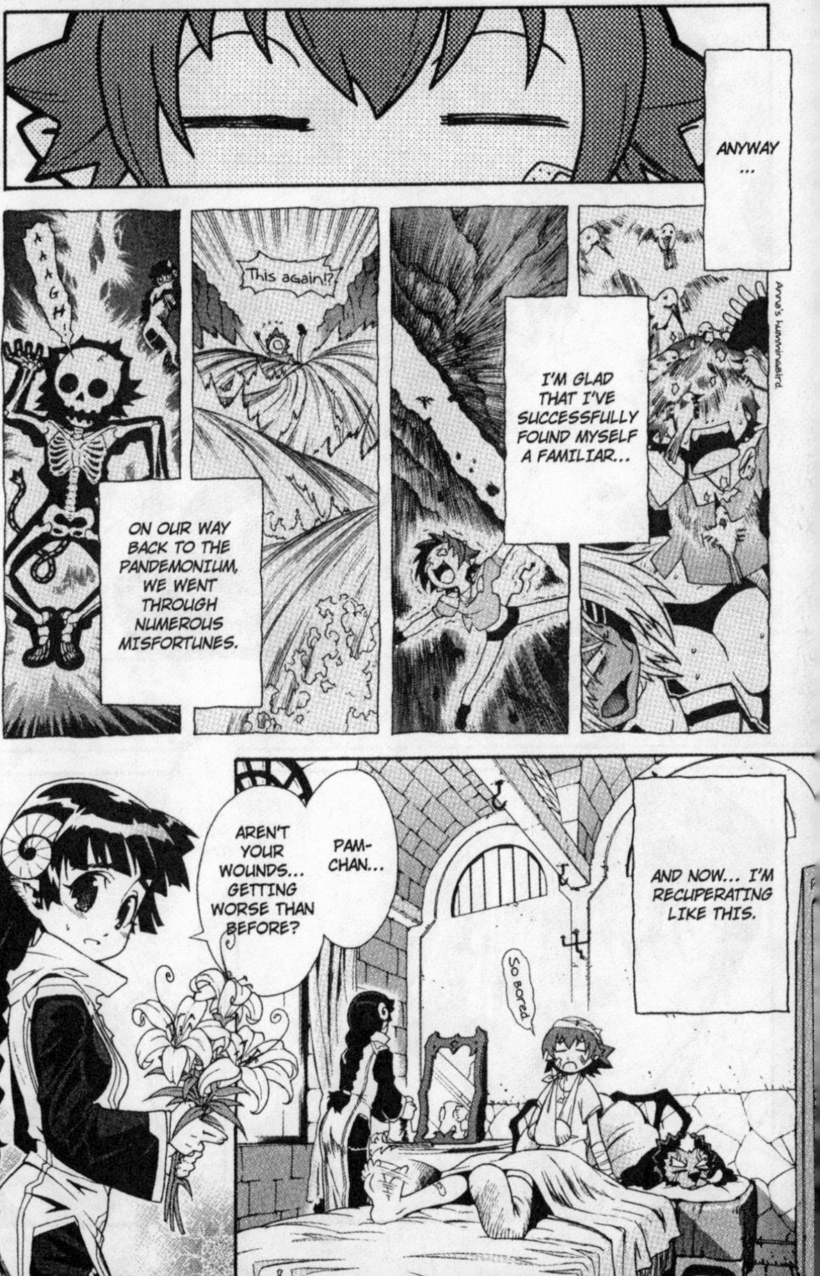

ANYWAY ...
I'M GLAD THAT I'VE SUCCESSFULLY FOUND MYSELF A FAMILIAR...
Anne's hummingbird.
This again!?
AAAGH!
ON OUR WAY BACK TO THE PANDEMONIUM, WE WENT THROUGH NUMEROUS MISFORTUNES.
AND NOW... I'M RECUPERATING LIKE THIS.
So bored.
PAM-CHAN...
AREN'T YOUR WOUNDS... GETTING WORSE THAN BEFORE?

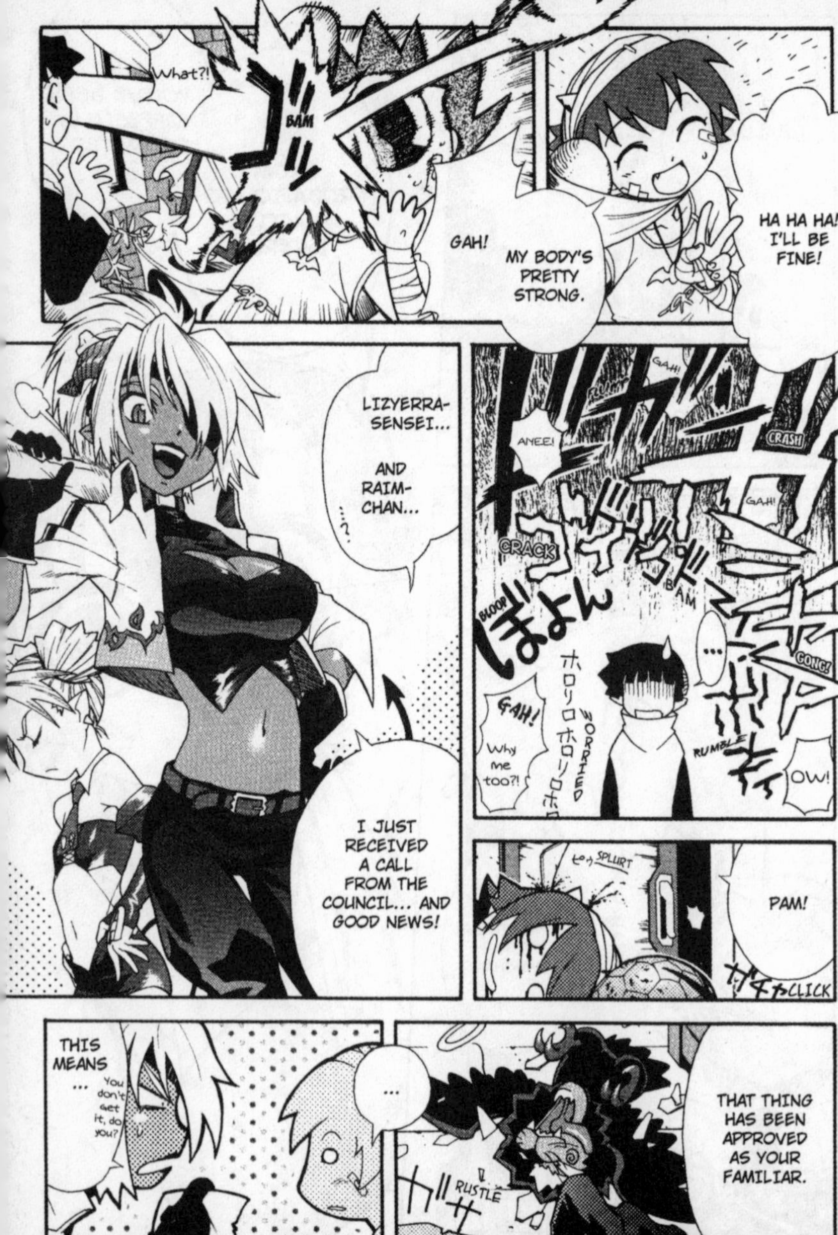
HA HA HA! I'LL BE FINE!
MY BODY'S PRETTY STRONG.
What?!
BAM
GAH!
GAH!
AIYEE!
CRASH
GAH!
CRACK
BAM
BLOOP
ぼよん
...
GONG!
GAH!
Why me too?!
WORRIED
ホロリロホロリロ
RUMBLE
OW!
SPLURT
PAM!
CLICK
LIZYERRA-SENSEI...
AND RAIM-CHAN...
...?
I JUST RECEIVED A CALL FROM THE COUNCIL... AND GOOD NEWS!
THAT THING HAS BEEN APPROVED AS YOUR FAMILIAR.
RUSTLE
Here's the approval form.
...
THIS MEANS ...
You don't get it, do you?

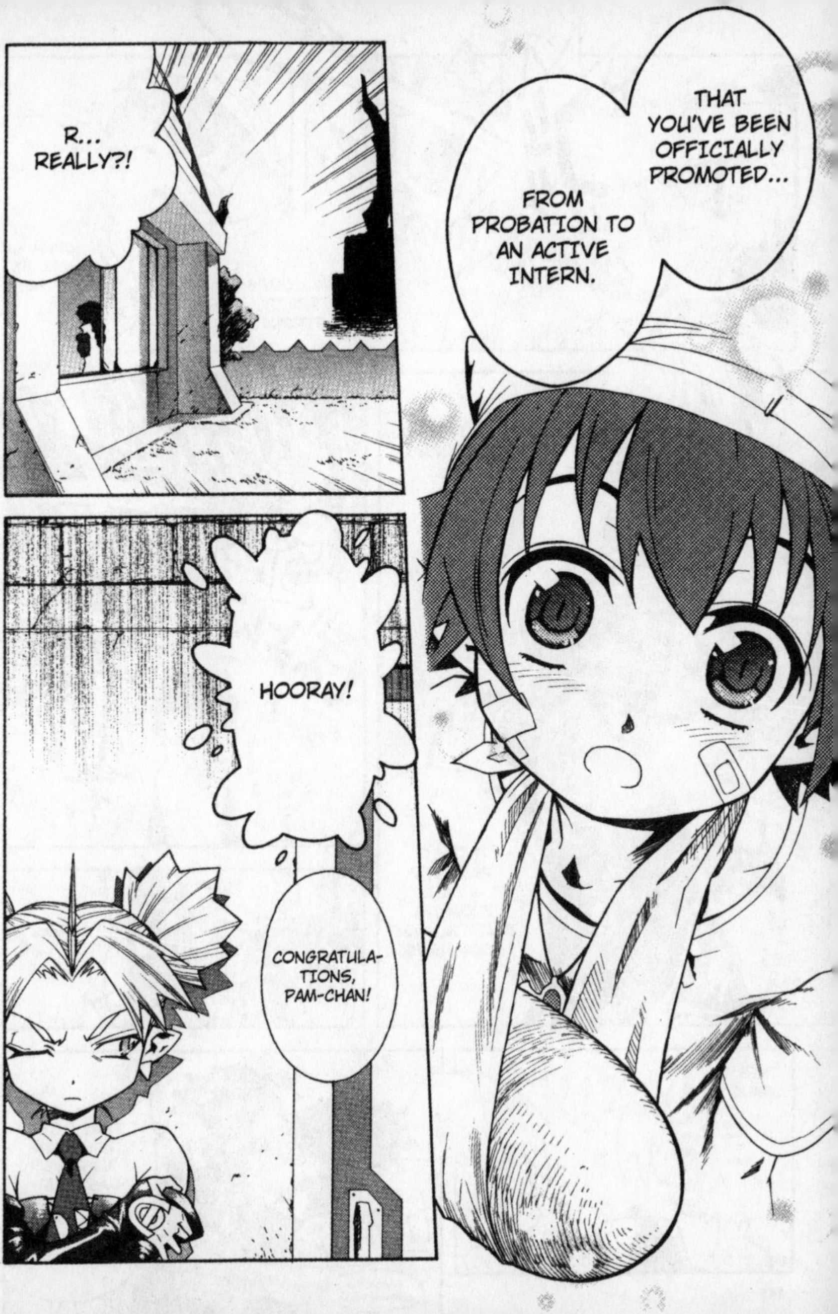
THAT YOU'VE BEEN OFFICIALLY PROMOTED...
FROM PROBATION TO AN ACTIVE INTERN.
R... REALLY?!
HOORAY!
CONGRATULA-TIONS, PAM-CHAN!

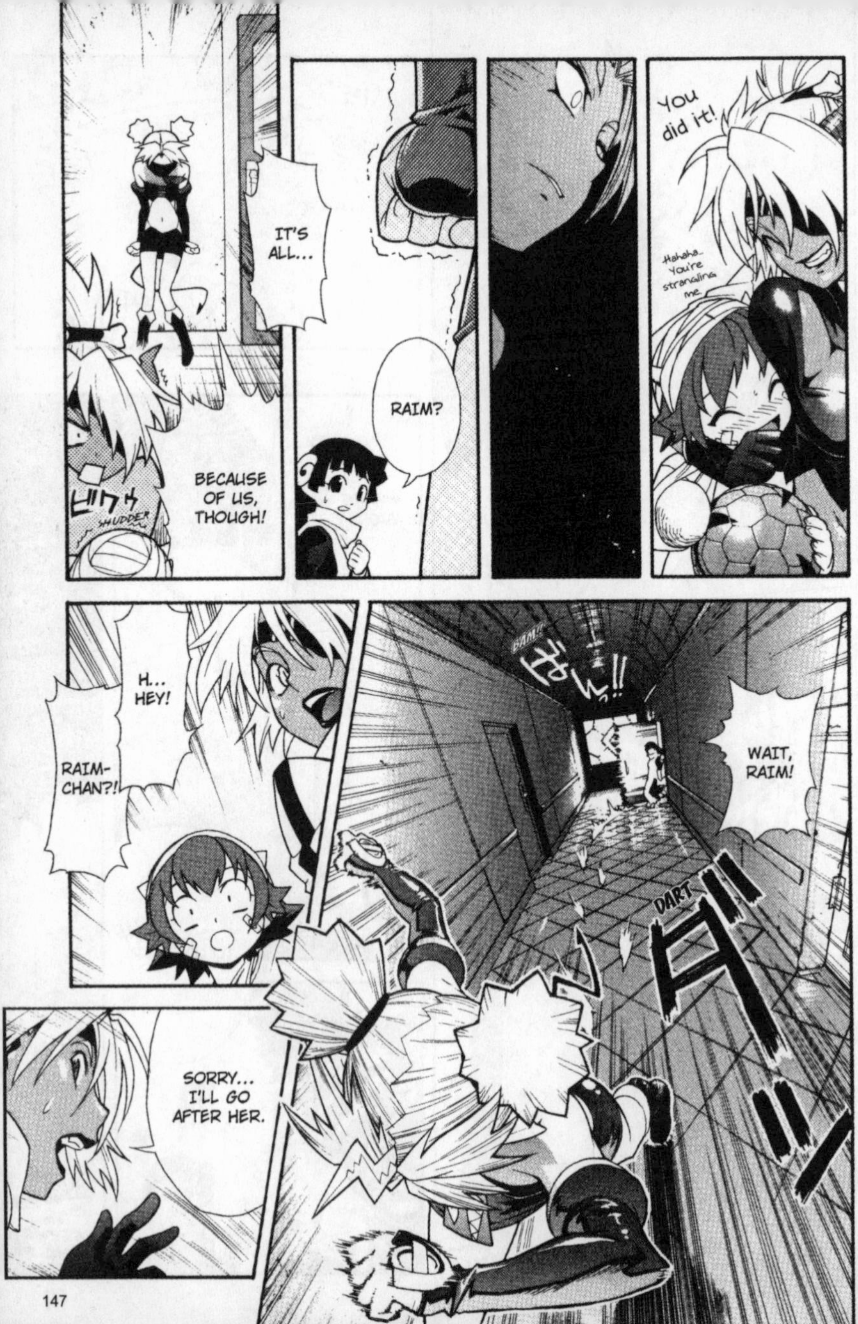

You did it!
Hahaha... You're strangling me
RAIM?
IT'S ALL...
BECAUSE OF US, THOUGH!
ビクッ SHUDDER
BAM!! ばん!!
WAIT, RAIM!
DART ダッ
H... HEY!
RAIM-CHAN?!
SORRY... I'LL GO AFTER HER.

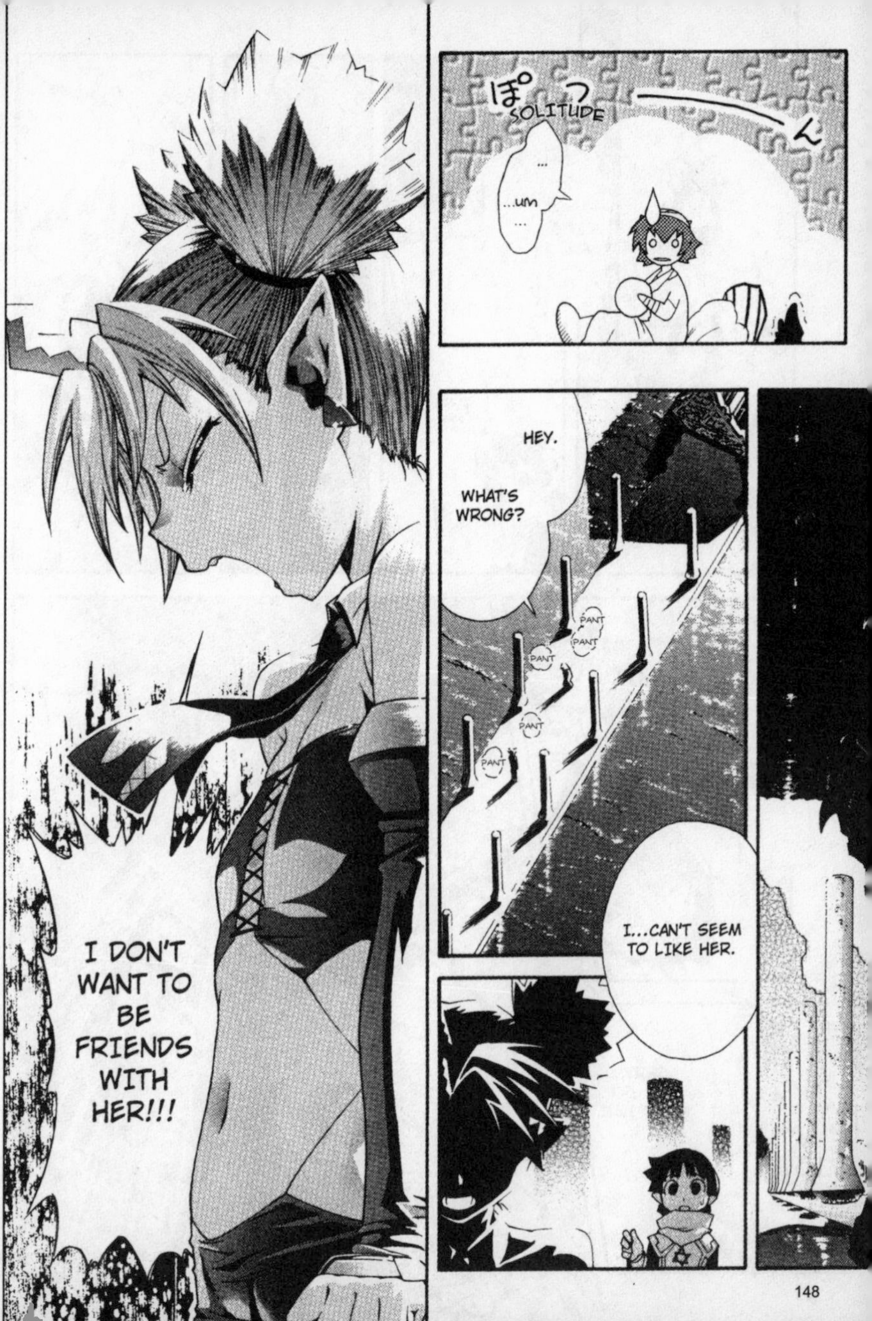
ぽつ
ん
SOLITUDE
...
...um
...
HEY.
WHAT'S WRONG?
PANT
PANT
PANT
PANT
PANT
I...CAN'T SEEM TO LIKE HER.
I DON'T WANT TO BE FRIENDS WITH HER!!!

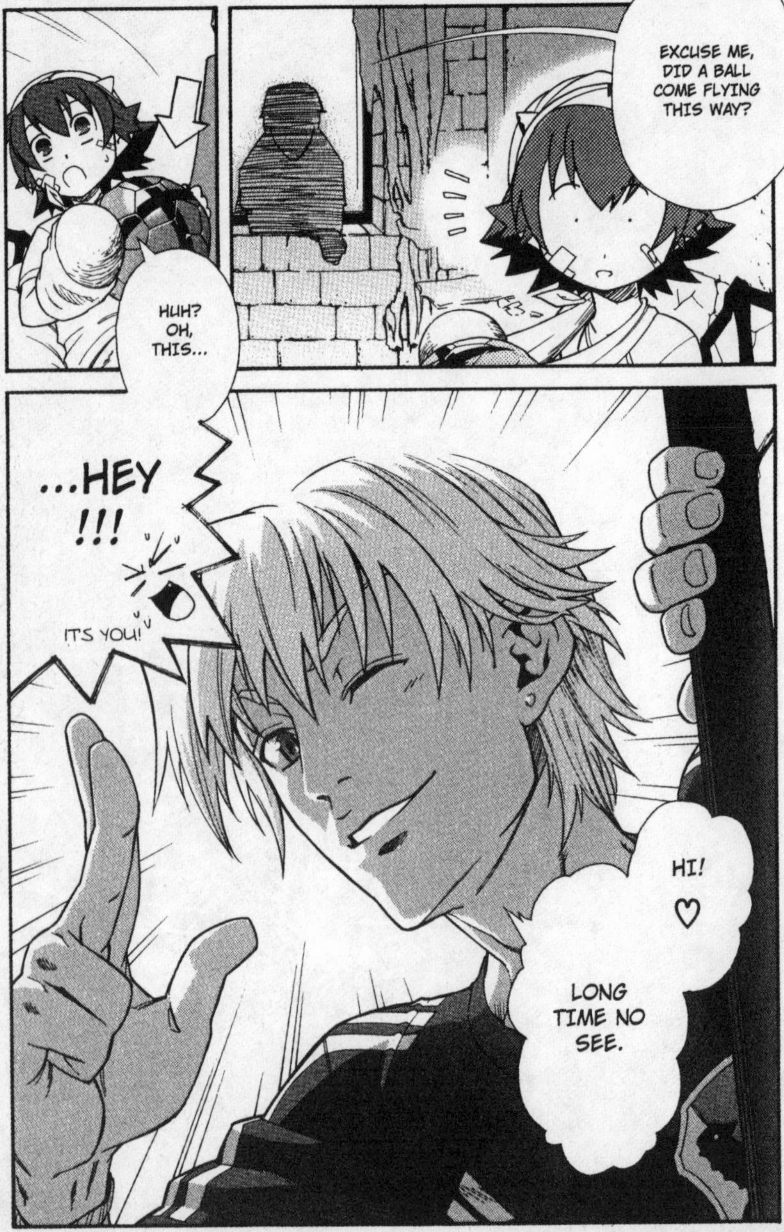
EXCUSE ME, DID A BALL COME FLYING THIS WAY?
HUH? OH, THIS...
...HEY !!!
IT'S YOU!
HI! ♡
LONG TIME NO SEE.

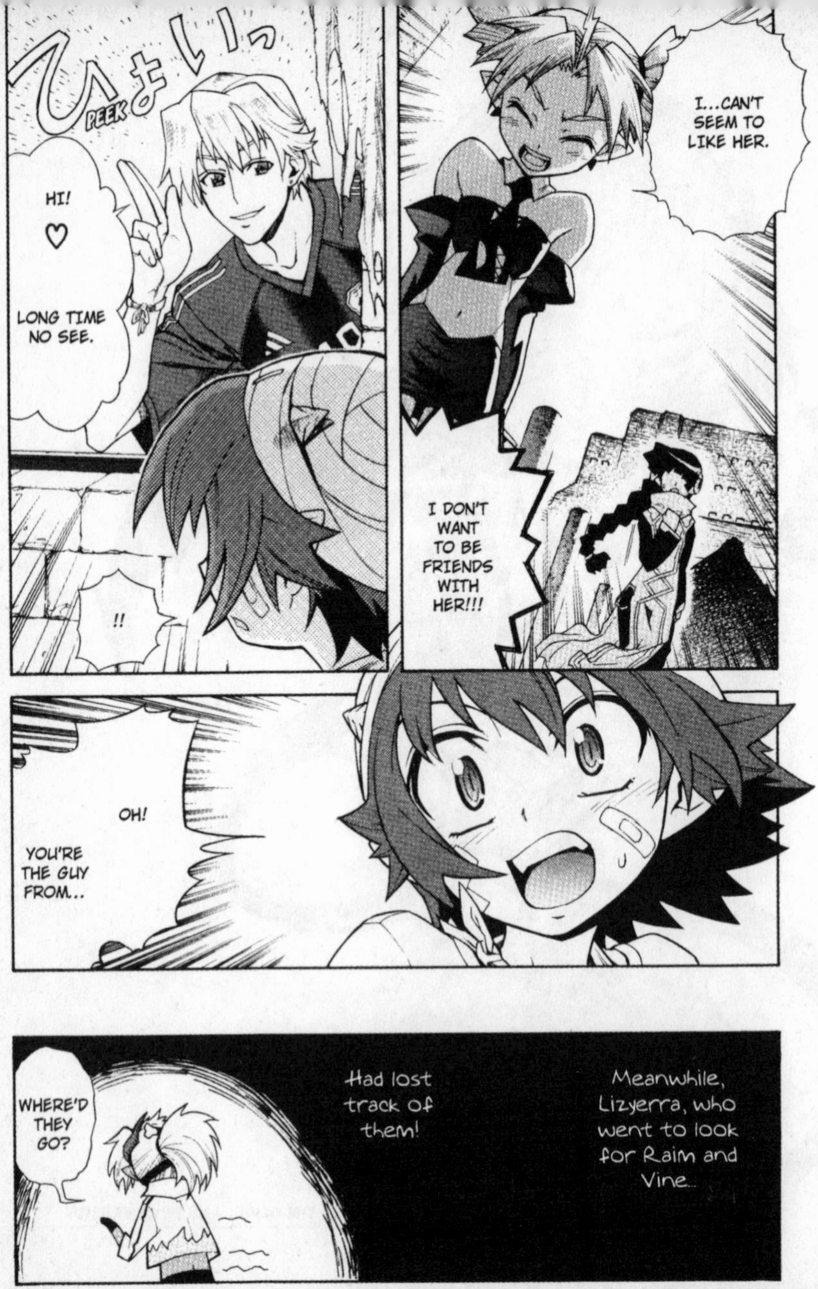
I...CAN'T SEEM TO LIKE HER.
I DON'T WANT TO BE FRIENDS WITH HER!!!
ひょいっ
PEEK
HI! ♡
LONG TIME NO SEE.
!!
OH!
YOU'RE THE GUY FROM...
Meanwhile, Lizyerra, who went to look for Raim and Vine...
Had lost track of them!
WHERE'D THEY GO?

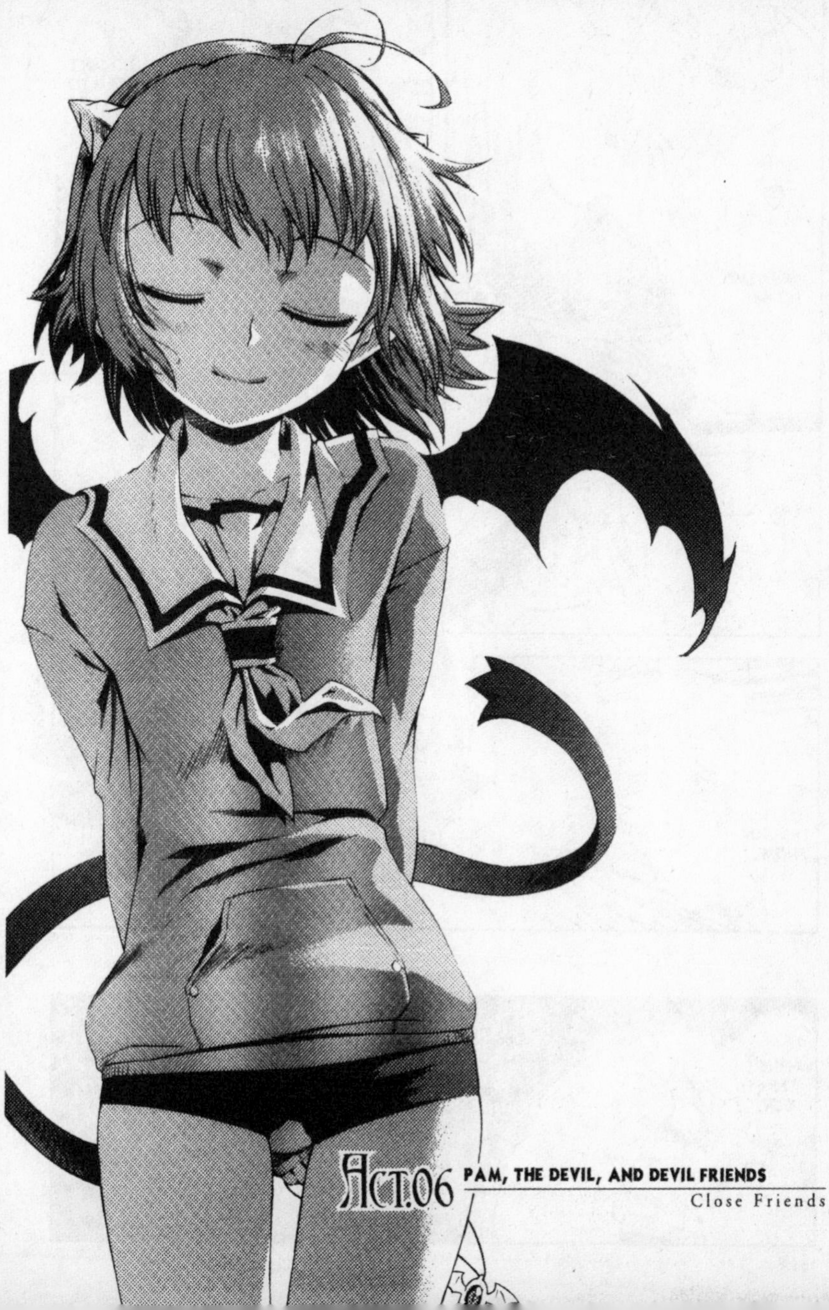
ACT.06
PAM, THE DEVIL, AND DEVIL FRIENDS
Close Friends

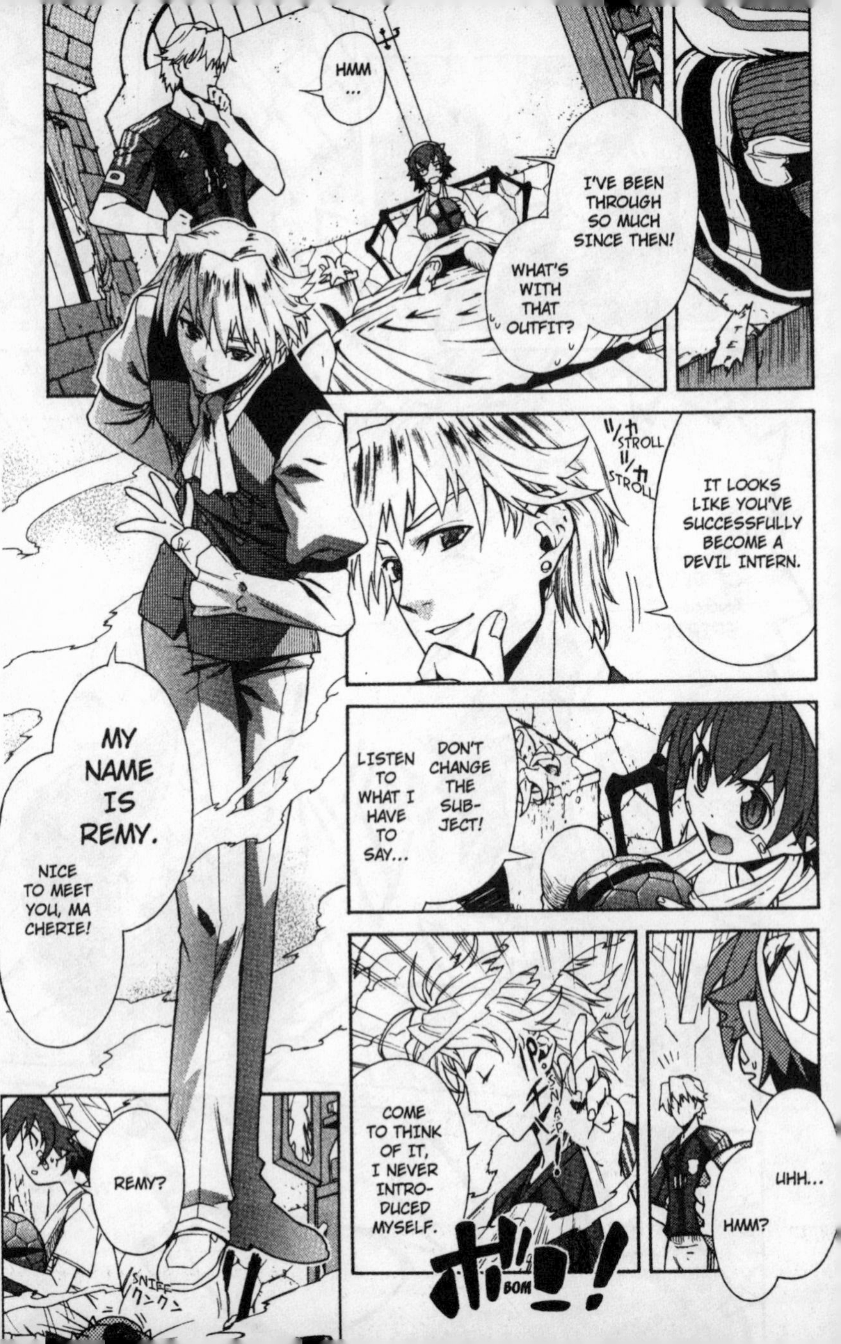
STEP
I'VE BEEN THROUGH SO MUCH SINCE THEN!
HMM ...
WHAT'S WITH THAT OUTFIT?
STROLL STROLL
IT LOOKS LIKE YOU'VE SUCCESSFULLY BECOME A DEVIL INTERN.
DON'T CHANGE THE SUB-JECT!
LISTEN TO WHAT I HAVE TO SAY...
UHH...
HMM?
SNAP
COME TO THINK OF IT, I NEVER INTRO-DUCED MYSELF.
BOM
MY NAME IS REMY.
NICE TO MEET YOU, MA CHERIE!
REMY?
SNIFF

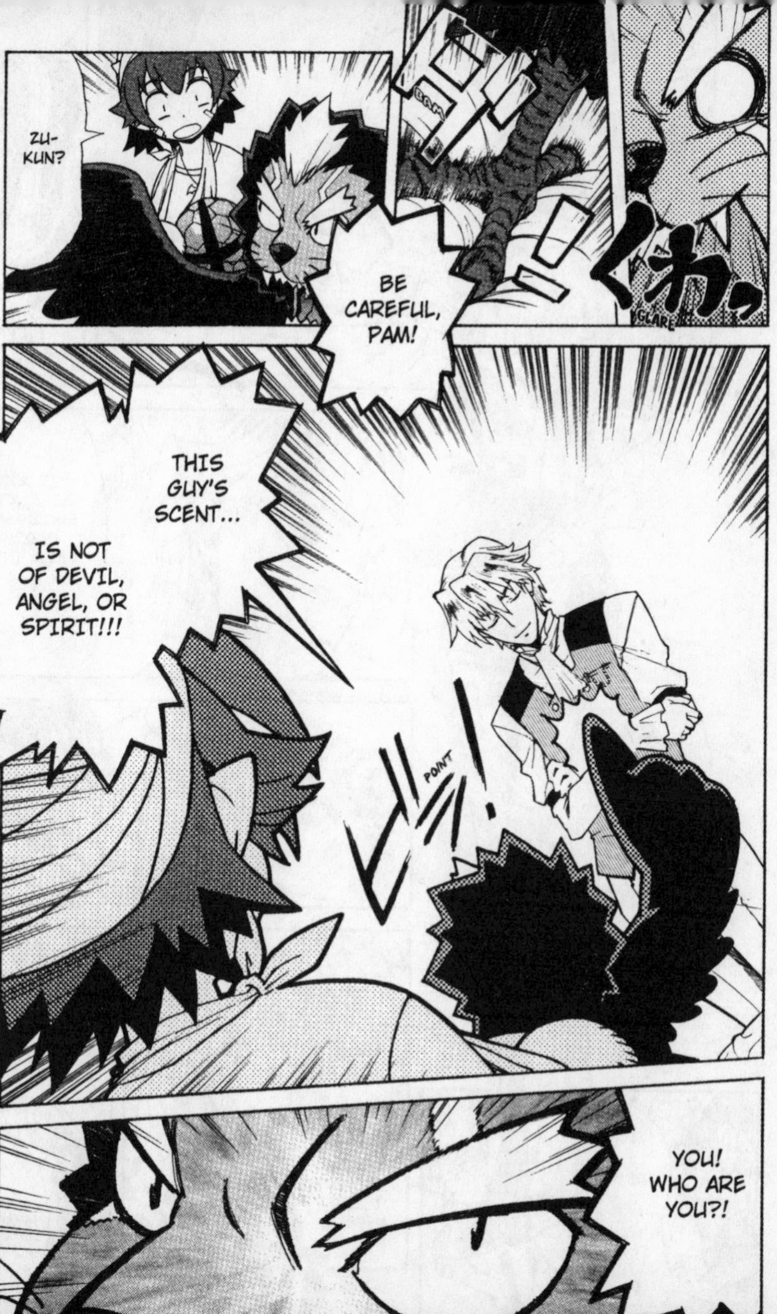
GLARE
BAM
ZU-KUN?
BE CAREFUL, PAM!
THIS GUY'S SCENT...
IS NOT OF DEVIL, ANGEL, OR SPIRIT!!!
POINT
YOU! WHO ARE YOU?!

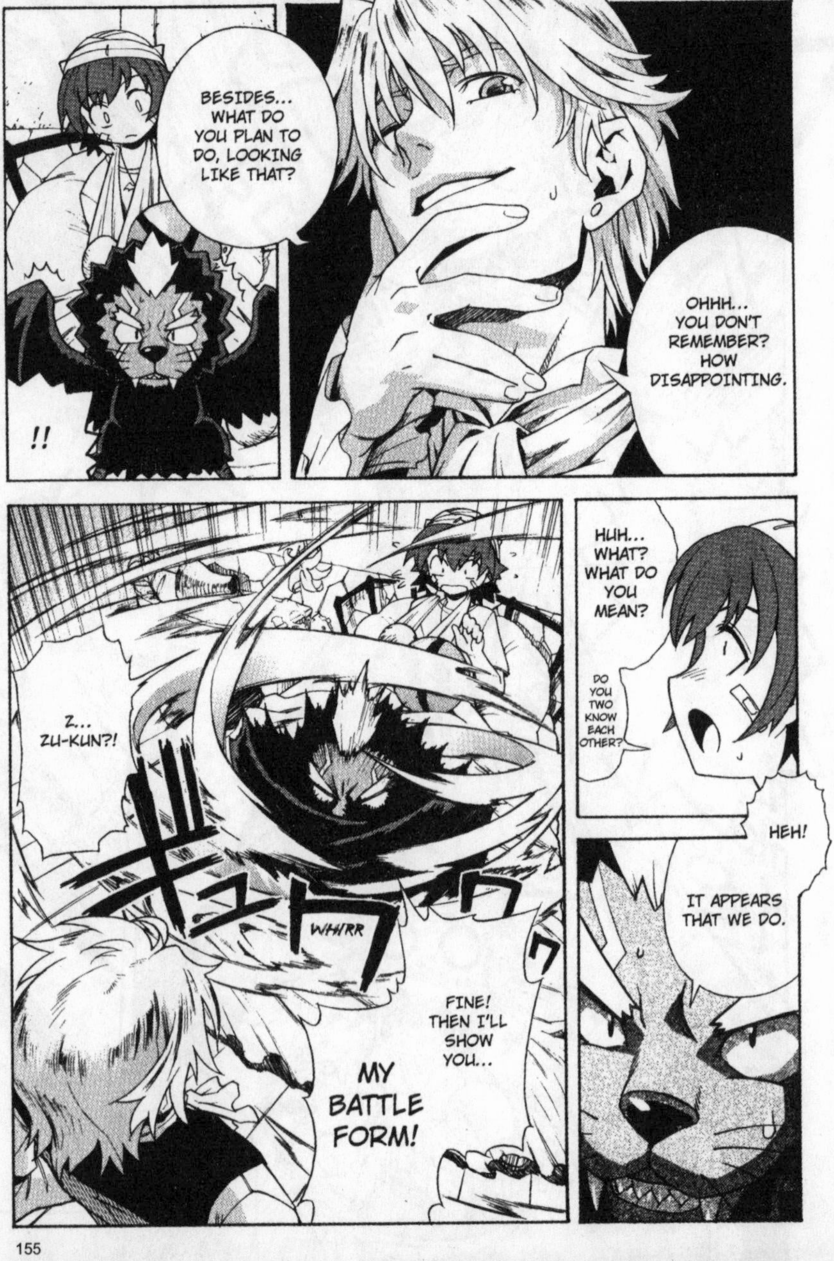
OHHH... YOU DON'T REMEMBER? HOW DISAPPOINTING.
BESIDES... WHAT DO YOU PLAN TO DO, LOOKING LIKE THAT?
!!
HUH... WHAT? WHAT DO YOU MEAN?
DO YOU TWO KNOW EACH OTHER?
HEH!
IT APPEARS THAT WE DO.
Z... ZU-KUN?!
WHIRR
FINE! THEN I'LL SHOW YOU...
MY BATTLE FORM!

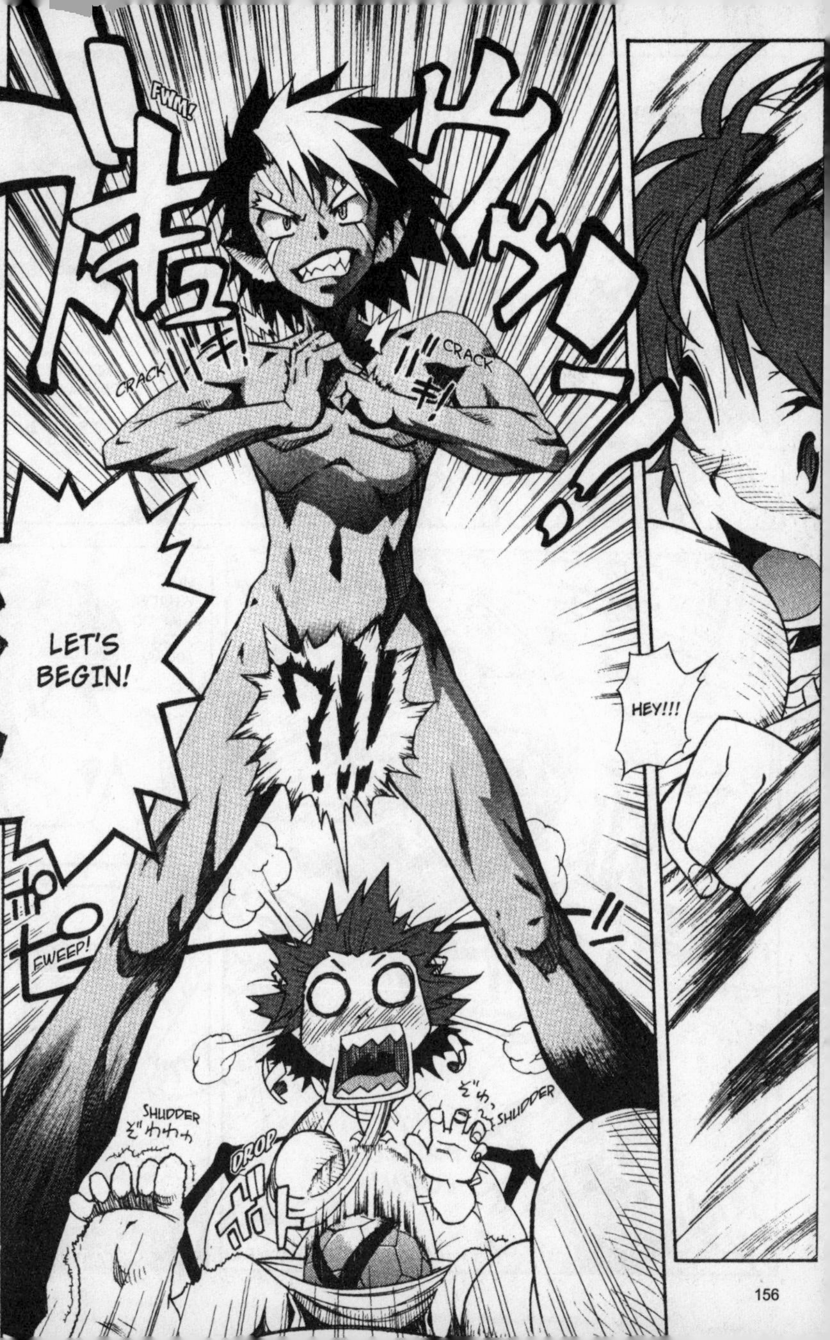
HEY!!!
FWM!
CRACK
CRACK
LET'S BEGIN!
?!!
FWEEP!
SHUDDER
SHUDDER
DROP

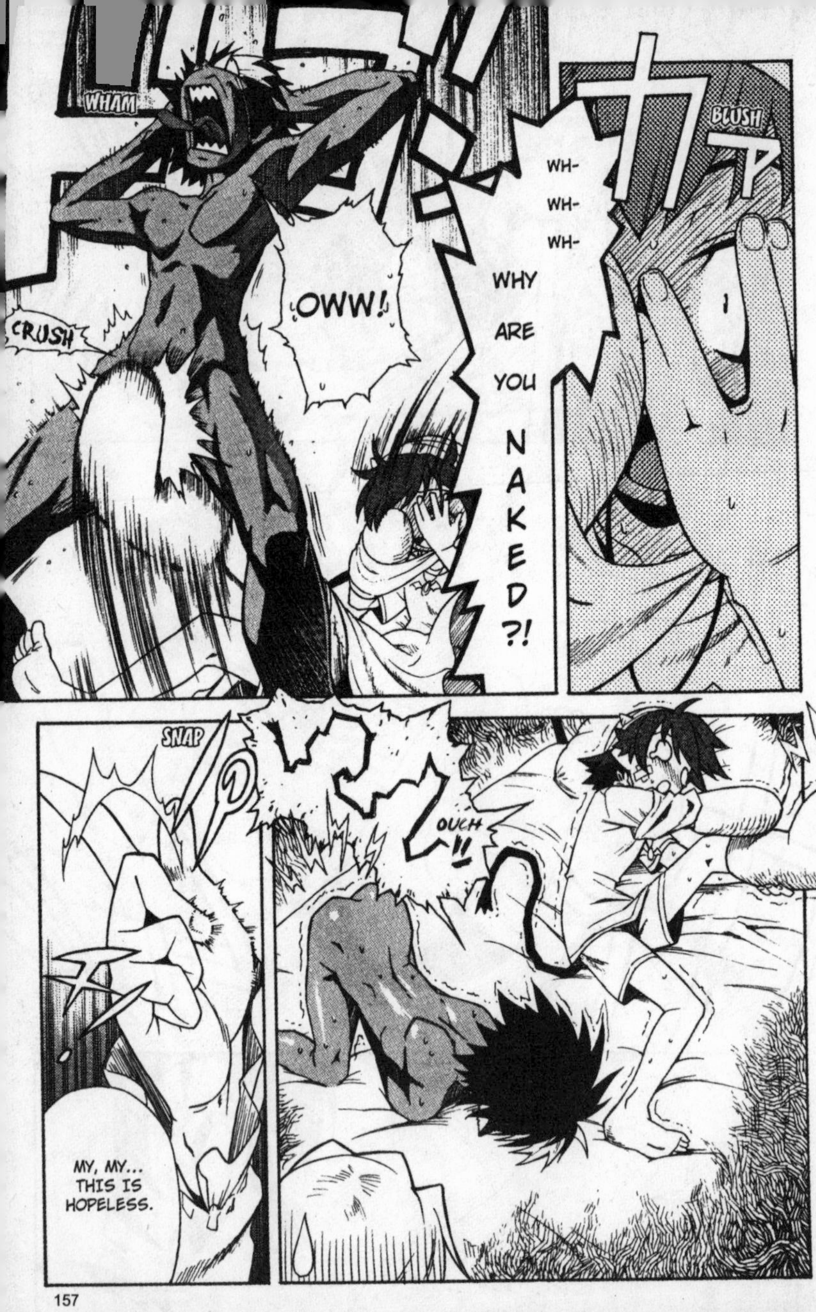
カァ
BLUSH
WH- WH- WH- WHY ARE YOU NAKED?!
WHAM
OWW!
CRUSH
OUCH!!
SNAP
MY, MY... THIS IS HOPELESS.

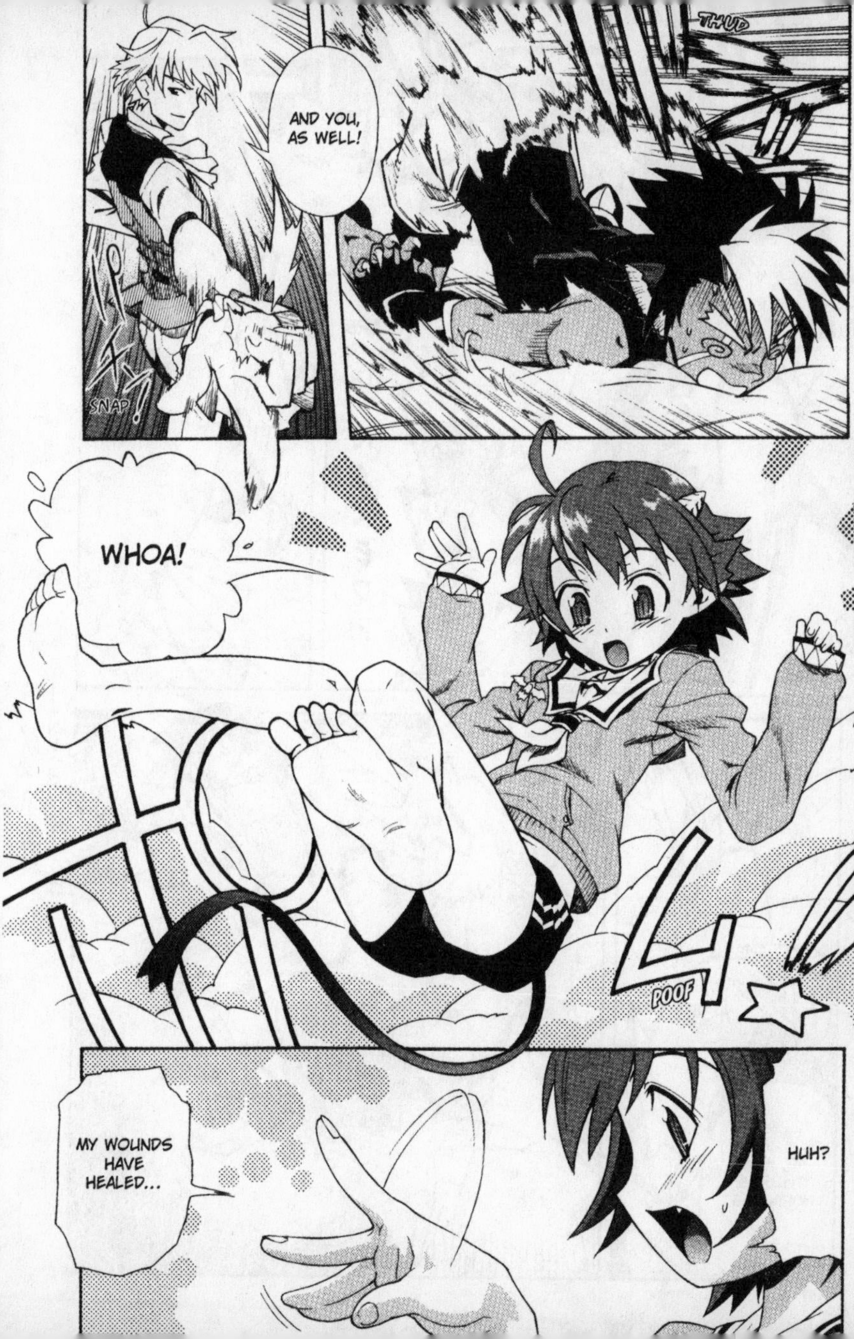
THUD
AND YOU, AS WELL!
SNAP
WHOA!
POOF
HUH?
MY WOUNDS HAVE HEALED...

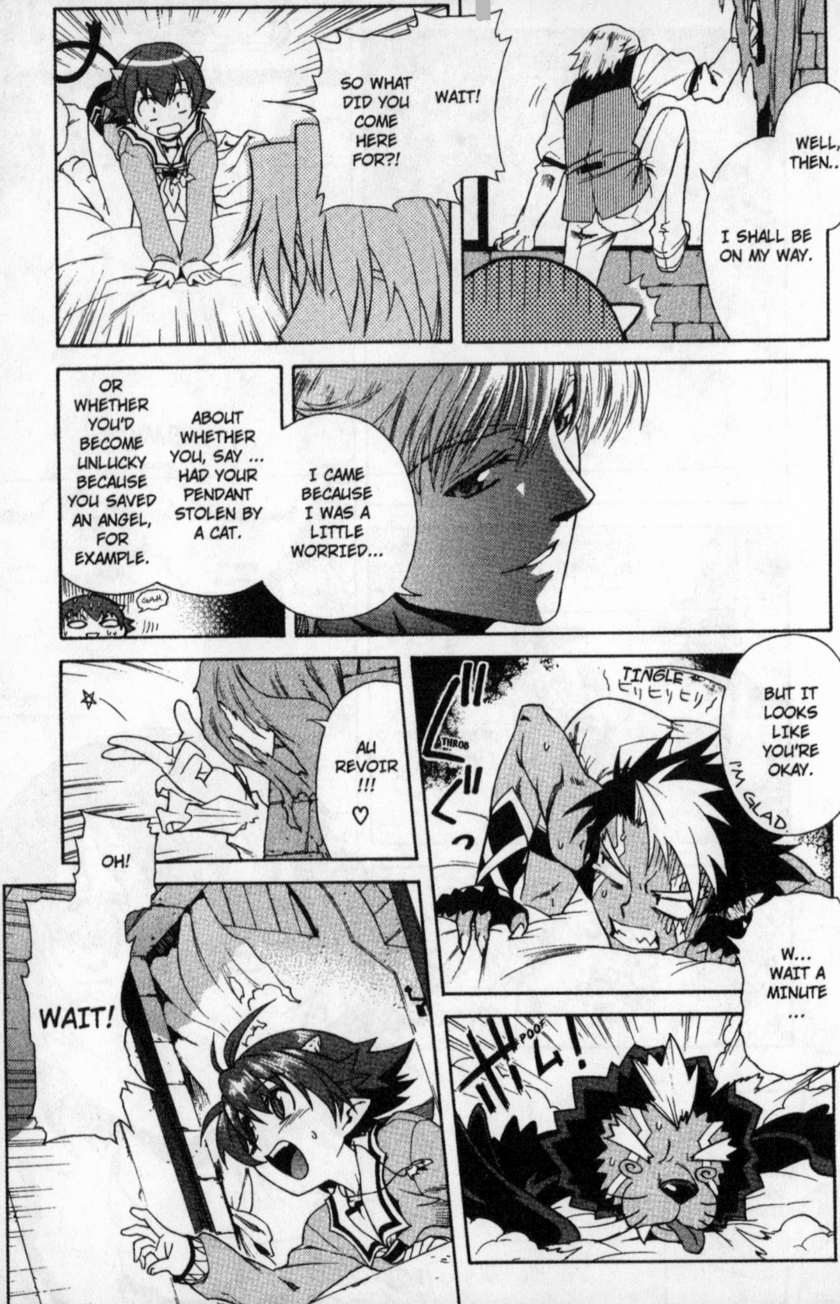
WELL, THEN...
I SHALL BE ON MY WAY.
WAIT!
SO WHAT DID YOU COME HERE FOR?!
I CAME BECAUSE I WAS A LITTLE WORRIED...
ABOUT WHETHER YOU, SAY ... HAD YOUR PENDANT STOLEN BY A CAT.
OR WHETHER YOU'D BECOME UNLUCKY BECAUSE YOU SAVED AN ANGEL, FOR EXAMPLE.
GAH.
BUT IT LOOKS LIKE YOU'RE OKAY.
I'M GLAD.
TINGLE
THROB
AU REVOIR !!! ♡
OH!
W... WAIT A MINUTE ...
POOF
WAIT!

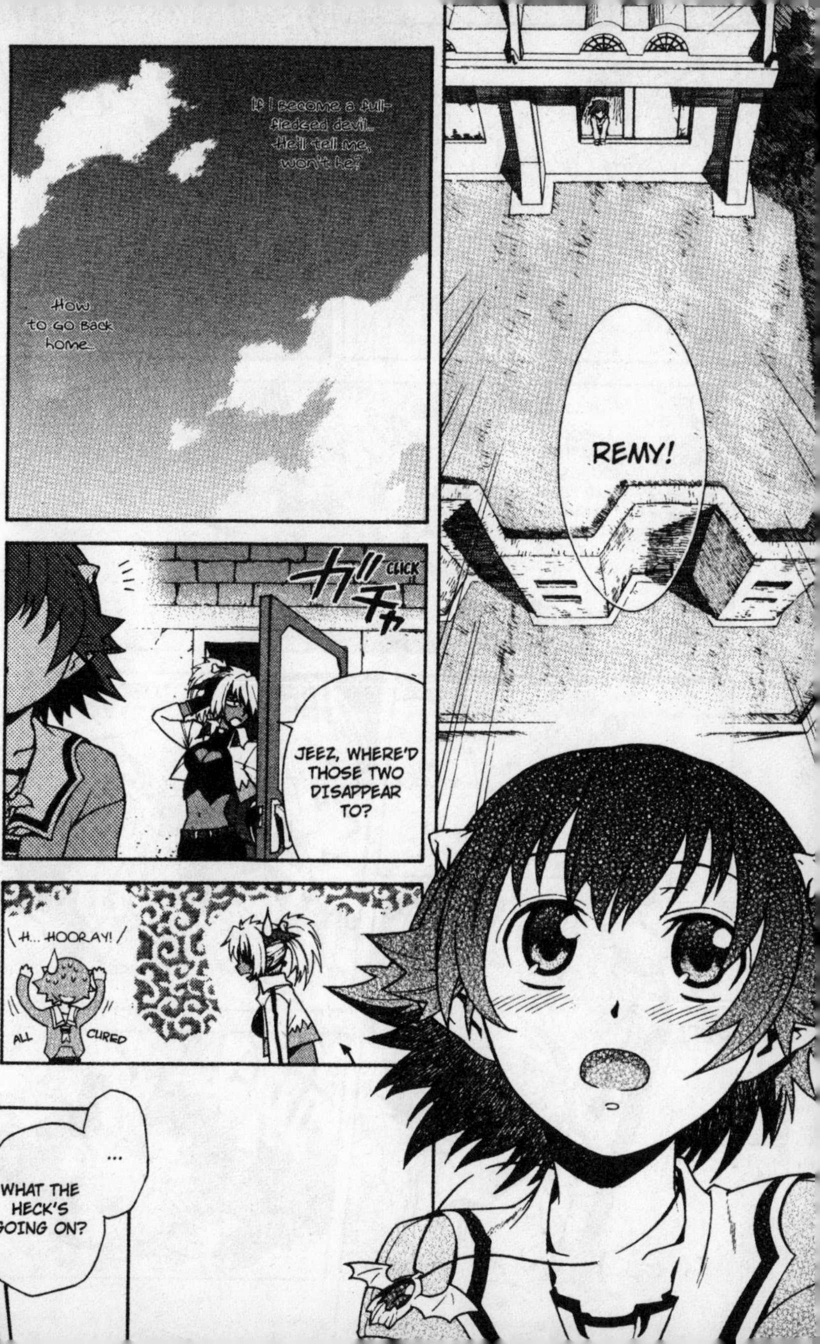
REMY!
If I become a full-fledged devil...
He'll tell me, won't he?
How to go back home...
CLICK
JEEZ, WHERE'D THOSE TWO DISAPPEAR TO?
H... HOORAY!
ALL CURED
...
WHAT THE HECK'S GOING ON?

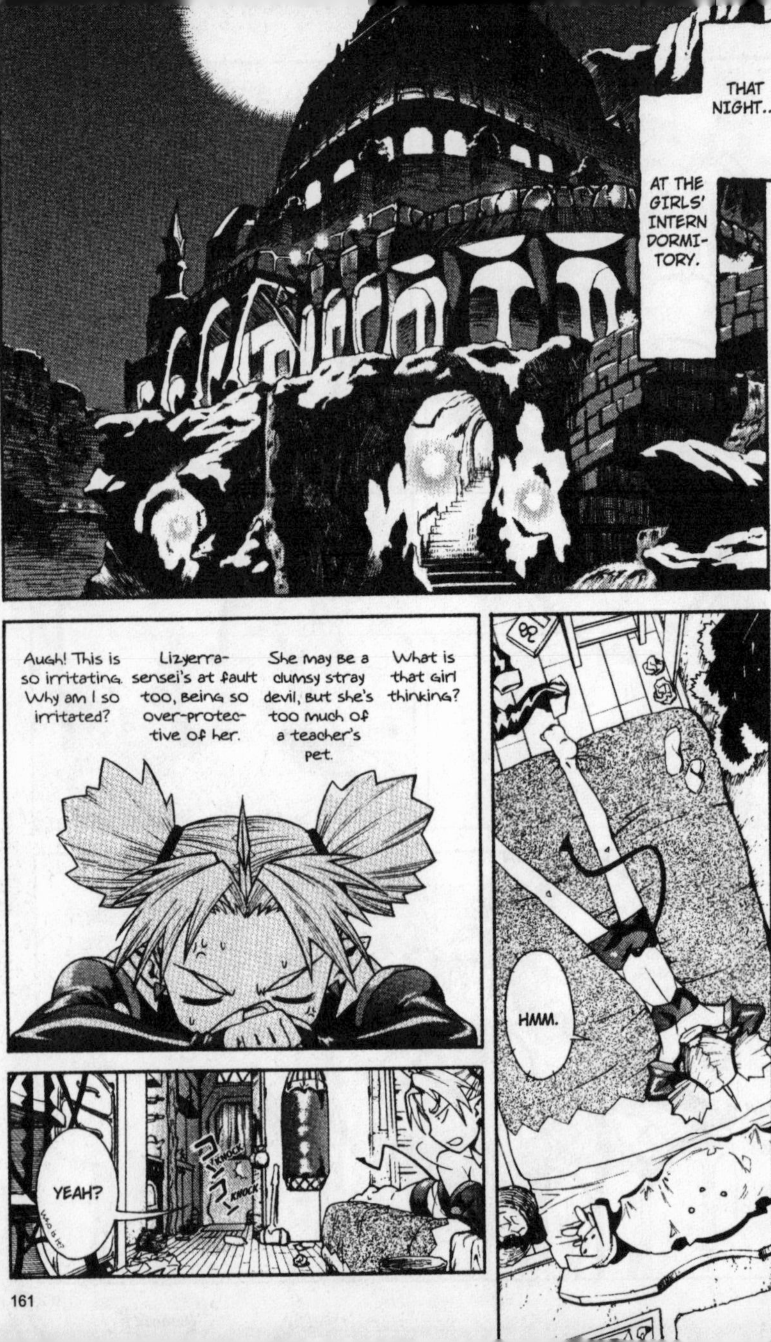
THAT NIGHT...
AT THE GIRLS' INTERN DORMITORY.
HMM.
What is that girl thinking?
She may be a clumsy stray devil, but she's too much of a teacher's pet.
Lizyerra-sensei's at fault too, being so over-protective of her.
Augh! This is so irritating. Why am I so irritated?
KNOCK
KNOCK
YEAH?

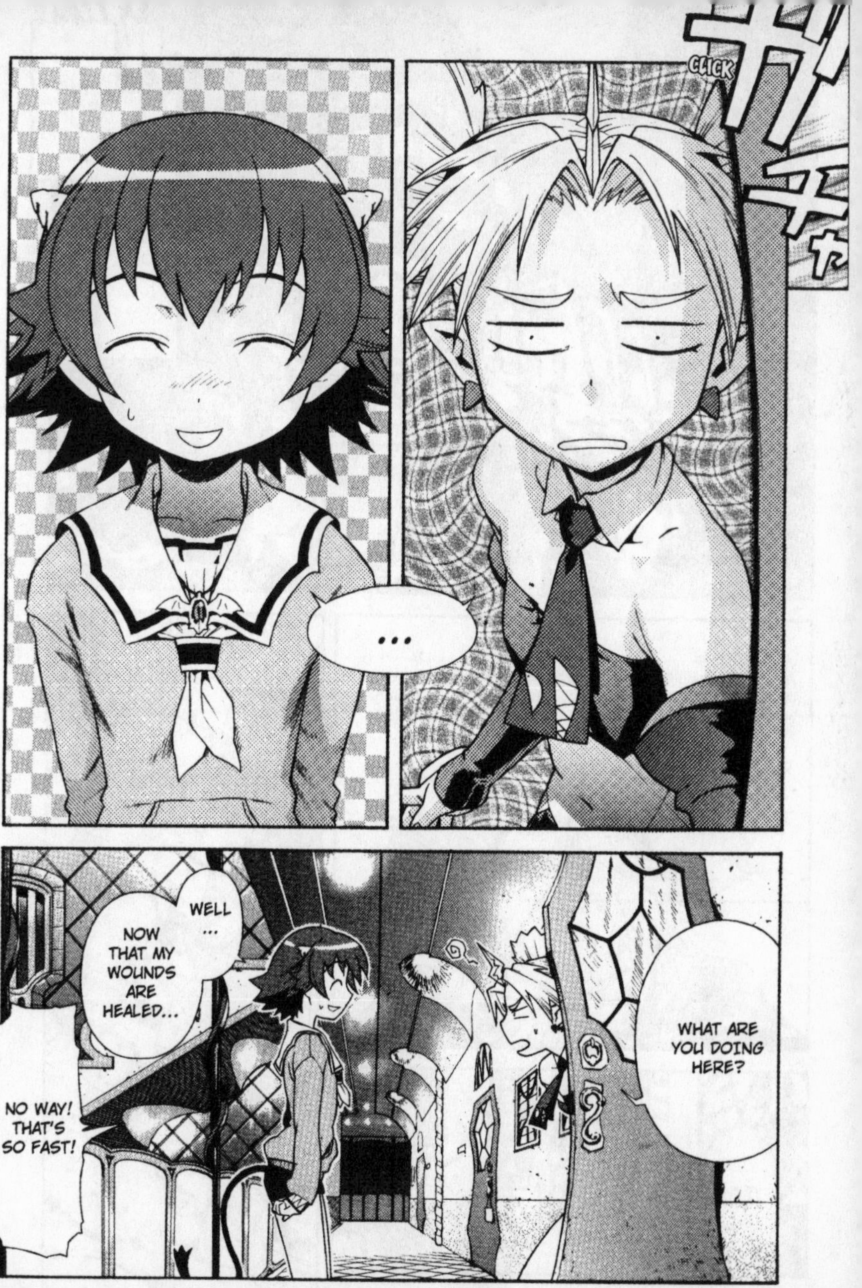
CLICK
ガチャ
...
WHAT ARE YOU DOING HERE?
WELL ...
NOW THAT MY WOUNDS ARE HEALED...
NO WAY! THAT'S SO FAST!

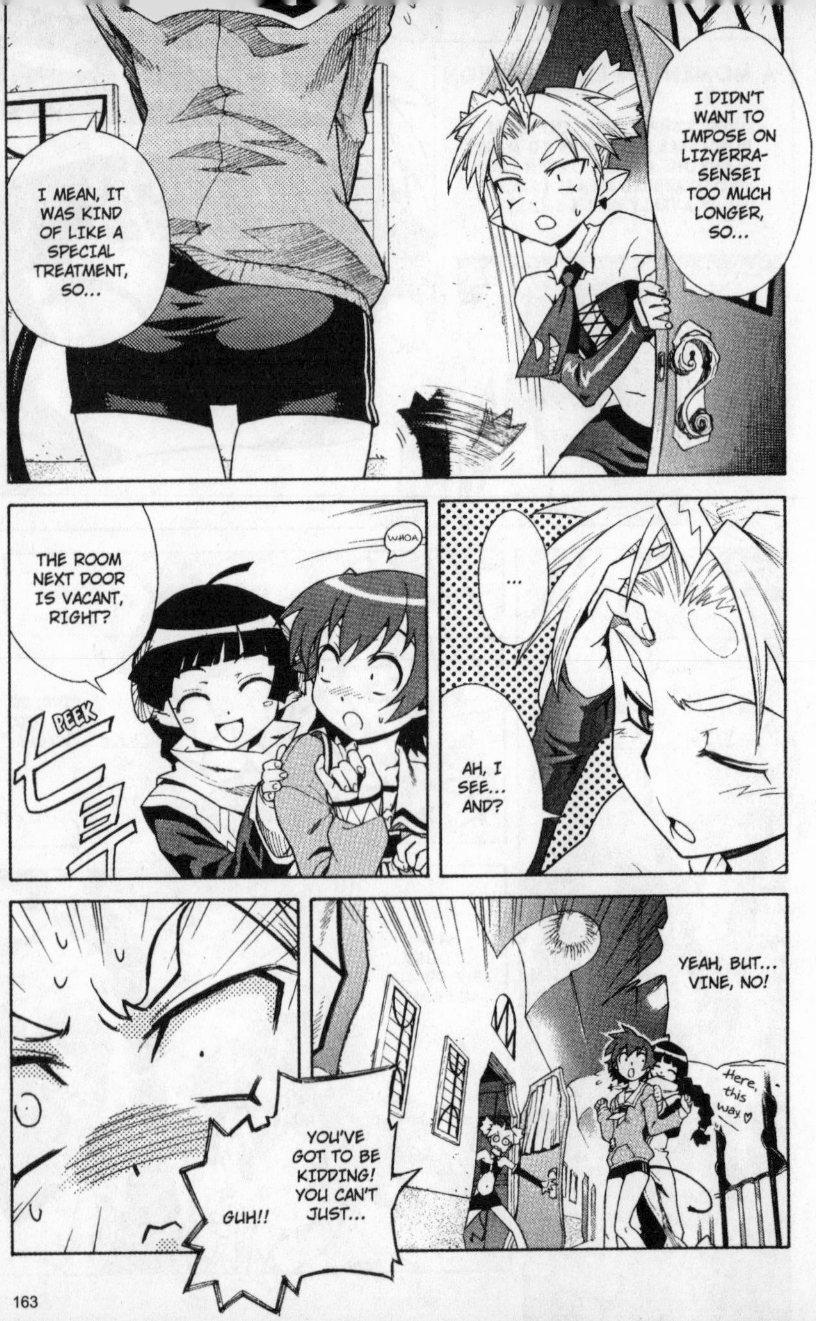
I DIDN'T WANT TO IMPOSE ON LIZYERRA-SENSEI TOO MUCH LONGER, SO...
I MEAN, IT WAS KIND OF LIKE A SPECIAL TREATMENT, SO...
...
AH, I SEE... AND?
WHOA
THE ROOM NEXT DOOR IS VACANT, RIGHT?
PEEK
YEAH, BUT... VINE, NO!
Here, this way. ♥
YOU'VE GOT TO BE KIDDING! YOU CAN'T JUST...
GUH!!

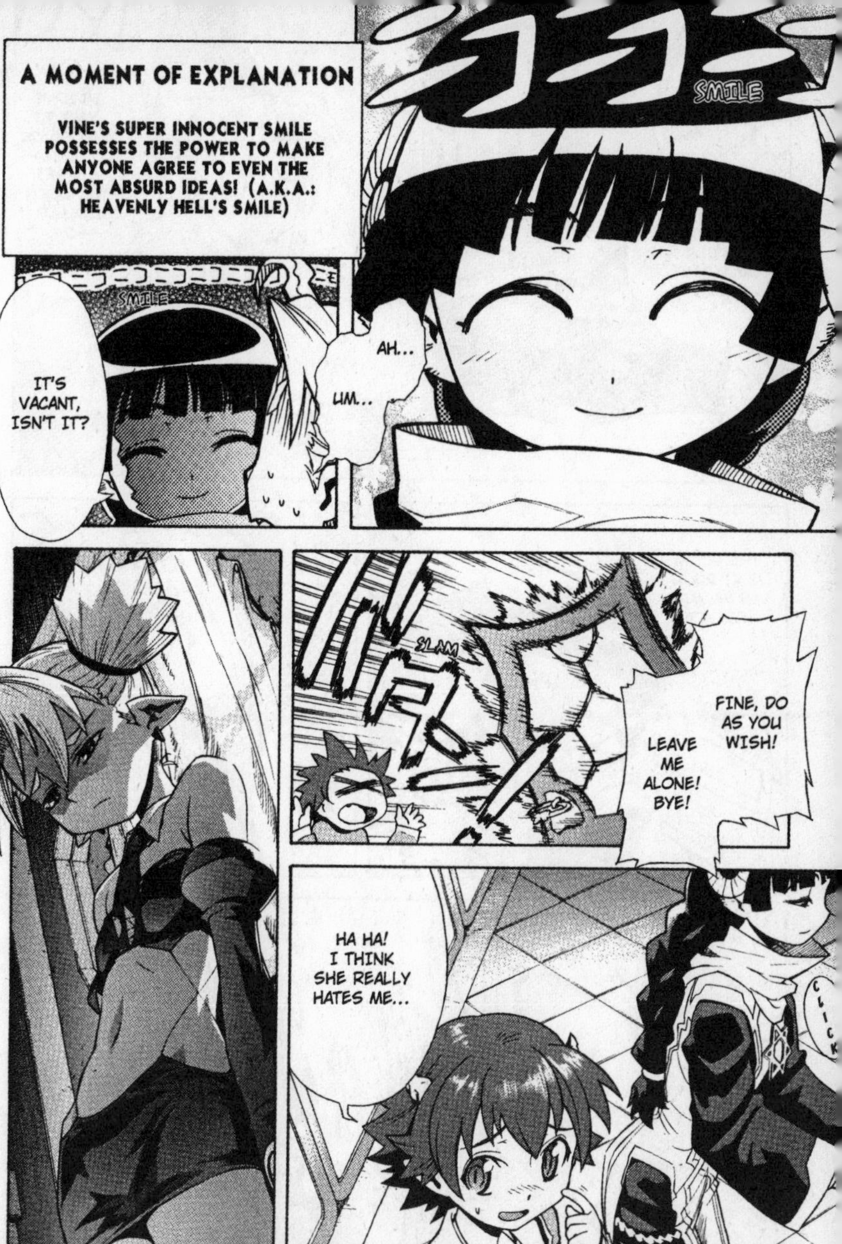
SMILE
A MOMENT OF EXPLANATION
VINE'S SUPER INNOCENT SMILE POSSESSES THE POWER TO MAKE ANYONE AGREE TO EVEN THE MOST ABSURD IDEAS! (A.K.A.: HEAVENLY HELL'S SMILE)
SMILE
AH...
UM...
IT'S VACANT, ISN'T IT?
FINE, DO AS YOU WISH!
LEAVE ME ALONE! BYE!
SLAM
CLICK
HA HA! I THINK SHE REALLY HATES ME...

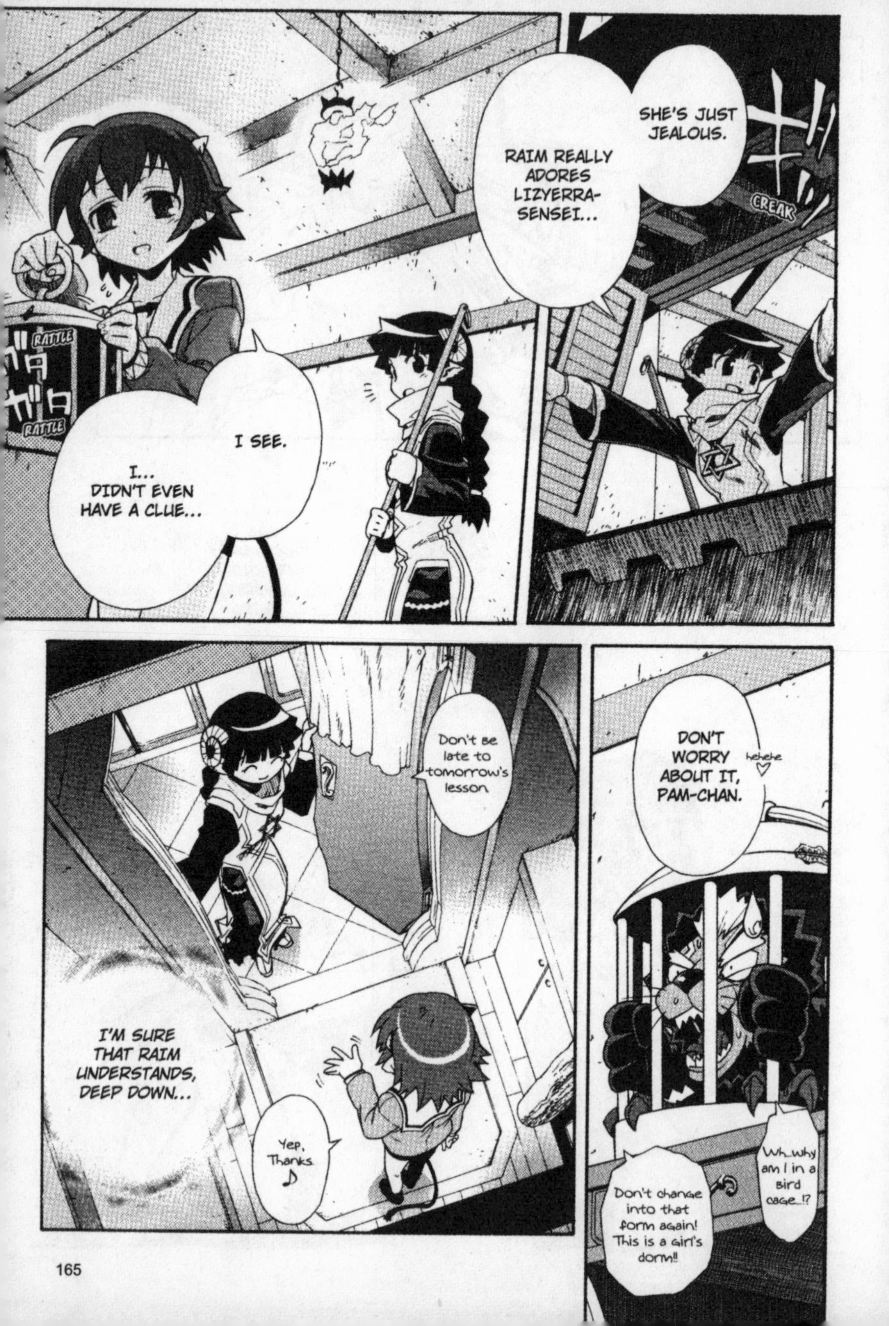
SHE'S JUST JEALOUS.
RAIM REALLY ADORES LIZYERRA-SENSEI...
CREAK
RATTLE
RATTLE
I SEE.
I... DIDN'T EVEN HAVE A CLUE...
DON'T WORRY ABOUT IT, PAM-CHAN.
hehehe ♡
Wh..why am I in a bird cage..!?
Don't change into that form again! This is a girl's dorm!!
Don't be late to tomorrow's lesson.
I'M SURE THAT RAIM UNDERSTANDS, DEEP DOWN...
Yep, Thanks. ♪

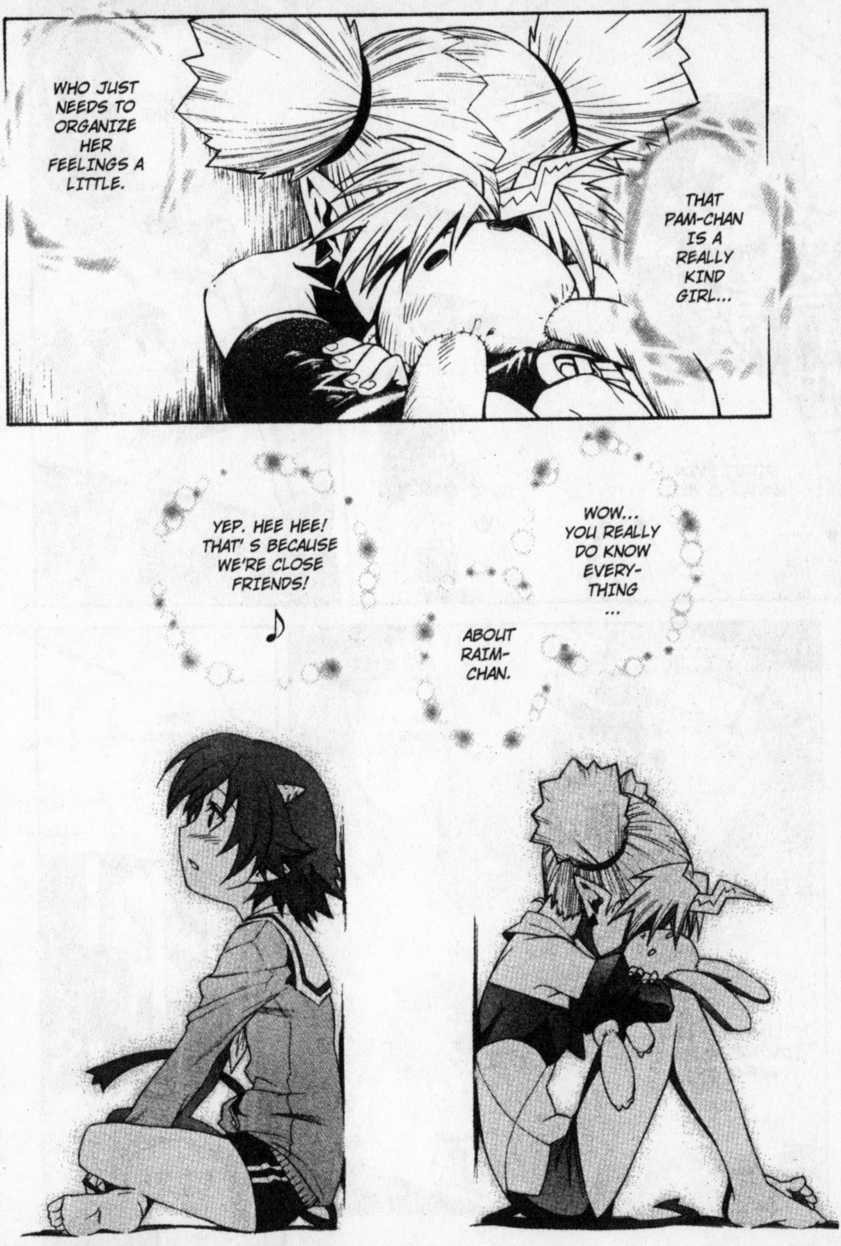
THAT PAM-CHAN IS A REALLY KIND GIRL...
WHO JUST NEEDS TO ORGANIZE HER FEELINGS A LITTLE.
WOW... YOU REALLY DO KNOW EVERYTHING ...
ABOUT RAIM-CHAN.
YEP. HEE HEE! THAT' S BECAUSE WE'RE CLOSE FRIENDS!
♪

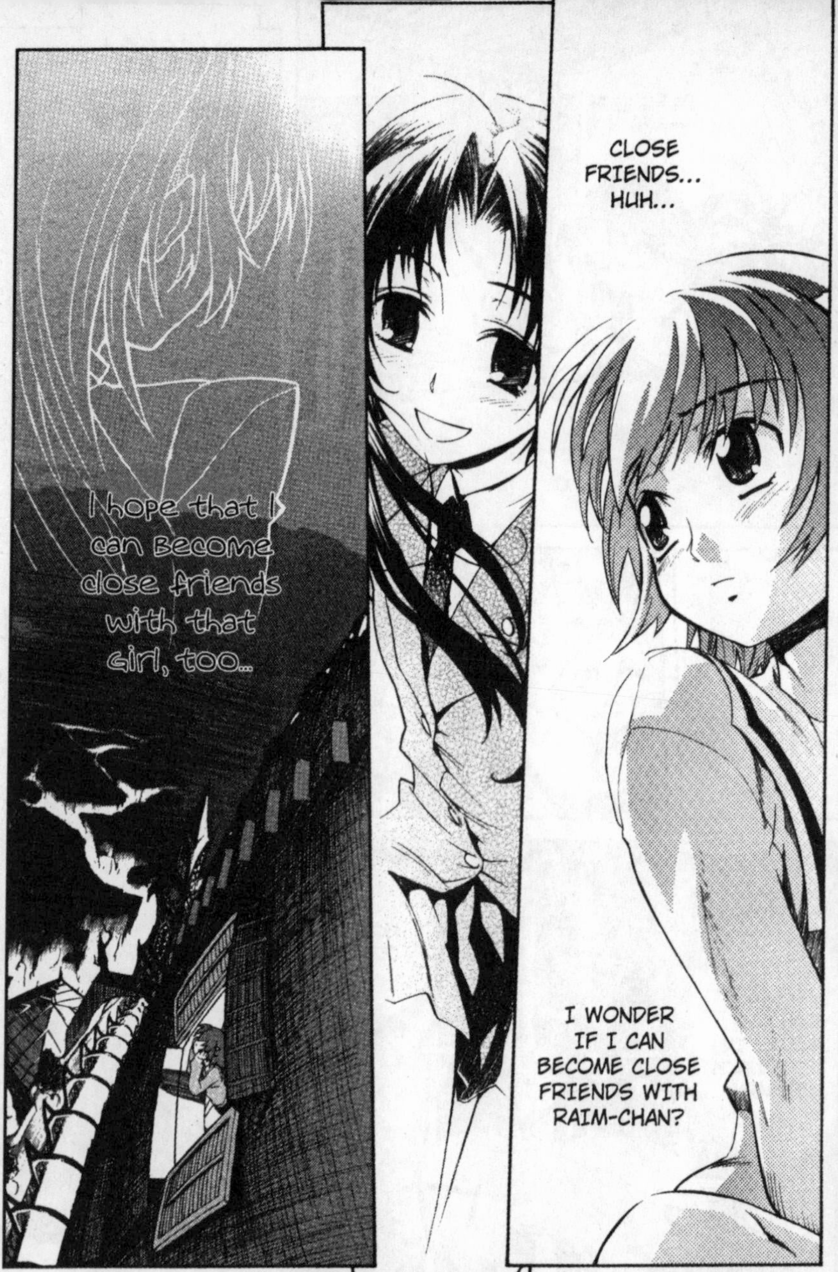
CLOSE FRIENDS... HUH...
I WONDER IF I CAN BECOME CLOSE FRIENDS WITH RAIM-CHAN?
I hope that I can become close friends with that girl, too...

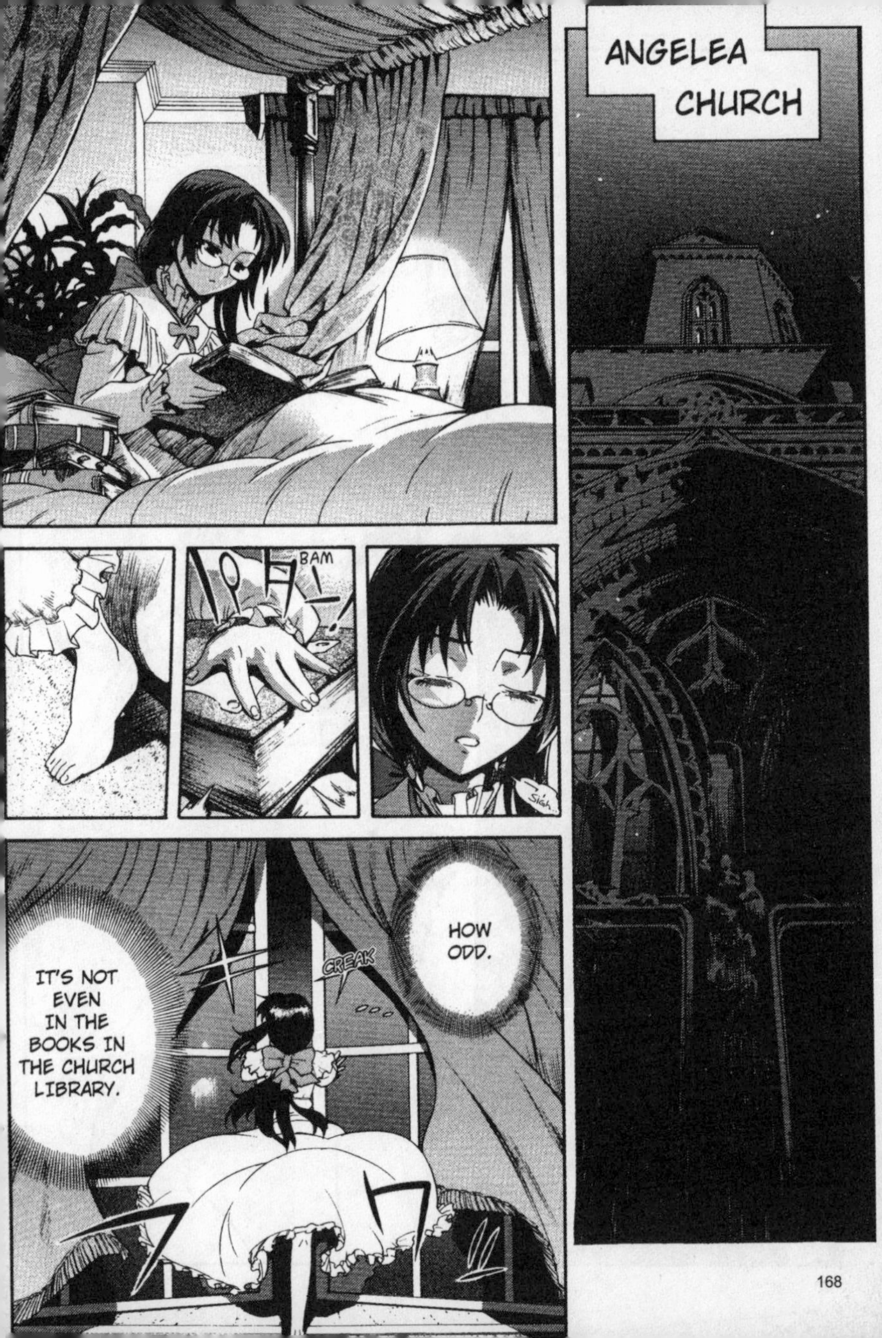
ANGELEA CHURCH
SIGH...
BAM
HOW ODD.
CREAK
IT'S NOT EVEN IN THE BOOKS IN THE CHURCH LIBRARY.

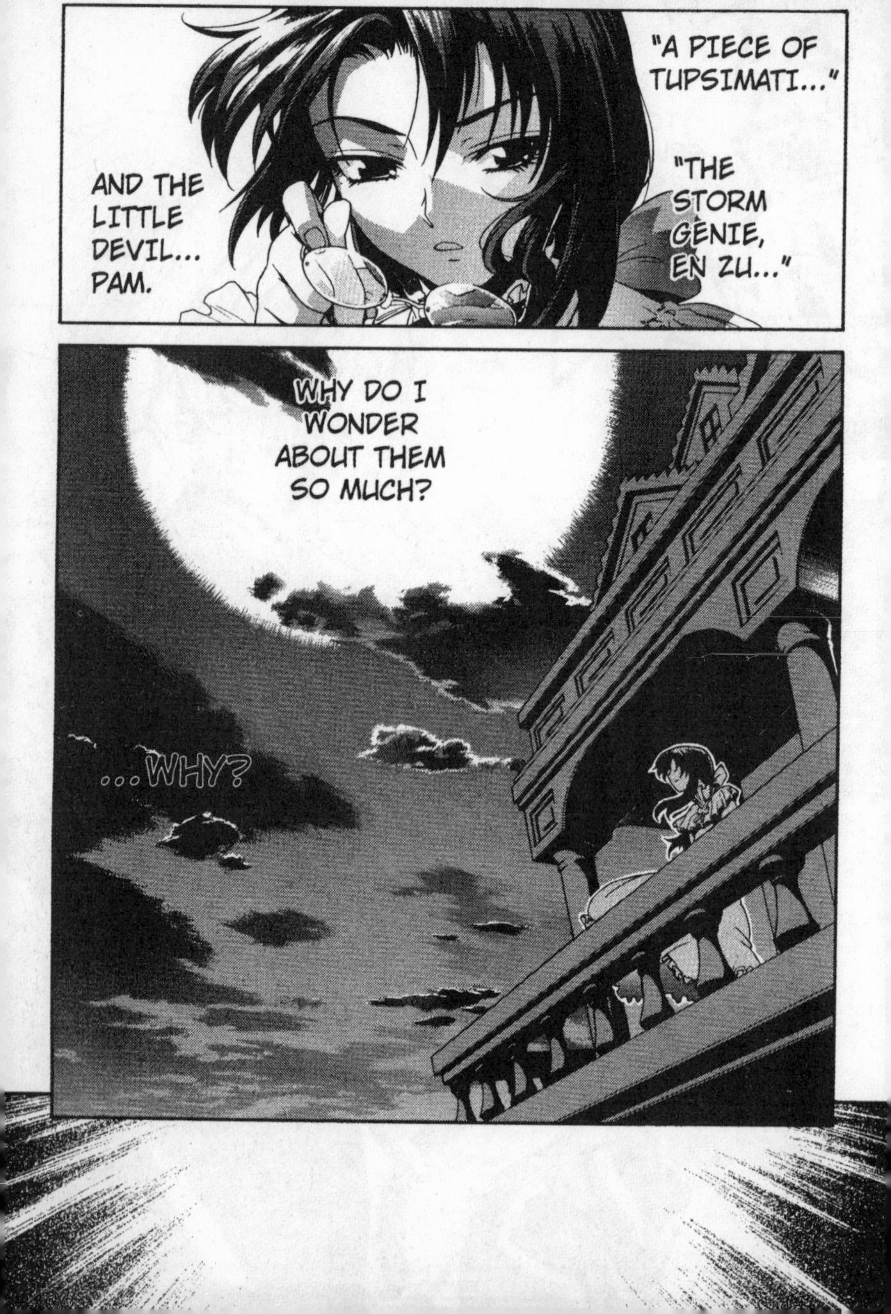
"A PIECE OF TUPSIMATI..."
"THE STORM GENIE, EN ZU..."
AND THE LITTLE DEVIL... PAM.
WHY DO I WONDER ABOUT THEM SO MUCH?
...WHY?

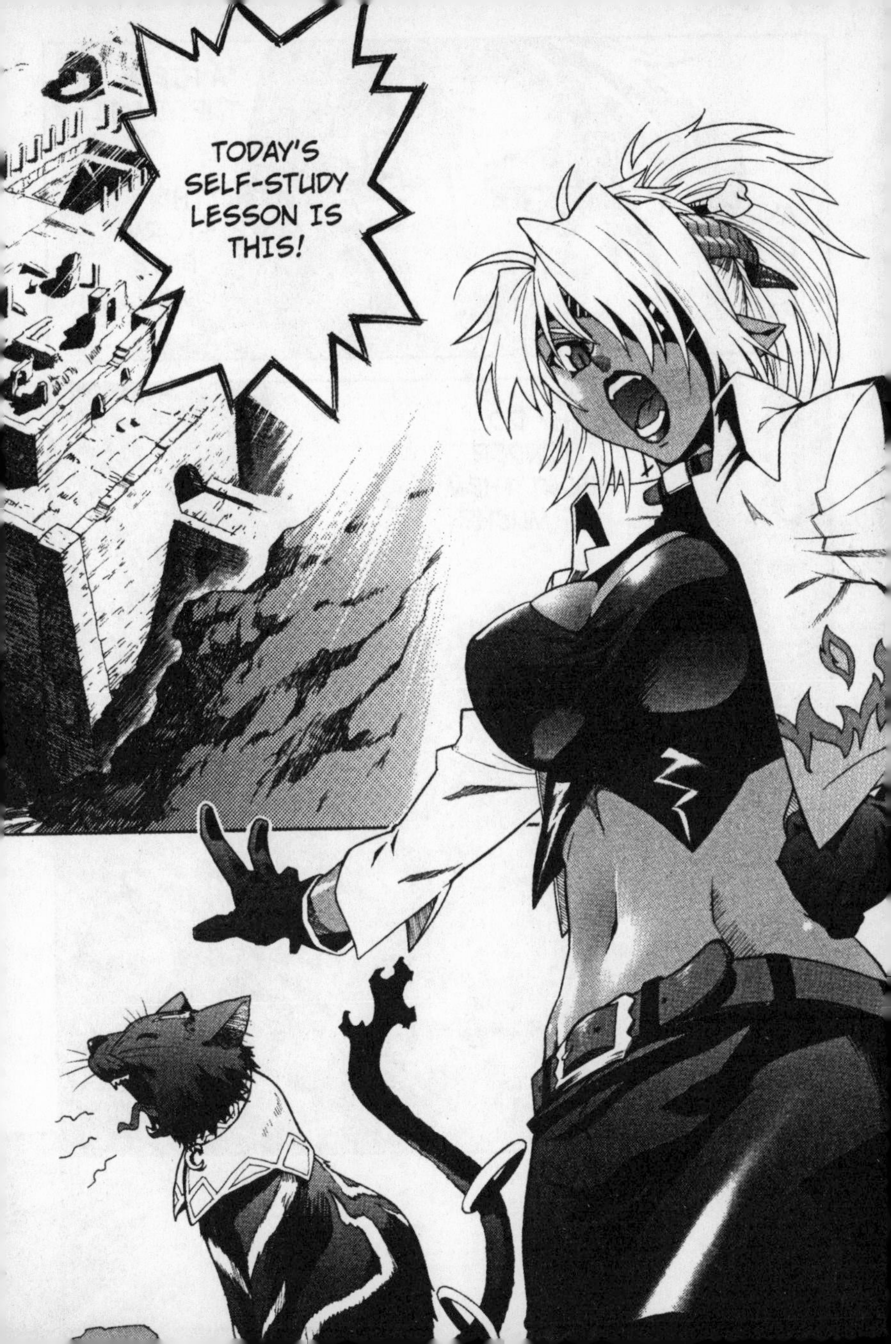
TODAY'S SELF-STUDY LESSON IS THIS!

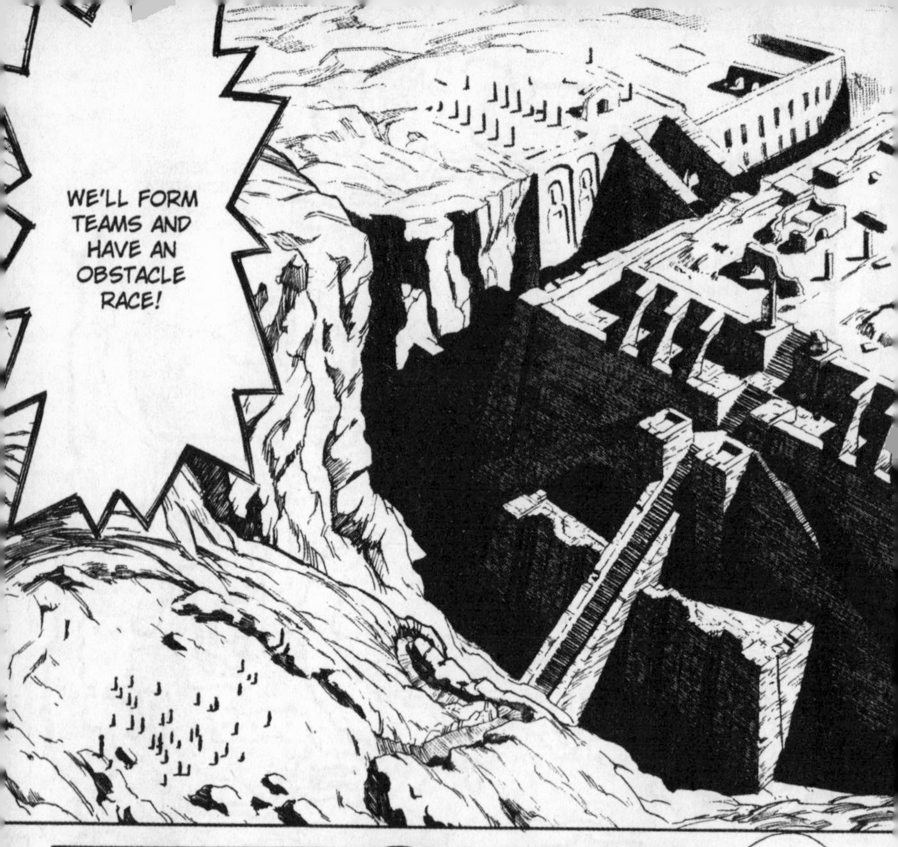
WE'LL FORM TEAMS AND HAVE AN OBSTACLE RACE!
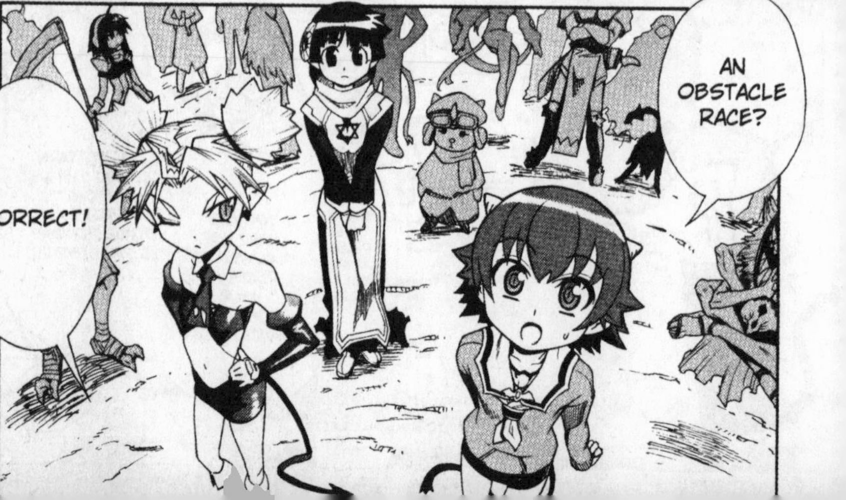
AN OBSTACLE RACE?
CORRECT!

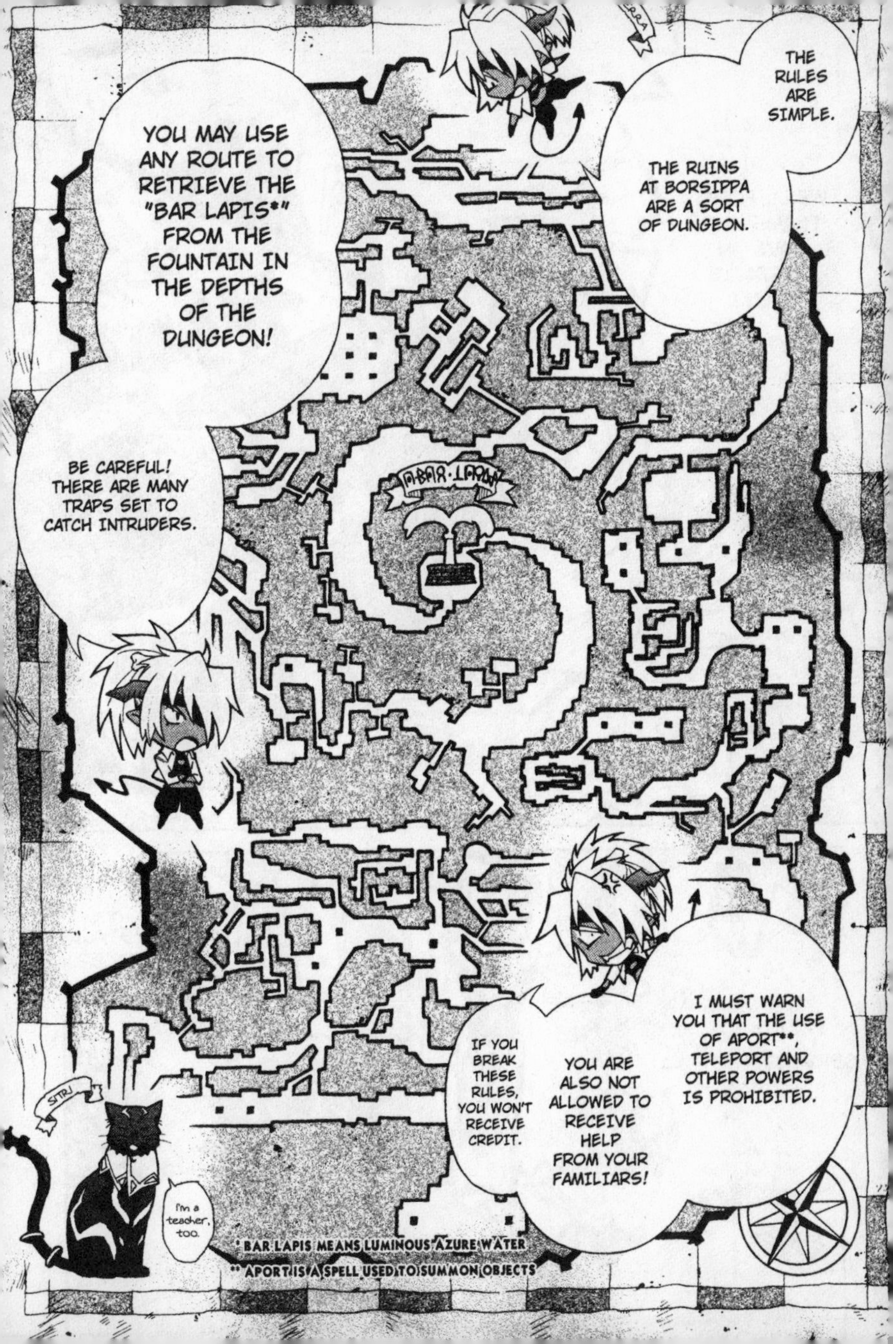
THE RULES ARE SIMPLE.
THE RUINS AT BORSIPPA ARE A SORT OF DUNGEON.
YOU MAY USE ANY ROUTE TO RETRIEVE THE "BAR LAPIS*" FROM THE FOUNTAIN IN THE DEPTHS OF THE DUNGEON!
BE CAREFUL! THERE ARE MANY TRAPS SET TO CATCH INTRUDERS.
I MUST WARN YOU THAT THE USE OF APORT**, TELEPORT AND OTHER POWERS IS PROHIBITED.
YOU ARE ALSO NOT ALLOWED TO RECEIVE HELP FROM YOUR FAMILIARS!
IF YOU BREAK THESE RULES, YOU WON'T RECEIVE CREDIT.
SITRI
I'm a teacher, too.

* BAR LAPIS MEANS LUMINOUS AZURE WATER

** APORT IS A SPELL USED TO SUMMON OBJECTS

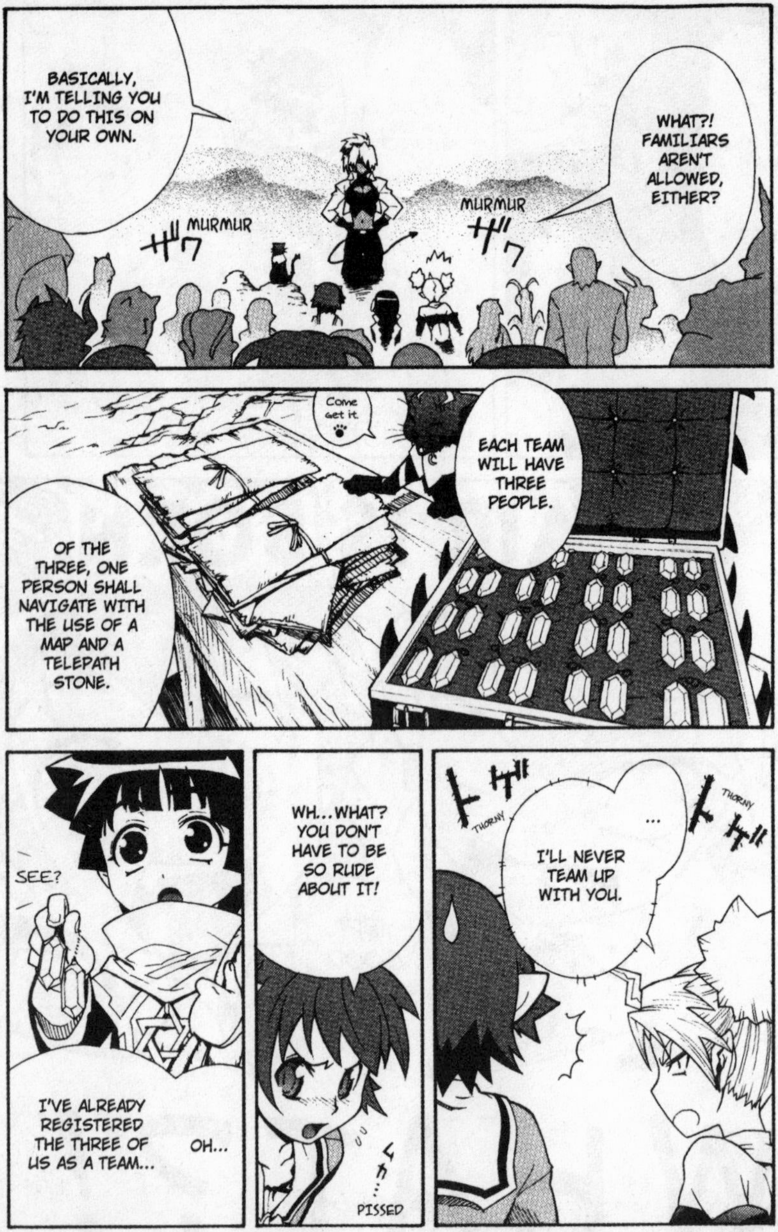
WHAT?! FAMILIARS AREN'T ALLOWED, EITHER?
ザワ
MURMUR
BASICALLY, I'M TELLING YOU TO DO THIS ON YOUR OWN.
ザワ
MURMUR
EACH TEAM WILL HAVE THREE PEOPLE.
Come get it.
OF THE THREE, ONE PERSON SHALL NAVIGATE WITH THE USE OF A MAP AND A TELEPATH STONE.
THORNY
...
I'LL NEVER TEAM UP WITH YOU.
THORNY
WH...WHAT? YOU DON'T HAVE TO BE SO RUDE ABOUT IT!
ムカ…
PISSED
SEE?
I'VE ALREADY REGISTERED THE THREE OF US AS A TEAM...
OH...

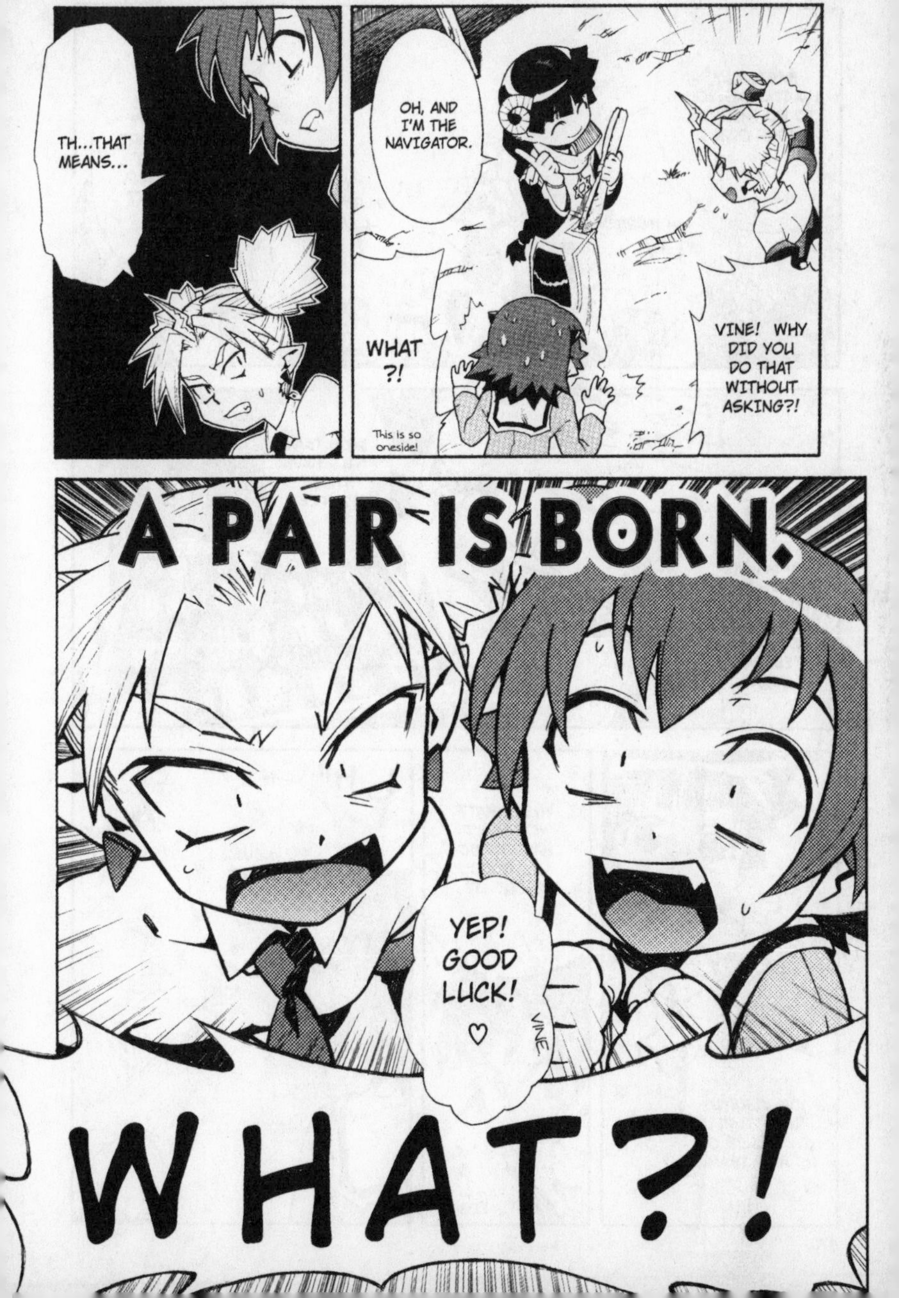
OH, AND I'M THE NAVIGATOR.
VINE! WHY DID YOU DO THAT WITHOUT ASKING?!
WHAT ?!
This is so oneside!
TH...THAT MEANS...
A PAIR IS BORN.
YEP! GOOD LUCK! ♡
VINE.
WHAT?!

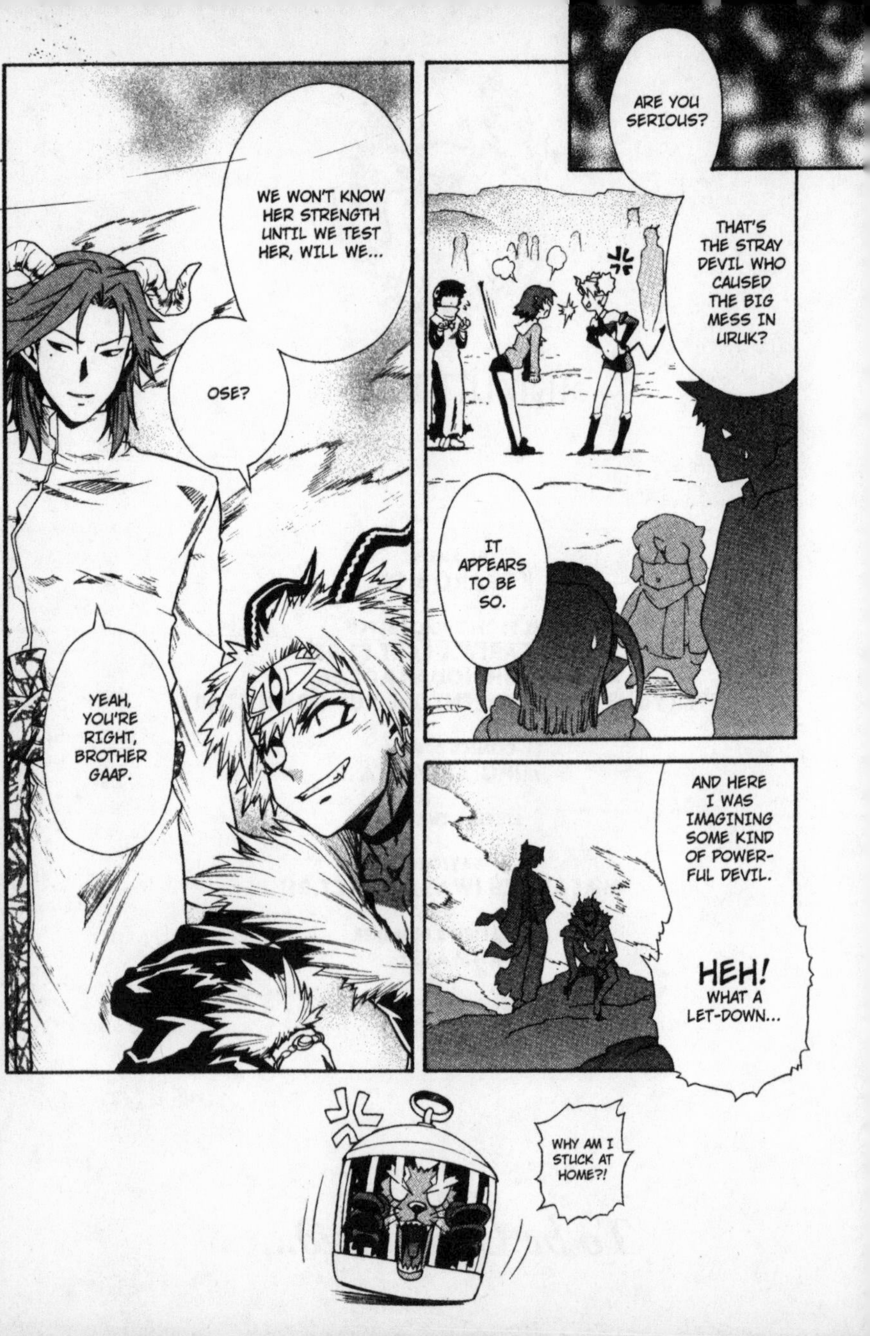
ARE YOU SERIOUS?
THAT'S THE STRAY DEVIL WHO CAUSED THE BIG MESS IN URUK?
IT APPEARS TO BE SO.
AND HERE I WAS IMAGINING SOME KIND OF POWER-FUL DEVIL.
HEH! WHAT A LET-DOWN...
WE WON'T KNOW HER STRENGTH UNTIL WE TEST HER, WILL WE...
OSE?
YEAH, YOU'RE RIGHT, BROTHER GAAP.
WHY AM I STUCK AT HOME?!

STRAY LITTLE DEVIL*
1

THE ARTIST
KOTARO MORI

THE PEOPLE WHO HELPED
YUKI KARIWA (ACT.01-05)
MIKIO SHINODA (ACT.06)
EVERYONE FROM SCREENTONE RUB-DOWN STARS

COMICS DESIGN
MIHO AKIYAMA

SPECIAL THANKS!

SAVIOR
MASAKAZU IWASAKI (ACT.01)

BABY SPIRITS DESIGNER
KUMAJET

VOLUME TWO PREVIEW
ON YOSHIDA

To be Continued...

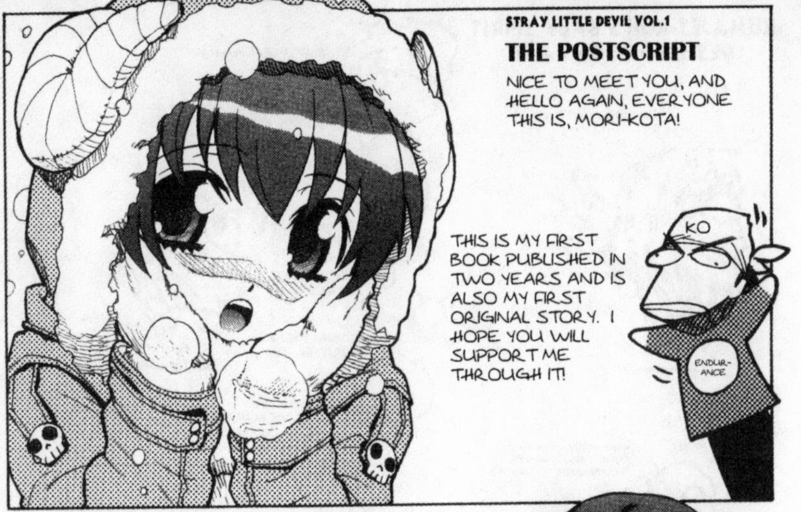
STRAY LITTLE DEVIL VOL.1
THE POSTSCRIPT
NICE TO MEET YOU, AND HELLO AGAIN, EVERYONE THIS IS, MORI-KOTA!
THIS IS MY FIRST BOOK PUBLISHED IN TWO YEARS AND IS ALSO MY FIRST ORIGINAL STORY. I HOPE YOU WILL SUPPORT ME THROUGH IT!
KO
ENDUR-ANCE

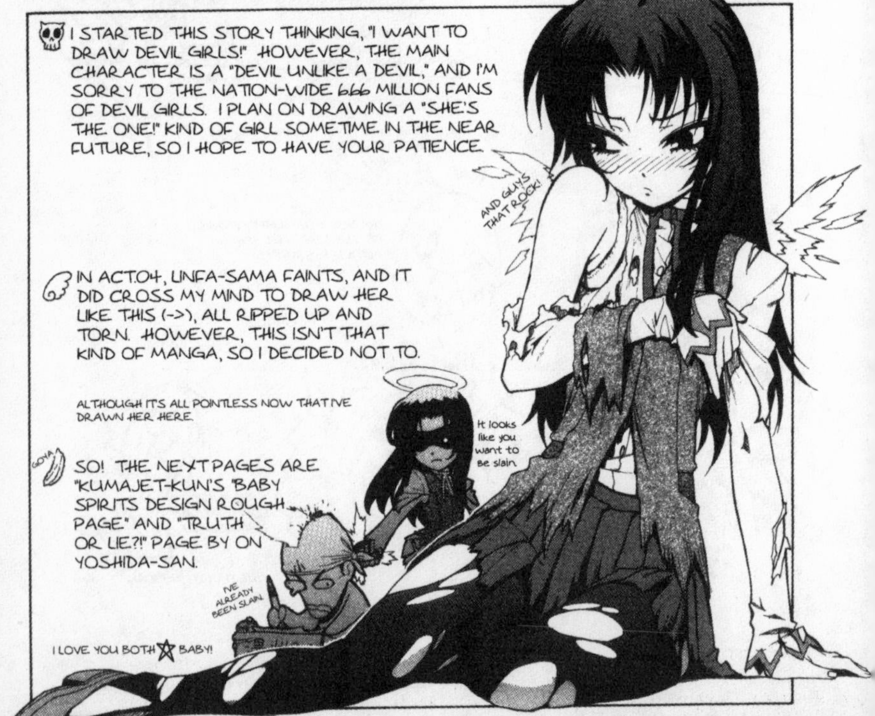
I STARTED THIS STORY THINKING, "I WANT TO DRAW DEVIL GIRLS!" HOWEVER, THE MAIN CHARACTER IS A "DEVIL UNLIKE A DEVIL," AND I'M SORRY TO THE NATION-WIDE 666 MILLION FANS OF DEVIL GIRLS. I PLAN ON DRAWING A "SHE'S THE ONE!" KIND OF GIRL SOMETIME IN THE NEAR FUTURE, SO I HOPE TO HAVE YOUR PATIENCE.
AND GUYS THAT ROCK!
IN ACT.04, UNFA-SAMA FAINTS, AND IT DID CROSS MY MIND TO DRAW HER LIKE THIS (->), ALL RIPPED UP AND TORN. HOWEVER, THIS ISN'T THAT KIND OF MANGA, SO I DECIDED NOT TO.
ALTHOUGH ITS ALL POINTLESS NOW THAT I'VE DRAWN HER HERE.
It looks like you want to be slain.
GOYA
SO! THE NEXT PAGES ARE "KUMAJET-KUN'S BABY SPIRITS DESIGN ROUGH PAGE" AND "TRUTH OR LIE?!" PAGE BY ON YOSHIDA-SAN.
I'VE ALREADY BEEN SLAIN.
I LOVE YOU BOTH ☆ BABY!

KUMAJET-KUN'S BABY SPIRIT DESIGN ROUGH PAGE

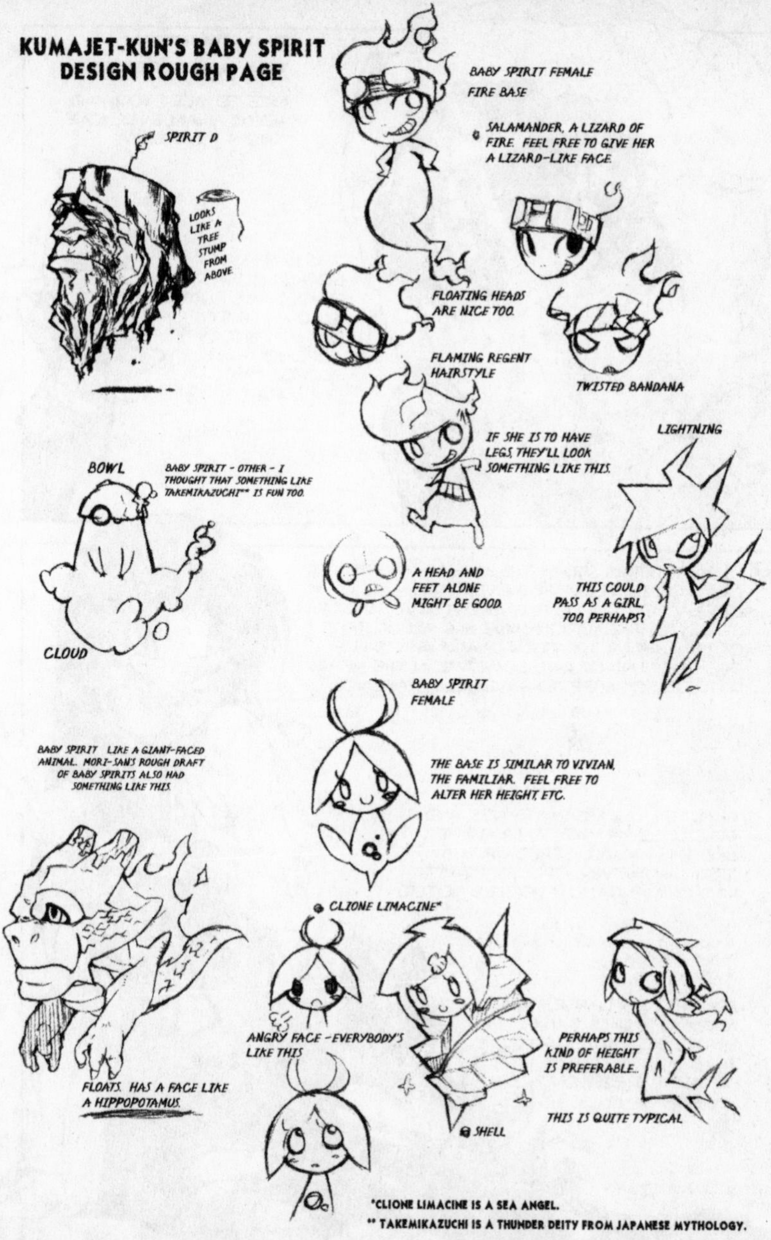
BABY SPIRIT FEMALE
FIRE BASE
SALAMANDER, A LIZARD OF FIRE. FEEL FREE TO GIVE HER A LIZARD-LIKE FACE.
SPIRIT D
LOOKS LIKE A TREE STUMP FROM ABOVE.
FLOATING HEADS ARE NICE TOO.
FLAMING REGENT HAIRSTYLE
TWISTED BANDANA
IF SHE IS TO HAVE LEGS, THEY'LL LOOK SOMETHING LIKE THIS.
LIGHTNING
BOWL
BABY SPIRIT - OTHER - I THOUGHT THAT SOMETHING LIKE TAKEMIKAZUCHI** IS FUN TOO.
A HEAD AND FEET ALONE MIGHT BE GOOD.
THIS COULD PASS AS A GIRL, TOO, PERHAPS?
CLOUD
BABY SPIRIT FEMALE
BABY SPIRIT LIKE A GIANT-FACED ANIMAL. MORI-SAN'S ROUGH DRAFT OF BABY SPIRITS ALSO HAD SOMETHING LIKE THIS.
THE BASE IS SIMILAR TO VIVIAN, THE FAMILIAR. FEEL FREE TO ALTER HER HEIGHT, ETC.
CLIONE LIMACINE*
ANGRY FACE - EVERYBODY'S LIKE THIS
PERHAPS THIS KIND OF HEIGHT IS PREFERABLE...
FLOATS. HAS A FACE LIKE A HIPPOPOTAMUS.
THIS IS QUITE TYPICAL
SHELL

*CLIONE LIMACINE IS A SEA ANGEL.

** TAKEMIKAZUCHI IS A THUNDER DEITY FROM JAPANESE MYTHOLOGY.

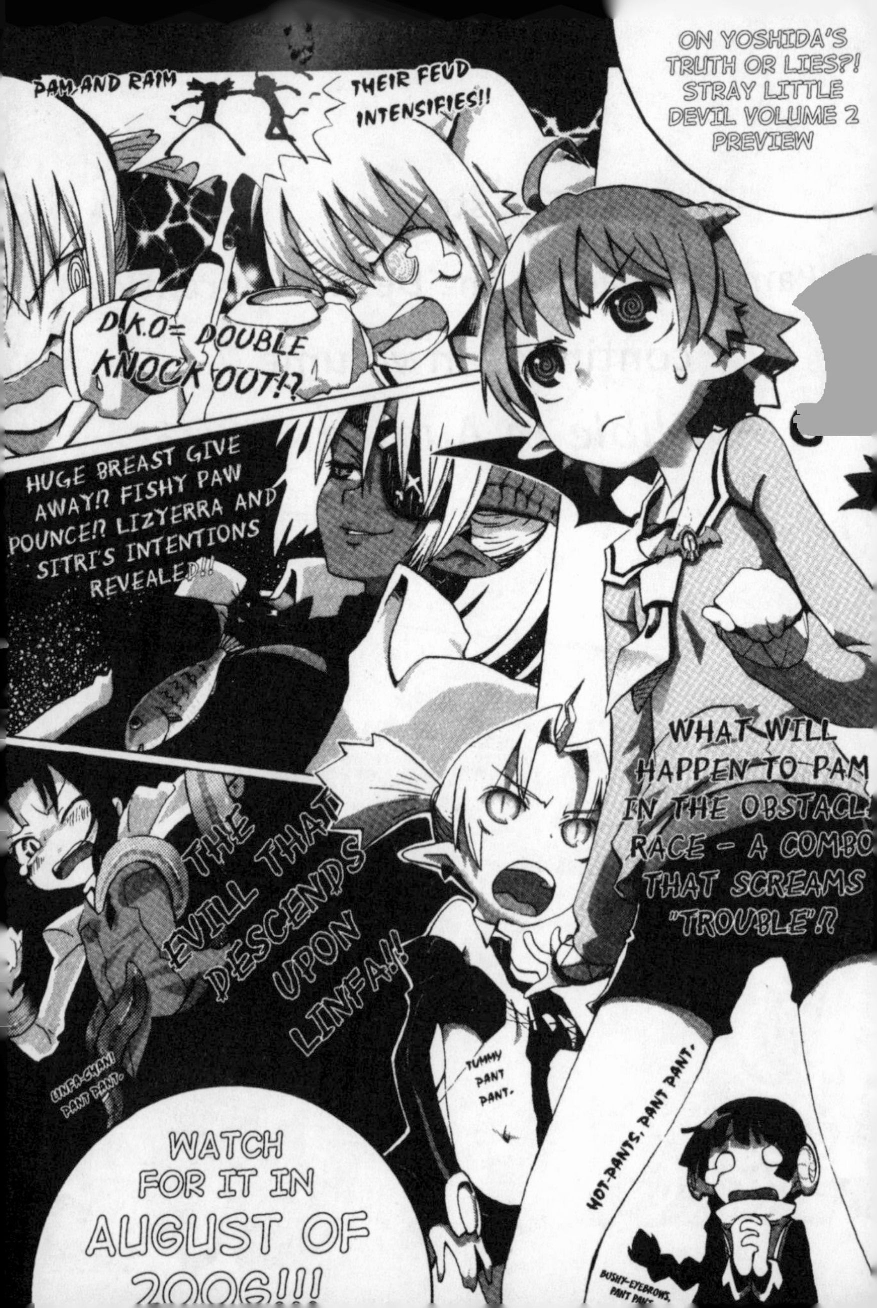
ON YOSHIDA'S TRUTH OR LIES?! STRAY LITTLE DEVIL VOLUME 2 PREVIEW
THEIR FEUD INTENSIFIES!!
PAM AND RAIM
D.K.O= DOUBLE KNOCK OUT!?
HUGE BREAST GIVE AWAY!? FISHY PAW POUNCE!? LIZYERRA AND SITRI'S INTENTIONS REVEALED!!
WHAT WILL HAPPEN TO PAM IN THE OBSTACLE RACE - A COMBO THAT SCREAMS "TROUBLE"!?
THE EVILL THAT DESCENDS UPON LINFA!!
HOT-PANTS, PANT PANT.
TUMMY PANT PANT.
LINFA-CHAN! PANT PANT.
BUSHY-EYEBROWS, PANT PANT.
WATCH FOR IT IN AUGUST OF 2006!!!

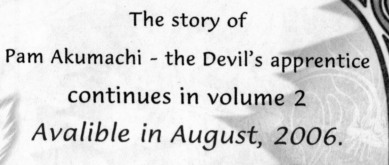

The story of
Pam Akumachi - the Devil's apprentice
continues in volume 2
Avalible in August, 2006.

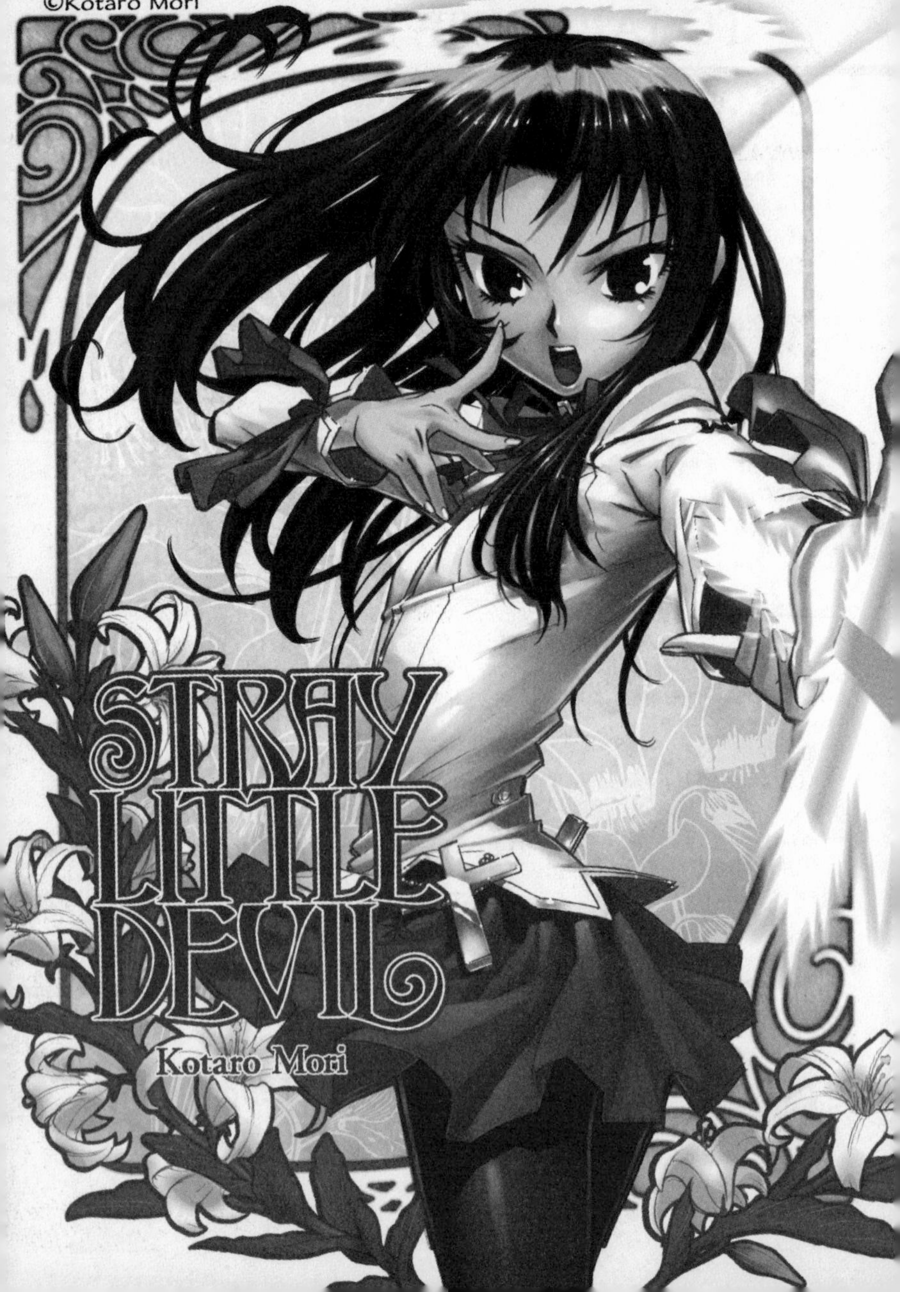
STRAY
LITTLE
DEVIL
Kotaro Mori

TO JAPANESE HONORIFICS

-SAMA. -SAMA IS THE MOST FORMAL HONORIFIC USED IN DAILY CONVERSATION IN JAPANESE. IT IS USED PRIMARILY IN ADDRESSING PERSONS MUCH HIGHER IN RANK, PROMINENCE OR IMPORTANCE THAN ONESELF. IT IS ALSO USED IN COMMERCIAL AND BUSINESS SETTINGS TO ADDRESS AND REFER TO CUSTOMERS.

EXAMPLE:
MAYA-SAMA,
ONI-SAMA,
AYATO-SAMA

-SENPAI. -SENPAI IS A JAPANESE TERM FOR A PERSON IN A CLUB OR OTHER ORGANIZATION, INCLUDING A SCHOOL OR COLLEGE, WHO IS A SENIOR. ANTONYM: KŌHAI ( ).

-SENSEI. -SENSEI IS A GENERIC JAPANESE TERM FOR "MASTER", "TEACHER" OR "DOCTOR". PERTAINING TO AND DENOTING PROFESSION, IT CAN BE USED TO REFER TO ANY AUTHORITY FIGURE, SUCH AS SCHOOLTEACHER, PROFESSOR, PRIEST, LAWYER, OR POLITICIAN. IT CAN BE USED ON BOTH GENDERS.

EXAMPLE:
MIZUHO SENSEI, I CAN'T STOP THINKING ABOUT YOU.

-CCHI. -CCHI IS ONE OF THE FEW NON-STANDARD INFORMAL HONORIFICS THAT HAS BECOME A HOUSEHOLD WORD USED TO REFER TO CLOSE FRIENDS.

THE MANGA READER' GUIDE

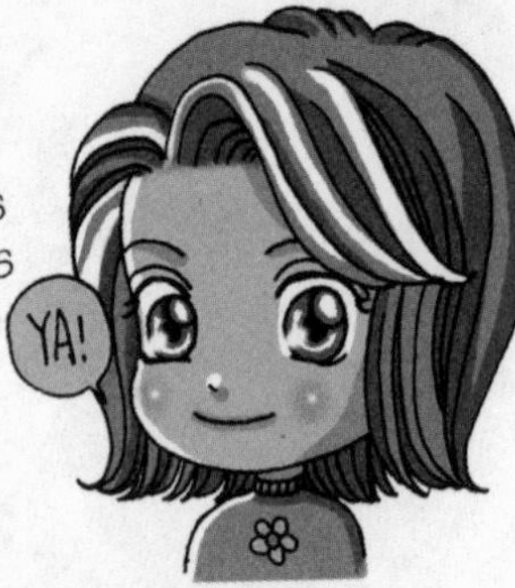
YA!

AT FIRST, WE WERE SKEPTICAL ABOUT LEAVING THE JAPANESE HONORIFICS IN OUR BOOKS. BUT, WE TOOK A LOOK AT GREAT WORKS OF LITERATURES AROUND THE WORLD (LIKE LES MISÉRABLES) AND WE SAW THAT LEAVING MONSIEUR AND MADEMOISELLE IN THE ENGLISH TRANSLATION WAS COOL AND WELL-ACCEPTED BY THE READERS. SO, WE SAID, "OK. WHY DON'T WE DO THAT WITH OUR BOOKS?"

SO, HERE IS THE LIST OF THE BASIC JAPANESE HONORIFICS THAT WILL HELP YOU TO ATTAIN A HIGHER LEVEL OF UNDERSTANDING AND APPRECIATION FOR READING MANGA AND JAPANESE NOVELS:

-SAN. *-SAN IS THE MOST COMMON HONORIFIC TITLE, AND USED IN ADDRESSING MOST SOCIAL OUTSIDERS (FOR EXAMPLE, NON-FAMILY MEMBERS). -SAN IS USED UNLESS WHEN SOME OTHER TITLE IS UNAVAILABLE OR UNLESS THE ADDRESSEE'S STATUS WARRANTS A MORE POLITE TERM. IT IS OFTEN TRANSLATED AS "MR.", "MS.", "MRS.", AND THE LIKE.*

-KUN. *-KUN IS AN INFORMAL AND INTIMATE HONORIFIC PRIMARILY USED BY SUPERIORS IN ADDRESSING INFERIORS, OR BY MALES OF ROUGHLY THE SAME AGE AND STATUS IN ADDRESSING EACH OTHER. IN BUSINESS SETTINGS, YOUNG WOMEN MAY ALSO BE ADDRESSED AS -KUN BY OLDER MALE SUPERIORS. SCHOOLTEACHERS TYPICALLY ADDRESS MALE STUDENTS USING -KUN, WHILE FEMALE STUDENTS ARE ADDRESSED AS -SAN. -KUN IS ALSO USED AMONG FRIENDS OF SIMILAR SOCIAL STANDING, AND BY PARENTS AND RELATIVES TO ADDRESS OLDER MALE CHILDREN (INSTEAD OF -CHAN).*

-CHAN. *-CHAN IS THE INFORMAL, INTIMATE, DIMINUTIVE EQUIVALENT OF -SAN, USED PRIMARILY BY CHILDREN TO REFER TO FRIENDS AND FAMILY MEMBERS BUT ALSO APPLIED TO SIBLINGS, TO CLOSE FRIENDS AND LOVERS, AND TO CHILDREN BY ADULTS.*

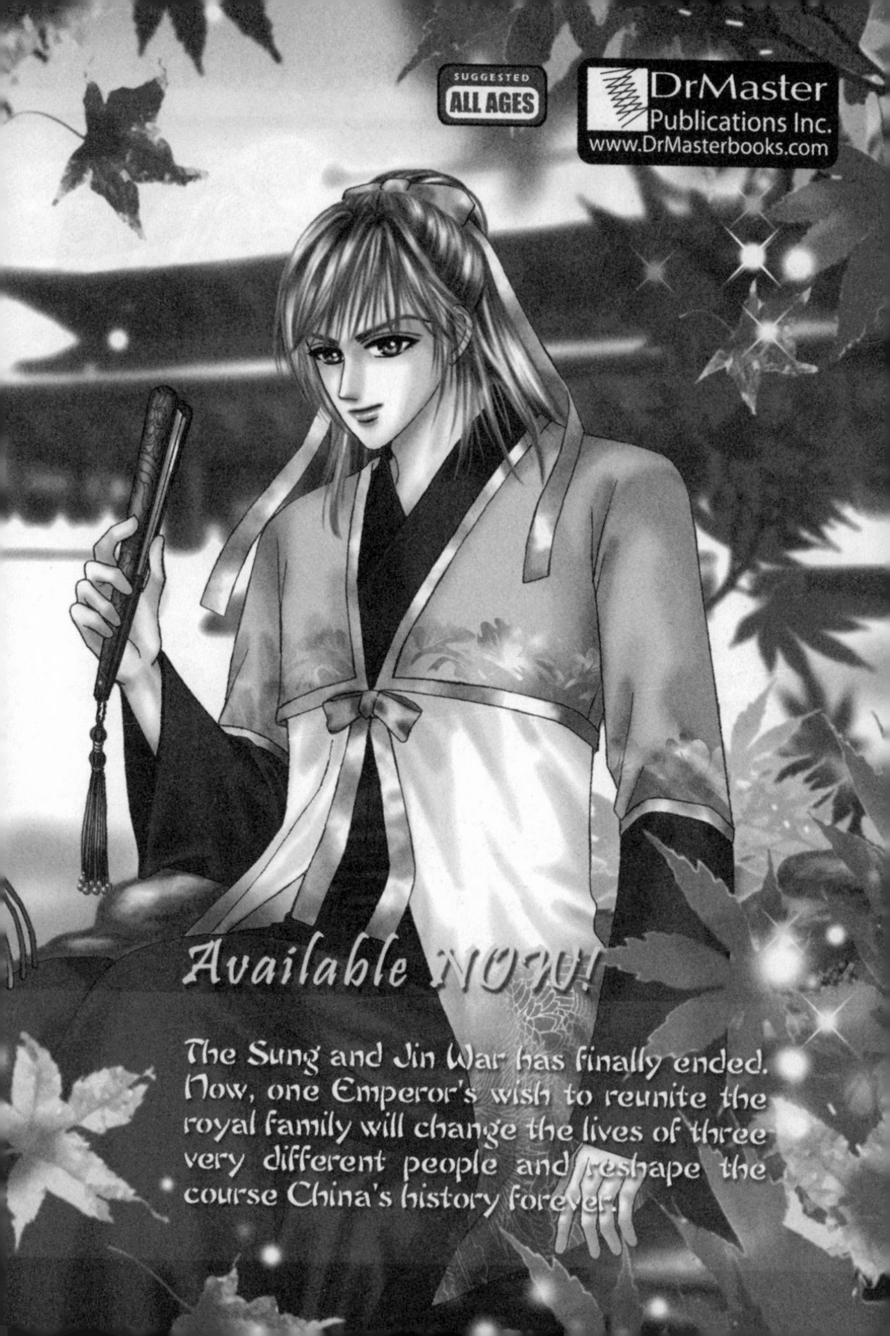
SUGGESTED ALL AGES
DrMaster Publications Inc.
www.DrMasterbooks.com
Available NOW!
The Sung and Jin War has finally ended. Now, one Emperor's wish to reunite the royal family will change the lives of three very different people and reshape the course China's history forever.

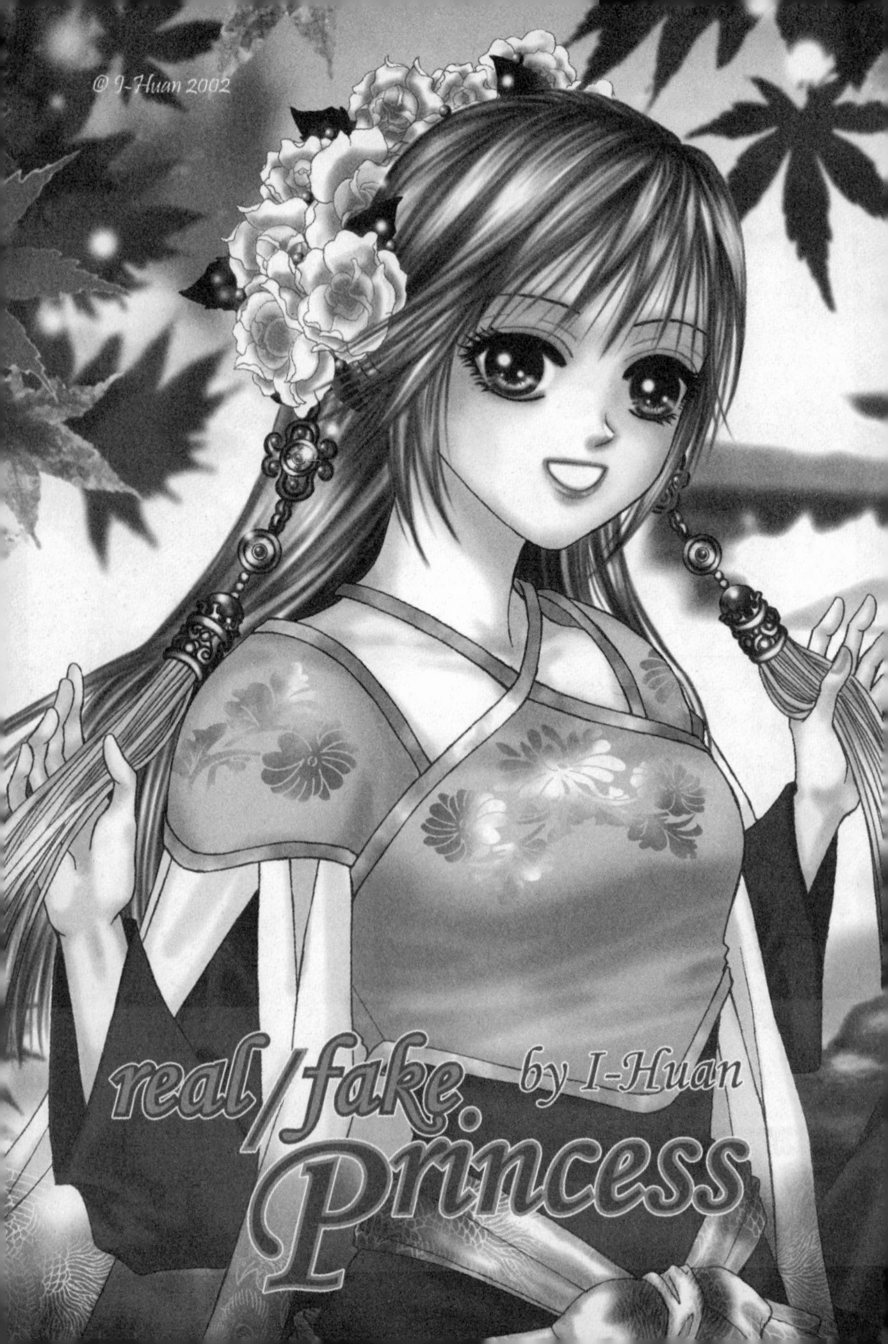
© I-Huan 2002
real/fake Princess
by I-Huan

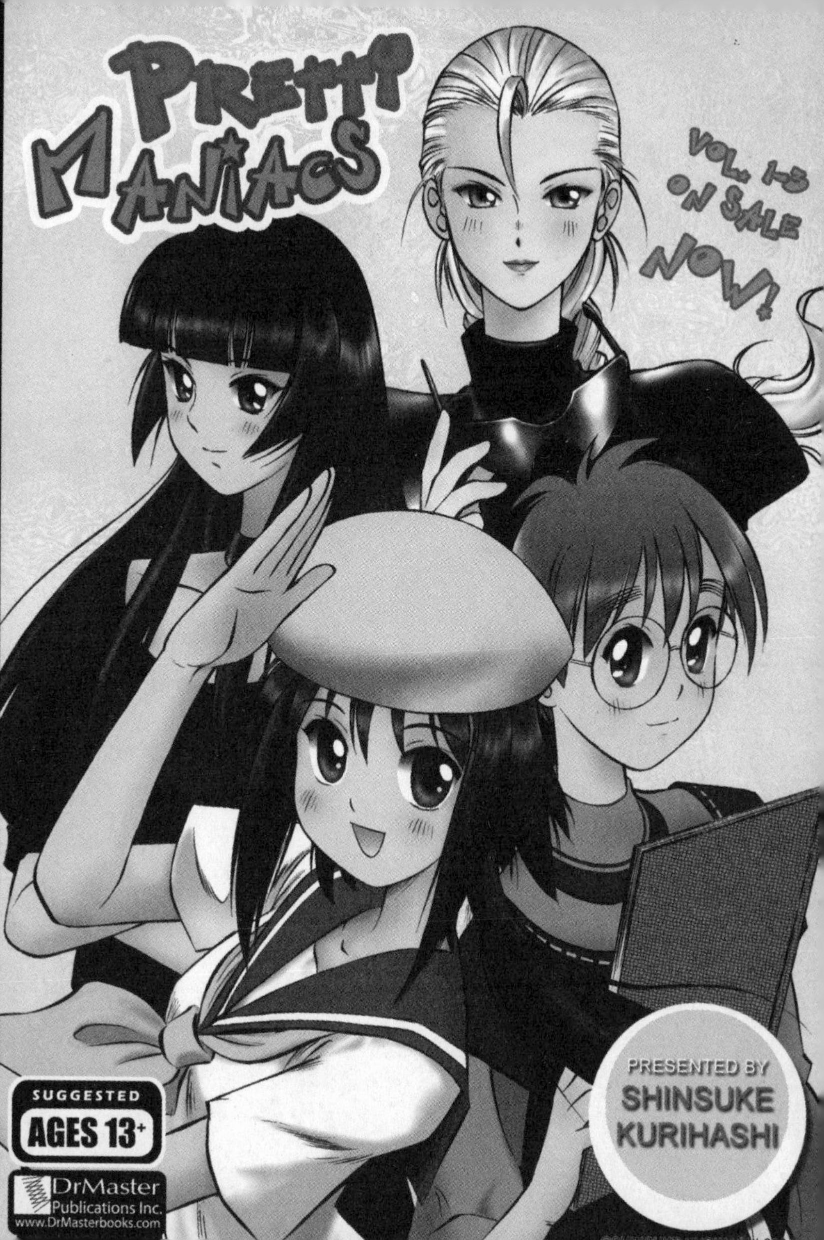
PRETTY MANIACS
VOL. 1-3 ON SALE NOW!
PRESENTED BY SHINSUKE KURIHASHI
SUGGESTED AGES 13+
DrMaster Publications Inc.
www.DrMasterbooks.com

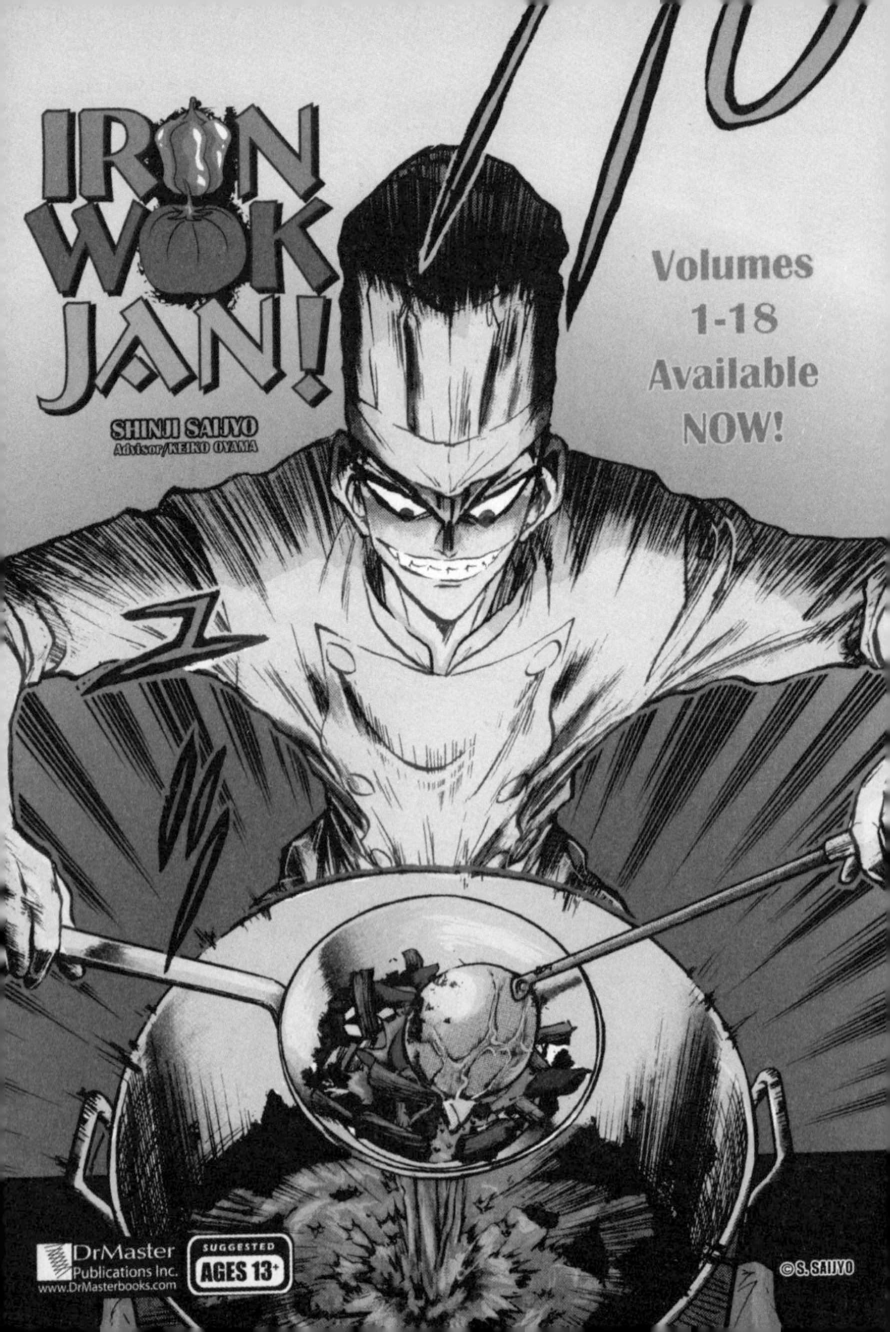

IRON WOK JAN!
SHINJI SAIJYO
Advisor/KEIKO OYAMA
Volumes 1-18 Available NOW!
DrMaster Publications Inc.
www.DrMasterbooks.com
SUGGESTED AGES 13+
© S. SAIJYO

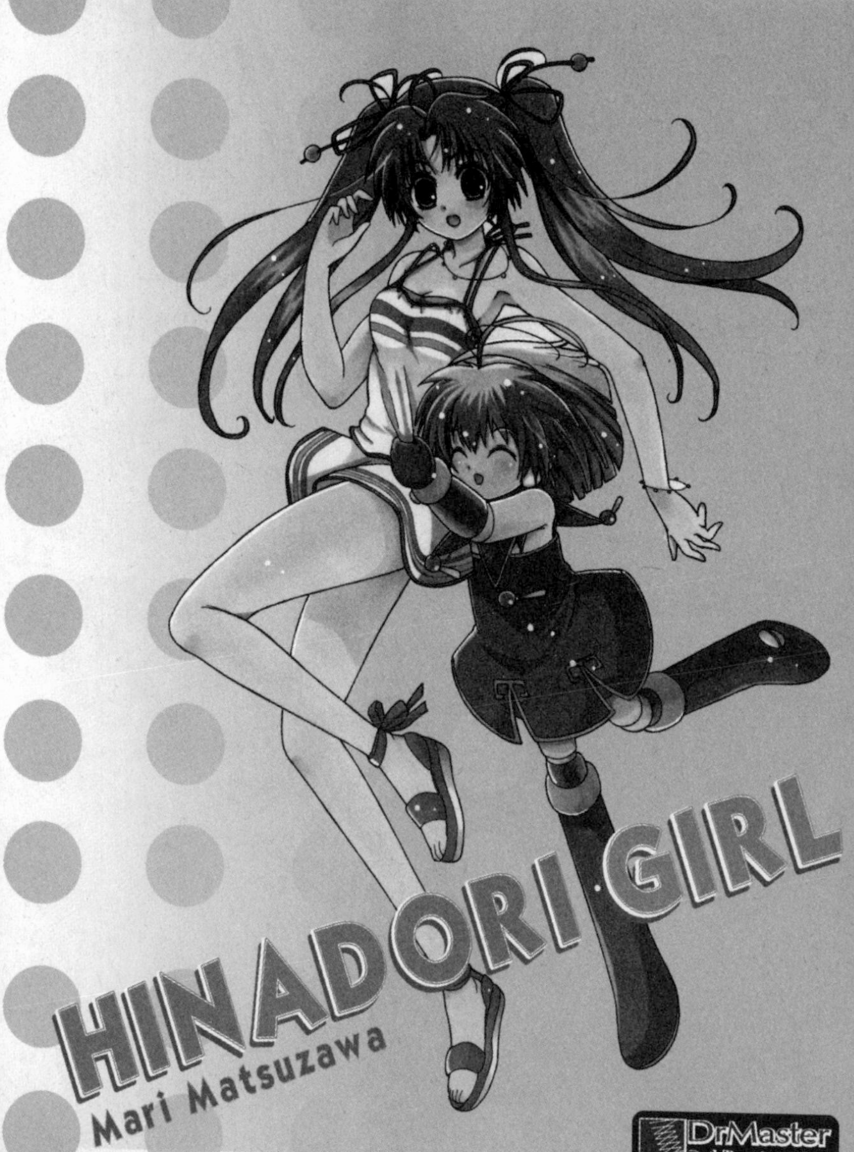
HINADORI GIRL
Mari Matsuzawa

DrMaster Publications Inc.
www.DrMasterbooks.com

NANKIN GUREKO

DrMaster
Publications Inc.
www.DrMasterbooks.com

IMPERFECT ★ HERO

YUJI MIDORIKAWA IS YOUR TYPICAL HIGH SCHOOL STUDENT WHO HAS A SECRET IDENTITY: HE IS "GREEN" IN THE HIGH SCHOOL BATTALION UNIT, GAKUSEI 5 (G5 FOR SHORT). G5 IS THE SPECIAL UNIT TRAINED TO FIGHT AND PROTECT EARTH AGAINST THE INVASION OF THE DREADED GALACTIC FORCE "GURDARK" AND ITS SEXY QUEEN MAYURA. BUT GREEN HAS A PROBLEM, HE REALLY CAN'T FIGHT, AND ALWAYS ENDS UP HIDING BEHIND HIS OTHER TEAMMATES. WHAT ENSUES IS A WITTY AND WILD RIDE AS OUR "IMPERFECT HERO" STRUGGLES TO MAINTAIN HIS REPUTATION AS A "GUARDIAN OF EARTH" WHILE KEEPING UP HIS GRADE POINT AVERAGE IN SCHOOL!

888

KUWATA NORIKO

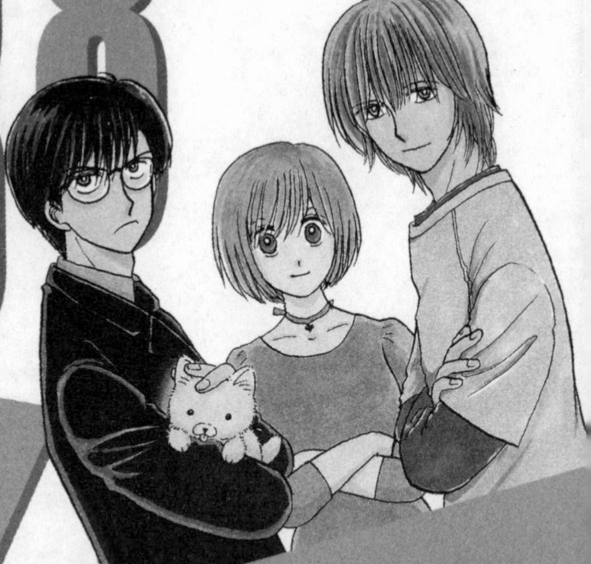

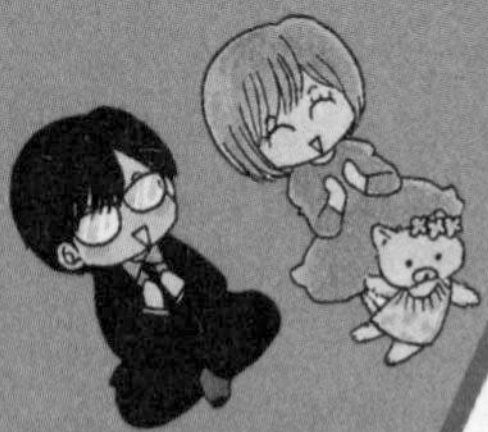

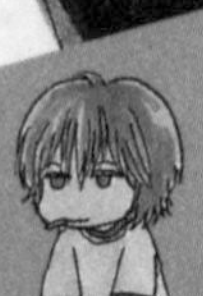

No work and a lot of play... 888 is a whimsical glimpse at detective life for a new Private eye agency. The problem is, detective Mori Shimeki his pet pomeranian and fellow coherts can't get a single case. Volume one consists of eight episodes of laid-back detective stories, that include Shimeki's past (his ex-wife, his long-lost brother), taking measures to increase clients, and the everyday scene at their workplace.

DrMaster Publications Inc.
www.DrMasterbooks.com

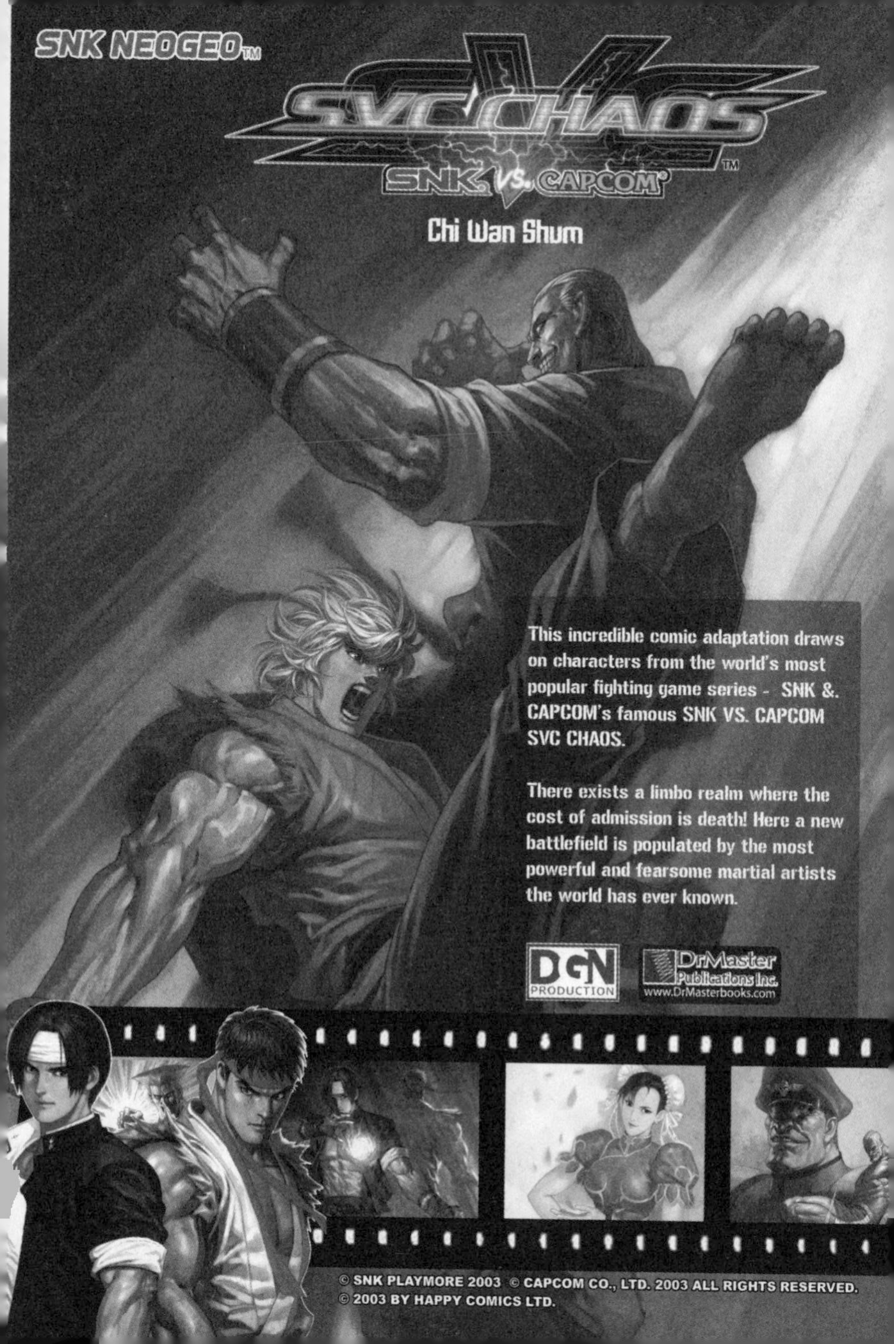
SNK NEOGEO TM
SVC CHAOS
SNK VS. CAPCOM TM
Chi Wan Shum
This incredible comic adaptation draws on characters from the world's most popular fighting game series - SNK &. CAPCOM's famous SNK VS. CAPCOM SVC CHAOS.
There exists a limbo realm where the cost of admission is death! Here a new battlefield is populated by the most powerful and fearsome martial artists the world has ever known.
DGN PRODUCTION
DrMaster Publications Inc.
www.DrMasterbooks.com
© SNK PLAYMORE 2003 © CAPCOM CO., LTD. 2003 ALL RIGHTS RESERVED.
© 2003 BY HAPPY COMICS LTD.

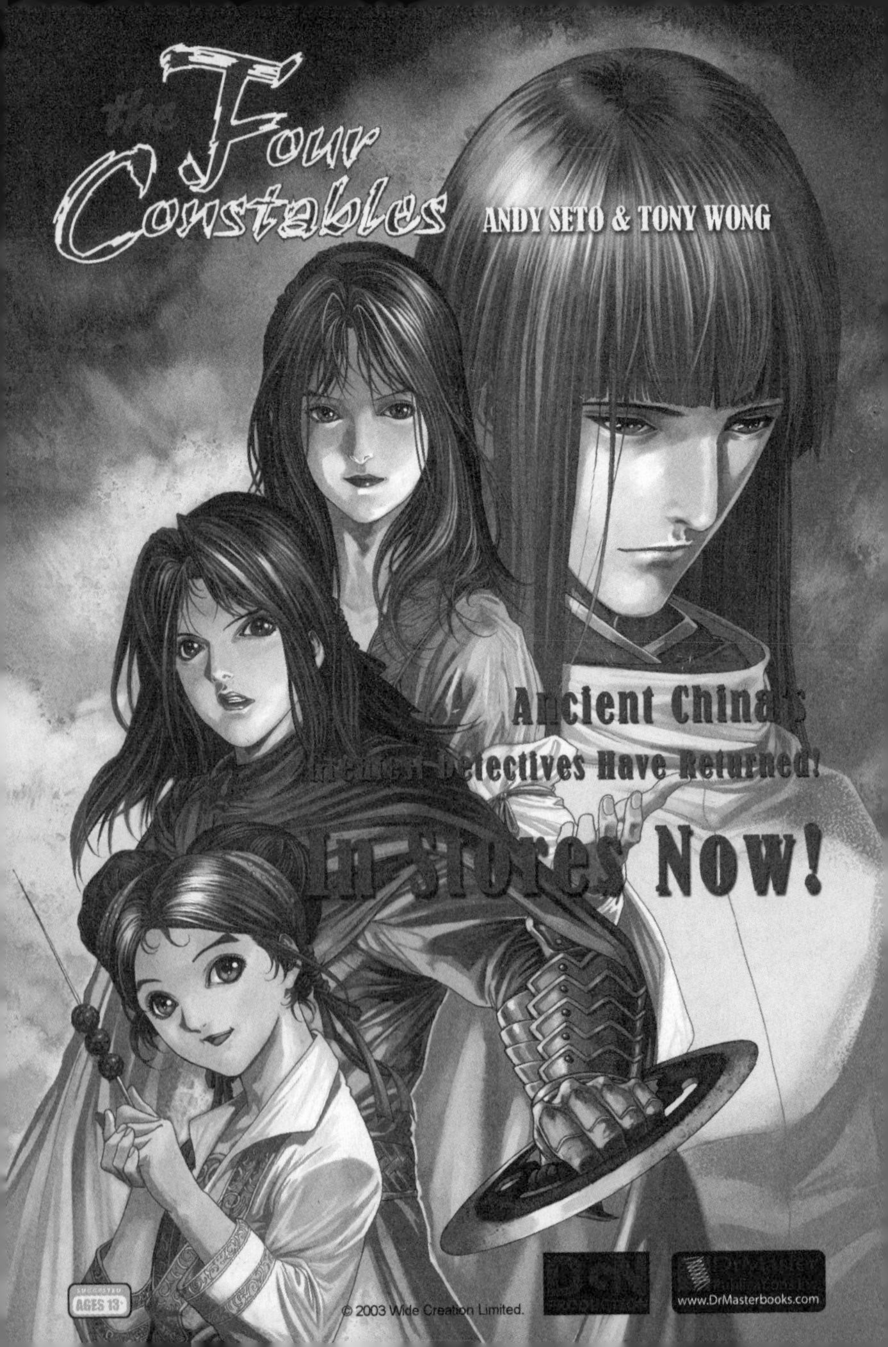

the Four Constables
ANDY SETO & TONY WONG
Ancient Chin
etectives Have Returned!
Stores Now!
SUGGESTED AGES 13+
© 2003 Wide Creation Limited.
www.DrMasterbooks.com

JUNK FORCE

Leave the planet and don't look back!

THE NOVEL

Delve deeper into the Junk Force universe with this first novelization of the hard hitting sci/fi manga! Follow the trials and tribulations of Liza, Wooty, Mill, Mamet and Louis as they strive to defeat the Z.T.P. while fighting off Martians and their own personal deviations. It's a literary adaption that knows

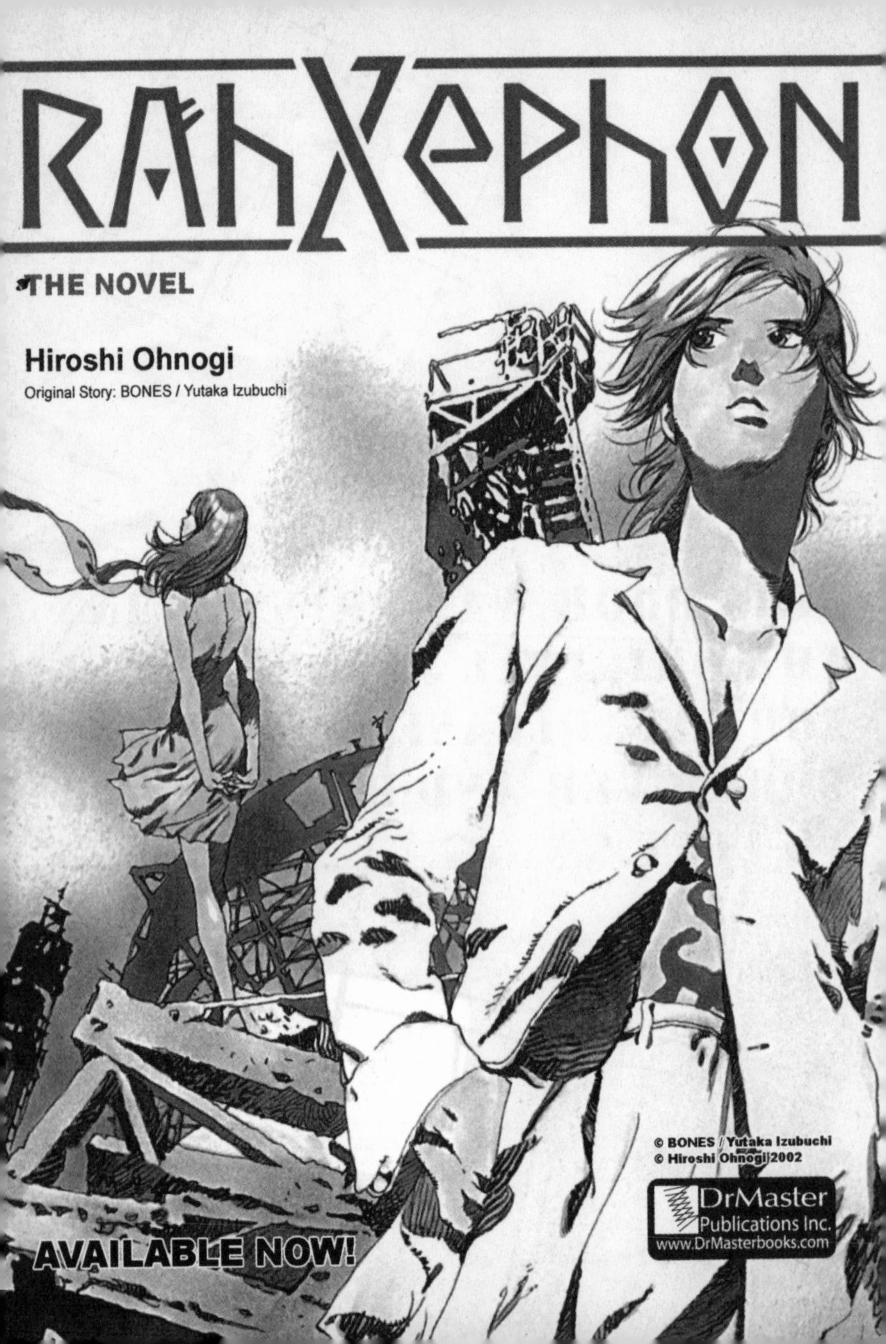
RahXephon
THE NOVEL
Hiroshi Ohnogi
Original Story: BONES / Yutaka Izubuchi
© BONES / Yutaka Izubuchi
© Hiroshi Ohnogi 2002
DrMaster Publications Inc.
www.DrMasterbooks.com
AVAILABLE NOW!

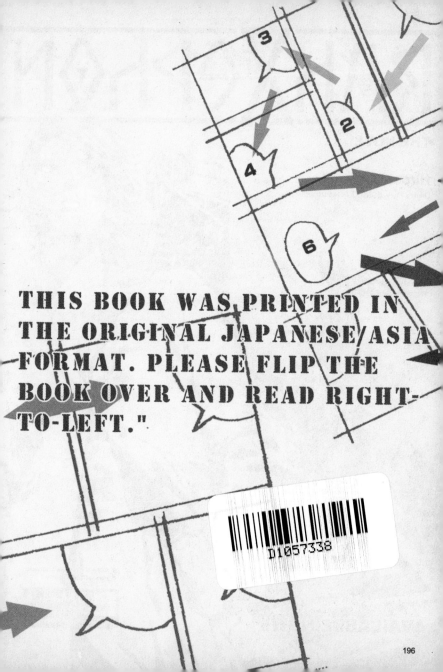

THIS BOOK WAS PRINTED IN THE ORIGINAL JAPANESE/ASIA FORMAT. PLEASE FLIP THE BOOK OVER AND READ RIGHT-TO-LEFT."